The Life
of
JOHN O'HARA

(Vytas Valaitas)

The
Life of
JOHN O'HARA

Frank MacShane

E. P. Dutton · New York

For information contact:
Elsevier-Dutton Publishing Co., Inc., 2 Park Avenue, New York, N.Y. 10016

Library of Congress Cataloging in Publication Data

MacShane, Frank.
The life of John O'Hara.

1. O'Hara, John, 1905–1970—Biography.
2. Novelists, American—20th century—Biography. I. Title.
PS3529.H29Z76 1980   813'.52 [B]   80-11949

ISBN: 0-525-13720-3

Published simultaneously in Canada by Clarke, Irwin & Company Limited, Toronto and Vancouver

Designed by The Etheredges

10 9 8 7 6 5 4 3 2 1

First Edition

FOR JEAN AND FRASER

CONTENTS

SIXTEEN PAGES OF ILLUSTRATIONS FOLLOW PAGE 146

PREFACE
and
ACKNOWLEDGMENTS

Although relatively unknown among young readers today, John O'Hara was one of the leading chroniclers of American society during the first half of the twentieth century. His novels and stories deal with the social and material ambitions of the middle and upper classes in the United States, but he is mainly concerned with the price people pay for having these values. O'Hara's understanding of individuals, especially his ability to give a vivid sense of the relationships between men and women, makes his work transcend its time and setting.

The purpose of this book is to renew an interest in O'Hara's work through a look at his life. He was more involved in public and social life than writers usually are, and at times he seemed to be more controlled by events than to be in charge of them. Yet he managed to be more prolific than most of his contemporaries. He stands out among them because of his volume of work and the high standards to which he adhered.

O'Hara's best writing went into his fiction. He was a good letter writer but not a superlative one, so while I have used his correspondence as much as possible to let him tell his own story, I have also relied heavily on interviews. John O'Hara's family has been most helpful in answering questions about him, and I am grateful for their assistance and encouragement. I particularly want to thank his daughter Wylie O'Hara Doughty for her patient help. I also want to thank his brothers and sisters, Mary O'Hara, Joseph O'Hara, Martin O'Hara, James O'Hara, Eugene O'Hara and Kathleen O'Hara Fuldner. Other members of the O'Hara family, Rebecca O'Hara, Ellen O'Hara, Polly McKee and John Delaney, were also most helpful. In addition, I am grateful to members of the Wylie family into which O'Hara married, and I want to thank especially Henry and Winifred Gardiner, Robert and Jane Wylie and Lucilla Potter. I am also indebted to Joan Gates and Courtlandt Dixon Barnes Bryan, whose mother was O'Hara's third wife.

I wish to thank O'Hara's many friends and acquaintances who agreed to talk to me about him, and in particular I should like to record the names of the following: Charles Addams, Roger Angell, Wodrow Archbald, Henry Baehr, Courtlandt Dixon Barnes, Jr., Mrs. Philip Barry, Luigi Barzini, Admiral John Bergen, Michael Blankfort, Mrs. Bertram Bonner, Gardner Botsford, Gerald and Kate Bramwell, John Brooks, David Brown, Joe Brown, Niven Busch, Noel Busch, the late Robert Cantwell, John Chamberlain, Hamilton and Jane Cottier, Mary Crosby, John Davies, Robin Denniston, Philip and Amanda Dunne, Geraldine Fitzgerald, Henry Fonda, Joan Fontaine, Edward Fox, Brendan Gill, Hayes Goetz, Emily Hahn, C. E. Halcomb, Nancy Hale, Dorothy Hellman, John Hersey, Leonora Hornblow, Governor and Mrs. Richard Hughes, John K. Hutchens, Gloria Jones, E. J. Kahn, Jr., Mrs. Norman Katkov, Morley Kennerly, Donald Klopfer, Rensselaer Lee, Warren Leslie, Stephen Longstreet, Robert and Adele Lovett, Mr. and Mrs. William Lord, Richard Ludwig, Gertrude Macy, William Maxwell, the late St. Clair McKelway, Louis Nizer, the late Joseph W. Outerbridge, Felicia Paramore, Robert Payne, Thelma Pemberton, the late S. J. Perelman, Dr. D. Pickering, James B. Reilly, Ruth Sato Reinhart, Allen Rivkin, Richard Rodgers, Gilbert Roland, Meta Rosenberg, the late Joel Sayre, Nora Sayre, Don Schanche, Budd Schulberg, Edgar Scott, Irwin Shaw, Marian Sheafer, Mrs. Kenneth Setton, Dr. Hamilton Southworth, Elaine Steinbeck, Peter Sterner, Irving and Jean Stone, Mrs. Russell Suender, Herbert Bayard Swope, Jr., Helen Thurber, Theodore Toussaint, Jean Valentine, Mrs. John Valentine, Phyllis Cerf Wagner, Graham Watson, Richard Watts, Katherine Bowman Werner, M. R. Werner, Alden Whitman, Lili Pell Whitmer, R. E. M. Whittaker, Isabel Wilder, Elizabeth Wilson, Dr. Benjamin Wright, Collier Young and Frank Zachary.

I also wish to acknowledge the help of those who in telephone conversations or letters answered questions and gave me information I needed. These include George Abbott, Walter Allen, Louis Auchincloss, Lauren Bacall, Carlos Baker, Nona Balakian, Nathaniel Benchley, Mrs. John Bradley, Joseph Bryan III, Mrs. Charles Caldwell, John Cheever, Alexander Clark, Marc Connelly, George Cory, Malcolm Cowley, the late James Gould Cozzens, Emmet Crozier, Mrs. Mosolino Deitman, Ralph deToledano, Lucinda Ballard Dietz, Richardson Dilworth, Jr., Edwin Earl,

Dr. Frank D. Elliott, Lessing Engelking, Don Ettlinger, Clifton Fadiman, William Fadiman, John Fante, Joseph Farley, Robert Galbraith, Felicia Geffen, Edgar Gemmall, Sheilah Graham, Mary Griswold, Philip Hamburger, Averell Harriman, Mary Hemingway, Verna Hobson, Ann Honeycutt, Gene Kelly, George Kennan, Norman Katkov, James Kerney, Jr., Florence Kriendler, Margaretta Archbald Kroll, the late Roy E. Larsen, Dorothy Laughlin, Ernest Lehman, Richard Lockridge, Henry Cabot Lodge, Jr., John Davis Lodge, Joshua Logan, Mary Longwell, Clare Booth Luce, Ann Martindell, William Marvel, T. S. Matthews, Faith McNulty, John McPhee, Robert B. Meyner, James A. Michener, Pamela Milburne, Alice Leone Moats, Mrs. L. B. Norris, Benjamin O'Sullivan, Ben Perrick, J. B. Priestley, Peter Quennell, Mary Reilly, Vincent Rodgers, Gloria Romanoff, Robert Root, George Rowan, Robert Rowan, William Saroyan, Gloria Sheekman, Mrs. Arthur Sherwood, Paul Shyre, Frank Sinatra, Datus C. Smith, Jr., Red Smith, Caskie Stinnett, Frank Sugrue, H. N. Swanson, Willard Thorp, Diana Trilling, Janet Camp Troxell, John Updike, John Wack, Ernest Walker, Irving Wallace, Robert Penn Warren, Jerome Weidman, Glenway Wescott, E. B. White, Kathrine K. White, Lucius Wilmerding and Mildred Gilman Wohlforth.

I am indebted to those who have written about O'Hara before me, in particular to Charles Bassett and to Finis Farr and Matthew Bruccoli whose biographies and editions of O'Hara's work have been most helpful to me and who have been patient and courteous in response to my inquiries. I also owe a great debt of gratitude to Charles Mann and his assistant Sandy Stelts of the manuscript and rare book library of Pennsylvania State University. This library houses O'Hara's papers and manuscripts, and I received every conceivable courtesy and kindness from its staff.

I am grateful to other libraries and public collections as well for their help in supplying manuscripts and letters that I needed. I should like to record my indebtedness to the library and archives of the American Academy and Institute of Arts and Letters, the American Academy of Motion Picture Arts and Sciences, the libraries of Boston University and Columbia University, the Library of Congress, the Historical Society of Saratoga Springs, the John F. Kennedy Library, the Newberry Library, and the libraries of Ohio State University, the University of Pittsburgh, Princeton University and the University of Wyoming. I am also grateful to Harcourt Brace Jovanovich, *The New Yorker,* Random House and the Screenwriters Guild for material made available. The following individuals made available their private collections of letters from John O'Hara: Charles Addams, Carlos Baker, Mrs. Philip Barry, Wylie O'Hara Doughty, Kathleen O'Hara Fuldner, Joan Gates, John Hersey, John K. Hutchens, Robert and Adele Lovett, Gertrude Macy, William Marvel, William Maxwell, Rebecca O'Hara, Edgar Scott, Diana Trilling and Phyllis Cerf Wagner.

In addition, I should like to thank a number of individuals who helped me in different ways during the course of my research and writing of this book. In particular, Vincent Balitas, Barbara Bedway, Patricia Blake, Sandra Booker, John Gregory Dunne and Joan Didion, George Dwight, Kathrine Jason, Peggy Jackson, William Jovanovich, Jascha Kessler, Murray Kempton, Kenneth Lohf, Richard Ludwig, Nancy Milford, Margaret Mills, Bob Nero, Tillie Olsen, Frank Platt, Estelle Powers, Debra Ratner, Mrs. A. B. Scotten, Charles Simmons, Ted Slate, Gay and Nan Talese and Rita Vaughan.

For their generosity in reading this book in typescript and for giving me suggestions for improvement, I am grateful to Jane Alpert, Carl Brandt, Wylie O'Hara Doughty, Joan Gates, John Macrae III, Debra Ratner and Rogers Scudder. I wish also to thank Cipriana Scelba and the Fulbright Commission in Rome, John D'Arms and the American Academy in Rome, the late Count Roberti and Countess Roberti Pasolini Dall'Onda, my son Nicholas and my wife Lynn for their understanding and help to me during the time that the book was being written.

Barberino Val d'Elsa

The Life
of
JOHN O'HARA

1. POTTSVILLE

At the age of sixty, John O'Hara summed up his life for a London journalist. "I can die tomorrow," he said, "and know that I have left some mark on the world. I can assure you that forty years ago you could have got very good odds that I would never do that." O'Hara had to work to make his energies productive, and often he had to struggle hardest with himself. He loved and hated enthusiastically, and he was volatile in his moods. He made well over a million dollars by his writing, but he also suffered humiliation and failure. In his late fifties he said that on the whole he had been a lucky man, yet characteristically he added, "but by God, I earned it." He was a man of contradictions and great sensitivity. In a moment of doubt he said, "I know so much better than anyone else that I have an inferior talent." Yet he could fly to the opposite extreme and openly announce that he was the best novelist of his generation and that he expected to receive the Nobel Prize for Literature. As a young man, he was notorious for being pugnacious. His nervousness made him touchy, and he would suddenly turn an amiable gathering into a brawl. Later, when he gave up drinking, he was like a tamed lion, polite and courteous, dull and withdrawn.

He was also warm and funny and almost blindly loyal to his friends. His often tumultuous life was held together by his capacity to give and

1

receive the love he shared with his wives. Because he was open and vulnerable, he suffered, but he also had enough warmth and sympathy to respond to the world he lived in. Despite his early roughneck appearance, he was intelligent and observant, and he was a born writer. He was blessed with energy and discipline, and no matter how bad things were, he kept on writing. Mentally restless, he was always experimenting, and in the process, his work matured and developed. His testament is a collection of thirty-three books in which he recorded his vision of American life. O'Hara was not the sort of Irishman who broods silently on his hurts; on the contrary, he poured out everything. The same impulse that made for his abundance also limits his achievement, however, for O'Hara wrote too much. Nevertheless, the short stories and the half-dozen novels and novellas in which he successfully fused the contradictory elements of his nature are sure to endure.

More than most writers, O'Hara was formed and nourished by his background. Psychologically, he never left the small Pennsylvania mining town of Pottsville where he was born on January 31, 1905. The people of this city of 25,000 and of the coal mining region that embraces Schuylkill County and other parts of northeastern Pennsylvania from Scranton to Harrisburg were the inspiration for books that rival in scope the work of Balzac, Trollope and Faulkner. O'Hara hated Pottsville because it was claustrophobic and narrow; he loved it for its physical beauty and familiarity. It was home, where he grew up, and the impulse that drove him to write about it was formed by love rather than by hatred. He was not a satirist but a novelist who wanted to reveal the lives of his subjects as fully and completely as he could.

O'Hara's divided feelings about Pottsville echoed the opposed forces that settled within the city and in the coal mining region of Schuylkill County. Built on two hills that are separated by railroad tracks and the main highway, Pottsville took its shape as a nineteenth-century company town. It had been a frontier post in the eighteenth century, when it was organized by John Pott, but when large tracts of anthracite were discovered in the surrounding country, it became an important mining center. Capital for development of the region came from Philadelphia, and soon large monopolies like the Philadelphia & Reading Coal and Iron Company and the Girard Estate imported miners from Wales, Ireland, Lithuania and Poland and settled them wherever mines were dug.

Because the companies controlled the banks, the railroads, the canals and even the towns where the men lived, they exploited their employees outrageously. The inhabitants soon grew to hate one another as the workers tried to form unions and the coal operators tried to suppress them. The worst violence broke out in the 1870s when the miners, frustrated by their failures, turned for support to an Irish organization called the Ancient Order of the Hibernians, which had experience in fighting landlords in

Ireland. Members of this group were known as Molly Maguires, and they terrorized and killed mine foremen and others associated with the owners. In collusion with the state, the operators fought back. A number of trials were held, and dozens of "Mollies" were hanged in Pottsville and other Pennsylvania mining centers.

The social, religious and economic hatreds that grew out of these nineteenth-century struggles were reflected in the social structure and physical appearance of Pottsville. On the one hand, the town prospered. Centre Street, with its brick and granite Episcopal and Presbyterian churches, the bank with its marble façade, its hotel and shops, reflected the wealth that came from coal mining. But the narrow streets that rose up the hillsides of the town revealed the poverty and meanness in which ordinary people were forced to live. Lined with wooden row houses painted white or gray, with front porches where people sat at night to smoke and chat with the neighbors, these streets were cramped and ungenerous.

Further up the hill, where the professional people, the lawyers, bank managers and representatives of the Philadelphia owners lived, the streets changed in character. Mahantongo and Howard streets, the more elegant thoroughfares, were lined by trees which softened the severity of the architecture. Towards the top of the hill, the houses were no longer attached but stood in gardens with lawns, and a few achieved some feeling of grandeur with wrought-iron fences enclosing the property.

In Pottsville, physical differences mirrored social. Living between the extremes of the two worlds, O'Hara grew to understand them both. The families that lived in the upper reaches of Mahantongo Street, with whom he most naturally associated, were Protestant and of English or German descent. They sent their children to Yale and Wellesley or Princeton and Bryn Mawr; they traveled to Europe and had summer places on Martha's Vineyard or Cape Cod. They were the "nobs" and without feeling any rancor, O'Hara and his Irish Catholic family were not part of their set. Instead, as he later noted, the O'Hara's were "proud, middle-class, and what is called 'lace curtain' Irish-Americans."

Yet their roots were as deep in this class-riven and divided society as almost anyone in "the region," as the coal mining area was called. O'Hara even enjoyed pointing out that his family went back to the tenth century in Ireland. Of Celtic stock, they were known for their military prowess and were prosperous people in the western counties of Mayo and Sligo until the time of Cromwell. O'Hara's grandfather, Michael J. O'Hara, was in fact born in Ireland, although he went to America as a child. He served in the Union Army as an officer in the Civil War, and afterwards visited Shenandoah, Pennsylvania, in order to tell the parents of a comrade of his that their son had died. He was offered a job working on the new railroad line that was being built between Pottsville and Shenandoah, so he decided to settle there. Soon afterwards he married Mary Franey, whose family were natives of the place. John O'Hara later made a point of saying that his Shenandoah grandparents were "the top people of Shenandoah, which is top of nothing much, but top." He also observed that the Franeys were "gentle Irish" whereas "the O'Haras were violent and spectacular."

Michael O'Hara raised his family by taking up the kind of hard work that was available to industrious and ambitious middle-class Irish. He did not have sufficient capital to invest in banks or land or coal mines, but he had a few horses and therefore opened a livery stable, which in turn led him into the undertaking business. He also became a building contractor and built the Shenandoah Opera House which his sons later renamed the O'Hara Theatre. He earned enough money to send his sons to the University of Pennsylvania and lived in a substantial wooden house in the town. Most of the other O'Hara children didn't amount to much—they were "all larceny" according to John O'Hara. But Patrick Henry O'Hara, John's father, took his medical degree at the University of Pennsylvania after doing undergraduate work at Niagara University, a Roman Catholic institution in New York State. He was a gifted surgeon. After a quarrel with his brothers in Shenandoah, he moved to New Orleans where he practiced briefly before returning to Pennsylvania.

First he settled in the small town of Schuylkill Haven, less than ten miles from Pottsville, where he became a surgeon at the County Hospital and superintendent of the local insane asylum. There he established his reputation for probity by refusing to charge his personal whiskey to the hospital. But Schuylkill Haven was no place for a vigorous young man like Patrick O'Hara, and in 1896 he moved to Pottsville, where he became a resident surgeon in the local hospital. A short stocky man with an aggressive jaw, he was very much his own man, independent and forthright. He had been forced to work hard in his father's livery stable, where he had learned to fight and swear, but he had been courageous enough to leave this boozy and slovenly world. Despite his violent language, he was a puritan, and when one of his brothers died from falling downstairs while drunk, he became a strict teetotaler.

In Pottsville, he lived at the Pottsville Club, and soon he established his own private practice. As an Irish Catholic, he naturally became physician to the many Irish miners who lived in "patches" near the coal mines outside of Pottsville. One of his main duties was to look after those who had accidents while working in the mines. He was under contract to the Philadelphia & Reading Coal and Iron Company, and he soon learned the need to master the art of trephining, an advanced form of trepanning, since so many miners suffered head injuries. But O'Hara's practice was not limited, and he treated people of all classes. A serious professional, he went every week to Philadelphia to observe his old mentor, Dr. John Deaver, as he performed operations at the Lackenau Hospital. Deaver operated in leather riding boots and had an imperious manner. He wore a stiff waxed moustache and had glinting eyes, and Dr. O'Hara may well have emulated his mannerisms.

After some years as a bachelor, Dr. O'Hara met and courted Katharine Delaney of Lykens, a small farming and mining town thirty miles southwest of Pottsville, towards Harrisburg. The Delaneys were also Irish Catholic but of older stock than the O'Haras, having come to America in the eighteenth century. They were also "gentle" Irish, like the Franeys. Katharine's father, Joseph Israel Delaney, was the proprietor of a wholesale grocery and hardware store in Lykens as well as the owner of a number of row houses in the town. The Delaneys were considered socially superior to the O'Haras of Shenandoah, but the difference is marginal, for both families were quite plain middle class. They were prosperous, but because of religion and race, were excluded from the highest circles dominated by English and German Protestant families.

Katharine Delaney was a staunch Roman Catholic, a graduate of one of the Sacred Heart academies, Eden Hall, outside of Philadelphia. She was well-read, spoke French and played the piano. She was small and gentle but had character and strength. In 1903, she married Dr. O'Hara at Our Lady Help of Christians Church in Lykens. Afterwards, she settled with him in Pottsville, where he had secured a combined house and office at 125 Mahantongo Street, one block up from Centre Street, where the main shops were, and across from the Pottsville Academy of Music.

About a year later, Katharine Delaney O'Hara gave birth to her first son. The baby boy, born at home on January 31, 1905, was christened John Henry O'Hara in honor of Dr. O'Hara's best friend, Dr. John Henry Swaving, a colleague. He was a big child, with protruding ears, his father's prominent chin and his mother's nose. He had striking blue eyes and even as a little boy, the delicate hands that his father was to think so suitable for a future surgeon. After the baby was born, Dr. O'Hara and Dr. Swaving went off to Europe to study modern surgery. They visited Berlin and Vienna, where surgical standards were highest, and attended lectures at Guy's Hospital in London. They also stayed in Rome and Turin long enough for Dr. O'Hara to buy a set of surgical instruments which he used for the rest of his life and to learn enough of the language to be able to speak Italian to the sick miners of Palo Alto, a small community on the outskirts of Pottsville.

As a child, O'Hara was jolly and full of energy. He was also spoiled by his adoring parents. Every week when Dr. O'Hara returned from Philadelphia, he would bring a present, and John is reputed to have been the first child in Pottsville to own a teddy bear. He was also bossy and unruly. At the age of seven he accidentally set the house on fire so that the fire trucks had to be summoned. When Dr. O'Hara found out that his son had been playing with matches, he was so furious he spanked him in public. For the most part, John spent his time with his friends inventing games which they played in the alley behind the house or on the sidewalk. They were simple, homemade games which he played with one other child since he never had any interest in group sports.

The O'Hara house at 125 Mahantongo Street—known to the locals as "Markie" or "Mackie" Street—was only partly occupied by the doctor and his family. The ground-floor front rooms were given over to Dr. O'Hara's office and surgery, and the upper floors on the street side were occupied by two tenants. The O'Haras lived in the back of the building, with living and dining rooms downstairs and bedrooms and bath above.

In due time, other O'Hara children were born. John's sister Mary and his brother Joseph were the first of seven other children to appear over the next fourteen years. The parents insisted that they all dress carefully. The boys wore Norfolk jackets and knickers or plus fours. John also wore an Eton collar and had his hair cut straight around in a Dutch bob.

When it came time to go to school, John and his sister Mary were sent to a private day nursery in the neighborhood, run by Miss Katie Carpenter. There were only a few children enrolled, which meant a good deal of private attention, and soon John was beginning to read. Miss Carpenter, to whom O'Hara was later to dedicate *From the Terrace,* was keen on theatricals, and she used the parsonage of Trinity Episcopal Church for that purpose. On one occasion, John O'Hara played Old King Cole.

In 1913, owing to the growing size of his family, Dr. O'Hara decided to move. He kept his office at 125 Mahantongo Street, but bought a larger house up the street at number 606. This house belonged to the Yuengling family, owners of a local brewery and members of Pottsville's society, who in turn built a large Georgian house further up the street. The O'Haras' new house was an attached town house, but it was spacious. It was also convenient for school and church, since St. Patrick's Roman Catholic Church and the parochial school attached to it were just across the street from the house.

O'Hara has written that his schooling at Miss Carpenter's was so Protestant that the first hymn he learned was "Onward Christian Soldiers" and that he recited the Lord's prayer with the Episcopalian ending, "For Thine is the kingdom and the power and the glory." A fervent Roman Catholic who went to mass every day of the year, Mrs. O'Hara was eager to have her children raised as Catholics, so after they finished at Miss Carpenter's, John and Mary "went to St. Patrick's and the Sisters of St. Joseph where," as O'Hara later remembered, "we became closely acquainted with the Studs Lonigans of our place and time, and I got a cassock and surplice and raised my mother's foolish hopes that she had produced a Jesuit." O'Hara was aware of the social differences between Miss Katie's and St. Patrick's, so to ensure he was accepted by the young toughs who would now be his schoolmates, he invited them all to see *The Perils of Pauline* with him at a local movie house. "The invitations were accepted, to a man, and in we trooped at a quarter to four, a single file of stalwart Irish and Italian inward troopers. We were not to be denied. We were not denied."

The book learning he received from the nuns was "mostly orthography, etymology, syntax, prosody—and geography," he wrote. His attendance at St. Patrick's also made him a religious enthusiast, and he became an acolyte. He served on Saturdays and Sundays as well as at funerals and weddings and also became a member of the St. Aloysius Society for altar boys. For a time O'Hara became a great Defender of the Faith. He would lecture his friends about religious matters and correct their errors. His remarkable memory helped him master the details of theology, and he enjoyed bewildering and confounding his friends with quotations from St. Thomas Aquinas.

Soon O'Hara's religious enthusiasm took an unexpected turn. While still quite young, he and a fellow acolyte, John Bergen, were caught by the happily named Father Melody drinking the communion wine. The deed was communicated to Monsignor McGovern, the priest in charge of St. Patrick's, who in turn reported the affair to the O'Haras. Because Bergen was older he was accused of leading the younger boy astray, but O'Hara had not lacked enthusiasm for the prank.

Meanwhile his social life was developing in more acceptable ways. With the other boys in the street, O'Hara joined the Fisk Bicycle Club, whose only requirement was that at least one member use Fisk tires. Not long afterwards, Dr. O'Hara bought his son a pony and a governess cart which made him popular with the girls. A dog cart, which seated only two, was even more to his purpose, so Dr. O'Hara obliged. "Shortly thereafter Augusta Yuengling became interested in ponies, an interest I have never since regretted," O'Hara later noted. "After school we would go riding in my dog cart and every Saturday she and Hippie, the Yuenglings' chauffeur, would drive up in their Lozier to take my sister Mary and me to dancing school. It was always easy to hide Mary's ballet slippers."

More than anything else, dancing school made O'Hara aware of the social structure of Pottsville. Along with his friends, he "felt a little smug and snobbish" when the pretty embossed cards arrived each September from the dancing mistresses, Miss Lettie and Miss Katie, for they were not sent to everyone. "If, for example, your father owned a saloon, you weren't invited, no matter how much money your father possessed. And if your father was a bank director and lived on Mahantongo Street and had a Winton and had given you a pony, but was Jewish, you weren't invited." O'Hara went to Philadelphia with his father to buy a blue Norfolk jacket and patent leather pumps, and visited a local shop to buy the white silk handkerchiefs young gentlemen used to protect the young ladies' frocks from their grimy hands. Above all, there was the music and dancing, with instruction in the bunny-hug, the turkey trot, the tango, the fox trot and the polka. O'Hara learned to be a skillful dancer, but as he later noted, it wasn't the dancing instruction that counted. "It was the poise you acquired by associating with the misses of your own age, the knowledge of what to do with a white silk handerchief."

O'Hara was also becoming aware of the coarser side of life in Schuylkill County. Special occasions, such as trips to his maternal grandparents in Lykens, opened his eyes to social conditions. He and his mother would begin their journey by boarding the Minersville trolley, which was in effect a local railway, one of many that for years linked the rural towns and villages with Pottsville and with one another. Sometimes when they changed at Westwood Switch, they would catch the miners' train, made up of wooden coaches, each with three rows of benches nailed down on the floor. There the miners sat, waiting to be dropped off after a day's work at Silver Creek, Good Springs, Donaldson or some nameless place where there was only a path leading through the woods to their houses. "All these years later," wrote O'Hara, "I can still feel the weariness of those men, with their blackened faces and their gruff silences. They were too tired for conversation or for the horseplay that the end of the working day usually releases on other jobs." They were Lithuanians and Poles, mostly, with some Irish and Welsh and Pennsylvania Dutch, but there was no cheerfulness in their lives, no singing or jokes. "I can still remember the smell of the miners' train, a mixture of human sweat and damp clothes and coal oil and burned wicks from the lamps the men wore on their caps, and chewing tobacco and rubber boots."

At Tremont, O'Hara and his mother changed once again, but this time the train had plush seats and acetylene lamps with frosted glass; "the window frames contained mother-of-pearl inlays, the varnish and the brightwork had a nice patina." The conductor, with a white linen waistcoat and a gold watch beneath his brass-buttoned coat and gold braid, would talk familiarly to O'Hara's mother with the Pennsylvania Dutch intonations of the region: "Well, Katharine is this your eldest? My gootness, he sure is growing up like a weet."

At Lykens they would be met by Ambrose Bupp, his grandfather's delivery man, and be taken to 665 Main Street, where Grandfather Delaney lived with his wife and with Aunt Verna, the spinster sister. O'Hara adored his grandfather: "He was the nicest man that ever lived, bar none." Built right on the street, the grandparents' house was a plain white frame structure with tall Victorian windows in front. On Sundays the grandparents would sit on the front porch and talk to the people on their way home from church. Watching these meetings, O'Hara "realized at an early age that older people do not treat each other as equals." This was to be crucial knowledge, but as a young boy he mainly enjoyed playing in the big yard behind the house and exploring the open countryside where he could take picnics and swim in the river.

Lykens itself was a poor mining town with a run-down hotel, a bank, some shops and a gasoline pump. Joseph Delaney's general store occupied the ground floor of a house, and in his yard he kept lumber and general hardware supplies. It was a wonderfully exciting place for a small boy, and in later years, O'Hara could remember "the sights and smells of a small-town store; the barrel of dill pickles and the Gail & Ax and the beautifully made chests of Number 50 cotton and Hecker's catalogue-almanacs and the brass tacks for measuring muslin and the Dietz lanterns and the dried figs and sugar coconut (that I used to pretend was Miner's Extra chewing tobacco)."

In the late afternoons, young John would make the rounds with Ambrose Bupp. Sitting in the wagon he was sometimes permitted to take the reins while going up steep hills or to take off the brake at the bottom. But occasionally Ambrose would not appear, and Grandfather Delaney would explain that he had asthma. "Several times my grandfather fired Ambrose for getting asthma too often, but he always took him back when it got cured."

Delivering groceries in the Polish section of Lykens, O'Hara had seen many unfamiliar sights, but Pottsville opened his eyes to an even greater world beyond Pennsylvania. On the day the circus train arrived, O'Hara would get up at four in the morning, put on his leather cowboy chaps and sombrero and ride down to the railroad yard on his Shetland pony. "The farmers who had come to town to see the circus unload would eye me with what I still like to think was envy and awe, asking me questions about which line the train was coming in on—the Pennsy or the Reading—and generally making me feel that I was at least a part owner."

O'Hara was an actively curious boy. A childhood friend of his remarked that "as a kid, he used to sit by the tracks and watch the freights go by. When he grew up he could tell you the name of every railroad in the United States. The same thing applied to horses, Christian creeds, cars, music and just about everything."

He was only twelve when America joined the Allies in the first World War, but he took part in whatever childlike way he could, "selling thrift stamps, and giving coffee and doughnuts to troops in the trains passing through my town, and carrying the flag of the Belgians in parades." He and a friend also did some amateur spying. They broke into a German-American club thinking it was beaming reports of troop movements to the enemy, but instead of a radio all they found were nude calendars and cases of beer and whiskey. O'Hara got up early on Armistice Day and found the streets full of people who had been celebrating all night. He saw a courtly young soldier pretending to be a trolley conductor and another "doughboy" lying in the gutter outside a bar holding a bottle in one hand. His other hand was missing, for he had lost it in France.

O'Hara made a point of talking to the veterans, doing what his friends would not do. One who talked to him freely was a big Polish steelworker called Mike. "A pal of his had been killed before his eyes by a German prisoner whom he had neglected to search for small arms. Mike literally cut the heart out of that German. It was a true story too; I verified it from other men who were in the same company. The nice boys, the boys who lived in my street, they wouldn't talk about it at all. Whatever it was they saw or did or felt, they avoided the war as a topic of conversation."

As the eldest of eight children, O'Hara had the responsibilities and privileges of the firstborn. He was the favorite and therefore much was expected of him. When the family moved up Mahantongo Street to number 606, he was given his own room on the top floor along the side of the house, while the large front room was shared by the five other boys. Downstairs was the master bedroom, the bathroom and a room for the two girls. As the house had been built by the Yuengling brewing family, "there was said to be a two-block-long tunnel connecting the brewery and the house," wrote O'Hara, "although I never was able to find it; the cut-glass chandelier in the parlor was delicate and beautiful; the speaking tube from the third floor to the kitchen was a nice thing to pour a pitcher of water down; some of the stair landings were so dark you could stand in a corner of one of them and not be seen by a person a foot away."

The day began with Mrs. O'Hara's solitary pilgrimage to six o'clock mass across the street at St. Patrick's. After breakfast, the children went to school and Dr. O'Hara set off on his rounds. Everyone came back at noon and gathered for lunch in the basement dining room. Afterwards, the Doctor—he hated the name Patrick and was called "Doctor" even by his wife—returned to his office for afternoon consultations. He was a forth-right and bristly person. Once a former patient came in pleading poverty and asking for free medical advice. Dr. O'Hara pointed to his visitor's expensive car parked in front of the office and told him that if he could afford the car he could afford a doctor and asked him to leave. Yet he was an exceptionally dedicated man. One night while attending a concert at the Academy of Music he heard people shouting for a doctor. He rushed out and found that a tram had run over a small newsboy. Disregarding his white tie and tails, he crawled under the tram to rescue the child. Once during a smallpox epidemic he alone treated a family whose house had been quarantined and roped off. He would take off his clothes and wear a sheet to go inside to visit his patients.

He allowed nothing to impede his medical work. Once he knocked down a policeman who arrested him for speeding while he was rushing to a sick person's bedside. Sometimes, in the middle of the night, he would call on his eldest sons to drive the car or sleigh to a sick patient. As his father's most frequent companion on these outings, John later recalled a memorable night: "A runaway train wreck, and I, as a kid of maybe 12, had to hold the hand of one man who was dying of burns and another man who was dying after amputation of both legs. These men just wanted a hand to hold on the way out. The nurses were busy."

Dr. O'Hara's medical work threatened to disrupt the household, but the drama of his life brought the family together. The children were warm and friendly with one another, although they tended to pair off according to age, starting with John and Mary, followed by Joe and Marty, Tom and Jimmy, Eugene and Kathleen. In the evenings, after dinner and homework, they would gather in one of the two living rooms on the ground floor. The larger of these, overlooking the street, contained a pair of fireplaces, a harmonium and Mary's harp. Mrs. O'Hara, herself a pianist, encouraged the children to play musical instruments. John took up the piano and later the banjo, and he also played the violin. Aside from family concerts, the parents and children would play parlor and word games.

The O'Haras were also great readers, and the second parlor in the back was filled with books. As a child, O'Hara was encouraged to read by the books he was given for Christmas. Every year he received an English annual called *This Year's Book for Boys.* It was "full of stories about Fuzzy-Wuzzy and the yachting at Cowes, bravely illustrated in color." He also read a great many of the books and magazines he found in the back parlor. Dr. O'Hara was a great admirer of Napoleon and had many books about him. As one of the leading professionals in Pottsville, he also received a free subscription to *Time,* and his son John devoured each issue as it arrived, delighting in its formula phrases and reverse syntax as well as its word inventions such as "relict" and "tycoon." The O'Haras also subscribed to the old *Life,* the *Review of Reviews* and *Judge.* Among the books John liked were Edith Wharton's novels, which he discussed with his mother, but mainly he was attracted by younger writers. He read the early fiction of Thornton Wilder and Ernest Hemingway and memorized whole passages from *The Cabala* and *In Our Time.* He also read William Lyon Phelps's literary columns. They made him impatient with the parochial views of his school teachers and may have kindled his interest in Yale where Phelps was a professor of English literature.

Horses also played an important part in Dr. O'Hara's household. Apart from those he needed for his rounds, he bought six Shetlands and a variety of pony carts for the younger children. There was also a mule called Billy. For his eldest son he bought a Kentucky mare by the name of Julia. The eldest boys had to look after the horses; they learned how to feed them and give them salt and water and the right kinds of grain. They had to curry them and rub their hooves with neatsfoot oil. There was a groom who also looked after the cow Dr. O'Hara kept in town for fresh milk, but the children were taught to be responsible.

O'Hara first learned how to ride from his father, but he also went to the state police barracks where the troopers gave him pointers. There, using his preferred English saddle, he taught Julia how to rise on her hind legs and how to count. He also trained her to move to right or left with only the pressure of his knees on her flanks. Horses suited O'Hara's temperament. He was not gregarious; instead, as he said, he "went in for solitary riding." Yet the race meetings he attended with his father in nearby towns and as far away as Allentown and Reading were lively, and as one of the few young people in Pottsville who liked horses, he went every year to the Devon Horse Show outside of Philadelphia.

Dr. O'Hara was proud of his son's progress. He let it be known that he thought his son was the best young rider in eastern Pennsylvania, but he never praised his son to his face. He found it difficult to express approval of his child's achievement, but had no trouble being critical. The relationship between the two was therefore always tense. One day, Mary and her father were watching John ride Julia down the street when a passing car frightened the horse and made her rear. Determined not to be thrown in front of his father, O'Hara kept his upright position in the saddle and brought Julia under control. Then he saluted Mary and his father, and rode off without a word.

Horses were a natural part of the farm Dr. O'Hara bought in the Panther Valley a few miles southwest of Pottsville in Pennsylvania Dutch country. There was a barn and a large white farmhouse with hand-cut beams that stood on the side of a hill above the meadow. In all, 136 acres, and the O'Haras had pigs, chickens, twenty-four Jersey cows and several horses. The family usually visited the farm on weekends and stayed for longer periods during the summer. Dr. O'Hara enjoyed playing gentleman farmer and didn't mind being cheated by the tenant farmer so long as he had fresh peas and onions, sweet potatoes, celery and tomatoes for his family. The children adored the farm: they would ride the ponies, collect fresh eggs for breakfast and lie under the trees by the stream that ran through the property, where the cows also went to stay cool.

The outdoor life was good for the children but it also introduced competition and rivalry. Dr. O'Hara encouraged physical exercise for the growing boys and was especially keen about boxing. He kept gloves at home and even at his office (where he also kept a gun), and he liked to spar with his young sons. He was a friend of a well-known professional boxer, Philadelphia Jack O'Brien, who trained outside of Pottsville at Tumbling Run. One day he goaded O'Brien into a match with himself, even though O'Brien didn't want to fight. After a brief exchange, the Doctor was knocked into the next room, unhinging a door along the way. Mrs. O'Hara was not pleased. The violence that accompanied boxing made it easy for Dr. O'Hara to be rough with his children when they disobeyed him. For minor offenses, even when the children were small, he would spank them with his rain rubbers.

O'Hara's difficulties with his father seem to have stemmed from the intense expectations his father invested in the relationship. He adored the little boy, spoiled him as a child and wanted him to grow up to be a doctor like himself. His great disappointment was that young John showed no interest in medicine. As a result, the Doctor resented his son's other achievements. When John was in the eighth grade at St. Patrick's School, one of the nuns told Dr. O'Hara that he ought to give up wanting his son to be a doctor. She had been struck by his literary gifts and said she thought he should be allowed to be a writer. But for Dr. O'Hara writing was nothing at all, a hopeless sort of job.

Once while making his rounds with Mary in the car, Dr. O'Hara began to complain about his son's refusal to study medicine. "He has marvelous hands and would make a fine surgeon," he said. Before he could go on, Mary interrupted and said that to be a surgeon or anything at all worthwhile, you first had to have an inner desire for it. Clearly, John lacked this desire. But Dr. O'Hara could never understand why his son would not want to enter so noble a profession. Even before John reached his teens, Dr. O'Hara approached him and said, "If you will give your word of honor that you will study medicine, I will put ten thousand dollars in the bank for you right now." But O'Hara would not make the promise.

Dr. O'Hara had a mild side, to be sure. He liked to sketch and would make charcoal drawings of the countryside as well as scientific sketches of operations to help other doctors. John inherited this artistic talent from his father, and it might have formed a bond between them. But he had also inherited his father's stubbornness, which made it difficult to communicate. Usually, he simply rebelled against his father's wishes. Even as a young boy, taken to Philadelphia to watch his father's old university, Pennsylvania, play football at Franklin Field, he made a point of rooting for the other team.

Far more serious was O'Hara's early drinking. After sampling the communion wine with John Bergen, he needed little inducement to continue. By the age of fourteen, he was a regular customer at Pat Joyce's bar in Logan Alley where he would go with two young Irish friends, Joe Devitt and Bud McDonald. Inevitably, he got into trouble. One day his father interrupted his morning calls by returning home, and there he found his son still quite drunk from the night before. In his fury, Dr. O'Hara picked up a heavy Tudor chair and started to beat his son over the head with it. Mrs. O'Hara came in and stopped the beating while the younger brother, Joe, helped clean him up since he was bleeding badly. But the damage was severe enough to keep John in bed for a number of days. These episodes became a feature of life in the household, and the other children were forced to intercede. O'Hara's younger brother, Tom, knowing his father's "fierce, skyrocket temper," came to the rescue in this way: "He once knocked John down and started to kick him and I burst into tears." Tom believed his interference may have "saved John a broken rib or spleen."

The violence could not and did not persist at this level, but there was always tension in the house, an armed truce between John and his father. Tom O'Hara later recalled a day when once again John was riding Julia down Mahantongo Street. Tom and his father stood watching and Dr. O'Hara praised John's horsemanship. "Then John stopped the horse at the door and was about to hitch her up and he said coolly, 'Want to ride her?' Daddy in his heavy, tweedy, scratchy pants and coat said yes and he got on and rode off for a block or two and came back. Then John took her back to the stable. Our father apparently was flattered that his son offered him a ride and John must have observed him observing him." Tom thought "it was good, those two hard heads covertly admiring one another but never showing the admiration," but the experience left a scar. In O'Hara's autobiographical story "The Doctor's Son," the father praises the boy openly. This so unnerves him that he starts crying and walks towards the stable with his head down, so that he "could let the tears roll right out of my eyes and down to the ground without putting my hand up to my face. I knew he was still looking."

2. SCHOOLS

Fordham Prep is the popular name for St. John's College High School of Fordham University. Located in the Bronx, the northernmost borough of New York City, it was founded in 1841 as a four-year school to prepare candidates for admission to Fordham University. Most of the faculty were members of the Society of Jesus. The buildings are made of gray stone with white trim around the doors and windows. The walls are covered with ivy, and wide lawns and shade trees soften the severity of the granite. In the 1920s, the university was surrounded by open country, and Fordham Road was like the main street of a village.

Here John O'Hara was enrolled as a student in February of 1920. By the time he reached fifteen years of age, he had exhausted the possibilities of St. Patrick's in Pottsville, so his parents decided to send him away to school. They were eager to have their son receive a Roman Catholic education, but this preference created a problem as it did for many middle-class Irish Catholics in America. The best schools and universities were either Protestant or nondenominational, and they offered better opportunities than the Catholic institutions did.

Having attended both Roman Catholic and Protestant universities, Dr. O'Hara knew the difference between them; moreover, he was something of a snob and he detested what he called "North-of-the-Mountain"

Irish—the loutish and ignorant Catholics who clung to their vulgar super-stitions. At the same time, he was proud of what he had accomplished without betraying his heritage. One day, while they were out driving together, his son Joseph pointed to a sign on a factory door that read, "No Irish Need Apply." He asked his father whether it referred to them. "No, we are Americans," answered Dr. O'Hara and then explained that the sign was intended for ignorant and unskilled immigrants. "The only way to get rid of signs like that," he continued, "is to change public opinion, and public opinion will change only if the Irish become hardworking and sober and overcome their national weaknesses, laziness and drink."

When O'Hara arrived at Fordham Prep, he was one of six hundred students, most of them boys with Irish and Italian backgrounds who lived in the Bronx. There were only fifteen boarders because the school authori-ties had decided to transform it into a day school only. Most of the boarders came from the eastern United States and from Central and South America. There was one other boy from Pennsylvania.

O'Hara found the daily routine a startling change from the relative ease of living at home. He had to rise at 6:30, attend mass at 6:55 and have breakfast at 7:30. The rest of the morning was devoted to classes. After lunch and a period for sports, there were more classes and study periods; following dinner there was one more study period, and after evening prayers, lights were put out at 9:30. The boarders were under the control of the prefect for discipline, a layman by the name of Shea.

O'Hara took courses that would prepare him to enter college and take a bachelor of science degree; he did not study ancient Greek as was re-quired of those desiring a B.A., although the school authorities emphasized the usefulness of classical studies "for all who desire a cultivated mind and keen intellectual power." During his first year, O'Hara took Latin, English, algebra and ancient history, and substantially the same his second, along with biology. The English course for his first year was devoted to a review of syntax, weekly compositions and short exercises. Selections from Long-fellow, Dickens, Hawthorne and Walter Scott were, in the words of the school *Bulletin of Information,* "carefully studied in the classroom, the main purpose being to awaken the literary imagination by forming vivid mental pictures of what is read." They read "Evangeline," *Tanglewood Tales,* "The Lady of the Lake" and the works of such authors as Gray, De Quincey, Tennyson, Macaulay and Cowper. The course also included the study of Julius Caesar.

As for writing, the school believed that the best way "to arouse the instinct for literary form" was to imitate the masters; "hence sentences and later in the year, paragraphs, from Irving are minutely studied, and then imitated by the class during every recitation period; this imitation is made to influence the weekly composition." At the same time, literary taste was to be molded by "an appreciation for the ideal in scenes and occurrences familiar to youthful experience. Irving, Goldsmith, Whittier, Coleridge and Bryant are read with this end in view." How O'Hara was influenced by this curriculum it is impossible to know. All writers begin by imitation, however, and it is possible that O'Hara's own style was formed by his study of Washington Irving's clear but relatively colorless prose.

Accustomed to the freedom of Pottsville, O'Hara disliked the isolation of Fordham Prep. The boarding students were restricted to the immediate neighborhood of the school, and for entertainment had to rely on school football and basketball games, debates, public elocution contests and an occasional visit to Keith's Fordham Theatre. If a student wished to leave the school, an invitation from a relative or guardian was necessary, and O'Hara had only some cousins in New Jersey to whom to turn. Had he been sent to a real boarding school, he might have enjoyed the experience, but the fourteen other boarders provided little company. The most they developed was a certain esprit through feeling superior to the day boys— the Day Hops, as they were called.

O'Hara did not become actively involved in his studies because he was bored and rebellious. Although he had begun to write in Pottsville, he contributed nothing to either of the school magazines, the *Beacon* or the *Rambler*. Nor did he take part in sports. What singled him out from the other students was his attitude towards the school. He disliked the discipline and resented having to follow a strict timetable. He preferred to sit at his desk and draw cartoons and caricatures of the other boys and masters.

The religious atmosphere of the school increased his hostility to it. Even before going to Fordham, he had learned to be skeptical about the Church and to believe that the priesthood was hypocritical. In Pottsville, Father McGovern preached pure thoughts and deeds, but O'Hara had seen him and Murphy, the sexton, drinking together at Rap Cardin's speakeasy. Now at school, he was under the guidance of the Jebbies, as the Jesuit fathers were called, and he disliked them. As a student, he was required to take part in many religious exercises. He belonged automatically to the Apostleship of Prayer and the League of the Sacred Heart, whose purpose was "to instil into the students that Apostolic spirit which, as public men, it is hoped they will later on exercise in the world; and secondly, to join the great work of reparation for the outrages daily offered our Lord by sinners." Every day there were recitations from the catechism and instruction in Christian doctrine, and at various times during the year, there were special three-day retreats. In addition, as at other Jesuit schools, there was an annual Novena of Grace in honor of the cofounder of the order, St. Francis Xavier.

These exercises irritated O'Hara and made him impatient. He was by nature independent and therefore skeptical about the teaching he received. One of his former teachers said of him, "He thought he knew it all. When things were explained to him, he thought his way was better. He was in no way disrespectful, but he had to say what he wanted to say." His brightness made him cocky. Once at confession when asked what he planned to do for penance, he answered, "Nothing, because it is not a mortal sin." The priest responded, "I see we have a smart young theologian here." O'Hara got up and walked away.

In the end, the teaching at Fordham Prep and its cloistral atmosphere made him so rebellious that he broke with the Church. For a time, he continued his formal observances and in later years he would send his mother an Easter telegram saying that he had made his confession and communion, but it was only a pretense, a gesture to please her.

Instead of being a step into a wider world of experience, Fordham Prep had proved to be a move into a more limited sort of life. After two years there he left. The school records show that he was "transferred" in November of 1921, but no reason is given. His grades had deteriorated during his stay at the school. He had done well his first year, with 81 in Latin and 83 in English, but in the second year there was a decline to a 67 in Latin, 69 in history and 49 in biology. It was not a good record, but it was not a disaster. It reflects the discontent and unhappiness which may have led him to risk expulsion by going away for a weekend without permission. O'Hara's departure from Fordham Prep was the first of a series of failures that were to mark his early years.

Little time was left before the beginning of the next school year, and Dr. O'Hara probably thought that the boarding department of Keystone Normal School at Kutztown, Pennsylvania, was the best he could find for his son at short notice. O'Hara believed that he was being sent there to do penance, while Dr. O'Hara expected that a year in such an obscure school would make him eager to do well so that he could go to a better place the year after. But the bitterness and hostility between father and son seems to have gone too deep, and John felt humiliated. All his friends were going to real boarding schools, and Keystone Normal was nothing at all. "I won't be there long," he told a friend.

The town of Kutztown was charming, although O'Hara was not in a mood to appreciate it. Founded in the eighteenth century, it was in the heart of lovely farming country and populated by people of German stock —Pennsylvania Dutch, as they are called. There were also a number of Mennonites, wearing dark clothes and long skirts, who went about in a horse and carriage rather than ride in cars. Kutztown was rather like an English market town, with houses and shops along the main street, and it was far more attractive than the coal mining towns of Schuylkill County. Keystone Normal—it is now called Kutztown State College—was founded in 1866 and it occupied some buildings in a leafy section of the town. The main structure was a Georgian hall of red brick with white columns and a bell tower, and there was a Greek revival library in gray stone with a pillared portico and a frieze bearing the names of Tennyson, Shakespeare, Milton and others.

Since Keystone Normal was a teachers' college, the boarding school attended by O'Hara was used as a laboratory by the apprentice school-teachers. Intellectually, it was not challenging. O'Hara was more sophisticated than the farmers' sons and daughters who were his classmates, and he soon became known among them. He was conspicuous in size and appearance, and in the student lounges and the local restaurant, he would often be found talking with fellow students. He showed some interest in writing and was elected to a literary society. Some thought him shy and tender; to others he seemed arrogant. His marks were mediocre, betraying boredom and unhappiness. One improvement over Fordham Prep was that girls were also enrolled. "The normal school was the more fun," O'Hara later recalled, "so much so that for reasons directly related to the presence of women students I did not last out the year. I played football and tennis and took a gentlemanly interest in Cicero and plane geometry, but being seventeen years old and having had two years at a stag prep school, I was not even repelled by those bloomers the girls wore to gym. This was the candy store, and I had a very sweet tooth." Evidently O'Hara's attentions to one girl got him into trouble. The principal of the school, Amos Rothermel, ordered O'Hara to stop courting Euphemia (Famy) Shumberger, whose father was a trustee of the place. Naturally, O'Hara refused to obey, and since his grades provided no convincing reason for his remaining, he was dismissed.

Back in Pottsville to face an angry father, O'Hara was immediately set to work. He had some experience from earlier summer jobs when he worked as a soda jerk in a drugstore and as a guard in a park, but this time his father wanted him to become a day laborer, perhaps as a punishment for his expulsion. His first job, which he took with his friend, Robert Root, required him to go out of town to Port Carbon, where a rail strike was under way. The two boys were hired as call boys to wake the crews of scab workers in time for their runs. They were paid five dollars a shift, but they received a good deal of abuse when they woke the men in their shacks, especially as the boys had to make them sign a card to prove they had been called.

This experience was O'Hara's real introduction to the industrial and coal mining life of eastern Pennsylvania. It was a rough and unpleasant world, and although O'Hara later joked that he "once held up the whole Sunbury Division by failing to rout out a bunch of crews" of railroad men, he was also being exposed to the reality of working-class life. To begin with, the landscape itself looked traumatized. Great mountains of slag, or culm as it's called in Pennsylvania, rose around the fringes of the mines and obliterated the gentle contours of the countryside. The nearby towns and miners' "patches" were dreary in another way. The streets were lined with frame houses, often built in rows, with green tarpaper facing. Goats and chickens wandered about at will. In a story O'Hara described the yard of one house as being "full of old wash boilers and rubber boots, tin cans and the framework of an abandoned baby carriage." The centers of the larger towns were made up of routine drugstores, goods shops and small department stores, a few run-down bars, a hotel with a metal awning over the door, and always churches—Roman Catholic, Russian Orthodox, Baptist, Methodist.

Working out of Pottsville, O'Hara saw how minimal and depressed conditions were. The spirit of the place seems to have encouraged narrowness and bigotry, with Protestants hating Catholics, with Irish and Poles and Lithuanians all separated from one another. With nothing to raise their hopes, the people themselves were reduced. Young people did not marry for love; they just married classmates from school who had the same origin and religion. The women stayed home with the children; the men went out with their chums and came home drunk. Then they beat their children. One miners' song contains the lines, "Please don't beat me, papa, for I've done no wrong, Please don't whip me, papa, for I won't be with you long." The life was brutal and without privacy. Another song written at the time of the "Mollies" ends, "In short, if you want to enjoy God's bounty, Go anywhere except to Schuylkill County."

Although O'Hara never wrote directly about working in the mines, he made use of his varied experiences as a day laborer. After working at Port Carbon, he was a "baggage smasher" or porter at the Railway Express office, and he worked at the open hearth of the Eastern Steel Mill in Pottsville. At another time, he was an assistant signalman for the Reading Railroad gravity system and worked in the marshalling yards at Port Carbon. There he handled the heavy switches and brakes that controlled the coal cars as they were sent down a long incline to Pottsville. He also worked in the Reading Railroad roundhouse, as a pit man, swabbing grease on the undersides of steam locomotives. This work made him so strong that in later years he was able to pick up in one hand a No Parking stanchion weighted in concrete and easily toss it aside. Apart from becoming strong, O'Hara got to know some of the toughest working men in America—the Poles and Lithuanians and Irish who worked in the steel mills and on the trains—and he also learned the deadening routine of physical labor, the petty terrorism of office life and the fear and vacuity that comes from working in a place where you have no power and no prospect of ever getting any.

Saturday night was practically the only time to relax, and when the mines were working, Pottsville was filled with miners and their families and girl friends coming in for a fling. There were restaurants, movie theaters and dance halls, and the sidewalks were crowded. O'Hara often went to the bars and dance halls and quickly got to know the rough underside of small-town life. The saloons were almost always kept by Irishmen, and there were plenty of loose girls and prostitutes. O'Hara hung around these places and saw the brutality of exploitation, the rough language and the debased currency of human relations. In a story he described a saloon called the Bucket of Blood which was in a tough Italian neighborhood that was "so feared by the town police that they ignored everything" that went on there. But O'Hara responded to the tremendous vitality and uninhibited humor that exists in such places. At home he had to be well-mannered and genteel, but he also knew how others lived.

O'Hara did not go to prostitutes because he was attractive enough to court the complaisant Polish working girls he met in Pottsville, Shenandoah and other towns. With his friend, John Bergen, who had a car, he would call on them at night. One of the places they would go to he later used as a model for his novel *The Farmers Hotel.*

The best places to meet girls were the dance halls which during O'Hara's youth were visited by the big bands from Paul Whiteman's to Tommy and Jimmy Dorsey's, who originally came from Shenandoah. These bands played at Charlton's dance hall in Pottsville, at Maher's in Shenandoah and at similar halls in other towns and small cities throughout the region. Other popular places were Lakewood and Lakeside, which were amusement parks out in the country. Thursday was the night to go, and young men and factory girls from Pottsville would ride out in the trolley to listen and dance to Kay Keyser, George Olson, Cab Calloway and the other "name" bands. Three or four hundred people would go, some in groups, some alone, hoping to meet others. They would pay fifty cents or a dollar to get in, and during intermission they would wander about the amusement park, play games and eat food from the stands. O'Hara later recalled what happened when an Irish tenor called Jack Gallagher began to sing. A former miner who had lost an arm in an accident, he had an immediate effect on the young boys and girls who gathered round the platform. "The sexual stimulation was universal," wrote O'Hara. This was especially true when he began to sing "Jazz Me Blues," which had a pounding rhythm: "after the first four bars the bellies were rubbing the bellies in obedience to the beat, but all the women had their eyes on Gallagher. When the number ended there would be a mass exit to the bushes."

Here O'Hara and his Pottsville friends would meet the mill girls whom they called "spivots." When the dances were over they would go to one of the neighboring nightclubs or speakeasies such as the Amber Lantern or the Rattlesnake, where once five Italians were murdered. There were prostitutes available, rooms for assignations and prohibition booze. The buildings were ugly square concrete structures that looked sinister without trying to.

It was a crude and harsh world, yet O'Hara drew energy from it. He enjoyed visiting the dives along Minersville Street in Pottsville which, with appropriate irony, has subsequently been named "John O'Hara Street." Yet he also felt guilty about it since he was one of the "nasty boys who went away to school and dances collegiate and had nothing better to do than bring shame and disgrace on the girls who worked in the mills." Mainly he associated with girls in the country club set. They too wanted to hear Ted Weems and Fred Waring's Pennsylvanians, so O'Hara and his friends would sometimes make up a party of six or eight and drive out for an evening. They would stick together as a group, and this created new problems. "As we were dirty little snobs, we would have a hard time the next week explaining to the spivots why we hadn't danced with them last Thursday. 'If I'm not good enough for you then, you don't get a dance with me tonight,' the spivots would say. They even had musical support for their arguments: two of the popular Scranton Siren tunes were *Aggravatin' Papa, Don't You Try to Two-Time Me,* and *You Gotta See Mama Every Night or You Don't See Mama at All."*

This was O'Hara's social dilemma: he understood both worlds but felt he belonged to neither. This knowledge would help him as a writer but would make him unhappy and dissatisfied as a person. The rest of the family shared few of O'Hara's social worries. Dr. O'Hara was self-sufficient and his professional life kept him busy. He was proud of his work in the community and was determined to be independent. Personally, he had always been socially accepted. He belonged to the Pottsville Club and to the Outdoor Club which was the antecedent to the Schuylkill Country Club, but he did not use them much. He preferred to amuse himself by going to the races, by riding and attending sports events. Mrs. O'Hara belonged to small women's societies, including a Cercle Français which she attended on weekday afternoons. Her religious pursuits and the need to look after eight growing children left her little time for ordinary social activity.

The O'Haras were aware of social gradations, however. When the children attended the parochial school across the street, they were told to come home by themselves, which was a way of saying that working-class children were not welcome. The other side of the coin was their discovery that they were in competition with other Irish Catholic families that wanted to rise in society. Of the various immigrants to move into a predominantly Protestant Anglo-Saxon country, the Irish had the advantage of speaking English. This made it possible for them to be assimilated more quickly than the Italians, the Poles or the Central European Jews. In Pottsville, one Irish contemporary of Dr. O'Hara's was more socially ambitious than most. Having made a great deal of money, he married into a Protestant family and, when the time came for the new Schuylkill Country Club to be built in the outskirts of Pottsville, he bought a substantial number of $1000 shares in order to be ingratiating. As a result, he became a prominent member of the country club.

On one occasion, Mrs. O'Hara, who also belonged to the club, decided to give a bridge luncheon for fifty women friends to whom she felt socially indebted. The day was set, the invitations were sent out and accepted, the Baked Alaskas were ordered. Then the wife of the social-climbing Irishman, jealous of Mrs. O'Hara's party, had her husband force the club steward to postpone Mrs. O'Hara's party so that she could have one of her own on the same day for many of the same people. Since those who did not belong to the club could accept only one invitation every six months, she succeeded in spoiling Mrs. O'Hara's party. It was a petty but brutal attack by one socially insecure family on another.

Pottsville's social activities took place mainly during the summer holidays and at Christmas when the young people came home from school and college. A group of them formed a "gang" of whom O'Hara was one. His best friends were Ransloe Boone, whose father was a doctor; Fred Hoefel, who was later to suffer from polio; and Robert Simonds, with whom he corresponded at Dartmouth and whose father was superintendent of schools. There were others as well, Eddie Fox, Robert Root and Jack Bergen, who was slightly older. They would "hang out" at a drugstore on South Centre Street and listen to the latest jazz records at home.

Dancing was important in their lives. Having been trained in deportment at dancing classes, the young ladies and gentlemen moved on to the club dances. The first social dance that O'Hara attended was held at the Outdoor Club, where the band, made up of local boys, was called the Tasmanian Tinsmiths. "I began to take girls to dances at the beginning of the Scott Fitzgerald era," O'Hara later wrote, "and I recall that when I came to my father for the necessary funds for my first formal dance he gave me so much for the dance subscriptions, so much for incidentals and so much for flowers. 'Flowers?' I asked.

" 'Flowers, of course,' he said, in a way that seemed to leave no room for argument. As a result I sent flowers to all the lucky girls in the early days until I began to get embarrassed by their profuse thanks. None of my friends sent flowers, so it looked as though I were putting on the 'dog,' so I stopped. The flower money went for Four Roses, and that, in a thimble, is the story of flaming youth."

During the Christmas holidays the young people all came home from boarding school. Those already returned would run down to the railroad station to meet the new arrivals and take them off to a party even before they went home to greet their parents. O'Hara was fascinated by the way in which everyone examined everyone else—for the stylish clothes they had picked up in the east, for their fraternity or club pins, for all the signs of growing up, and growing away, from Pottsville. Then came questions about who was going to what dance. "A certain delicacy in human relations was observed in this phase: all the boys who were going to the Assembly knew which others would be going and which would not. Same was true of the country-club Christmas dance."

O'Hara always linked the delight of Christmas with social competition; together they represent his mixed feelings about his childhood home. "The cold air was exhilarating, and the heavy fall of snow did its best to create beauty, even to the extent of covering up the gouges that coal mining had made in the hillsides and hiding the squalor of the company houses. Wherever you went you had the snow to contend with, shoveled and drifted high on the sides of the streets and roads; and if you were going anywhere off the heaviest traveled path you first called up to ask how the roads were. Thus, when you got there, you had some sense of accomplishment; you earned your fireplace, your drink, your furtive kiss."

But with O'Hara, the pleasures were always modified by yearnings. "Some thirty years ago," he wrote in 1947, "in a little coal-mining town in the anthracite region of Pennsylvania, there lived a boy, a boy of 12. He was tall for his age, and in many ways precocious. He looked forward to the day when, like Clint Sheafer, he would own his own Mercer; when, like Al Cullum, he would be on his way to Yale; when, like Bill Ulmer, he would know the 16th Arrondissement better than he knew the Third Ward."

For most of 1922 and 1923, while in exile from school, O'Hara kept himself amused by going to parties. "My record for a week is four dances," he wrote, "which really gives *Pottsville* sufficient cause for gossip." One of the girls he courted was Gladys Suender from Frackville, who was known as "the Wonderful Wench" and "the Captivating Creole." O'Hara went out with her frequently, often to the annoyance of her family. O'Hara enjoyed showing off, and at dinner parties he would light kitchen matches with his thumbnail. People were supposed to be impressed, but when he failed to pull off his trick, he would be crestfallen and sometimes fall into an Irish depression.

He could also be irritating: once when courting Gladys, he borrowed her family car even though he had been told not to. Then, when the car had a flat tire, he phoned her brother, whom he disliked and, complaining about the state of the car, told him to come and arrange for the repairs. He was annoying but also witty and original. He took sophomoric pleasure in making aphoristic remarks such as "Gratitude is the lively anticipation of further favors" and "Your insolence can never hope to reach the height of my disdain." His boredom and instability occasionally made him turn to drink. "I'm going to continue to get drunk as much as I can," he told a friend, adding, in a mood of self-pity, "I can see that I'll be the only genuine failure in the gang."

There were also signs of productive restlessness. Relations with his father were bad, but they led to a desire to get on with his education. "All

I crave is two years in college," he said. Since his father was skeptical about his scholarly aptitudes, O'Hara considered becoming a car salesman in order to make enough money to become independent and then perhaps go to a university. "I have made up my mind to get out of Pottsville, but when, I can't say." He was reading a lot and his intellectual curiosity made him introspective. "Every damn thing imaginable has come in for a share of inspection by me," he wrote, "and this may sound queer, but one thing I blame it on is learning to arrive at the meaning of a word by recalling its Latin root. Bend that!" He was also delighted to be learning new words, one of which was "protagonist," which he picked up from a piece of theater criticism by Robert Benchley.

With his friend Simonds off at Dartmouth, O'Hara did his own reading at home. "Did you ever read any of John Galsworthy's thrillers (?)," he wrote. "I've finished 'In Chancery.' Liked it immensely. Also read two other English authors,—Beresford and Frances Hodgson Burnett. The more I read modern English authors, the more I think we Americans are sadly lacking in pen-wielders. I've assayed Balzac and am compelled to admit that he held no interest for my temperamental nature. Christopher Morley amuses me with his one act plays." O'Hara's interest in words and in other writers suggests that he wanted to record the emotions of his own life.

Meanwhile, there were practical questions about his own future. "I've done a lot of serious thinking," he wrote Simonds. "Why not? Here I am at 18 with several years of school and nothing to show for it; perhaps some latent ability which I fear will remain latent; no liking for the work I've done or am doing; no desire to enter medicine, business or the Army, (sounds English, what?). Added to all this, I'm in that awful coma—the Pottsville lethargy. Something must be done." In another letter he told Simonds that he wanted to go to a university, but mainly for its social advantages. He wanted to join a national drinking club, win a varsity letter in sports, take part in a play and belong to the literary magazine. There was no cant about school spirit, which he thought was so much "horse shit" or "apple sauce" and he ended his letter with an apology: "I hope I'm not being iconoclastic and smashing any cherished ideals of yours, but when one says 'frankly,' one feels that almost anything is permissible."

After his sojourn at home, O'Hara was sent off in September of 1923 to Niagara University Prep School, near Niagara Falls in New York State. Having been an undergraduate there, Dr. O'Hara was able to arrange for his son's admission. Founded in 1856, the school was operated by the Vincentian Fathers, a less rigorous order than the Jesuits of Fordham. Although he "felt about 55 years older than everyone else in the school," O'Hara soon entered into the life of the place. The many religious activities of this Roman Catholic institution may have been distasteful to O'Hara, but as he later said, he "had a good year there. Nearly every afternoon I went for a walk to Lewiston, all by myself except for a book and a pipe, and I always used to pause for the view from the Niagara Falls Country Club and watch the Toronto boat come in from the Lake. Some days I would walk all the way to Fort Niagara, where a former chauffeur of my father's was a regular army sergeant. He was a wild Irishman called Foxie Cole, and at Fort Niagara he would lecture me on drinking and smoking, to both of which my father was fanatically opposed, but he and I would then light up a couple of Piedmonts and he would take me to the canteen and treat me to a bottle of pop."

O'Hara did well in his studies. He received an average of 97 in English literature, the highest ever achieved at the school. His talents were recognized when he was selected to be class poet and valedictorian. He was still iconoclastic, however, and spent much time sitting about and talking. One of the authors he enjoyed was Clarence Buddington Kelland, a popular writer who wrote a series of books for boys in the style of *Tom Sawyer* as well as adult novels of manners with such titles as *Conflict, Hard Money* and *The Great Crooner*. Like most writers, O'Hara read widely and indiscriminately, without academic prejudice. He was more attracted to novels dealing with contemporary life than to books on the school syllabus.

At Niagara, O'Hara fulfilled for the first time the promise he had always shown. In June of 1924, his pleased parents drove up to the school for the graduation exercises. Then, on the night before the ceremony, in celebration of the end of school, O'Hara and two of his classmates went out on the town. They went from bar to bar and were brought back to the school by two state policemen at six o'clock in the morning, in full sight of the Fathers who were up early for their religious exercises. O'Hara went to his dormitory to sleep it off. A few hours later his father came to his room and told him to go home immediately, by train. The school had stripped him of the honors he was to receive and he left without his diploma. "Father never really spoke cordially to me after that," O'Hara later said.

3. APPRENTICE JOURNALIST

The *Pottsville Journal* was housed in a narrow and rickety building on South Centre Street, down the hill from the O'Haras' house on Mahantongo Street. The newsroom was on the top floor and there John O'Hara had a desk. Every day Mrs. O'Hara would prepare lunch for him, including a special lemon or apple pie in its own little dish, and it would be delivered, rain or shine, by his younger brother Tom. After the disgrace at Niagara and the loss of all possibility of going to Yale, Dr. O'Hara had made no punitive efforts to force his son to become a day laborer. Instead, he had spoken to his friend Harry Silliman, the owner of the *Journal,* and John had begun to work as a "utility reporter" at a salary of "zero a week to start."

The *Journal* was an evening paper, a rival of the more powerful morning *Republican*. It emphasized local news. O'Hara's first story was about a man in Port Carbon who had shot his father to defend his mother. The editor, William Kehoe, told him to "get the facts and get details," and this advice influenced O'Hara for the rest of his life.

About thirty-five people worked for the *Journal,* among them, Walter Farquhar, a talented columnist and sports editor who became O'Hara's counselor. Soon O'Hara was covering high school football games on Saturdays and professional football games on Sundays. Over the years the coal mining districts of Pennsylvania produced many burly players, and Pottsville had developed a mania for football. At the time O'Hara was at the *Journal,* Pottsville even had a team in the National Football League, playing against the New York Giants, the Green Bay Packers and others. O'Hara enjoyed writing about sports, but found it difficult to be interesting, since so much of it was the same. He therefore studied Ring Lardner and Grantland Rice and learned from them about narrative methods.

In sports he could rely on statistics, but O'Hara was less good as a general reporter. David Yocum, the news editor, remembered in later years that "he was also shy about interviewing people. Once I sent him over to Schuylkill Haven to get a story about what we used to call a goose-bone weather prophet. Well, John came back and said he couldn't find the fellow. Another time he missed covering a church banquet because he had a date. But there was a certain kind of story John liked to do and did well. For instance there was a cigar store where everyone would hang out in those days. One day we heard it was going out of business. John wrote a nice story about that."

Not having interest in most of his assignments, O'Hara grew lazy and soon found himself in trouble. He didn't worry about it, however, claiming he wouldn't be fired because his father was a friend of the owner's. He was also a great tease, especially of Katherine Bowman, who worked in the society department. One day Silliman, the owner, came into the part of the office where O'Hara and his friend Ransloe Boone worked and found Katherine Bowman teaching the two men how to do the Charleston. "For God's sake," was all he said, before leaving. On another day while Katherine was clipping society items from other local papers to use in her own column, O'Hara, whose desk was in front of hers, leaned back and hooked his arm over her typewriter so she could not work. Exasperated, she told him she was working against a deadline. He then set fire to the papers she was clipping, which so annoyed her she poked him in the stomach with a pair of shears. Pretending to be mortally wounded, he grabbed her hand and accidentally dislocated her thumb.

Despite the horseplay, O'Hara had real ambitions. He wanted to get a job on the *New York World,* believing that he could then move anywhere he liked at a good salary. For country newspapermen, the *World* meant Franklin Pierce Adams—F.P.A. as he was known—whose daily column, "The Conning Tower," was awaited eagerly at newsstands. Katherine Bowman's future husband, himself a small-town newspaper columnist, wrote that "all over the country, lonely persons in little towns looked to his humor as an escape from Main Street and Winesburg and Spoon River; in country newspaper offices he was a god."

O'Hara believed that if he were to have a column of his own it would improve his chances of getting a job on the *World.* On April 1, 1925, he was given permission to have a column in the *Journal.* It was called "After Four O'Clock" and was signed Trewq, the five letters in the upper left-hand corner of the keyboard in reverse order. As F.P.A. did, O'Hara tried to get others to contribute to the column, but he teased them so about the work they submitted that they lost interest in writing for him. The title gave some unity to the column which was mainly about afternoon and evening amusements. O'Hara told his readers where they might go and described his own experiences of driving around the countryside.

Despite his belief that his position at the *Journal* was impregnable, O'Hara was fired twice. He was supposed to be at the office by eight in the morning, but often he didn't appear till noon and his work had to be made up by others. He was original in his excuses, claiming that he had bumped his head while bobsledding and therefore had overslept, but they weren't good enough. Following his departure from the *Journal*, he got a job at a smaller paper, the *Evening Courier*, in Tamaqua, a small mining city with a main street lined with churches and saloons. O'Hara took a room in a cheap hotel, but since the town had little to offer and was only sixteen miles away from Pottsville, he decided to commute by trolley. He worked at the *Courier* for only a few months and once again was fired. It was the usual trouble. "I always seemed to be in the corner saloon when the story broke," he later explained. "I got licked on a story in my own home town by a *Philadelphia Bulletin* man. He was in the State Police headquarters while I was out feeding sugar to the horses."

Almost all of O'Hara's friends lived on Mahantongo Street, which was also known as "Liver Street" because the residents were known to be eaters of calves' liver, locally thought of as an exotic viand. O'Hara was keen to emphasize the special quality of his neighborhood friends as well as their social superiority. This was most easily done by wearing expensive and unusual pieces of clothing. At the *Journal*, when O'Hara, Katherine Bowman and Ransloe Boone appeared together, they would create a sartorial stir. "I know one thing about this paper," said the editor. "I'll bet it's the only paper that has three reporters that wear 'coon coats." Dr. O'Hara loftily observed that while raccoon coats were suitable for coachmen who had to sit out in bad weather, they were vulgar for gentlemen. But it was the 1920s, and they were the height of style in Cambridge and New Haven. In Pottsville, fur coats and exaggeratedly collegiate clothing just irritated O'Hara's elders, who correctly thought that he and his friends were putting on airs.

Not long after his return from Niagara, O'Hara and his friends formed an association which they mockingly called The Purity League. They drank together and enjoyed pranks, such as placing empty gin bottles on a noted teetotaler's porch. The members of the group had nicknames such as Beanie and Deacon; O'Hara was known as Doc. Then, when his friends went away to college, O'Hara tried to set up a fraternity back home in Pottsville. To be called Lamda Delta Alpha, it was supposed to include "the gang in its entirety" and was intended to give a focus to the social activities of the "fratres." O'Hara wrote enthusiastically to the would-be members, but since most of them were already away at college where they belonged to real fraternities, the plan failed and the club was never formed.

Meanwhile the O'Haras had an intermittent family membership in the relatively new Schuylkill Country Club, which professed to be exclusive. There O'Hara would meet the upper-class girls from Pottsville he had known since dancing school days. Although the rest of his family cared little about social advancement, O'Hara did and had grown increasingly disturbed about not quite belonging to the world of the "nobs" because he was an Irish Catholic. Although he admired their style, he resented the rich who lived at the upper end of Mahantongo Street and was sometimes scornful of their values. This emotional conflict led to excesses. Sometimes he dressed so much in the style of the young collegian, with flannels that were baggier than anyone else's, that he seemed a caricature of fashion; on other occasions he would appear at a country club dance wearing white knickers and a tweed jacket, and if a letter came from the club president reminding him to wear a dinner jacket, the next time he would appear unshaven and wearing a dirty shirt and unpressed trousers.

As an outsider who insisted he wasn't one, he earned himself a bad reputation, especially with a group of war veterans who had served together as members of the Pottsville Troop. They were genteel with a vengeance, and they disliked the uppity young Irish Catholic with his scornful airs. O'Hara reacted to their hostility most often when he had had some drinks, which made him contentious. There were fistfights, and more than once he was thrown out of the Schuylkill Country Club.

Once, in what was plainly an effort to discredit him, O'Hara was accused of having stolen a watch at the country club. His friend Jack Bergen asked him whether he stole it, and O'Hara answered, "What do you think?" In a column years later, he wrote of being "brought up to tell the truth. The word honor meant a lot in my family, and still does." Dismissing George Washington's "I cannot tell a lie," O'Hara observed, "Our version would have been: 'I did it,' and take the licking." O'Hara never forgot the false charge at the country club. In a story derived from it, he spoke of the accuser as the "bastard, the dirty bastard."

He also attended the smaller parties that were given by the younger members of the Archbald, Sheafer and Suender families who lived high up on Mahantongo Street. There were progressive dinner parties which moved, course by course, from one house to another; there were bridge parties and dinners followed by an evening at the movies. Because there were more girls than boys, O'Hara was often invited to these parties. He had a bad complexion and big ears that stuck out from the side of his head; in his rebellious moments he was so rough-looking that some of the older girls called him "dirty-neck O'Hara." But he was always perceptive and witty, and this made him attractive. More than most young people of his age, he also had a clear idea of what he wanted to do. He was ambitious and literary; he spoke of the books he read and especially of the writers he admired. One of his favorites was F. Scott Fitzgerald. He also read Elinor Wylie, Joseph Hergesheimer and Carl Van Vechten; on the whole he preferred the wittier, lighter writers to more solemn chroniclers such as Theodore Dreiser.

The chief attraction of upper-class Pottsville society was Margaretta Archbald, a tall, slender girl who was the daughter of Colonel James Archbald, the representative of the Girard Estate in Pottsville and a prominent member of the town's society. O'Hara and Margaretta met first in dancing school, and although she was some years older than he, they continued to see each other over the years. Like the O'Haras, the Archbalds kept horses, and John and Margaretta often went riding alone. They also went to the same horse shows together. By 1923, they were seeing so much of each other that the gossips were saying that they were engaged. O'Hara denied this, but admitted seeing her a good deal. "Last week I had three and this week two dates and two auto rides with her," he wrote.

In O'Hara's eyes, the Archbalds were the embodiment of social grace. A Yale graduate and Protestant with money and position, Colonel Archbald and his family represented all the things O'Hara admired and yearned for. Compared to his own stolidly middle-class household, they were experienced and at ease in the world beyond Pottsville. Colonel Archbald was even an expert in one of O'Hara's favorite subjects, college fraternities, and gave him information about them. But O'Hara's enthusiasm was not returned. Although they knew one another, the Archbalds and Dr. and Mrs. O'Hara were in different social worlds and met infrequently. Unlike some of their neighbors, however, they were not anti-Catholic. One of their own daughters was a convert and later became a nun. But they did not wish to encourage O'Hara as a suitor. There was the age difference and they disapproved of his drinking. By sending Margaretta off to boarding school and college they hoped to blunt the romance.

But for O'Hara, the relationship was everything. The more he saw of Margaretta and her world, the more his own felt claustrophobic. "I go through cheap shame when the O'Hara side gets too close for comfort," he later wrote to F. Scott Fitzgerald. Meantime, the first year of his love for Margaretta was "a great year." He kept a diary and was alive to his surroundings; love made him notice the latest songs, the movies, the new expressions and jokes. It was all thanks to Margaretta, for as he wrote at the time, "she's all that makes Po. bearable."

Meanwhile, in 1924, Dr. O'Hara found himself in conflict with some of his colleagues at the Pottsville Hospital. His rectitude in questioning the inflated fee scale the Philadelphia & Reading paid for mining accidents and his skill as a surgeon made his colleagues angry and jealous. They were also offended by his outspokenness and lack of tact. Beneath the crisis lay

religious bigotry, and the result of the quarrel was a schism between
Roman Catholic and Protestant doctors. Although Dr. O'Hara was chief
surgeon and chief of staff, he was forced with some of the other Roman
Catholic doctors to leave the hospital and set up a new one. Where formerly Pottsville had one hospital in which Catholics and Protestants
worked together, it now had two, and the Catholics were in the inferior
building. Dr. O'Hara worked hard to set up the new hospital and had the
help of a Protestant, A. C. Millikan, who donated a building. There were
frequent meetings in the O'Haras' front living room and Dr. O'Hara had
to supervise the buying of new equipment and the administration of the
new hospital in addition to taking care of his regular patients.

The crisis brought out John's loyalties. He was so angry he wanted to
beat up the Protestant doctors physically. The episode distressed him on
a deeper level, for it showed how big a handicap his Irish Catholic heritage
was. He could also see that his father was exhausted by overwork, and he
was worried about his health. In February of 1925, Dr. O'Hara decided to
take a holiday by himself and went south to St. Petersburg, in Florida.
Within a month word came that he was seriously ill. He was put on a train
to Philadelphia and then transferred to a Pullman for Pottsville. John went
to the station to meet him. He waited in the roadster, and when his father
got off the train, he "went up to him and kissed him because he was my
father. I took him by the hand and drove him home. I got him upstairs to
his bedroom and helped him undress—he had no luggage on the train—
and put him to bed."

Dr. O'Hara was only fifty-eight, but he knew he was dying. He had
uremic poisoning and a visit from a Philadelphia specialist confirmed the
suspicion that he had Bright's disease. He told his wife that John, who was
only twenty, could not be relied on as head of the family but could always
be counted on in emergencies. Dr. O'Hara had never made a will, and now
it was too late to do so. The younger children were sent away to stay with
their aunt in New Jersey, and John fetched Mary from her boarding school
in Philadelphia. At this point John also fell ill. He stopped by his father's
bedside before going upstairs to bed himself, and his father said "Poor
John." These were the last words he ever heard his father speak. Late at
night, six days after his return from Florida, Dr. O'Hara died. The family
gathered by the bedside, but John wouldn't go in to join the mourners.
When his sister Mary asked him why not, he answered, "I've already shed
many tears for my father."

There was a big Irish Catholic funeral—"almost as big as a gangster's
or a politician's," his son was later to remark. "But the people who turned
up at the church—the Protestants and Jews as well as the Catholics—were
not there only for the spectacle." A week later, O'Hara wrote to his friend
Simonds that his father's death had a "sobering effect" on him. It was the
end of any hope of marrying Margaretta Archbald; it meant the end of

European travel plans and even of Yale, insofar as that was still a possibility. His father's death also made him think about values. "No one knows better than I what sort of life the governor led. Hard work, a clean life and so little pleasure. No one can tell me he derived a lot of satisfaction from the knowledge that he was doing good and that alone. It's all out of proportion."

Since there was no will, the state took charge of the O'Hara estate, and it amounted to very little. Dr. O'Hara had some cash; most of his property was tied up in real estate, including some slum tenements, and there was a safe full of German marks, which inflation had made worthless. Fortunately, Mrs. O'Hara had enough money of her own to prevent any immediate sacrifices, but in the meantime, there were terrible adjustments. John and his mother had to go to Philadelphia to pick up the little children who had been staying with their aunt in New Jersey. When they rushed out of the station to the car and saw that it was empty, they cried out, "Where's Daddy? Where's Daddy?" They had not been told.

The family bereavement brought John and his mother close together. Both had good senses of humor which allowed each to see through any tendency the other had to put on airs. When they played bridge together, O'Hara would sometimes invent elaborate theories about bidding and attempt to disrupt the game with his proposals. His mother would pull him down to earth by saying, "Just follow the rules, please." In the past, she had always been a buffer between his father and himself. When he had come home late at night and crept unsteadily up the stairs, fearful of waking his father, his mother would joke about it with him in the morning. She also discussed books with him and was the first to encourage him to write.

She was only forty-five when she found herself in charge of the family. To some of her Pottsville neighbors she was known as a "saint" for so cheerfully undertaking the children's upbringing, but her son was more perceptive. It was not easy, for as he later wrote, "Sometimes I would come home and find her doing household arithmetic, trying to figure out how to pay taxes, grocery bills, etc. but there would be no complaints, although God knows she must have stayed awake many nights wondering and worrying." Yet she enjoyed what she had to do. "She baked cakes and sold them for $5, she gave French lessons and did crocheting, and she was active in the D.A.R., gave recitals with The First Piano Octette of Pottsville, Pa., and not too humbly heard herself described as 'Katharine O'Hara is a remarkable woman.' She loved it." O'Hara did what he could: he helped his younger brothers with their schoolwork and contributed from his meager salary. But he resented seeming to be at the head of the family without being able to play the role properly. When the farm was sold and the horses were auctioned, he also felt that his own position in Pottsville was being undermined. It was no disgrace to lose your money, but O'Hara felt that it was. His own snobbery came home to roost, and he imagined that his enemies were now enjoying his discomfiture. It was a traumatic experience and it helps explain his harsh judgment of his father: "He may have been a good surgeon, but in money matters he was a fool."

O'Hara was affected by mixed feelings of rebellion and remorse. Once when his sister Kathleen asked him why he and his father had always fought, he became furious and said, "Never forget that Daddy loved you and he loved me." Then he choked up and his eyes filled with tears. "I was proud of my father," O'Hara wrote afterwards, "and went around bragging about how he was going to get into Who's Who. Then one day I asked him if he had filled out the blank and sent it in. He said he certainly had not." But the father's indifference to public fame made O'Hara take the opposite line. "From that moment on I was attracted to Who's Who," he wrote. Later on, in the midst of an argument, John told his father he would be in *Who's Who* by the time he was thirty, to which the response was, "The way you're going you won't be alive by the time you're 30." But now Dr. O'Hara was dead, and there was no way for him to prove himself. He would always suffer from feelings of inadequacy that grew out of the intensity of the relationship with his father and the way it was so abruptly terminated.

But to trace all of O'Hara's frustrations to his feelings about his father would be absurd. A week after the funeral he was still hoping to spend at least a year in college, and he was determined to leave Pottsville. He was bitter about the accidental quality of his misfortune, but he was also ambitious. To some degree this made him careless of the feelings of others, and he was easily critical of many whom he dismissed as "creeps." He began to concentrate on doing his own work and that made him increasingly independent of the opinions of others. He was not interested in being a "nice guy." He knew what he wanted and set about doing it.

In an article he wrote for the *Pottsville Journal* while still only twenty, O'Hara said, "I have every hope of winning a Pulitzer Prize, and if I ever get to it, I intend to write The Great American Novel." It was partly a joke, but he also meant it. His literary talents had been noticed early at St. Patrick's by Sister Calista. As a teenager, he had written a patriotic essay on "Our Flag" and been awarded a German helmet as first prize. Unlike most young writers, O'Hara wrote little poetry, and his work was free of imagery. This may have been caused by his color blindness, which was so bad he mistakenly wore a red tie on the day of his father's funeral. Color blindness made him insensitive to some forms of nature; there is hardly any mention of flowers in his work. O'Hara's schoolboy writings were mainly humorous and satirical. One of his first pieces was a sketch based on a tapestry in the O'Hara house that contained a number of esoteric symbols. O'Hara wrote a skit about it in the manner of a musical comedy act and pinned it to the back of the tapestry in a shy first act of family publication. He also revealed an editorial gift when he helped his brother Joseph write an essay on "How to Wash a Car" for his school class. O'Hara told him to eliminate every unnecessary word, wherever possible including the word "I," and to reduce the piece to one page.

From the beginning, O'Hara did most of his writing at night. He would come home after work at the newspaper, make himself a peanut butter sandwich, go upstairs to his third floor room and start typing. He was always exceptionally disciplined. He would read and analyze the stories he found in magazines and then send in his own work to the *Saturday Evening Post* and others that he admired. He would be cast down when his work was rejected, as it always was at the beginning, because he was convinced it was as good as the stories being published, but he kept submitting new work. He also corresponded with writers he admired such as F. Scott Fitzgerald, and from some of them he received replies. Walter Farquhar encouraged his writing at the *Journal,* and further incentive came from his competition with Ransloe Boone and Katherine Bowman for the honor of being the first to be published in a national paper or magazine.

O'Hara later observed that "practically all good writing is a form of protest." Certainly his own was. At the *Journal* he began to sign his pieces "Petronius" in honor of the Roman satirist who was known as the *Arbiter Elegantiae.* The satirist wants to improve society by making people laugh at their own foibles. O'Hara's use of "Petronius" was an imitation of the pseudonymous contributors to F.P.A.'s "The Conning Tower" who had the same purpose in mind. Dorothy Parker was "Dolly," Louis Untermeyer was "Daffydowndilly" and Deems Taylor was "Smeed." It was a period when humor magazines were flourishing and the wit of such writers as Dorothy Parker, Alexander Woollcott and Robert Benchley was highly valued. O'Hara's natural bent was not satirical, but by imitating actual speech mannerisms, he found that he could be amusing. In a few years, he was to write that "kidding Rotary clubs went out with Mencken," but he himself began as an imitator of Sinclair Lewis, who did just that. He made no attempt to hide the source of his first parodies, for one purported to be a speech by "George F. Gabbitry" and another article was called "The Man Who Knew Sinclair Lewis."

O'Hara was first published in "The Conning Tower" in March of 1927, just after being fired from the *Tamaqua Courier.* In most of the pieces he wrote for this column, O'Hara seems to have been interested mainly in imitating American speech. Where Sinclair Lewis makes sarcastic judgments about his characters, O'Hara lets them reveal themselves through their own words. Many of his sketches are devoted to Babbitt-like businessmen and boosters, but he also enjoyed recording the language of bootleggers and telephone operators. Here is the operator at the law firm of Holmes, Watson and Holmes: "G'morning, Mr. Smudge, how's things in the Sandusky branch. Justaminute till I get this . . . Holmeswatsonandholmes. No, Mr. Watson is not in town. Spell that, please. N,o,w,o,k k for klan, yes, I understand, one k,l,e,w,i,c,z. Nowokeswis . . . Oh, Novoka-vitch. Very well, thank you. . . . Miss Smither is not in yet. Whitehall tharrrreee-thrrrrree-niyun-niyun. Is that correct. . . . " The pleasure comes from seeing how ridiculous familiar sounds become when put down on paper. In his early sketches, O'Hara relied heavily on tricks of spelling. His Babbitt figure says "reelize" for realize; "innaresting" for interesting, and he speaks of the "speert of cawoperation." Sometimes O'Hara's spelling variants become unreadable and the humor is lost. Lewis and O'Hara both used dialogue to reveal character, but O'Hara had a much better ear. In his sketches for "The Conning Tower" he began to learn how to use this astonishing gift, the most important he had as a writer.

O'Hara was encouraged by F.P.A.'s acceptance of his work; it made up for the many rejections he had received from the *Saturday Evening Post, Scribner's* and other magazines. But contributors to "The Conning Tower" were not paid. O'Hara was as far away from leaving Pottsville as ever, and without a job. He had hoped to find work as a newspaperman in Missoula, Montana, because Margaretta Archbald had accepted a job teaching Flat-head Indians on a reservation near there. When that failed, he tried to get a job on a paper in Allentown, Pennsylvania, where his friend Bob Si-monds was living. Asking Simonds to help find him a room, he warned him to tell the landlady he was Catholic: "There's so much prejudice in Allen-town, you know, and there are people otherwise normal who feel that to harbor a Papist is to defy the great god Janus." When this prospect fell through, he turned to his uncle in New Jersey, John McKee, to help him find a shipboard job through his own connections as a customs official.

In July, he was hired as a tourist class steward on board the United States Line ship *George Washington*, sailing for Germany by way of Ireland. The trip took thirteen days and the work was rigorous. "I was not seasick," O'Hara later recalled, "but I was afraid I would be, which is almost as bad, especially when we ran into some heavy weather and most of the passen-gers were unable to look at food." At Cobh, he unloaded laundry during the brief stay there, but he was given some leave in Germany and was able to run over to Hamburg from the port of Bremerhaven. It was not a pleasant experience—"I once was known as one of the most undesirable paid hands that ever got drunk at the Rotesan," a bar in Bremerhaven. He sent F.P.A. a couplet that reflected his homesickness:

The Times is 80 pennies in Hamburg:
But you can't buy the World for a mark in this damn burg.

Back in Pottsville within the month, he was soon looking for other jobs that would take him away. He refused to be a steward again, but he applied to work as an assistant purser on the *Leviathan*. Other possibilities included a job as overseer of a banana plantation for the United Fruit Company in Central or South America and working for the Firestone Company in Liberia. Nothing came of these exotic prospects, so with the help of Colonel Archbald, he began to negotiate with Yale about admissions requirements. "I suppose I'll get this college bug every year until I'm 30," he noted, "but I really should like to go, get a degree, take an M.A. and teach."

Continuous frustrations made him desperate to get away from Pottsville. "Everything seems to be going all ways but the right," he wrote Simonds, "and I'm ready to light out for any place." In another letter, he remarked, more threateningly. "I simply must get out of Pottsville or I'll buy a gun and use it." Finally, in October of 1927, he hitchhiked west from Pottsville to State College, where Pennsylvania State University is located, and where his friend, Robert Root, was living. He stayed at Root's fraternity over the weekend and then set off for Pittsburgh with the idea of continuing west to Columbus, Ohio, where he hoped to find a job. If that failed he was to go on to Chicago. Beyond that, his plans were vague, although he wanted to visit New Orleans for the Mardi Gras and hoped to end up in Missoula, Montana. Without money, he had a miserable time. In Ohio, he went to the Salvation Army and was turned away because he was too well dressed. Finally, a Catholic priest got him a hotel room and a meal. In Chicago, he was forced to seek employment as a groom, but the man wouldn't hire him. "What's a young man in a Brooks suit trying to get a job as a groom for?" O'Hara answered, "To eat." But it was no good: he stayed at a "fleabag at 600 West Madison Street" and got free drinks from a friend who was otherwise unhelpful. "It was fun but no fun, if you know what I mean."

A month after leaving, he was back again in the "adorable hamlet" of Pottsville and deeply discouraged. Everything was going wrong: no money, no job and a crisis with Margaretta Archbald. "At my present rate," he wrote, "I'll end up in a joint in Tia Juana with a bullet in my left ventricle." Tony Mosolino, the local bootlegger, then made a proposal. "You belong to that country club," said Mosolino. "I'd like to sell my booze to the guys who belong to that club. How would you like to go to work for me? Fifty bucks a week." The money was tempting, but everything else about it was demeaning, and O'Hara turned it down.

By the early spring of 1928, he had drifted into a pointless job in Lykens, working in the office of the American Briquet Company and acting as part-time chauffeur to his grandmother, the "Queen Mother" in whose house he was staying. By now he had registered with a placement office that was housed at the Yale Club in New York. Too late he heard of a possible job at *The New Yorker*. "Thank God I can laugh," he said, "for I'd otherwise go crazier."

Then his sister Mary announced that she was leaving Pottsville to go to New York for a job. That made him act. Determined to be the first to leave, he arranged with his brother Joe, who was then in funds, to drive him to New York so he could arrive a day before his sister. It was the kind of last minute push that was required. It took courage to go to New York, where good jobs were harder to find than in other parts of the country. The competition was tough and the risk of failure ominous. He was twenty-three years old and he had seventeen dollars in his pocket.

4. NEW YORK

Within a week of his arrival, O'Hara was standing in Bleeck's, a speakeasy next door to the back entrance of the *New York Herald Tribune* on West Fortieth Street. He had just been offered a job by Stanley Walker, the paper's city editor. Walker was now introducing his new "word painter" to other employees who at the end of the day made a practice of going "downstairs" to Bleeck's. Pronounced "Blakes," known formally as the Artist and Writers Club and patronized by journalists from all over the neighborhood, it was an unpretentious restaurant with plain wooden furniture and a low ceiling. The back rooms were a speakeasy where regulars gathered for cheap drinks, plain food and mannish talk. Until 1935 women were not encouraged to enter the premises. On the walls were hunting prints and a set of drawings by James Thurber depicting the match game whose losing players had to buy drinks for all the others.

As O'Hara was being introduced to others from the *Herald Tribune,* he was pleased to have his name recognized as a contributor to F.P.A.'s column. "The place was exciting to a fresh young reporter from Pottsville, Pa." for it contained such writers as Ring Lardner, Grantland Rice, Percy Hammond, Alva Johnston and Heywood Broun. O'Hara soon found himself at home in this world. "Last night," he wrote his brother Tom, "I was on a party with Dick Watts, the movie critic; Frank Sullivan, the World humorist, Don Skene, the boxing writer for the H.T. and later, Noel Busch, of Time, Lynn Segal, of Time (a girl) and many others. We started at the Artists and Writers Club and then went to Tony's, another speakeasy where all the celebrities go. There I met Frank Sullivan, whose stuff you may have seen in the World. He gave me a big howdedoo and congratulated me on my stuff, etc. It was great fun and I had a lovely time."

O'Hara's sudden success in New York had been assisted by his experience and buoyancy. His father had taken him to Philadelphia and New York as a boy, and he had ridden a double-decker bus up Fifth Avenue to look at the smart cars parked in front of the big houses overlooking Central Park. The memory of these early trips was enough to give him a feeling of "defenseless optimism. New York would take care of the newcomer."

After settling with Mary at the house in East Orange where his uncle John McKee lived, O'Hara had gone into New York to call at the Yale Club's placement office. He also phoned F. P. Adams, who remembered his contributions to "The Conning Tower" and invited O'Hara to visit him in his office at the *World*. He went downtown to Park Row. When he entered the *World* building with its famous gold dome, he was sent to the twelfth floor. There Herbert Bayard Swope, the editor, presided over what was one of the most prestigious newspapers in America. Owned by the Pulitzers since the 1880s, the *World* gradually established a reputation for having first-rate men on its staff. The "Op. Ed." page, which Swope initiated, ran regular contributions by such writers as Alexander Woollcott, Heywood Broun, St. John Ervine, Deems Taylor and F.P.A. himself. Adams greeted O'Hara and after quizzing him brusquely—"Where *is* Pottsville?"—he phoned round to introduce him to other papers including the *Post* and *The New Yorker* since there were no openings on the *World*. He impressed O'Hara with the violence of his language—"every other word is damn or hell"—and with his kindness: "Never saw me before," he wrote his friend Simonds, "and did more for me than anyone but you would do. With him cheering for me I'll get along. Remember what I told you about 1929 vs. 1927? This time next year I'll *be* somebody."

In less than a week, O'Hara had a job at the *Herald Tribune*. Stanley Walker, who had hired him, was a lean Texan of about O'Hara's own age. As city editor, he was responsible for making the *Herald Tribune* the most readable paper of the 1920s and 1930s in New York. A family paper, owned by Whitelaw Reid, it had an upper-class bias and accepted the prevailing values of society in a light-hearted manner. Many of its employees were graduates of eastern universities, notably Yale. Without being snobbish, the paper had a clublike atmosphere. Where *The New York Times* as the "newspaper of record" would send five or six reporters to cover an event and produce a committee-written story, the *Herald Tribune,* which had some of the best rewrite men in the business, would send only one or two, and the stories it published were lively and original.

At first, O'Hara did some local reporting, a specialty of the paper, which slighted foreign news. He happened to be in the subway station at Times Square when a bad accident occurred, and he had the presence of mind to phone the paper and relate everything that was happening to a rewrite man. O'Hara was complimented for his resourcefulness, but soon he was working as a day rewrite man, as he had done before at the *Pottsville Journal*. He worked at a desk in the office, editing stories sent in by reporters and transforming them into publishable articles.

Herbert Bayard Swope said that "journalism is life reflected in ink" and he believed that there was no better place for a writer than a newspaper. "It is, for him, like attending some fabulous university where the humanities are studied to the accompaniment of ribald laughter, the incessant splutter of an orchestra of typewriters, the occasional clinking of glasses, and the gyrations of some of the strangest performers ever set loose by a capricious and allegedly all-wise Creator." Stanley Walker had similar views and identified a talented newspaperman as one who has "a restless and searching mind" and who is capable of soaking up the "smells and information and significant trivia alike from the policeman on the corner and the bibliophile in his study." Although he never remained long in a newspaper office, O'Hara fulfilled Walker's requirements, especially his alertness to trivia. He recognized this tendency when comparing himself to another newspaper writer whose superiority he acknowledged, "except for versatility of information and an intense interest in trifles."

In the 1920s and 1930s newspaper journalism was an unusually social occupation. The hours were long and irregular, which meant that many of those employed by the seventeen daily papers then published in New York found that their social and professional lives overlapped. Paradoxically, the social side was given an impetus by the passing of the Volstead Act in 1919, which prohibited the sale of alcohol. Soon speakeasies—unlicensed restaurants where "bootleg" liquor was sold—came into existence all over New York and elsewhere. Because they were illegal and their patrons had to be known to the management, they soon developed a more friendly and clublike atmosphere than was ever found in an ordinary restaurant. Many were also neighborhood establishments where the same people went, which meant that the customers would find familiar faces and friends. One such establishment favored by *Herald Tribune* employees was the Type and Print Club, farther towards the river on West Fortieth Street. It was a small place in a brownstone, where drinks and a simple meal could be obtained for about a dollar. In addition to reporters, the Type and Print was patronized by newspaper compositors who wore the paper caps they used at work. Most speakeasies of this kind were simple, often run by

Italians who served continental food on small tables covered with red checkered tablecloths. Others, like Moriarty's on East Fifty-eighth Street and Costello's on Third Avenue, were Irish and preserved the jolly atmosphere of the pub where everyone knew everyone else, and no one was anonymous.

Certain speakeasies such as Tony's on West Fifty-second Street and Jack and Charlie's at 21 West Fifty-second Street were visited by people from all over town, for lunch and dinner and after the theater. Of the two, "21" was known for the high quality of its food and drink and was patronized by theater and newspaper people, writers, sports editors, Hollywood actors and producers, stockbrokers and lawyers interested in the arts, and Yale undergraduates. Tony's, across the street, attracted much the same clientele, but it was considerably less expensive.

Speakeasies helped lower the class barriers that had already fallen to some degree during the war when in the army, Americans of all kinds made friends with those they would not ordinarily have met. The ease and intimacy of the speakeasy made it possible for a young man such as John O'Hara to become friendly with people he would normally never have encountered socially. Speakeasies also discouraged the sort of professional isolation that is common today. Novelists, racetrack operators, theater owners, book reviewers, bankers, sports writers—they all gathered easily and talked to one another over drinks. The common subject of conversation was usually New York itself, for almost everyone who was sufficiently sociable to go to a speakeasy was involved in some way in the city's public life. For a writer like O'Hara, this world was a marvelous source of material. It was vivid and energetic and devoid of nostalgia. As A. J. Liebling observed, New York "is one of the oldest places in the United States but doesn't live in retrospect like the professionally picturesque provinces."

O'Hara's salary of twenty-five dollars a week was not enough to pay for the sort of life he was beginning to enjoy, so he arranged charge accounts at Bleeck's and the other places he frequented. This gesture typified his instability. His clothes were contradictorily messy and elegant. He wore unpressed gray flannels with a tweed jacket over a shirt that was often in need of washing; yet he also went out in a raccoon coat and always carried a malacca cane. His appearance and manner unsettled his colleagues. "His ears stuck out," wrote Joel Sayre, then a fellow employee of the *Tribune,* "and now and then his deadpan look and cold blue eyes made you think of a young trooper in the Coal & Iron police." He soon found that his style of living interfered with his job. At five o'clock, when he was through for the day, he would go downstairs to Bleeck's for a few drinks with Richard Watts or Wolcott Gibbs from *The New Yorker.* Then they moved on, perhaps with others, to dinner at Tony's. This was followed by the theater, more drinks afterwards and some work of his own at home before going to bed at two or three in the morning. After such a night, he was often unable to appear at the *Herald Tribune* until ten or eleven in the morning. Inevitably, Stanley Walker had to fire him (with tears in his eyes, according to O'Hara): "The experiment didn't work out well," Walker later recalled. "He didn't last long. I said goodby to O'Hara without prejudice to his talent, or possible genius, but in the conviction that he was sadly misplaced on the paper. While with us he wrote nothing at all of any distinction."

By now O'Hara had the expenses of living in the city, for he had found it troublesome to commute from New Jersey. At first he shared an apartment with a Pottsville friend called Bayerle, but soon he moved into a small rooming house on West Forty-third Street. "It was supposed to be for men only," he later recalled. "A room with running water cost $9. As I cannot sleep in a room where there is running water, I lived in a $6 room." At another time he lived and worked as a receptionist and telephone operator in a flophouse in the same neighborhood. "It was full of fairies, a couple of gangsters, and people like Cary Grant, Alan Mowbray, Cesar Romero et al."

After leaving the *Herald Tribune,* O'Hara learned from the Yale Club's placement office that there was an opening at *Time,* then a three-year-old magazine with offices in the same building as the even younger *New Yorker* at 25 West Forty-fifth Street. O'Hara went for an interview and found himself talking to Noel Busch, whom he had already met at Bleeck's. He was hired on a two-week trial basis. In the early days, *Time* relied almost exclusively on the reporting of others. Stories were culled from newspaper and wire service clippings and then rewritten by staff editors in the snappy, wisecracking style the magazine then affected. The articles were written by men using material gathered by female researchers and checkers who worked alongside them. O'Hara was first put to work in the "People" section, where he extracted human interest items from rejected news stories. He had a desk in an office with Noel Busch and Kathrine White, who was a researcher. After his probationary period, he was hired on a regular basis and made religion editor, although he also contributed to a number of other departments and even made up fake correspondence for the letters column. His salary averaged $162 a month.

O'Hara was a capable writer for *Time.* He mastered the magazine's silly backwards style known as "Timese" that Wolcott Gibbs parodied in his famous sentence, "Where it all will end, knows God!" It was all right as a gag, but tiresome for anyone with a developed sense of his own style. "I suppose one reason that I was never a great success at Time was that you have to write one word at a time. You have to think in single words, not in sentences," he wrote. Moreover, O'Hara noticed that his efforts to be a writer on his own were resented, and he observed that few real writers stayed for long. Years later, wondering out loud why Yale University produced so few writers in modern times, he wrote, "Yale men who want to write usually fall comfortably into the hands of Harry Luce. Poor little lambs that have lost their way—in a Borden's bottling plant."

After a few months at *Time,* O'Hara was put in charge of the sports department. Assigned to write about a World Series baseball game, O'Hara actually attended the game at Yankee Stadium. Individual reporting was not customary at *Time,* and as the game fell on the same day the magazine was put to bed, his action infuriated John Martin, who was soon appointed managing editor. "His first official act was to fire me," O'Hara recalled. Martin was an unstable man, but O'Hara's departure from *Time* was predictable. Noting that O'Hara "had a strong distaste for sunlight and preferred to stay in bed until the worst of it was over," his friend Wolcott Gibbs said that Henry Luce had backed up Martin "with the virtuous comment that Luce publications had no use for a man who lolled in bed after nine o'clock in the morning." O'Hara's departure from *Time* was no disgrace, for journalists are migratory, but the pattern was ominous and recalled his school expulsions.

O'Hara's instability rose from his drinking and his relationships with women. At the beginning, he was fortunate. Soon after he arrived in New York he met a girl who was his own social and intellectual level, who also agreed to sleep with him. This had never happened in Pottsville, so he was ecstatic. "I am in a fair way to having the compassionate mistress I used to talk to you about," he confided to Simonds. He met her in Greenwich Village and he liked her so much he was afraid to ask her for a date. Then on a Thursday, "for the first time—having seen her just three times previously—I slept with her. God! What a body! And what a brain!" It passed, but he got to know many other girls, mainly on the newspapers and magazines where he worked and had friends.

Kathrine White, who knew him at *Time,* remembers him as being scruffy with a "mean beard," a young man who looked as though he bought his clothes at a rummage sale in the vicinity of an Ivy League college. He got on with the girls at *Time* because he treated them as people and generally did not patronize them. He was prankish and enjoyed playing jokes. He also liked to generalize. Once he wrote a piece for *Vanity Fair* in which he summed up his requirements of the female sex. A woman, he wrote, "shouldn't extravagantly praise a man whom she knows the present man despises. She doesn't discuss *ex cathedra* books and plays which he knows nothing about. She doesn't say, 'You're getting tight,' especially when he *is* getting tight. She is probably non-existent." At the same time he could be sympathetic and understanding. He was a good listener, and if someone was in trouble, he wouldn't try to ignore it but would propose a definite line of action. In a good mood, he was carefree and without self-pity. Because he cashed his paychecks at bars he tended to spend everything he earned right away and looked upon the resulting impoverishment as an act of God over which he had no control.

But drinking could quickly change his disposition and threatened to ruin his career and happiness. He was forced to admit that Stanley Walker was right to fire him: "I was drunk most of the time and was never punctual." O'Hara's heavy drinking had begun after his father's death in 1925. Prior to that he had not been a compulsive drinker. After he moved to New York, he was less depressed, but by then alcohol was a habit. When things went wrong, especially in his relationships with women, he would drink heavily and without let-up. Sometimes late at night, he would appear at the apartment of a girl who had spurned him. The drink gave him the courage to go there but made him unpredictable when he arrived. He would stagger in and unless he was treated gently and tactfully, he became violent. He took refusals hard. Every part of him was involved, for he was a very physical man and suffered more than most when his sexual drives were frustrated. Drink was intended as a solace, but it turned his masculinity into acts of physical violence instead of sexual satisfaction.

Sometimes, he seemed to be so consumed by furies that his violence and self-destructiveness were frightening to those he was with. His own unhappiness gave him insights into the troubles of others and made him exceptionally kind and thoughtful, but he did not know how to comfort himself. He was often beside himself when upset. His appearance made him look tough and uncaring, for he was a big man with a plain, coarse face, but in fact he was exceptionally sensitive. He was often deeply troubled. Once, after a night on the town, he shared a hotel room with Stanley Walker. In the middle of the night, Walker heard a noise and woke up to find O'Hara kneeling beside his bed with his head bent in prayer.

But O'Hara was generally suited to the full life and variety of New York and he responded to it. "I was a latecomer, to be sure," he noted, "but I grew up in the Jazz Age and I became a post Jazz Age author." Dancing school and listening to the big bands in Pennsylvania paved the way. "When I was a young man," O'Hara later wrote, "I learned that girls liked two things about me: one, I was a good dancer; two, I made them laugh." New York put him in the heart of music in America. Paul Whiteman, the Dorsey brothers and Guy Lombardo all played at the hotels, and at the smaller nightclubs, which he preferred, O'Hara could listen to jazz and dance in more intimate surroundings. Even before moving to New York, he had gone to the Pré Catalan, which was known as the "Pre Cat" and located on West Thirty-ninth Street. It had a reputation for being "the glamor spot for collegians and prep school types from Charlottesville to Cambridge." By the time O'Hara was living in the city, nightclubs were entering their best period. Like speakeasies, they were suited to young people who for the most part lived in single rooms and wanted to get out and have a good time. O'Hara often went to nightclubs with girls he met at the *Herald Tribune, Time* or *The New Yorker,* and he preferred little places in midtown Manhattan. The atmosphere was what mattered. He liked clubs that had only twenty or thirty tables grouped round a small dance floor in the center of the room. The lights were subdued and the tables often had low candles burning in glass containers. Cigarette girls in satin trousers moved from table to table, and there were usually two orchestras, one of them playing Latin American music. Sometimes there were floor-shows with professional dancers and singers, but often not. The best clubs had a character of their own reflecting the owner's personality. The Trocadero had Emil Coleman's music with Fred and Adele Astaire dancing; the Perroquet was owned by Otto Kahn's son; Jimmy Durante presided at the Club Durant; the Mirador had a Fokine ballet as part of the entertainment.

The food served was relatively inexpensive, with filet mignon and lobster newburg for less than two dollars; but drinks were high. A pint of whiskey would cost ten dollars and a little bottle of soda water, one. O'Hara went as often as he could afford it. One night he encountered the notorious gangster "Legs" Diamond in one of the "cribs" he frequented; at another, Jimmy Walker, famous for his advice: "Don't stand up if you can sit down; don't sit down if you can lie down." Over the years as the Stork Club, El Morocco, Larue and many other clubs were established in New York, O'Hara became a frequent late-night customer. "I guess I like them," he conceded. "I wouldn't spend so much time in them if I didn't."

O'Hara was also caught up in the prankish atmosphere of the decade. Wolcott Gibbs recalled that one day he was sent on an assignment to go up in "an airplane to fly over the city and then write a story about it. It turned out that John, nervous about airsickness, had taken sensible precautions against it, so that when he came down he was in a state of mild confusion, and when the plane started to taxi away across the landing field, he somehow got the impression that there was no pilot in it and broke a window with the heroic intention of climbing in and shutting off the motor before somebody got hurt." On another occasion he introduced a young girl, disguised as a man, into the Yale Club bar without being caught and then wrote a piece about it that was published under a pseudonym in the *Herald Tribune*. Sometimes when drunk, he would buy a supply of newspapers from a vendor and then hawk them in the street, crying out, "Extra! Read all about it! Hoover turns Catholic!" He spent a picturesque summer staying with Noel and Niven Busch at their mother's apartment on East Seventy-first Street. He was always having trouble with the keys: they were supposed to be left for him in the mailbox, but sometimes he couldn't find them. One night he smashed all the mailboxes in his search for them, but usually he would pile up the metal trash cans outside of the building in order to reach the fire escape, and then he would climb up to the apartment.

But New York wasn't just a matter of dancing at the Algonquin or listening to music at Rudy Vallee's nightclub. It also affected O'Hara as he walked across a street in midtown, peering at the menu cards in the windows of restaurants, or went window-shopping along Fifth Avenue where the displays are more enticing than paintings in the galleries, or when he stopped at a florist and found a whole garden of pink and red azaleas and poinsettias and roses bursting out of the shop at Christmastime. Certain sights were peculiar to the city—the fire escapes that cling to the sides and fronts of so many houses, the old elevated railway that until the mid-fifties ran up and down Third Avenue, encasing the street below in noisy gloom but, as John McNulty observed, helping drunks who were trying to cross the street to one of the Irish bars. In the twenties and thirties, you could still dine outside, at the Marguery at 270 Park Avenue or at one of the many roof gardens. On the St. Regis Roof you could also dance. In winter, the wind off the Hudson was bone-chilling, but New York apartments were warm and cozy. It was a stop-and-go city, in the elevators of the buildings as in traffic along Park Avenue. In midtown, where O'Hara lived, there were still many brownstone houses that gave a human scale to an environment that was otherwise marked by soaring skyscrapers. New York was a village that had suddenly been transformed into a futuristic landscape. Nancy Hale described a predawn moment that captures this feeling: "The sky was dull whitish dark and the shapes of a few high buildings stood out, their edges blurred; in some of the towers an occasional light burned far away, single and remote; who was there, in this lonely hour, and what did they do? Whoever they were, they too were awake and living, across the air."

All of this was material for O'Hara's writing, and from the beginning his contributions to *The New Yorker* were devoted to the social foibles and customs of New Yorkers. His first piece appeared in May of 1928, two months after his arrival in New York, and in letter after letter to Harold Ross, the magazine's editor, and to Katharine Angell, his assistant, he suggested subjects that related to city life. He proposed profiles of curious and interesting citizens such as Al Smith's son, the clerk of New York City and a Jesuit seismologist at Fordham. He read old newspapers in search of ideas for pieces for "The Talk of the Town" section that occupies the opening pages of the magazine. "I have lots of spare time," he wrote Mrs. Angell, "and interesting thoughts and ideas and I am not going to California for just years and years, if at all."

O'Hara's instinct to emphasize the journalistic side of his nature helped establish him as a contributor to *The New Yorker,* for although this magazine is best known for its stories and cartoons and was a direct successor to such humorous magazines as *Vanity Fair* and *Life,* it grew out of Harold Ross's own experience as a journalist. Ross had worked on the armed forces newspaper *Stars and Stripes* in France. After the war he was employed by some veterans' magazines in New York. Following a brief stay at *Judge,* he founded *The New Yorker* in February of 1925. From the beginning, the magazine was an extension of Ross's personality, and that meant that it adhered to high journalistic standards. William Shawn, who succeeded him as editor of the magazine, wrote that Ross "was not at home with ideas, theory, speculation—abstract thought of any kind. He liked what he regarded as pure information. His working assumption, at least, was that there was such a thing as objective reporting. He wanted to know about events; he did not want to know what a writer's subjective response to the events was." *The New Yorker* was not a daily paper: "We don't cover the news," said Ross; "we parallel the news." But he wanted to be as accurate as the best newspaper. "Facts steadied him and comforted him," wrote Shawn. "Facts also amused him. They didn't need to be funny facts —just facts." As editor, he naturally allowed no tampering with facts, and he was opposed to writing that obscured them. He saw, as Shawn recalled, "no excuse for ambiguity or obscurity in prose. He wanted every sentence of prose in the magazine to be intelligible, and he struggled hard to achieve that aim."

The New Yorker's journalistic bias did not mean dullness, for the best newspaper writing of the 1920s and 1930s was far more individual and personal than it is today. At the *World,* Herbert Bayard Swope urged his reporters to use colorful anecdotes, and Stanley Walker at the *Herald Tribune* gave his writers plenty of space in which to express themselves. The most admired newspaper writers were such men as Richard Harding Davis and Ring Lardner who were not only accurate, but literate and amusing or, if the occasion demanded it, dramatic and moving. O'Hara had been brought up in this school of journalism, and although the *Pottsville Journal* gave him few opportunities for memorable writing, he was in a tradition that went back to Charles Dickens, Mark Twain, Stephen Crane, Willa Cather, Theodore Dreiser and Jack London, who all worked for newspapers. As Ben Hecht put it, "It was as natural for a police reporter to start writing a novel or play as it was for an ant to climb a grass blade."

O'Hara's first contribution to *The New Yorker* was a short sketch printed in the back of the magazine and entitled "The Alumnae Bulletin." It is intended to be the monologue of a Vassar or Smith graduate as she reads the class notes about her friends, now six years out of college. There is a dramatic contrast between the woman's avid comments about her class-mates and her closing remark, "I wonder why anybody reads this stuff in the *Bulletin* for, anyway." During the following months, O'Hara published a number of similar sketches—a telephone conversation that marks the breakup of a romance, a monologue on tennis by a country club bore, two Yale men at a bar who try to think of someone they know in common, the frustrations of someone who thought he could reach the police commis-sioner by phoning the local precinct station.

These sketches go beyond the satirical purposes of the Babbitt imita-tions published in F.P.A.'s column, and establish O'Hara as an authentic recorder of conversation. "Dialog is not written around a peculiarity," said O'Hara. In an article in which he compared O'Hara with Sinclair Lewis, Wolcott Gibbs observed that the characters in *Main Street* and *Babbitt* spoke in a way that "was frankly heightened to absurdity since they were little more than animated symbols of Mr. Lewis' general contempt for American thought." In contrast, O'Hara's people are "reasonable approximations of human beings." O'Hara's conversations were thus able to reveal a whole world without any descriptive prose at all. You can see the Irish cop sitting at his precinct desk when he picks up the phone and says, "Wukkan I do fya?" and you can picture the perplexed gentleman in his town house through the mannered convolutions of his speech.

In September of 1928, *The New Yorker* published the first of a series of longer contributions by O'Hara that purported to be transcripts of the proceedings of a women's club in New Jersey. This series allowed O'Hara to create a cast of characters who are carried over from one sketch to another. Simply by what they say, the speakers at the meetings reveal their limitations and prejudices, as well as the social ambitions and conflicts of provincial society. The speaker's grammar is "often tangled up in its own draperies," as Wolcott Gibbs put it, and the characters frequently utter non sequiturs. These errors in language are not only meant to be funny. They also show how ignorant, prudish, hypocritical and small-minded Americans often are.

The proceedings of the "Orange County Afternoon Delphian Society" owe their origin to Pottsville and in particular to a women's group of that name to which his mother belonged. Returning to Pottsville for Christmas in 1928, O'Hara noted in a letter to Katharine Angell of *The New Yorker* that on two occasions he "was very frigidly greeted by members of the After-noon Delphian Society. So I am a social as well as a financial success." One sketch specifically relates to Pennsylvania. Entitled "The Coal Fields," it is the report of one of the ladies who went to Scranton and Pittsburgh to report on recent coal mining strikes. In fact, she speaks mainly about the country clubs, hotels and attractive homes where she stayed along the way. As to the coal miners, "The things Mrs. Yocum told me were almost unbelievable! The arrogance of some of the coal miners in refusing to leave their homes when they were evicted, and their strikes and so on. Really, dear friends, it is astounding. And most of them were so dirty."

O'Hara also created a series dealing with the staff of a paint manufac-turing company in the Yorkville section of Manhattan, called Hagedorn & Brownmiller. These sketches are monologues pronounced by Mr. Wood-ring, the manager, who speaks the same language of boosterism and pep that is associated with the Babbitts of the Middle West. They mark a considerable advance in O'Hara's technique, however, for they allow the creation of other characters. Irv Rosenthal, an old regular in the company, and Mr. Cleary, the sophisticated son of a former vice-president, come to life through what Mr. Woodring says about them. "Most of us," he says, "aren't much of a golfer although I understand Mr. Cleary there belongs to the New York A.C. and they have a golf course. Is that right, Mr. Cleary? I guess Mr. Cleary is the only one of the Hagedorn & Brownmiller, Incorporated, staff that belongs to a golf club, except of course F. W. and the directors, although I understand even some of them don't feel they can afford any extravagance like that."

By indirectly creating characters through dialogue, O'Hara stretched the technique of reporting actual speech as far as it can go. Step by step he moved from simple to more complex forms. He wrote profiles which required exposition and narrative in addition to dialogue. Then he moved on to writing portraits of representative types. Yet in all his early work, O'Hara never lost interest in surfaces, in public life, social class, customs and habits. To make his world authentic, he used the techniques of the journalist, recording the telling detail, the concrete fact, and above all, the character's voice. O'Hara's ability to render speech patterns accurately reveals something of his own nature. Unlike certain contemporary poets, who listen almost exclusively to their own voices, O'Hara listened to others.

Despite his success with *The New Yorker*, O'Hara was still very poor, for the money he earned as a contributor hardly made up for the loss of his job at *Time*. He received fifteen dollars for his first contribution to *The New Yorker* and was generally paid at the rate of ten cents a word. The magazine was never prodigal with money, and O'Hara only earned a few hundred dollars a year from his writings.

He was still living in single rooms at hotels where he could pay by the week. One of these was the Belmont on Forty-fourth Street, where his bedroom overlooked a theater where R. C. Sherriff's *Journey's End* was playing. The gunfire that ends the play was a startling interruption to his work. His continuing poverty affected him deeply and within two years of his arrival, as he later wrote, he "was literally starving, by which I mean that for one three-day stretch I went without anything to eat. The experience of those first two years did not make a banker out of me, and they were not all as disillusioning or as difficult as those three days. But you never quite get over the degrading, debasing experience of going hungry. (Henry R. Luce chose that particular moment to dun me for $50 I owed him.) You learn to see things very plain, and not only things but people, and not only people but a city."

Yet his financial misfortunes never made him servile, and he always treated Ross in a forthright manner. He could also be charming and used his humor to good effect. When he sent in the Delphian Club piece on the Pennsylvania coal miners, he spoofingly reminded Ross that "most of the stuff that is being said about the Pennsylvania coal fields is liberal poppycock." Ross was not stuffy, so he did not repulse O'Hara's efforts to push his own writing, but the two men never really hit it off. In personal relationships, Ross was bothered by his position as editor, for he had to deal with people who were ambitious and often neurotic as well. He felt besieged by contributors. "What I am running here is a goddam bughouse," he once said. "Not a man in the place without a screw loose." His writers respected his insistence on clarity and simplicity, but he was often defensive. "God, how I pity me!" he said. Ross admired O'Hara's work, otherwise he would not have published it, but O'Hara also needed help from others, especially in the beginning. Katharine Angell, who was one of the fiction editors, was a champion of his work, and for a time, at least, she was O'Hara's confidante as far as ideas and proposals were concerned. "Why am I telling you all these things?" he asked at the end of a letter reporting on his activities for *The New Yorker*. "Ah, well. You are a mother, and you will understand."

In 1931, Ross hired O'Hara on salary to write for "The Talk of the Town" department along with B. A. Bergman, who was in charge of it. He was given a drawing account of seventy-five dollars a week to cover expenses. O'Hara worked well, according to Bergman, and submitted "some excellent pieces—tightly written, graceful, revealing." But then, continues Bergman, "For reasons I never discovered, Ross took a dislike to O'Hara from the day he was hired and rejected every O'Hara piece I turned in." At the end of a month, Ross noticed that O'Hara had run up $300 in his drawing account with no credits for work accepted. He told Bergman to fire him, and Bergman had to face a justifiably irate O'Hara and give him the news. Ever afterwards, when they met, O'Hara made a point of saying, "You're the son of a bitch that fired me!"

Living in the same neighborhood as the office of *The New Yorker* and other magazines, O'Hara became part of a group of writers that went around together. Although personally shy, he was generally at ease with fellow professionals. Often a number of them would have lunch together at one of their usual hangouts, Martin and Mino's on East Fifty-second Street, or Tony's on West Fifty-second. Among the regulars was Wolcott Gibbs, who at the time was a fiction editor at *The New Yorker* and later its drama critic. He and O'Hara became good friends at this period. Neither had gone to college, and felt it, although Gibbs came from an old New York family and had none of O'Hara's social insecurity. Gibbs also knew Pennsylvania, having gone to school there. When O'Hara came to write his Pennsylvania novels, he used Gibbsville as the name for his fictional version of Pottsville. They had good times together, and Gibbs recalled some of their joint adventures. "It was a queer time—" he wrote, "the fact that everybody was part of the same general conspiracy against a silly law [the Volstead Act] broke down many barriers so that it was hard to tell what might happen before any night was over—and the things I remember about it are queer. I recall John complaining in a puzzled way because a lady had taken away his coat and mandolin—God knows what he was doing with a mandolin—and given them to her janitor. There was also the odd affair of the cheese knives. This was when John, grimly determined to assassinate a man who had brought him to the end of his negligible patience, secured for the purpose a long, deadly blade from the free-lunch counter. Alert friends, however, took the knife away and in a little while everybody in the bar, including John and the potential corpse, wandered off amiably to Child's for a cup of coffee. Everything went quietly until they got up to go, when a second and totally unsuspected cheese knife fell from somewhere onto the floor. John, it appeared, had simply decided to be prepared in case any further unpleasantness came up. Finally, there was the Italian voice, inexplicable but menacing, which exactly at four o'clock every afternoon for about a week, came over the telephone in his hotel room.

" 'All right, O'Hara,' it would say softly, darkly. 'Just watch out, that's all.'

"This horrible warning so unnerved him at last that he fled by night to another hotel, changing from one taxi to another on the way as adroitly as any Pinkerton. The voice desisted, but it was never explained."

O'Hara and Gibbs were friends mainly to have adventures together, but when Gibbs's second wife committed suicide by jumping out of a bathroom window, O'Hara was so concerned about his friend that he stayed with him and even adopted Gibbs's phobia about not sleeping in an apartment on the upper floor of a building. But O'Hara himself was a private person who increasingly built a shell to protect him from the world. One Christmas eve Gibbs and his friend Ann Honeycutt, in a rush of sentiment to bring cheer to the neglected, went to see O'Hara. He was at home, in a low state, drinking Scotch all by himself. They soon realized they had made a mistake in coming, for they had found him with his defenses down. The nonchalant man-about-town had been discovered in his essential loneliness.

After leaving *Time,* and while he was free-lancing for *The New Yorker,* O'Hara began looking for another job. He worked briefly as an occasional contributor to *Editor and Publisher,* a trade paper, and then in July of 1929 he was hired by the *Daily Mirror,* an evening paper that had been started by William Randolph Hearst to compete with the *Daily News* and Bernarr Macfadden's popular *Daily Graphic.* A tabloid, it was a comedown from the *Herald Tribune,* but when Gene Fowler was its editor, it was a lively paper. It appealed mainly to the emotions of its readers, who were from all classes, and was known for its vivid reporting of human interest stories. Walter Winchell wrote for the paper, and O'Hara supplied him with material for his columns. In general, he enjoyed his job. "The moment I enter a newspaper office I am at home," he later wrote, "not only because the surroundings are as familiar to me as backstage is to an actor, but because, like an actor, I am ready to go on in any part. I could write a headline, take a story over the telephone, cover a fire, or interview a movie queen, and if I had to make up the front page I could do that too." His talents weren't required for so many roles at the *Daily Mirror,* but he wrote at least one article under his own byline, an account of the sentencing of a man who had been convicted of fraud. Mainly he was employed as a night rewrite man. "The job paid well," O'Hara recalled, "the company was a rather jolly group, and at least we could say we weren't working for the *Graphic.*" Despite its appearance, the *Mirror* had some style. The city editor wore silk shirts and drove a Pierce-Arrow, and there were a number of pretty girls who cheered up the routine of work. O'Hara was supposed to report at six in the evening, but found it a difficult hour. "Unfortunately for journalism, although happily for my social life, the day side of the *Mirror* would be at Racky's [a local restaurant], on their way home, just when I was on my way to work. Consequently the crack night rewrite battery of the *Mirror* was usually not fully manned until 7 P.M. And in due course they got another boy."

O'Hara's departure coincided with the Stock Market crash that brought on the depression. He first tried to get a job on a newspaper in Trenton, but when that failed, he wrote to Heywood Broun to ask if he could help him with the campaign he was running through his column at the *World* to encourage people to hire the unemployed. Broun immediately engaged him to answer mail, conduct interviews and write material for his broadsheets and columns. O'Hara found Broun a generous and open man. He was married to a noted feminist and was often at rallies and protest marches against one or other form of injustice. A Harvard graduate, he bitterly attacked President Lowell for the part he played in ensuring the execution of Sacco and Vanzetti. "I ate lunch at his penthouse every day the first week I was with him," O'Hara later recalled, "and incidentally it was usually the big meal of the day for me. At the end of the week I was genuinely surprised to receive a pay check for $35, which he gave me all the time I worked for him. And it came out of his own pocket, because I knew, through my job with him, quite a bit about his current financial situation, his checking accounts, etc." O'Hara considered Broun "the best-writing newspaperman I ever knew of," but more than that, "He was a gentleman. He was what *I* mean by a gentleman, and what my father and mother meant when they tried to bring me up to be one. He was kind, courteous and square. Generous, considerate and big. Broun honored Harvard by going there, continued to keep it respectable by continuing to like it. I know I still have a raccoon coat for the excellent reason that at my age Heywood Broun had one too. He made a lot of people seem right by letting it be known that they were his friends. He honored me, by God, by letting me sit with him, work for him, drink to him."

By May of 1930, O'Hara found another job, this time with the *Morning*

Telegraph, a daily paper devoted to sports and entertainment. Like *Variety,* it contained professional news as well as reviews. O'Hara began as second-string drama critic, reviewing amateur productions at the Ninety-second Street YM/YWHA and at Columbia University. Soon he was put in charge of a daily radio column, one of the first in the country. Having no radio of his own, he did his listening at a speakeasy. He wrote about jazz and reviewed the music of Guy Lombardo, Emil Coleman, Ted Husing and Louis Armstrong. He was chatty and personal as he told his readers about one of his first encounters with radio: "Way back in 1922 when we were working on an engineering corps in Pennsylvania we used to listen and listen to WSAP. Sitting there in that dreadful little mining town (name on request) where you couldn't get a drink except some corn that never had seen a charcoal keg, that decrepit set, which had been assembled by one of the exiles, saved us white men from going to pieces altogether. That and the fact that we always dressed for dinner." By June, he was also made the paper's film critic, so he adopted a pseudonym, "Franey Delaney," from the female side of his family for the radio column. Movie reviewing gave him more scope and pleasure, and he used to attend screenings with his friend Richard Watts. But within three months, his tenure at the *Morning Telegraph* came to an end. He was probably fired since he signed his last column, "Te morituri salutamus."

O'Hara's job failures and general hard times forced him to return to Pottsville in the early part of 1931. He wrote a friend, "I'm suffering horrible nostalgia for 21 west 52nd and New York generally. I was in New York for the past three years but the going was too tough. Job trouble. My family live here, so I am playing Artist In The Family." He spent his time writing pieces for *The New Yorker, Scribner's* and other magazines. But the burden of an extra mouth to feed was hard on his mother, so his sister Mary, who was working in New York for the *Daily News,* urged him to leave. He returned to New York within the month.

Having worked with press agents while at the *Morning Telegraph,* O'Hara soon found a job as public relations man for Warner Brothers film studio. Most of Hollywood's talent came from Broadway, so the film companies kept big offices in New York during the 1930s, and O'Hara found himself in the middle of the theater world. It was a further step down from the *Herald Tribune,* but it was varied and sometimes amusing. One of his jobs was to arrange what he called "cozy little luncheons for the press" to which he would bring leading stars who were in town from the coast. He also wrote background copy and discovered how phony was the information printed in the columns of those who wanted to "out-Winchell Walter." He attended screenings in order to prepare publicity and also wrote advertisements. His ads pleased his boss, Charles Einfeld, who thought they were "the damnedest ones you've ever seen. They were offbeat, provocative and great." Through his work O'Hara became familiar with the world of Broadway. He got to know what Mark Hellinger called "chorus girls with dying mothers and chorus boys with dyed hair," and he wrote a profile of a chorus girl for *The New Yorker* called "Of Thee I Sing, Baby." After the customary brief period, O'Hara moved from Warner Brothers to Benjamin Sonnenberg, a public relations consultant whose accounts included the Bergdorf Goodman store on Fifth Avenue. O'Hara's tenure with Sonnenberg was typical. "You don't fire people like that," Sonnenberg later remarked. "They just dissolve."

O'Hara's early promise as a newspaperman had come to little. Many journalists move from one newspaper or magazine to another, but O'Hara's progression was steadily downhill. Generally he was fired for laziness and indifference rather than incapacity. His contributions to *The New Yorker* interested him and also helped make money, but there was a financial gap. Although he was recognized for his gifts, O'Hara was still in the early stages of his development. Also, the attractions of nightclub and speakeasy life disrupted his writing and burdened him with debts. He was known about town, but his life lacked focus.

O'Hara's economic plight was made more difficult to bear by the uncertainties of his love life. New York had been liberating insofar as he had found intelligent women who were sexually uninhibited, and he had enjoyed a certain amount of romantic success. But what troubled him most was his frustration with Margaretta Archbald. She had moved from Pottsville to New York at the same time he did, and they had made plans to see a great deal of each other in New York. But as so often happens, Margaretta's accessibility reduced the charm of their relationship. It was also unsettled since O'Hara was meeting lots of girls through his jobs and Margaretta had many beaux of her own. Soon after he arrived in New York, he wrote a friend that "Marg and I have agreed, amicably, to disagree." They were still special to each other, however. When O'Hara fell into a despairing mood, he would sometimes appear late at night at the apartment where Margaretta and her cousin Mary Brooks were living. He would usually be drunk and resentful, so that it would take all the persuasive powers of the girls to get him to leave. Because the relationship deteriorated so gradually, it was especially painful. "If I had had enough sense to break it off early in 1928," O'Hara later wrote, "or if she had had sense enough to leave me alone in 1929, we'd have been spared 1930, the worst year in my life."

Years later he invoked his despair in an article about loneliness and fidelity. "But with all men the awful thing is the fear of not being loved, of being dismissed, brushed off, forgotten. No man can stand that. There are men who have had all the time in the world for the self-torture of imagining their women making love to somebody else. Some of these men have so expertly set the scene that they have expressed their appreciation of their own artistry by the supreme accolade, suicide." O'Hara threatened suicide several times in his life, but when his rejection by Margaretta was added to his being fired from the *Morning Telegraph,* he just went home to Pottsville, like a dog seeking shelter. His brother Tom later described what it was like: "I watched him sitting in that big square chair, the one with the upholstery that changed its shade of green when you rubbed it. He seemed to hunch down as if he wanted, more than anything, a feeling of shelter. I couldn't do anything to help him except by trying to make him aware of my love and admiration. Somehow he found inside himself what it took to get well, at least enough to go on with the walking wounded." Help came also from friends in New York, and when the emotional depression finally lifted he returned to the city.

There, by chance, his luck changed, for early in 1931, he met Helen Ritchie Petit, a young girl in her mid-twenties who had graduated from Wellesley and done graduate work at Columbia. She had begun a career as an actress and teacher, and she was very pretty. Her Wellesley friends recalled "her golden hair to the waist, her deep blue eyes, her delicate features and her Alice-in-Wonderland air." She had beautiful bone structure and seemed "all fluff" in her animated blondness. O'Hara noticed that "she had a shine all around her." He was also attracted to her because of her brains. "She has the best taste of anyone I know," he later wrote.

She was also a gay and spontaneous person who loved to drink. She accompanied O'Hara on his visits to speakeasies and appreciated his pranks, such as his riding off on a mounted policeman's horse while the policeman was having a drink at Tony's. Helen—or "Pet" as O'Hara called her—came from a well-to-do Episcopalian family in Brooklyn. O'Hara knew that religious differences would be a problem with her mother. But in the meantime he found Pet enchanting. He also noticed her fastidiousness and believed that it signified that she was kind and imaginative.

Soon O'Hara and Pet were living together, and Mrs. Petit became alarmed. O'Hara was not what she had in mind for her daughter: he had no job, few prospects and was a Roman Catholic. Once again, O'Hara found himself patronized by a possible parent-in-law. The only solution was to get married quietly and expeditiously. Through his newspaper connections, O'Hara knew a number of New York politicians such as Samuel Seabury, the district attorney, and Jimmy Walker, the mayor of New York. As plans for his marriage to Pet were laid in Tony's on Fifty-second Street, O'Hara told everybody that they were to be married by Jimmy Walker at City Hall. But on the chosen day, "the late Mayor of New York" as he was known for his lack of punctuality, failed to show up and they were married by a clerk of court. Mrs. O'Hara knew nothing of this, and neither did Mrs. Petit. O'Hara knew that his mother would be opposed to a marriage outside the Church and that she would be upset to learn of her son's wedding on Walter Winchell's evening radio broadcast, to which she always listened, but he apparently lacked the courage to send her a wire or to telephone. Instead, he asked a former Niagara Prep School friend, now a priest, to bless their marriage on the following day. Pet agreed and they called on Father Beatty in Brooklyn for the ceremony. Unfortunately, the priest observed that Pet and O'Hara had been "living in sin" and Pet angrily pointed out that her own church recognized civil marriages. There was an unpleasant scene, and the couple left without the ceremony.

Settled in an apartment at 41 West Fifty-second Street, perhaps too convenient to Tony's and "21," O'Hara resumed work on his own writing. Pet's support made a big difference to his confidence. He began a new series for *The New Yorker* based on the Idlewood Country Club, a provincial establishment similar to the Schuylkill Country Club of Pottsville. Again he used the device of the monologue. The speaker is a Mr. Duffy, chairman of the Greens Committee. A vulgar ignoramus, hardheaded and un-imaginative, he dominates the club through his aggressive provincialism. Duffy represents the complacent mean-spiritedness O'Hara found perva-sive in small-town America.

More and more he turned to Pennsylvania for subject matter. Living mainly on occasional checks received from *The New Yorker* and on the allowance Pet's family agreed to give her, O'Hara began a longer piece called "The Hoffman Estate" which appears to have been a treatment of a number of middle-class characters of the sort he had known in Pottsville. He was encouraged by Kyle Crichton, the associate editor of *Scribner's,* to submit this longer work for the Scribner's Prize Novel contest, which carried an award of $5000. To complete "The Hoffman Estate" required a period of uninterrupted work, so with money borrowed from the bank, Pet and O'Hara sailed for Bermuda in the summer of 1931, intending to stay there for three months.

They had wanted to go to Paris, but the little house in Paget East, a few miles from Hamilton, suited them ideally: "Living room, two master's bedrooms, maid's room, dining room, kitchen, electric refrigerator, and about ⅓ of an acre of woodsy ground, all for $50 a month. Food is comparatively inexpensive (although we haven't got the bills yet). The drinking question is by way of being an exclamation: we just don't drink. No resolutions or anything. It just doesn't seem to occur to us." O'Hara was so enchanted by the place he wanted to live there permanently but Pet was less enthusiastic. He therefore had to remonstrate, as he told Robert Simonds, "Sweetheart this is so heavenly that we must spend most of our time here, and if you don't like it I'll knock your God damn block off, sweetheart." The daily routine of writing, cycling into Hamilton for mail and newspapers, having a bottle of beer or porter in the evening, was productive. O'Hara worked on his long piece and also wrote some short stories which he sent to Crichton at *Scribner's.* The process of "being crea-tive and neglecting my bride of four months" paid off, and the story "Alone" was accepted for publication. He was paid seventy-five dollars and was delighted with "the honest-to-God thrill and encouragement I got out of selling my first piece to Scribner's." He worked even harder, and on August 18, he sent "the short novel by that amazing young genius, O'Hara, who will be hurled into the literary spotlight by winning the Scribner's contest, and who will be promptly hurled into durance vile by his many creditors who will attach the five-grand prize." Despite Crichton's support "The Hoffman Estate" was rejected by Max Perkins, Scribner's senior editor. O'Hara admitted that "the piece has been written so fast (it's really journalistic) that there hasn't been much time for Influences," and speed may have been the fault. He had evidently overreached himself without properly conceiving the work as a whole. Crichton urged him to elaborate the social aspect of the novel and to make "the erotic story a subsidiary rather than an all-enveloping thing."

O'Hara took the disappointment well. He was working on many other things including the long autobiographical story that became "The Doctor's Son." He was afraid of forgetting the details of Pottsville life. In a letter to Simonds, he said it was important to "keep writing, no matter how badly or how bad you think it is, because you'll never forget what you set down in writing or on a typewriter." Imagining what he and his friend might accomplish, he added, "Between us we might make Winesburg, Ohio take a back seat. Imagine the vote of thanks we'll get from the Chambers of Commerce at Pottsville and Shenandoah." He thought of combining his new story with "The Hoffman Estate" to make a book. "My idea is this: make a few changes in both stories; that is give them a definite common locale, (such as referring to Pottsville by a fictitious name, but using the same name in both stories), and writing a third story, also with the same locale, and putting them in one book together. It would be a post-war picture of The Region, from the standpoint of three classes: the Sheafer aristocrats, the middle class O'Haras, and the Schwackie [Polish, East European] gangster type. You'd have the three classes and the predominating races in just about the right periods."

Meanwhile, the honeymoon phase of his life with Pet had come to an end. When they returned from Bermuda, they stayed with Mrs. Petit in Brooklyn, and it was "all that the comic supplements reveal." After two weeks in her disapproving presence, they found an apartment at 19 West Fifty-fifth Street and had the assurance of $100 which Mrs. Petit agreed to provide. O'Hara took a job briefly with the publicity department of RKO Pictures, but there was no steady income and they found themselves, in this early year of the depression, expecting to carry on as before without the money to do it. "We eat a cheap table d'hote dinner," wrote O'Hara, "and proceed to a first-night. We buy two 'quarts' of cordial shop gin and the evening turns into a swell party. I try without success to get a $50 a week job, and a few minutes later am promised tickets for the Beaux-Arts Ball. Maybe this isn't a depression at all. Maybe it's just L-i-f-e."

The financial strain created problems at home. Irritated by his failure to provide, Pet resented the time he spent on his own writing. "Pet gets bored when I talk about The Region," O'Hara noted, "and I get sore when she gets bored, and so on." Having to depend on his wife made him truculent, with the usual results. "Mrs. O'Hara and I have done a good deal of drinking since Bermuda, you will not be interested to know," he told Simonds. The drink made him jealous and he convinced himself that Pet was disloyal. "If there wasn't any stress," noted Finis Farr, who knew him at the time, "he appeared, often enough, to be trying to create some." He was often violent and abusive. His friends were appalled for, as Farr observes, "he was in obvious psychic anguish, and causing pain for others, thus building up a load of guilt that he could hardly carry around without continuous and crippling emotional discomfort."

Towards the end of the second year of their marriage, Pet discovered she was pregnant. What might have brought them together estranged them, however, for Pet gave in to her mother's suggestion that she have an abortion. In stressing O'Hara's unreliability as a potential father, Mrs. Petit succeeded in destroying the marriage. O'Hara weakly agreed to the abortion and so contributed to his own humiliation. As the marriage unwound, O'Hara grew restless. "I'm pretty well fed up with myself at this juncture," he admitted to Simonds. "I wish I could take a vacation from myself. I have, of course, taken quite a number of overnight vacations; getting so cockeyed drunk that twenty hours elapse before I recover. But that's just the trouble." The glamour of New York had vanished and he needed a change. "A few years ago—say seven or eight—I could go to a town like Philadelphia, stay at a hotel, and get a swell kick out of listening to the city noises. I could get a kick out of uniformed delivery boys, and electric motor trucks and elevated trains and orchestras unobtrusively playing at luncheon in the hotel dining rooms; mounted police and shops that sell $20 shoes. Maybe I could recapture that swell feeling in another city."

By the early part of 1933, O'Hara had reached a crisis. He had no job, his stories were unsold and his marriage had collapsed. Characteristically, he sought to blame New York instead of himself, and hearing of a job as editor of a magazine in Pittsburgh, Pennsylvania, he decided to apply for it. He wrote a long letter analyzing the publication for the proprietors, and they were sufficiently impressed to hire him. From his hotel room in Pittsburgh, he wrote a letter to F. Scott Fitzgerald with whom he had recently begun to correspond. It ended with these words: "My pretty little wife is rolling out to Reno next week, and the girl I loved from the time I was 17 got married in Haiti last month, to a Byronic lad she's known about two months. And she was the shadow on the wall that broke up my marriage. Oh, my."

5. APPOINTMENT IN SAMARRA

Arriving in Pittsburgh in the late spring of 1933, O'Hara took a room at the William Penn Hotel in the center of the city so as to be convenient to the office of the *Bulletin-Index*. A newspaper in the nineteenth century, this periodical had been converted into a local society magazine. It was loosely imitative of *The New Yorker* and was one of several similar journals then flourishing in Cleveland, Detroit and other cities in the United States. It contained photographs of weddings and coming-out parties and published local news, cartoons and a weekly calendar of events. O'Hara told the owners, Henry and Paul Scheetz, that the magazine lacked focus. It was witty but had no consistent point of view. It was also amateurish and inaccurate. O'Hara believed that people only subscribed to magazines they trusted. "Every average reader knows a little more about one thing than he does about all others, whether his specialty be philatelics or philology. And when he comes upon a story dealing with his specialty, he wants it to be right. In a well-written publication, he gets that."

To give the *Bulletin-Index* an identity and to clear up inconsistencies, O'Hara decided to imitate a device used by *Time* in presenting information. He established departments covering such subjects as business and finance, education, music, sports and society. He also ran feature articles on subjects of local interest such as a recent Rhodes scholar, a prominent polo player and a gifted newspaper columnist. He gave the photographs irreverent captions and even borrowed "Timese" to enliven the language of reporting. Pittsburgh readers began to see their institutions in a new light when they read, "A leonine person in appearance, temper and will, was Henry Clay Frick, bearded Pittsburgh steel & coke master, Carnegie friend & foe; but a very gentle lion when he thought of children."

O'Hara had an editorial staff of two, one of them a young boy of eighteen named Frank Zachary, who later became editor-in-chief of *Town and Country*. Not drinking, O'Hara appeared at the office on time in the morning, and he was an efficient and energetic editor. He treated his young assistant in a friendly way, took him along on interviews and taught him how to edit a paper. Although he had only a small salary, O'Hara appeared at the best places and was soon known in Pittsburgh. He played golf at the public links but also went to Sewickley and was considered an amiable man-about-town. He soon regained the confidence he had lost in New York. He carried on a lively correspondence with editors and writers in New York, and the staff was impressed when envelopes arrived bearing the return addresses of *The New Yorker, Vanity Fair* and *Scribner's*. Sometimes, to the astonishment of his assistants, he would sit down at the desk and, with one leg over the arm of the chair, type out a story for *The New Yorker* without pause or mistake. O'Hara also enjoyed appearing knowledgeable. On press night he would close the magazine late, in imitation of the national weeklies, and take his staff across the street to a local bar to celebrate. Pointedly he would order Bronx cocktails, and when the bartender, not knowing this exotic drink, apologized for his ignorance, O'Hara would graciously accept a substitute.

Thanks to his extraordinary memory, O'Hara soon mastered Pittsburgh. On an interview, he never took notes; he simply remembered everything he heard. He collected an enormous amount of information about Pittsburgh without even seeming to try, and he soon understood the city's political and social structure. O'Hara led a quiet life in Pittsburgh. He did not drink much, although he kept a bottle in his hotel room. Mainly he read, and his room was filled with books. He made friends with the nightclub singer in the hotel and wrote about her for his magazine, but mostly he was alone. Once or twice he was visited by Pet. Despite the divorce, they were still in love, and they hoped to marry again. But Pet insisted that he have a well-paying job that would make them independent of Mrs. Petit. Then after four months, he suddenly left.

O'Hara's departure was unexpected despite some tension between him and Paul Scheetz, the business manager of the magazine. At one point, Scheetz decided to open all mail addressed to the office, including private letters addressed to O'Hara. Naturally, O'Hara was outraged by this practice and told Scheetz to stop. For a while he did, but then he started again. When O'Hara found his letters from Harold Ross and others lying open on his desk, he simply walked out of the office and did not return. Frank Zachary helped him pack his few possessions and sent his books on ahead by mail. O'Hara's decisiveness in leaving Pittsburgh came from a deeper level than annoyance about the mail, for he had come to realize that what he needed was uninterrupted time for his own work.

Back in New York, he took a room for eight dollars a week at the Pickwick Arms Club Residence at 230 East Fifty-first Street. The room was tiny but decent, and the hotel's only drawback was the noise from the Third Avenue el. He was somewhat at loose ends. He saw Pet, who had returned, divorced, from Reno, and he often went with her to a movie in the late afternoon. He slept for most of the day. In the early evenings he would go to Tony's on West Fifty-second Street and talk to Dorothy Parker, whom he had come to know and who encouraged him in his work. Sometimes he would go to Ira Gershwin's for backgammon before returning late at night to the hotel. Although he was not drinking, he was still very discouraged. "I have a feeling that all this is time-out preparatory to something terrible happening to me, but I almost don't care," he told his brother Tom. He did some football reporting for *The New Yorker,* and wrote that these articles were "the only things that make the difference between my being dead and alive. I don't mean only that the money keeps me alive. I mean I do nothing else, and except for them I might as well be dead." When *Scribner's* rejected a story, he wrote, "I *accept* this mantle of mediocrity, from whatever source it came, without even bothering about whether it fits."

Dorothy Parker was his main source of support. "John was broke and depressed and needed to be nagged," she later remarked. "He was a talent that blazed, but he hadn't yet steadied himself as a writer." She had tea with him several times a week, lent him money when necessary and was generally so helpful that he said, "Right now I think she is the best friend I have in the world." She read his work, and it was probably she who urged him to write a full-scale novel about Pottsville instead of a book of linked stories. He worked in the little cubicle of a room he had in the Pickwick Arms. "There was no desk—only a chair, a bureau, and the bed. I used the bed as a desk—put my typewriter on it—and each night I'd work until my back began to hurt." Usually he began at midnight and often didn't stop till seven in the morning. "I work in jags," he wrote to his brother Tom, "I work like the devil for days at a time, and then suddenly I dry up or get stale, or get physically too tired to go on."

He had most of the book that was to be *Appointment in Samarra* worked out in his head. "The locale of the novel is Pottsville," he told Tom, "called Gibbsville in the novel. Mahantongo Street is called Mantenego Street [later changed to Lantenengo]. All points in Schuylkill County are given fictitious names—Taqua, for instance. And others you will recognize. Points outside Schuylkill County—Hazelton, Easton, Reading, Wilkes-

Barre—are mentioned by their right names. The plot of the novel, which is quite slight, is rather hard to tell, but the story is essentially of a young married couple and their breakdown in the first year of the depression. I have no illusions about its being the great or the second-great American novel, but it's my first. And my second will be better."

After a while, O'Hara ran out of money, so with 25,000 words completed, he wrote to three publishers who had shown interest in the work, saying to each that if he would read the typescript overnight and offer a subsidy until the book was completed, he could publish it. "I finished these letters early in the morning, put them in the mail and came up to Times Square and went to the movies. I spent the whole day in 10 and 15 cent movie houses along Forty-second Street. When I went back to my room about 5:30 that afternoon I found messages to call all three publishers. There was nothing wrong with the mails that day—Cap Pearce of Harcourt, Brace had read my letter and called me at 11.30 that morning." Since he was the first to call, O'Hara gave him the typescript to read, and within twenty-four hours, he had an agreement for an advance to be paid in weekly installments of fifty dollars until the book was completed in three months' time.

F. Scott Fitzgerald was very much in O'Hara's mind while he was writing *Appointment in Samarra,* and that year the two men met in New York. O'Hara read the galley proofs of *Tender Is the Night* as a favor to Fitzgerald. "You helped me finish my novel," wrote O'Hara to Fitzgerald, crediting their talk together. "I reasoned that the best parts of my novel will be said to derive from Fitzgerald." While denying any intention to imitate, he acknowledged that "the best parts of my novel are facile pupils of The Beautiful and Damned and The Great Gatsby. I was bushed, as Dottie says, and the fact that I need money terribly was enough to make me say the hell with my book until you talked to me and seemed to accept me. So then I went ahead and finished my second-rate novel in peace. My message to the world is Fuck it!"

O'Hara was right in thinking that he would be compared to Fitzgerald, but years later he commented on a fundamental difference between *The Great Gatsby* and his own novel: *"Gatsby* is a great book," he wrote, "but *Gatsby* is satirical. *Appointment in Samarra* is not satirical; it is, literally, deadly serious. It is not a sarcastic comment on the time; it is *of* the time." The time was the two years before Roosevelt's inauguration: "the nation was stunned by the first blows of the depression, with other blows yet to come . . . the hope was not for a bright future; the hope was for the resumption of the immediate past."

Appointment in Samarra occupies three days in the lives of Julian English and his wife, Caroline, an upper-class couple in the small city of Gibbsville. On Christmas eve at a party at the country club, Julian grows tired of the pretensions of an Irish social climber called Harry Reilly and throws a glass of whiskey in his face with such violence that an ice cube gives Reilly a black eye. Reilly, to whom Julian owes money, refuses to accept his apology and the Catholic community turns against Julian. Caroline is also irritated with him, but he promises to make up to her the following night. Instead, he gets drunk again and flirts with a nightclub singer, the girl friend of a local mobster. On the third day, he quarrels with his friends at the Gibbsville Club, and has a final fight with his wife, who tells him she is leaving him. Julian goes home alone and after a few drinks, he enters the closed garage, sits down in his Cadillac and turns on the ignition.

The excessiveness of Julian's suicide is what makes *Appointment in Samarra* so much a part of its time. Julian doesn't belong to Fitzgerald's Jazz Age; he is ten years younger and belongs to what came to be called the hangover generation, the young people who grew up accustomed to the good life without having to earn it. This is the generation that had so little to defend itself with when the depression came in 1928. Fitzgerald believed that there was already, the year before, a "widespread neurosis" that was beginning to kill off the members of his generation. "A classmate killed his wife and himself on Long Island, another tumbled 'accidentally' from a skyscraper in Philadelphia, another purposely from a skyscraper in New York. One was killed in a speakeasy in Chicago; another was beaten to death in a speakeasy in New York and crawled home to the Princeton Club to die; still another had his skull crushed by a maniac's axe in an insane asylum where he was confined. These are not catastrophes that I went out of my way to look for—these were my friends."

Julian English is like one of these, a person formed by his environment and by lack of willpower. A nice young man with well-to-do parents, he goes to college, joins the right fraternity and comes back home where, instead of going into one of the professions, he takes over a Cadillac car agency. He cashes in on the prosperity of the mid-twenties and spends much of his time drinking and dancing at the country club with his equally nice but more conventional wife. Julian has grace and wit and the manners that come with inherited money. He is charming, but when his troubles begin he has no way of coping with them. Without any sort of interior life, without values formed through hardship, he has nothing to rely on. After throwing the whiskey at the country club, he has a conversation with the local Catholic priest. "I never was meant to be a Cadillac dealer or any other kind of dealer, Father," he says. Asked whether he had a secret ambition, Julian replies, "Oh, no, I'm not anything. I guess I should have been a doctor."

O'Hara draws on his own experience of both high and low life in Pottsville. In his portrait of Julian, he shows what he loved and hated in the upper classes. He admires the style of those who live on upper Mahantongo Street, but he also shows how their lives depend on having friendly relations with criminals such as Ed Charney and Al Grecco. They are people too, and O'Hara shows how sometimes the worm can turn. Writing the novel so soon after the death of his own relationship with Pet, O'Hara treats Caroline with imagination and understanding. Like everyone else in the novel, she is not a symbol but a person. One of O'Hara's greatest achievements is the way in which he gets under people's skins: he peels off layers of pretension so that the little lies his characters live by are discredited. Writing about sex, he is especially courageous, for he is not afraid to write scenes in which a woman taunts a man in a nightclub by revealing her breasts to him, or in which a married man sexually excites a college girl he is dancing with. O'Hara was almost alone in writing about these things. Moreover, he presents many scenes from the woman's point of view, and no modern American male writer understood or created women more convincingly than O'Hara. His understanding came from his fundamental desire to be fair to them, even though he mistreated them when drunk. He expressed this view once in a letter of advice to his brother Tom: "Never forget that your girl or your wife is every damn bit as much a person as you are. She regards you as another person, just as you regard her as another person. She thinks the world revolves around her just as you do around yourself, just as anyone does. She has a vote in life as well as politics, she eats and sleeps and suffers and loves and thinks (regardless of how badly you or I may think she thinks) like you and me. She was born, she lives, she's got to die; and for you to attempt to dominate her, to pinch her personality, is some kind of sin."

O'Hara best reveals his sense of women's equality in conversations where each person can speak openly. His understanding of the tragic plight of men and women is revealed beautifully in the last conversation Julian has with Caroline before he goes home to kill himself. Caroline naturally does not know his intentions. She is sitting in her car, with Julian standing in the street alongside it, and she tells him she won't see him again.

> "Oh, yes, you will. You will, all right."
> "You're pretty sure of yourself, but this time you're wrong. It's no go."
> "I didn't mean that. I didn't mean I was sure of myself. What I meant was, you'd see me. You wouldn't be able to help it."
> "Why should I want to?"
> "To gloat, probably. Either you'd want to gloat, if you were absolutely out of love with me, or you'd want to see if you still loved me."
> "You're so wrong it isn't even funny."
> "It isn't even funny. Lord and Taylor! Wouldn't that jar you? I'll say. You tell 'em casket, I'm coffin. I'll tell the world. Don't take any wooden nickels. . . . I'm going."
> "Oh, go ahead. But remember, I'm not going to be home tonight.

Not me. I'm going to call off the party, unless you want to have it. Anyway, I won't be there."

"That's all right. It only makes it a different kind of party."

"Oh, there's no need to tell me that. But you'd better be careful with your torch singer. She knows how to handle people like you."

"You're a dear. You're a sweet girl. I knew you'd be a good sport about it. I knew all along you would be."

"Oh, go to hell, you and your cheap sarcasm."

With almost everything he says, Julian is sending out signals to Caroline, but she doesn't receive them. She is on a different wavelength.

What is exceptional about *Appointment in Samarra* as a first novel is its own identity. There are debts to other writers, to Theodore Dreiser and Sinclair Lewis. O'Hara found his interest in details foreshadowed in the work of John Galsworthy and Sir Arthur Conan Doyle whom he admired "because he can transport you back to the England of his time, the sights and sounds and smells of London and the countryside, so economically and so truly." Although by temperament different from F. Scott Fitzgerald, he was grateful to him for being a writer who "could come right out and say Locomobile instead of high-powered motor car, Shanley's instead of gay cabaret, and George, instead of François, the *chasseur* at the Paris Ritz." O'Hara wanted *Appointment in Samarra* to have a similar authenticity, so he filled it with the names of popular songs, politicians, sports figures and cars of the period. Probably the greatest influence on his work was that of Booth Tarkington, whose *Alice Adams* describes small-town class struggles in a way O'Hara understood, and whose dialogue is masterful. Tarkington also knew how to present sociological information adroitly and indirectly. His fault is that he was sentimental. O'Hara thought he had "a fastidiousness that in my opinion should be no part of an author's equipment, at least if it makes him cheat even a little bit. The old thing about no omelet without breaking eggs, no surgery without letting blood." Like all writers, O'Hara used what he could from his predecessors, but throughout his first novel his voice is very much his own.

O'Hara's originality as a writer lies in the way he uses the facts of his own experience as a young man in a small American city without taking the easy path of ridicule. His *New Yorker* sketches were often satirical, but O'Hara soon abandoned this habit without losing his interest in accurate reporting. He continued to record the voices and mannerisms of his characters, but he also tried to present their feelings as completely as their humanity demanded. He wanted his readers to know what his characters' "vote in life" might be, whether they are able to exercise it or not.

While the book was being written, O'Hara used *The Infernal Grove* as a working title: it was taken from a poem by Blake. Then he came across a passage from Somerset Maugham's play, *Sheppey,* in which a merchant from Baghdad, fearing that Death is seeking him, flees to Samarra, not knowing that Death has an appointment with him there. The publishers objected to the allusiveness of the new title O'Hara suggested. One editor suggested *Swell Guy* as an alternate. But O'Hara stuck by his choice and helped prove Raymond Chandler's assertion that "a good title is the title of a successful book."

Some cuts reducing sexual explicitness were required before Harcourt would publish the book, but they were minor. They related to a point that would continue to plague O'Hara as a novelist, however. Even so unlikely a person as Sinclair Lewis attacked the book, when it appeared, as "nothing but infantilism—the erotic visions of a hobbledehoy behind the barn." Lewis' article, appearing in the *Saturday Review* along with H. S. Canby's review entitled "Mr. O'Hara, and the Vulgar School," increased a prurient interest in the novel although, as O'Hara later remarked, "it was quite a blow for a first novelist. It was probably good training for me, although it hurt at the time." The book went into three printings and received considerable attention, largely thanks to the support of fellow writers. Dorothy Parker said, "It stands, a fine and serious novel, of shrewd and inevitable pattern and almost unbelievable pace. Mr. O'Hara's eyes and ears have been spared nothing, but he has kept in his heart a curious and bitter mercy." Fitzgerald wrote that "John O'Hara's novel indicates the tremendous strides that American writers have taken since the war," and Hemingway, in a note in *Esquire,* said, "If you want to read a book by a man who knows exactly what he is writing about and has written it marvelously well, read Appointment in Samarra by John O'Hara."

The success of *Appointment in Samarra* naturally attracted attention in Pottsville. Walter Farquhar reviewed it favorably in the *Journal,* but most of the townspeople were unhappy. The response of the town's librarian, Edith Patterson, was representative: "I'm not holier-than-thou. Like others in Pottsville I was shocked. He brought a foreign vocabulary to our people, one they were not used to." O'Hara expected a hostile reaction, for he knew that a truthful writer was the enemy of the smug. Urging Farquhar to follow his own course, he wrote, "If you're going to get out of that God awful town, for God's sake write something that will *make* you get out of it. Write something that will automatically sever your connections with the town, that will help you get rid of the bitterness you must have stored up against all those patronizing cheap bastards in that dry-fucked excrescence on Sharp Mountain."

The townspeople of Pottsville also tried to identify the incidents and characters in *Appointment in Samarra,* certain that they were based on actual people and events. O'Hara was astonished upon returning to Pottsville soon after the novel was published "when people I knew very slightly and who were certainly never in my mind as characters in the book, came up with fire in their eyes, calling me names for holding them up to the ridicule

of all their friends and threatening to sue me for defamation of character."
They were probably led to this behavior because, unlike Sinclair Lewis,
who invented a whole city, Zenith, for his novel *Babbitt,* O'Hara was
content to use Pottsville as it was, only changing some of the names. It is
curious he was so uninventive: perhaps he needed the physical reality of
a place for his fictive world. With characters, his approach was more
complex. He did base his characters on people he had known but only to
ensure their authenticity. They were convincing, he said, because "they are
all real people, people who are living or who have lived. I use the psychological pattern of the real people, then I put them in different locations and
times, and cover them up with superficial characteristics, etc. In the case
of Julian English, the guy in real life was a fellow named Richards, who
was definitely not country-club, but had charm and a certain kind of native
intelligence, and who, when the chips were down, shot himself. I took his
life, his psychological pattern, and covered him up with Brooks shirts and
a Cadillac dealership and so on, and the reason the story rings so true is
that it is God's truth, out of life." Elsewhere, O'Hara expanded his comments: "The use of the psychological pattern of a real person is not a short
cut to the creation of characters. It can be very dangerous, and far from
being a short cut, it entails a lot of work, more work, possibly, than is
involved in the creation of a character out of, as they say, whole cloth—
a metaphor that I only vaguely understand."

Thinking it might give him an opportunity to finish *Appointment in
Samarra* in peace, O'Hara took a job as editor of the ship's newspaper on
board the Swedish-American liner *Kungsholm* for a three-week Caribbean
cruise in March of 1934. The job came to him through his friend, John
McClain, shipping correspondent of the *New York Sun,* who was unable to
go. Since most of the material for the paper was already prepared by the
company, all O'Hara had to do was write a column in which he commented
on the passengers in a friendly, gossipy way. There he asked, archly, "Who
is the pretty girl who looks so much like Karen Morley?" She turned out
to be Ruth Dill, a secretary from Detroit, and she took care of the free time
that was supposed to be devoted to finishing the novel. O'Hara's column
was breezy and amiable, reflecting his own good mood, but now and again,
he reported a telling conversation, as when a steward goes up to a couple
standing on the deck and hands a message to the man. " 'Anything interesting?' says solicitous Miss B. 'No, it's from my wife,' says tactless
Mr. A.—and then remembers too late that Miss B. didn't know he had
a wife."

Interviewed on his return by John McClain for the *Sun,* O'Hara was
reported as an enthusiastic traveler: "So we went to a group of places.
Barbados. I like Barbados. Trinidad. Trinidad is just lovely. Then in fairly
rapid succession, Caracas, Curaçao, Panama, Kingston, Port-au-Prince,
Nassau. I thought they were dear. I saw the Caribbean. In fact I spit in the
Caribbean. I saw the Pacific Ocean, and I can't think of many oceans that

are nicer than the Pacific. I set foot in South America. Dear South America."

When *Appointment in Samarra* was still in galleys, it was offered to a number of Hollywood studios. None of them bought it, but Paramount asked O'Hara whether he would go to Hollywood for three months during the summer of 1934 to work on various movies already in progress. Since the salary was $250 a week, an enormous sum to O'Hara, he accepted. He had a renewable three-month contract. "I'm so excited about the trip," he wrote his brother Tom, "and the prospect of being able to buy a Ford phaeton of my very own, and a new suit, and some razor blades."

He took an apartment at the Ravenswood, an eight-story apartment hotel at 570 North Rossmore in Hollywood, only a few minutes' walk from the Paramount studio on Melrose Avenue. The work was routine, although new to O'Hara. No one paid much attention to him until one day in a conversation with a producer, O'Hara revealed his knowledge of horsemanship, whereupon he was assigned to help write a cavalry picture for Richard Arlen and Carole Lombard. Like most new writers in Hollywood, O'Hara was more interested in the place than in the work, and he was alert to his surroundings: "The biggest automobile in town was a Lincoln town car, license number MW-1, owned by my neighbor, Mae West; it was against the zoning ordinances to put up a building more than fourteen stories high; Toby Wing was a starlet at Paramount; Mary Pickford was still married to Douglas Fairbanks and Pickfair was a quasiofficial Blair House to which Will Hays would take visiting notables. Irving Thalberg was the reigning genius at Metro and they had not yet built the Iron Lung, as they called the main office in Culver City. Sound was here to stay, and along La Cienega and Fairfax and on the side streets of Hollywood, little bungalows had been converted into studios where veteran singers and Shakespearean troupers were giving lessons to people who wanted to learn to enunciate and project."

O'Hara was soon seeing friends from Manhattan, many from *The New Yorker,* who had gone to California to write for the movies. They included Herbert Asbury, Nunnally Johnson and Joel Sayre, all with their wives, and also Arthur Kober and his wife, Lillian Hellman. On weekends they went out together to a beach club at Santa Monica and also played tennis. O'Hara played golf at the Brentwood Club and he often went to the Coconut Grove where there were tea dances attended by college students; at night it was popular with the movie set. In his free time he visited Stanley Rose's bookshop on Hollywood Boulevard, which was the best literary bookshop in Los Angeles, and met Meta Rosenberg, who worked there. He would often take her to lunch at the nearby Musso and Frank's restaurant where many New York exiles gathered, including James Cain. In the evenings they would go dancing. "The chic restaurant that year," O'Hara later recalled, "was the Vendome, the nearest thing Los Angeles had to the Colony in New York, and a sort of predecessor of Romanoff's, where the food and beverages were expensive and good, and where the women could show off their I. Magnin garments. And, of course, the men could show off their women."

O'Hara was in a sunny mood. He wasn't drinking and he was an amusing and witty companion. He spoke a lot to Meta Rosenberg about Hemingway and Fitzgerald and was serious about his own work, but never self-important. He would take an imaginative interest in the lives of the women he was with and treat them with a sympathy and understanding that made him likable. In telling them about his own troubles without feeling sorry for himself, he would get them to tell him theirs, for he was a good listener. Often he would go out of his way to be of use to someone who needed him, and he was generous with little presents that signified something pleasant or recalled an agreeable occasion. In comparison to most Californians, he was somewhat stiff, and Irving Stone, who met him at the time, recalled that he was always reserved, wearing a waistcoat and tie as though they were a suit of armor. Yet he was well liked. When *Appointment in Samarra* was published that summer, Herbert and Helen Asbury gave a party to celebrate the event at their house in Beverly Hills. They invited most of the expatriate *New Yorker* crowd, including S. J. Perelman, who happened to be in town, as well as some Hollywood people. At ten o'clock their chauffeur went out and bought fifty copies of the *Los Angeles Examiner* which contained a good review of the book, and distributed them to the guests. "By that time," O'Hara later remembered, "some of them couldn't read—I was on the wagon—but it was a wonderful party."

In September, he asked to be released from his option with Paramount and returned to New York. Although he was having a good time, he was lonely. "Pet is the one I pine for," he told his brother Tom, "because she was my wife and still is, really." Arriving in New York, he stayed briefly at the Pickwick Arms but then moved into an apartment in the East Fifties near Park Avenue, which he shared with Quentin Reynolds. He was soon caught up with work, selecting stories for a collection to be called *The Doctor's Son* that was being published by Harcourt, Brace as a result of the success of *Appointment in Samarra*.

He was thirty years old, had earned $5000 from his writings and was accepted in *Who's Who,* as he'd promised his father he would be. He was well known in literary circles, and through Dorothy Parker had become acquainted with some of the older writers in town, including Robert Benchley and others who had belonged to the Algonquin Round Table. But O'Hara was never a joiner: he usually stood alone at the bar of Tony's or at "21," and was at his best in intimate conversation with one or two other people. His solitude was painful but it was artistically beneficial, for he could study the habits and listen to the people he wanted to write about.

With the coming of the depression, the casual meetings that had formerly taken place at speakeasies now occurred at parties in private houses. A number of people began to entertain regularly at home, and invitations to their functions were sought after. One popular place was the house of Howard Dietz, the songwriter, on Eleventh Street in Greenwich Village, where people from theatrical, film and literary circles would gather. For their all-night parties, the Dietzes would have all their furniture moved out of the house and brought back the next morning. Mrs. Dietz was one of the first hostesses to encourage O'Hara in his writing, but even more important to him was Adele Lovett, the wife of Robert A. Lovett, who at the time was with the banking firm of Brown Brothers, Harriman. She first met O'Hara at Dorothy Parker's apartment and found him shy and withdrawn. Then she read *Appointment in Samarra* and one day, finding O'Hara alone at Tony's, she told him that she thought it was a masterpiece. After that, they were friends for life: O'Hara gave her the typescript of the novel and if ever he was difficult, she would remind him that he had "incurred" her friendship and that she would not fight with him.

The Lovetts were also important to O'Hara because they introduced him to New York society. Mrs. Lovett often went to first nights at the theater. Afterwards she would invite twenty or thirty people to her apartment overlooking the East River at Eighty-third Street. A typical evening would include such people as Robert Benchley, Howard Dietz, Dorothy Parker, John McClain, Hoagy Carmichael, Louise Macy, Archibald MacLeish, Robert Sherwood, Russel Crouse, F.P.A. and Frank Sullivan. Robert Lovett would come up late from the bank, perhaps with his partner, Averell Harriman. The Lovetts were also great friends of Philip Barry and his wife, and O'Hara later came to think of Barry as his best friend. At the Lovetts' O'Hara became acquainted not only with the older generation of people in the arts but also with members of an upper class who were beyond anything Pottsville could offer. Averell Harriman preferred the company of artists and writers to the bankers he knew on Wall Street; James Forrestal and William Lord, another businessman O'Hara met at the time, were at ease with the arts and certainly did not belong to the "booboisie" derided by Sinclair Lewis and H. L. Mencken. O'Hara was immediately attracted to these people because they were worldly and without religious prejudice; they had taste and were not ostentatious with their money. Books were not alien to them, nor was the theater; many of them belonged to the Democratic party and went into politics. This was the world O'Hara thought he belonged to. In his eyes, these people were the best America had produced and he wanted to associate with them. They in turn admired him, and he was relaxed and natural in their company.

At the same time, he never abandoned the Broadway world he had first known as a newspaperman. With John McClain, with whom he now shared the ground floor of an apartment building at 103 East Fifty-fifth Street, and with Jimmy Cannon, the sports writer, he often went out with three chorus girls, Colette Francis, Dorothy Van Heyn and Toni Sorel. There was a good deal of gossip about them in Walter Winchell's and other newspaper columns. In later years O'Hara occasionally mentioned Toni Sorel when she became an actress as one whose figure was so attractive "that the other people on stage could have shot one another dead and the audience would have paid no attention." He also went to Billy Rose's Casino de Paree, a large theater restaurant and nightclub which had a lavish revue and Benny Goodman's orchestra playing for dancing. One of the chorus girls there was a Japanese-American by the name of Ruth Sato, and O'Hara saw a good deal of her. At four o'clock in the morning, when the show was over, he would call for her in his yellow roadster, wearing his raccoon coat, and take her back to his apartment for something to eat. Often he would read her bits of dialogue from what he had just been writing and ask her opinion of it. Sometimes he would tell her to come in a taxi and pick up some food on the way. Once he sent her a telegram saying that he expected "the shipment of opium at 4 A.M." During this time he was at work on his second novel, *Butterfield 8,* and since he wanted to have his details right, he took Ruth Sato with him to visit some Park Avenue apartment buildings, pretending they were a married couple in search of a place to live.

O'Hara had no shyness about telling the girls he knew whom he had slept with and he earned a reputation as one who liked to "kiss and tell." His view was that they had been willing partners and that it was hypocrisy to deny it. Occasionally he suffered from gonorrhea because he was careless, and he would talk about his affliction as though it was an interesting fact of life. Yet he was annoyed when he found a note on the window of his car in Hollywood where he had parked in front of the office of a well-known specialist in this ailment. S. J. Perelman, recognizing the car, had written, "Don't worry, it's no worse than the common cold."

Partly O'Hara was just curious about sex. He wanted to take Ruth Sato to a sexual exhibition put on in Greenwich Village by a woman and her daughter: lesbianism was just another interesting phenomenon. The pervasive sexuality of his life sometimes led him to lose control of himself. One morning while he was still lying in bed in a hotel, a pretty chambermaid came in, and before he could help himself, he had her in bed with him. This experience made him worry about the strength of his own sexual impulses, but generally his partners were obliging. On another occasion, having forgotten about a luncheon engagement he had made with John McClain and Mildred Gilman, he went to his front door in a disheveled state. He told his friends to come in while he finished something, returned to the bedroom where he had a girl, and without closing the door, completed his noisy lovemaking. Afterwards, they all went out to lunch as though nothing had happened. Sometimes, there were comic overtones to his behavior. Annoyed that Howard Dietz was leaving a nightclub with a girl he liked, he called out, "I've slept with that woman!" To which Dietz replied, "Well, I'm going to sleep with her now."

Gradually these activities destroyed what remained of O'Hara's relationship with Pet. She lived close by, in her mother's apartment on Park Avenue, and occasionally she would come by with a little dog she owned. These impromptu visits began to irritate O'Hara, and if he had other plans he would ask her to leave. Caught up in his new social life, he didn't want to be tied down as he had the year before. Ruth Sato asked him why he didn't go back to Pet and O'Hara replied that she wouldn't have him. Both came to realize that it was no longer possible to revive the feelings they once had for each other.

He was now working on his second novel, *Butterfield 8.* The advance from Harcourt, Brace lessened his financial worries but he wasn't making much progress and was "stalling around." As he wrote to Ruth Sato, "The other novel, about a small town, was written in New York. The next one, mostly about New York, probably should be written in a small town, except that I can't live in a small town for more than a week at a time. New York is the best place for me because it takes longer for me to get tired of New York than any other place." To get away for a few days, he convinced *The New Yorker* to give him an advance for two or three articles on Ernest Hemingway. He drove down to Miami in February of 1935, with the intention of interviewing Hemingway at Key West, but learning that Hemingway had guests, he gave up the idea. Instead, he stayed in Miami for "my relaxation and thinking-out process" for the new book and spent his time "working on one of Earl Carroll's problem children. It took me a week to find out she was a Lesbian. They have to wear suits and smoke cigars before I recognize them."

Meanwhile, in England, Faber and Faber brought out *Appointment in Samarra* to good reviews, and *The Doctor's Son* was published by Harcourt, Brace in February of 1935. The book contained 37 of the 112 stories O'Hara had written since 1928, of which the greater part were published after 1932. Most of them are portraits of individuals or explorations of the relationship between two people—a married couple, the owner of a Chinese restaurant and his waitress, two employees in an office, coproprietors of a coffee shop, people in a club. There is little plotting beyond anecdote and the narrative is far less important than character development. Many of the characters suffer from loneliness, and there are sometimes inexplicable barriers that ensure isolation. O'Hara doesn't give reasons for the way things are in his stories; he simply presents the facts. Sometimes, the point is that there is no explanation.

O'Hara avoided tightly plotted stories because he did not believe that life is only an affair of cause and effect. Writing about the endings of stories and novels, he rejected the logical pattern of the syllogism as "a little too conclusive a form for the modern novel or short story. My half-baked theories on these forms of literature arrive at the ultimate opinion that life goes on, and for the sake of verisimilitude and realism, you cannot positively give the impression of an ending: you must let something hang. A cheap interpretation of that would be to say that you must always leave a chance for a sequel. People die, love dies, but life does not die, and so long as people live, stories must have life at the end."

One of the last stories in *The Doctor's Son*, "Over the River and Through the Woods," takes its title from a children's poem about visiting grandfather's house. The real story begins at the end when, alone in an upstairs room in the house he used to own, the not-so-old grandfather decides that "for a while he would just sit there and plan his own terror." He has been accused by one of his granddaughter's friends of being a dirty old man because he opened the bathroom door and found her naked. The girl is cruel and mistaken, nothing more than that. But the grandfather had been thinking about her, and no matter what anyone could ever say to explain or ameliorate things, the damage cannot be undone.

Two stories in the collection are autobiographical and allow O'Hara to express the warmth that is absent in his stories of lonely wives and hustlers. The title story, which is really a novella, uses as narrator a character called Jimmy Malloy who is a stand-in for O'Hara himself, although not in every respect. The story occurs in Gibbsville and its neighborhood during the famous influenza epidemic of 1918. Jimmy Malloy's father, exhausted from many all-night stands tending the stricken miners and their families, is replaced by a young doctor from Philadelphia whom Jimmy drives from one miners' "patch" to another to visit the sick. The drama, however, involves a flirtation between the young doctor and the wife of a mine supervisor outside of Gibbsville, and the relationship between Jimmy and the daughter of that house, who is a couple of years older than he. In the middle of the epidemic, these two loves run their different courses. There is no logical relationship between the setting and the passion that is born; they merely exist simultaneously. Looking at life without a literary bias, without trying to see patterns where none exist, O'Hara explores the delicate realm of human feelings and shows us the electricity in the air. Because his writing seems so true, the stories work.

After returning from Miami, O'Hara remained in New York for a month before deciding to leave town once again to work on *Butterfield 8.* This time, with spring approaching, he went to the Oceanside Hotel in East Sandwich, Massachusetts. In the off-season, Cape Cod was dreary, for the summer hotels and shops were closed. But without temptations, it was a good place to work. O'Hara had a room overlooking the sea and was close to the beach with its surf. "The food is good and plain," he wrote his New York publisher, "and I am the only guest. I pay $25 a week. There is no sex, no nothin'. I work in the afternoon and in the evening and quit at one A.M." He worked fast, and by May completed 25,000 words of the first draft. But it was not much fun: "Did you ever write a novel and break in two pipes at the same time?" he asked his publisher. "And grow a beard? And live ascetically?"

His solitude made him conscious of his unsatisfactory single state. He began to feel the need for someone to take the place of Pet. Although he had enjoyed himself in Hollywood and New York, the life was unsteady. "I am no happier here than ever," he had written his brother Tom from California, and it was becoming a chronic state. Then while still in Massachusetts, he met a young college student who seemed to be the answer to his need. He described her later to Scott Fitzgerald: "I am in love with a 19-year-old, a sophomore at Wellesley. Her name is Barbara Kibler, and she is 5'3, dark, beautiful figure, and looks younger than she is. She is from Columbus, and her family are nouveau riche and Protestant." Despite the discrepancy in age, they suited each other. "She is pretty wide-eyed now," O'Hara noted, acknowledging his comparative maturity, "but she has good Ohio common sense," adding that she could help give him the stability he needed. In June, along with John McClain, he drove out to Ohio to visit Barbara and her parents. "O'Clain, or Good Company, as we are calling him for just this trip," wrote O'Hara to Adele Lovett from Washington, Pennsylvania, "has been dying all day with a hangover that has taken all historical interest away from the Kansas dust storms, the last days of Pompeii, and the month or so immediately preceding the Ark's call on Mt. Ararat." Whether it was his age or his unsteady career, Barbara's family were, in O'Hara's reckoning, "against me." The Kiblers were Jewish in origin, related to the Lazarus family of midwestern merchants, and once again, O'Hara was distasteful to the family of the girl he wanted to marry.

To ease the tension, O'Hara abruptly left New York in July and sailed to Italy on the *Conte di Savoia.* The ship passage was unremarkable except for his winning the skeet shooting competition, and O'Hara worked on his novel. He did not go to Rome, but visited Florence for a couple of days, intending to mail the completed book back to New York on the return voyage of the *Conte di Savoia.* Unable to meet the deadline, he took the train to Paris in order to send it by another ship. "I have only seen Paris from the taxi window," he wrote his publisher, "from the station to the hotel. I am not seeing it until I can write Finis to the novel. I am not leaving this room. So far I've had all my meals sent up."

O'Hara's brief exposure to Europe seems to have made little impression on him. There is a great difference between O'Hara and the earlier generation of American writers—Hemingway, Fitzgerald and others—who used Europe as a background for their fiction. By 1935, the depression and the rise of Hitler and Mussolini had robbed Europe of its glamour, and O'Hara seemed to lack curiosity about its history. Staying at the Georges

V, he did not explore Paris but saw a few American friends. He considered taking a brief trip to London to see his publishers, but there was not enough money to do so. Mainly he was busy completing his novel. "I have finished Butterfield 8, or Wrong Number, as it soon will be called by foe and friend," he noted in a letter to Adele Lovett. He was still worried about money and Barbara Kibler: "I keep not forgetting that I have made this trip on borrowed money, that the money has to be repaid, and that it is too much of a mental hazard to get hitched on a bankroll of $7, which I did once before. All that we can do now is agree and decide, or disagree and decide, or decide and/or agree and/or disagree."

O'Hara sailed back to New York on the *Normandie* where once again he demonstrated his prowess in skeet shooting. John McClain met the boat and interviewed the returning author who showed him the prize he received for his shooting, a glass clock, with N–O–R–M–A–N–D–I–E embossed around the dial in place of numbers. "Unfortunately this treasure slipped from Mr. O'Hara's fingers as he was undergoing baggage examination, and shattered on the cement pier floor," wrote McClain. " 'Oh, for pity sakes!' said Mr. O'Hara, or words to that effect."

By the end of August, he was busy with the galley proofs of *Butterfield 8* and also with Barbara Kibler. Adele Lovett gave a party to introduce her to his friends, so she could get an impression "before it's too late." He invited Scott Fitzgerald who could not come and Ernest Hemingway who did, and the party was a great success. Barbara Kibler had eyes for no one but O'Hara. Yet there was tension, for some of O'Hara's friends had doubts about the marriage. O'Hara had hoped to sign a contract with a Hollywood studio and leave "for the Pacific littoral" soon after getting married, but the contract fell through and O'Hara's own doubts rose again to the surface. His sister Mary asked him whether he was in love with her. "What business is it of yours?" was the reply. "I have to know in order to let you know whether I approve or not," she answered. O'Hara paused. For two years he had been on the wagon and had devoted himself to a girl he wanted to marry. But now everyone else was doubtful or skeptical. "I'll let you know," he said.

In October, the same month as the party, *Butterfield 8* was published. Fearful that, like Fitzgerald's, his second novel might be badly received, O'Hara had decided to be ambitious and "to make plain what I had seen" in New York. Faced with the choice of writing a panoramic novel in the manner of Dos Passos' *Manhattan Transfer* or a book in which the characters represent types, as Dreiser's *Sister Carrie,* O'Hara had decided to try to combine the two approaches. To do this, he limited his range to a relatively small group of middle- and upper-middle-class characters living in Greenwich Village or the upper east side, the section of town served by the telephone exchange of the title, Butterfield 8. He based his novel on a sensational story about someone from this world that took up space on the front page of New York's newspapers for weeks during the summer of 1931.

In June of that year, Starr Faithfull was found mysteriously drowned off Long Beach, just beyond Far Rockaway on the south shore of Long Island. She was the twenty-five-year-old daughter of a moderately prosperous manufacturer who lived three doors down from Mayor Jimmy Walker on St. Luke's Place. The efforts made to discover whether she had been murdered or had committed suicide revealed a number of lurid episodes from her past. She was a pretty single girl who was well known in various speakeasies, and she had a reputation for sleeping around with men. There were links with important people, including Andrew Peters, the former mayor of Boston. Some of these went back to the time when she was a student at a boarding school in Massachusetts and suggested that she had been led astray as a very young girl. She drank a lot in order, as she said, "to like people," and then she took sedatives to forget what she had done with them. She kept a diary and left letters that revealed her desire to end her "worthless, disorderly bore of an existence before I ruin anyone else's life." She had charm and beauty and little else: she was a narcissist who let herself be used, and she floated aimlessly through life until her violent end.

O'Hara's representation of Starr Faithfull is Gloria Wandrous, and the emotional center of his novel is her love for Eddie Brunner, a decent impoverished artist, the only one of her men friends she does not sleep with. Had she met Eddie early in her life, she might have been all right, but now it's too late: "It's awful," she says, "when you think that you've stayed with so many men and made such a mess of your life, and then someone you really want to stay with because you love him, that person is the one person you mustn't stay with because if you do he immediately becomes like the rest, and you don't want him to become like the rest. The thing he has that the rest haven't is that you haven't stayed with him." So instead of staying with Eddie, Gloria drifts along from one man to another. Corrupted as a schoolgirl by an older man who introduced her to drink and drugs and sex, she found she liked them, or at least didn't dislike them. When she meets Weston Liggett, a rich man who is married with two daughters, she is overwhelmingly, and fatally, attracted to him. She then begins to move towards an end that seems at once accidental and inevitable.

To give Gloria's life a background, O'Hara introduces a number of other characters whose stories provide the book's social atmosphere and give a feeling of New York life. His failure to relate these lesser characters to Gloria creates a problem. In the narrow world of Gibbsville, O'Hara was able to move from character to character and not lose his focus on Julian English, but New York is so large that the emotional impact of the novel is diffused by the peripheral episodes.

O'Hara went out of his way to make it clear that Gloria Wandrous was not a "symbol of modern youth," even if there were such a thing. "It could be said," he wrote, "that she was a person who in various ways—some of them peculiar—had the ability to help other people, but lacked the ability to help herself." Gloria's childhood experiences robbed her of a normal youth. Her corruption deprived her of the magic of real love, and she was driven to despair. This is the theme that interested O'Hara. It had echoes in his own experience, and he was eager to give it expression. William Saroyan said that O'Hara's "preoccupation with the most intimate relations between male and female suggests the extent and depth of his separateness, isolation, and essentially inconsolable despair about a failure to heal loneliness."

A friend of O'Hara's smuggled a copy of D. H. Lawrence's *Lady Chatterly's Lover* into New York and he read it to see how Lawrence combined the physical aspects of love with the emotional. Although he did not follow Lawrence's lyrical methods, preferring dry mechanical descriptions, in *Butterfield 8* he extended the treatment of sexual relationships to many of the lesser characters as well as to Gloria. They are often sexually deprived or frustrated, but O'Hara shows how aware they are of their human and sexual possibilities, even if they can't or won't use them. This outspokenness caused him to be vigorously attacked by the critics. John Chamberlain in *The New York Times* was the only one to observe that the book was "a highly moral tale." At the other extreme were O. O. McIntyre who said it was "swill for the garbage man" and a small-town reviewer who wrote, "My objection to the book isn't that it's dirty. It's lousy." Although he was angered by these adverse comments, he knew what caused them. Writing to Scott Fitzgerald, he said that "writing an honest book is like suddenly closing your fist when you've been sparring with someone for fun. In its effect, I mean. The readers being the ones who are on the receiving end of the surprise punch. They like to fool around with an idea, and take it lightly, but if you give it to them the way you want to give it to them, you are a shit, and they get sore."

The New Yorker, which O'Hara considered his "own paper," also joined the attack with a review called "Disappointment in O'Hara" by Clifton Fadiman. Despite its venomous title, the review was temperate and called attention to a genuine weakness in the book, the shallowness of most of the characters. Fadiman wondered "how Mr. O'Hara, generously gifted, intelligent, witty, can possibly care to spend so much of his time with them." O'Hara's point was precisely that his characters were superficial and without interior lives, but Fadiman touched on a problem of conception O'Hara had to face—how to write interesting fiction about uninteresting people.

Butterfield 8 sold well, but the critical reception hurt him. It was degrading to be pilloried as an author of dirty fiction, and he began to feel he was doomed to failure. He was also getting bored: he "ratted around New York," as he later wrote, "until I was sick of New York and New York was sick of me." He suggested to Ross that he write a series of travel pieces for *The New Yorker,* to come from a trip he thought of taking to the south and California. Ross did not commission this "footloose reporter" series, but O'Hara and John McClain decided to set out anyhow, for McClain wanted to visit his parents in Ohio and O'Hara wanted to see Barbara Kibler. They picked up O'Hara's brother, Eugene, and then headed south. Driving down through Virginia and Georgia, they stopped in Tuskegee, Alabama, before going on to New Orleans, where Dr. O'Hara had practiced before moving to Pottsville. They stayed there for a couple of days before heading north. In Columbus, O'Hara and his brother visited the Kiblers who were distressed by the notoriety that accompanied the publication of *Butterfield 8.* O'Hara earned more than $8000 in 1935, a respectable figure for the time, but he had no immediate plans or job, and the Kiblers did not consider that his prospects were improved.

Nothing was decided by the time McClain and O'Hara returned to New York by plane, but early in 1936, Barbara Kibler broke off the engagement. This was a great blow to O'Hara. He missed her terribly, and his whole world seemed on the verge of collapse. Two months later he wrote that "that little girl in Ohio has had a far worse effect on me than I expected her to have, so there is nothing left for me but work."

6. HOLLYWOOD

By February of 1936, O'Hara was in Hollywood. He used the Roosevelt Hotel for his mail, but in fact stayed with his old friend Dorothy Parker, and her husband, Alan Campbell. "They have a large white house," O'Hara wrote, "Southern style, and live in luxury, including a brand new Picasso, a Packard convertible phaeton, a couple of Negroes, and dinner at the very best Beverly Hill homes." O'Hara was suffering from the aftermath of a flu attack in New York and was without a movie contract to justify his presence in Hollywood. Dorothy Parker put in a good word for him at Paramount and MGM, and soon he was talking to Clark Gable and Merle Oberon about the possibility of doing a screenplay of *The Great Gatsby*. The project interested O'Hara since he had never written a complete screenplay, but nothing came of it. Meanwhile, he found an apartment of his own at 10735 Ohio Avenue, which is in West Los Angeles, close to Santa Monica and the beach. In the 1930s, this part of Los Angeles still contained many open fields remaining from the farms that once covered the valley, and oil derricks were scattered here and there over the landscape. The country atmosphere was emphasized by the palm tree and two large oak trees that stood in the garden. O'Hara's small apartment building was built in the Spanish style with wrought iron balustrades covered with bougainvillea.

O'Hara's plan was to live on the $300 a month that Harcourt, Brace provided him as an advance against his next book. He also hoped to take movie jobs if they were available. He set a minimum of $1000 a week as his fee, however, and since that was high for a person as inexperienced as he was, he did not receive many offers. He worked briefly for Samuel Goldwyn on the treatment of a work called *Murder in Massachusetts* by Joseph Dineen, but it was boring. "I could write a serial for Cosmopolitan, I suppose," he wrote his New York publishers, "but between their kind of crap at one price and this kind of crap at a higher price, I choose this kind. At least this is anonymous crap, and it is also part of the business of finding out about Hollywood." This desire led him to ask his friend Lewis Milestone for a walk-on part in *The General Died at Dawn*, a film he was directing for Paramount that starred Gary Cooper and Madeleine Carroll. O'Hara played the role of a foreign correspondent in the restaurant car of a train in China, where the action takes place. His job was to say, "Oh, hello, O'Hara" to Gary Cooper, who was playing a character of that name. This always caused confusion: Cooper would muff his line and then protest, "That's wrong. He can't call *me* O'Hara. *His* name's O'Hara." Milestone would then explain: "We've been shooting this picture for 43 days, and all that time you've been O'Hara, remember?" And they would shoot the scene again.

Meanwhile, O'Hara was also working at home, and at first he sent encouraging news to Harcourt, Brace. Scott Fitzgerald, who thought that *Appointment in Samarra* was too much "in the same key" had urged him to try something different: "Your effects might show to advantage through a very quiet theme just for a change—I mean practically a bucolic idyl interrupted by the high pitched mood you handle so well—but to make it effective remember that you would have to believe in the bucolic idyl." The idea of a change in pace was attractive to O'Hara, but Fitzgerald had touched on a weakness that O'Hara also recognized in himself. "It isn't that I don't feel things," he said in a moment of self-doubt, "but when I begin to write out of hate, I find myself being diverted into tolerance; and when I write about love, or from love, I get critical and nasty." This time, although it would be "middle class to a low degree," he hoped to write a sustained story in which "there is some Hope for the characters." He told Fitzgerald that it was "about freshmen and their girls and cars, in California, now. It is young love." The book was tentatively called *So Far, So Good*, although it was finally published as *Hope of Heaven*. Both titles are suggestive, considering his own despair. Hope was what he needed, but it was hard to be convincing about it since he was again full of doubt about himself and believed his own life was a failure.

When O'Hara first arrived in California from New York, he was on the rebound from Barbara Kibler. Almost immediately he slept with someone from whom he caught gonorrhea. This condition hindered his relations with other women. He confided to Scott Fitzgerald, "I have no relationship with these exciting creatures. And I am lonely. I have no social grace, either. I lack the Princeton touch. People do not invite me out much, and the only way I can climb is down." Hollywood can be an exceptionally lonely place. Much of the social activity depends on work. While a film is being made, the actors and directors and cameramen are together all of the time, in and out of the studio. This is what Leo Rosten called "the controlled delirium of movie making," which is made especially difficult by the early and long hours involved. When the film is completed, the group disperses and nothing happens at all. To fill this void, Hollywood people tend to be exceptionally gregarious. "The craving for company at almost every hour of day or night," says Rosten, "exposes the great loneliness which lives under Hollywood's façade of gaiety." Such a world is difficult for a serious writer who wants to accumulate work steadily and who needs a routine and quiet to get it done.

But if Hollywood was neurotic, it was also full of opportunities. Like so many other single men living there, O'Hara was in a favored position. Every Friday afternoon, the Super Chief would pull into the Los Angeles station with two or three carloads of girls who wanted to make their reputations in the movies. Only a handful ever succeeded in doing so; hundreds more, like the characters in Nathanael West's *The Day of the Locust*, lived marginal lives as models, salesgirls, secretaries and call girls. One place where writers met girls was Stanley Rose's bookshop on Hollywood Boulevard; O'Hara had met Meta Rosenberg there the year before, and now encountered her friend and schoolmate Betty Anderson.

O'Hara was in a beguiling mood when they first went out together. "I am the shyest writer there is," he would say, "and Hemingway is the second shyest." On their first evening out, O'Hara took Betty Anderson to Dorothy Parker's, where the other guests included Donald Ogden Stewart and his wife. The party was pleasant and everyone behaved well. On the way home afterwards, Betty Anderson told O'Hara that she already had a regular boy friend, and he replied, "Well, let me give you a chance to see whether you wouldn't like somebody else." So they went out together, but when O'Hara made physical advances, she rebuffed him, and there were terrible fights. Once she had to get out of the car in the San Fernando Valley and hitch a ride back home. After that, O'Hara would come into the bookshop and make sarcastic remarks that could be heard by the other customers. He would also appear in his car at closing time and offer to take her home. She refused, so he would drive along beside the sidewalk, calling out her name and urging her to get into the car. He was often drunk and would create a traffic snarl on Hollywood Boulevard. Finally, after some months, he came into the bookshop and said, "You'll be glad to hear that I'm going back to New York." When she said, "Good riddance," he struck her, knocking her down in the aisle with such fury that she banged her head against the back wall of the shop. Then he left.

O'Hara was already well known for his sudden rages, which were often out of proportion to what caused them. Once he was banned from "21" for having "decked" a woman who was late for lunch with him. O'Hara himself commented rather elliptically on this sort of behavior: "Although I may often have felt like belting a woman, I have never actually taken a poke at one except in anger."

Little can be said to excuse this brutish behavior. Sober, O'Hara treated women imaginatively as equals, but drink made him throw away his gentlemanly code. In his mind, he may have justified his violence by believing that if women and men were equal, there should be no cant about treating them in a specially chivalrous way. But the attitude isn't convincing. At this time in Hollywood, O'Hara was frequently nasty to women, even those he did not know. Once, at a gambling place called the Clover Club, he was having drinks with Allen Rivkin, a fellow writer. Rivkin saw some friends of his, including a young girl, who were visiting California from Minnesota. He went over to say hello and when asked, he told them whom he was with. The young girl was an admirer of O'Hara's and said she would like to meet him. Rivkin, with some hesitation, brought her over to the bar, where O'Hara was standing, and introduced her as a friend from home. O'Hara turned to her and said, "Why don't you go and fuck yourself?"

One of his women friends, learning that he was having an affair with a married woman, decided to caution him to be discreet: she was afraid the husband might find out and sue for divorce. O'Hara and the friend met at a restaurant, and as they were sitting down, they saw a girl they both knew. "I slept with her last night," said O'Hara. With that the friend realized that he could not be relied on for discretion. Then, after the meal, O'Hara said, "Shall we go to your house or mine?" presuming that was the reason they had met in the first place.

O'Hara's ill treatment of women almost always came about when he was drunk, and in Hollywood during the summer of 1936 he often was. "I regret to report," he wrote his publishers, "that since returning to California I have been living at the bottom of a bottle." Alcohol released his inhibitions and allowed his deep resentments to come to the surface. He felt that he had been drained by women. From Margaretta Archbald to Pet to Barbara Kibler, there was an unbroken series of women whom he loved and who rejected him. Scott Fitzgerald wrote of his wife Zelda, "I gave her all the youth and freshness that was in me," and O'Hara, now thirty-one years old, must have felt the same bitterness about his own early loves. But O'Hara did not hate women, for he enjoyed being in their company. What he hated was something in himself that made them reject him. He thought that he was not accepted because he was a crude Irish mick, so when the pressure grew unbearable, he relapsed into being one. His deep frustrations blocked his energies until alcohol allowed them to explode. The self-hatred that was signified by his violent behavior was not only caused by his disappointment with women. He had never been able to justify himself in his father's eyes; he did not fully believe he was socially acceptable; his work did not receive the approval of the cultivated whom he admired; he was chronically unemployed. On various occasions, his cumulative despair drove him almost to the point of suicide. He would sit in a room high in a skyscraper with one leg out the window, half-inclined to leap. More often, with the cheap courage of alcohol, he would try to destroy himself by striking out at others.

Fortunately, not all of O'Hara's time in Hollywood was consumed by violent episodes; nor was he always content to remain working at home in "a tiny study that had windows placed so high that I could not look out." One place he often visited was the Garden of Allah, a hotel at 8152 Sunset Boulevard, where many of his friends stayed, and which for years was a center of the literary life of Hollywood. Built by the silent movie star Alla Nazimova, it was given a spurious Arabian flavor by the addition of the letter *h* to its name. There was a main hotel building, but most of the guests lived in small bungalows built in Spanish Colonial style round a swimming pool. The air was filled with the scent of mimosa and sprays of bougainvillea hung from the tiled roofs. Stone paths bordered by palm trees led from one cottage to another, and the place was lush and exotic.

The Garden of Allah was mainly for people staying a short time in Hollywood, and its pool became a meeting place for displaced writers from New York. Dorothy Parker and Scott Fitzgerald lived there off and on, and in 1936, the residents included O'Hara's friends Robert Benchley and John McClain. O'Hara had known Benchley from New York where he become famous for his humorous writings and for his drama criticism for *The New Yorker.* For O'Hara he was a kind of ideal. A graduate of Exeter and Harvard, he was immensely charming and also a man of letters. "The famous and some of the rich of those days," O'Hara wrote afterwards, "had to have someone to be beholden to, and they were lucky indeed that in their midst, at the very center of it all, was a man who had the professional qualifications through his writing and acting, and the social qualification through the infrequently mentioned fact that he was a gentleman."

John McClain recalled that the years he shared a bungalow with Benchley at the Garden of Allah "were filled with beautiful insanity and delight." Benchley operated a kind of literary salon, and on almost any late afternoon, at the cocktail hour, such people as Dorothy Parker, John Steinbeck, Mike Romanoff, Humphrey Bogart, Monty Woolley and O'Hara would gather at his place for drinks. Afterwards they would go to LaRue or the Vendome or the newly opened Chasen's, and then perhaps move on to a nightclub or gambling joint. O'Hara was generally a member of the party, although Sheilah Graham recalls him as being somewhat apart from the merriment. "I can see him standing against the wall in Benchley's villa, a glass in his hand, listening intently to the conversation but not joining in. Benchley did not love O'Hara, although he did not object to him hanging around. He always seemed ill at ease. He never smiled. He never laughed."

One evening, the two men fought. As Nathaniel Benchley tells the story, "O'Hara was drunk and was at his near worst, putting wrestling holds on ladies and otherwise acting churlish, and finally my father decided to put a stop to it. He went up to O'Hara who had a hammerlock on some woman, and said, 'All right, John, isn't that about enough?' to which O'Hara replied, 'Yeah, and that goes for you too,' and swung at my father, knocking the cigar out of his mouth. My father replied that he would get a new cigar if it was the last thing he did, and everyone subsided. The next day O'Hara telephoned, and the conversation as my father reported it to me, went something like this:

o'HARA: I just wanted to say I'm sorry.

BENCHLEY: For what, John?

o'HARA: For what I did last night.

BENCHLEY (all sweetness): Look, John, please don't apologize to *me*. You're a shit and everyone knows you're a shit, and people ask you out in spite of it. It's nothing to apologize about.

o'HARA: Do you mean that?

BENCHLEY: Of course I mean it, John. You were born a shit just as some people were born with blue eyes, but that's no reason to go around apologizing for it. People take you for what you are.

O'Hara was weeping by the end of the conversation, and my father maintained his gentle voice throughout."

Along with Benchley, McClain and an actor named Charles Butterworth, O'Hara was one of a group of bachelors who instead of limiting themselves to Hollywood, enjoyed going to Pasadena and Santa Barbara —or more precisely, San Marino and Montecito, those special enclaves where Spanish Colonial mansions stood at the head of long palm-lined driveways surrounded by lawns as extensive as those in Locust Valley or Greenwich. Although they made their money in "dirty celluloid," they preferred the society of these more settled communities and were almost the only Hollywood people to be welcome there. Almost everyone had eastern connections, and the young men went to Harvard, Yale and Princeton as well as Stanford. As a group, Benchley, O'Hara and McClain would go out for lunch at the Midwick Country Club, which was then famous for its polo teams. There were also luncheon parties with tennis, and weekend dances and house parties.

O'Hara enjoyed playing the role of tough guy, but he was generally better behaved in Pasadena or Santa Barbara than he was in Hollywood and was known for his good stories, his laugh and his good dancing. Here O'Hara also met a number of men and women ten years younger than himself who gave him some relief from his self-absorption. Admirers of his books, they looked up to him and gave him some of the praise and attention he craved. One of these young people was a Yale undergraduate, Alfred Wright, whose father was a Pasadena lawyer. He became a companion of O'Hara's at the various house parties to which they were invited in Santa Barbara and Palm Springs and was also a drinking buddy in Hollywood. O'Hara enjoyed belonging to this world, for there was plenty of money and the people who belonged to it were well mannered and cultured. Like Benchley and McClain, O'Hara also kept a "boy," a Philippine valet and chauffeur who looked after his domestic life and drove him back and forth to these parties in his yellow phaeton. It was part of the style and economics of the time, for even in New York O'Hara had shared a valet with McClain.

Meanwhile, O'Hara continued to see some of his friends from the previous visit, Joel Sayre and his wife, Nunnally Johnson, Ted and Felicia Paramore. One place where they met was the West Side Tennis Club in Westwood, close to O'Hara's apartment. Driving over in his yellow roadster, pipe in mouth, O'Hara would change into his white flannels and play doubles or singles with whoever was available. This was the era of dressing up for tennis. The women wore stylish tennis dresses, while the men had white sweaters with red and blue bands round the neck. O'Hara was never a very good player, despite a strong serve, but he played with a number of actors at the West Side Club and became a friend of Erroll Flynn and Gilbert Roland.

Another player at the West Side Tennis Club was a young writer by the name of Budd Schulberg, who was just beginning his career. The son of an important producer at Paramount, Schulberg used his knowledge of the studios in *What Makes Sammy Run?,* one of the most authoritative novels ever written about the film world. Schulberg was involved in politics and encouraged O'Hara to become actively concerned with some of the issues of the 1930s.

Alarmed by the rise of fascism in Spain, Germany and Italy and at the same time encouraged by Franklin Roosevelt's New Deal, most Hollywood actors and writers were on the Left. Nineteen thirty-six was an election year, so there was more action than usual as well as a desire on the part of many to get even with the studios. Two years before they had forced their employees to make "voluntary contributions" to the Republicans in order to defeat Upton Sinclair, the Democratic candidate for the governorship of California. In 1936 a group including Donald Ogden Stewart, Dudley Nichols and Alan Campbell, Dorothy Parker's husband, founded the Hollywood Anti-Nazi League. It was soon attacked as a Communist-front organization and subjected to a congressional investigation. A new group, the Motion Picture Democratic Committee, took its place, under Melvyn Douglas and Philip Dunne, but its moderate policies were sabotaged by extremists.

Schulberg was deeply involved in these activities as well as with efforts to re-establish the Writers Guild as the bargaining organization for screenwriters in Hollywood. He was articulate about the issues and O'Hara responded to his enthusiasm as well as to that of Clifford Odets, whose play, *Waiting for Lefty,* had been produced the year before. He was in the mood to get involved, for even before he met Odets and Schulberg he had written his publishers, "I am also getting radical again, more so than I was before." He gave money and went to meetings, and Schulberg was even asked whether he thought O'Hara suitable for membership in the Communist party. He replied that he thought O'Hara would not join, even though he was to the left of Roosevelt.

Despite his distaste for capitalist bosses and dictators, O'Hara became suspicious of some members of the Hollywood literary world who were involved in left-wing causes. In particular, he had doubts about Donald Ogden Stewart and Alan Campbell. He thought that these two, and others like them, were just pretending to be liberals, that they were playing at it because it was stylish. Reporting a conversation with Stewart, he wrote, "Don talked to me for an hour one afternoon about how he makes a much better radical than—well, than I. Because, he pointed out, he'd *had* Skull & Bones, he'd *had* the Whitney plantation, he's *had* big Hollywood money. He is certainly scared about something, and it isn't only the Revolution. But he is such a horse's ass that it doesn't matter much."

O'Hara's political activities forced him to consider his own position as a writer and his attitude towards proletarian fiction. He realized that Scott Fitzgerald's work was being ignored mainly because it dealt with upper-class life, and he had frequent conversations with Odets and with William Saroyan, whose *Daring Young Man on the Flying Trapeze* had been published two years earlier. But O'Hara found it difficult to have much sympathy for the plight of the working man. Physical labor had been his punishment when he was expelled from school, and the life of the day laborer was a nightmare he wanted to escape. He therefore had trouble making an imaginative leap to the world of the steelworker or coal miner, whose values he knew to be even more primitive than those of his neighbors on Mahantongo Street.

The issue came into focus in 1936 when he was asked to make a play from John Steinbeck's labor union novel, *In Dubious Battle,* which had just been published. O'Hara went to see Steinbeck at Pacific Grove and the two men became immediate friends. Steinbeck wrote his agent that he didn't like collaboration, but of O'Hara he said, "I liked him and his attitude. I think we could get along well." The plan was for O'Hara to do a draft and return for a conference. This never happened, but in later years O'Hara recalled the "warm and good friendship that began that warm afternoon in Pacific Grove, A.D. 1936, with some Mexican dish cooking on the stove, an English saddle hanging on a peg, your high school diploma on the wall, and you trying to explain about phalanx man."

O'Hara abandoned the *In Dubious Battle* project, "when I found that in those moments of truth when a writer must believe what he says, a thing is not finally true because another has said it is true. What was true for Steinbeck was not true for me. I had read Silone and Malraux as well as Steinbeck, and I was seeing Odets almost daily, giving money and lending my name to liberal causes, and I had worked with my hands and been miserably poor. Yet I could not, or stubbornly would not, write a novel that depicted all men in Brooks Brothers shirts as fascists and all men in overalls as crusaders for freedom, decency and truth. My memory of fascists in overalls and genuine liberals in button-down shirts was always getting in the way, whenever I was tempted to follow the trend of the proletarian propaganda novel and thereby escape the fate of Fitzgerald."

What counted for O'Hara was the rendering of human behavior and the delineation of character. Along with Budd Schulberg, O'Hara spent, as he put it, "hundreds of hours" with Clifford Odets, who was almost his exact contemporary. "We talked about politics, women, music, painting, manners, luxuries, writing, the things that had happened to us when we were young. We were men of passion, of violence; intemperate in matters that had nothing to do with alcohol. It was he, the Jew, and not I, the Irishman, who would shake his fist in the other's face. It was I, the Irishman, and not he, the Jew, who kept the peace. We would *inform* each other, without ever once changing the other's mind about anything. About *anything.* Whatever he wrote, I listened to every word and fought with him later, if I had to. But I wanted to know every word he wrote, because here was a man and a spirit you could respect and admire."

During the same period in 1936, O'Hara first saw the girl, then in her mid-twenties, who later became his wife. They were together on a transcontinental flight from Newark to Los Angeles and exchanged glances. The plane stopped at Wichita, in Kansas, and during the stopover, O'Hara, who was wearing a dashing trench coat, tried to talk to her, but she was too shy to respond. At Los Angeles they parted without speaking. A few days later, O'Hara was invited by Lucilla Potter, the wife of a Hollywood director, H. C. Potter, to come to a party in honor of her sister. He accepted, and the sister turned out to be the girl on the plane. Her name was Belle Wylie. They immediately hit it off, left the party early and O'Hara did not bring her back to the house until dawn.

Belle Wylie came from New York, where she had gone to Brearley before finishing at St. Timothy's School in Maryland. Her mother was the widow of a prominent physician, Dr. Robert Wylie, who had decided to remain in the northeast after completing his studies at Yale and Columbia instead of returning to his native South Carolina. Belle was a thin and delicate young girl, with curly brown hair and a slightly Asian look to her eyes. She was graceful, an excellent dancer, and was independent-minded, although on the surface shy and retiring. Not glamorous in the Hollywood manner, she was nevertheless stylish and designed her own clothes. She suffered from a congenital heart ailment but never held back or complained. Her physical condition made her cautious, however, and she knew her capabilities better than most people do. She developed strong likes and dislikes and loyalties and was in some ways like her mother, who was a strong woman and matriarch of the family. Mrs. Wylie was in no sense domineering, however, and Belle was allowed complete independence, even to the point of taking flying lessons and obtaining a pilot's license. With those she liked, Belle was original and gay, a creative and very feminine young girl.

Staying with her sister in Brentwood, Belle saw a good deal of O'Hara after their first meeting. They often went to the West Side Tennis Club, where Belle would play, and they went to Chasen's and the various little restaurants that line the "strip" on Sunset between Hollywood and Beverly Hills. They were deeply attracted to each other, for even before she saw him on the plane, Belle had admired O'Hara's work and she later told friends she had thought of him as someone she'd like to marry. But Belle did not act on this impulse, and after a while she returned to New York where she lived with her mother.

At Christmas, O'Hara decided to go to New York to visit Belle. On the way, he stopped in Pottsville to see his mother and his younger brothers and sisters. O'Hara never had a close relationship with the junior members of his family. In New York, he saw a good deal of his sister Mary, who would tease and chaff him for drinking too much and feed him breakfast when he had hangovers. The only member of the family he corresponded with much was his brother Tom, who had moved to Philadelphia where he was a reporter on the *Evening Ledger.* The other brothers, except for Joseph who lived in New Jersey, had remained in Pottsville, as did his younger sister Kathleen. Although Mrs. O'Hara had managed to survive decently in the years immediately following Dr. O'Hara's death, by 1936, she was in a bad way, as John was to discover on his visit. Her savings had been used up, and during the depression, it was hard to provide for the younger children. Mrs. O'Hara did not want her elder children to feel responsible for the younger ones, however, so she did not ask them for money. But when John appeared from Hollywood, he realized how difficult her life had become. Trying to make a long-distance telephone call to Belle, he found that the service was cut off. Kathleen told him there had been no money to pay the bill, so O'Hara went to see a friend of his who was head of the telephone company and gave him a check. Learning that the electric light bill was also long overdue, he paid that as well.

On Christmas eve, Mrs. O'Hara had no food for the family and no money either, but a farmer friend the O'Haras had known since the days of their own country farm came by with a chicken and some eggs which he left without asking to be paid. That was Christmas dinner. O'Hara naturally gave his mother some money, and continued to do so later on. But with the younger children—Martin, James, Eugene and Kathleen— time and distance had built up a barrier. O'Hara had cut his ties with Pottsville and had moved to a world more glamorous than theirs; they had remained and because of economic pressures had slipped down the scale from where they had begun as children.

On his first night in New York, O'Hara took Belle to a new nightclub on West Fifty-second Street called the Onyx. At one point, returning from the men's room, O'Hara found Belle in tears. "What's the matter?" he asked. "This used to be our kitchen," she replied. The brownstone in which the nightclub was located had been the Wylie house, and she had only just realized it. O'Hara took Belle to many nightclubs. Soon he was drinking heavily again. Late on New Year's eve, O'Hara phoned Adele Lovett to wish her well, and since she happened to be alone, she invited him and Belle for a drink. O'Hara was so drunk he fell asleep while sitting at the table where they were having champagne. Belle had never met Adele Lovett before, but she showed no signs of embarrassment or irritation. She and Mrs. Lovett simply talked until O'Hara woke up; then they had a final glass of champagne and went home.

In the new year, O'Hara decided to stay on in New York. He took an apartment in a new complex called the London Terrace on West Twenty-fourth Street beyond Eighth Avenue in the Chelsea district of New York. Although he had no job, he was able to live on money saved from Holly-wood and from new earnings from *The New Yorker*. Still, his life was uncertain and unsettled, as was his relationship with Belle. His drinking now became habitual, and when he went to New Haven to visit his young friend Alfred Wright at Yale, he would often pass out at the Fence Club. Wright later recalled his New York routine: "John had a regular circuit around town, and he was as methodical about it as a night watchman. Bleeck's, '21,' the Stork, and finally Dave's Blue Room for a bowl of cornflakes. And always in a trench coat and a big felt fedora. Also the white Brooks Bros. shirt."

During the summer of 1937 O'Hara rented a house in Quogue, a small town on the south shore of Long Island, between Westhampton Beach and Bridgehampton. He had known of Quogue as a boy, but was now going there because it was where Belle Wylie and her family spent their summers. It was a quiet place in the style of New England, with wide streets lined by white clapboard and shingle houses. Most of the old houses were shaded by maple trees and enclosed by picket fences or hedges. The village had only a post office, a police station, a grocer and general store, and a combined newspaper shop and luncheonette. The Wylies were old residents and lived in a big shingled house with separate servants' quarters and a barn. It was near the Field Club where tennis and golf were available. The same families went to Quogue year after year.

On the sea side of the town, across an inlet large enough to allow yachts to pass through, was the beach, and there, on Dune Road, O'Hara rented the furthest cottage from the town, overlooking the sand and sea that skirts the Long Island shore for miles. There was no telephone, but he had a car, a set of golf clubs and a case of Scotch given him by Sherman Billingsley of the Stork Club. If he thought Quogue was a place where people liked to have a few drinks before lunch, he was wrong, as he discovered when he was invited for the first time to the Beach Club. "Imagine my surprise when I went in and asked for a Scotch sour," he later wrote. "Imagine their surprise." For that kind of sociability he had to go to Southampton or Westhampton Beach. But mainly he wanted to settle down to a quiet summer of writing.

In Quogue, O'Hara gradually got to know the Wylies. Once again, he was not approved of, not for his drinking nor for his nominal Roman Catholicism, but because Mrs. Wylie thought Belle would be happier with someone she was accustomed to from her own "set." Personally, O'Hara got on well with Mrs. Wylie, who had been a nurse and who was a warm and charming woman. They had the medical world in common and were able to talk freely and openly with each other. O'Hara spoke to her about his problems, including his drinking.

O'Hara and Belle were falling in love, but Belle was hesitant about getting married. She had a sense of rectitude and wanted to do the right thing by herself and O'Hara. She was also fiercely loyal and knew that marrying O'Hara would probably separate her from her more conventional friends. More than a year went by before she made up her mind, and she even went abroad to think it over while staying with her sister, Winnie. O'Hara knew the risks he ran in marrying again, and the unhappiness he might cause, but he persisted in his quest. Finally, in December of 1937, Belle agreed to elope. They drove down to Elkton, Maryland, a place where marriages could be arranged quickly, and had a civil ceremony. The bridal couple returned late at night and told Mrs. Wylie their news. She let out a shriek, which was more of surprise than dismay, and then welcomed O'Hara into her family. Belle's brothers and sisters were upset by the elopement and felt sorry for Belle, but for the most part, they liked O'Hara and considered him a part of their family.

Robert and Adele Lovett offered the O'Haras the use of their house at Hobe Sound in Florida for their honeymoon. They put the car on a boat to Savannah and then drove the rest of the way south. O'Hara sent Adele

Lovett his reaction to the house: "It was dark when we got here, and for a while we did not know how to take it. After about eight seconds, however, it began to grow on you. It isn't a house you like right away, is what I'm trying to say. You live in it a while, and then suddenly, after seven or eight seconds, you begin to realize that it is the house perfect. Now I never want to leave it, and it may take a court order to oust me. At first I went around admiring things. The *Chinese* prints, and the *Chinese* statuettes, and the *Chinese* bowls and other things you picked up in *China* last year—I liked them. I like the lamp near the fireplace, the glass and chromium one. I like the hardware, and the colors even; me that has to say vibgyor to remember what's in the rainbow. A few minutes of going around liking things, and I said to hell with that. Find a flaw. So I have been going around for three and a half hours looking for a flaw. And I have found it! Baby, have I found a flaw! It may not be a flaw to you, but I think it is a flaw. At least, if I ever build a house it will have something that this house lacks. You are a sick woman, so I will not try your patience any longer. Bluntly, this house has no elevator."

The O'Haras spent their time sitting in the sun, playing tennis at the Jupiter Island Club, and reading. O'Hara bought a .22 rifle and he and Belle sat on the sun deck and took pot shots at floating wood in the surf. They went on day trips to Palm Beach and drove down to Key West in hopes of seeing Ernest Hemingway, but the house was padlocked and no one was home. The honeymoon couple had Christmas dinner at the local inn and O'Hara wrote Mrs. Lovett again to thank her for the pearl studs she sent him for Christmas: "Yes, it is a frivolous gift," he wrote, "adorable but frivolous, and so I have decided to have my ear-lobes pierced. I've always secretly thought of myself as the swashbuckling type, and I think a simple pearl in each ear would help. Don Juan O'Hara y Delaney, de bes' damn caballero as ever burned two generators in all New Mehico." They were pleased, and somewhat surprised, to receive a wedding present from Harry and Clare Luce, and O'Hara wrote Mrs. Lovett for their home address to thank them: "I'm just *lost* without a Social Register!" Later, he and Belle "delivered the new year, held it up by its legs and gave it a good whack in the back, and I join everyone in thinking that so far as the world in general is concerned, it will be one of those years that we ought to have a rebate on." Money problems, as well as the threat of war, lay before them. There might be a job in Hollywood or a position on *Fortune,* but they were only possibilities.

Nevertheless, O'Hara was cheerful, for he had finally completed the book, *Hope of Heaven,* begun two years earlier under the title of *So Far, So Good.* The delay had arisen partly because he was working on a novel about studio life in Hollywood for which he had a contract with Harcourt, Brace. He had hoped to write this book while in New York, where he could consult film magazines and other sources of information about the movies, but he eventually abandoned it. *Hope of Heaven* caused him enough trouble as it was. Wanting to write a "bucolic idyl," he had read Thomas Mann's stories, *Mario and the Magician* and *Disorder and Early Sorrow.* They gave him the idea of infusing his work with an allegorical meaning of the kind found in the Mann story where the magician becomes a symbol of political demagoguery. O'Hara was also attracted to the novella form, to see what could be accomplished by reducing a story to its essentials, with minimal narration and description. O'Hara's impulses were dramatic: he hoped to present in fiction the sort of interaction between characters that can come to life in the theater. He admired *Disorder and Early Sorrow,* which is about a little girl and her father, because Mann succeeded in making a trivial episode reveal the essential qualities of their relationship.

In *Hope of Heaven,* O'Hara focuses his attention on Peggy Henderson, a pretty girl who works in a bookshop in Beverly Hills and who is obviously based on Betty Anderson, and on his familiar narrator, James Malloy, who is employed as a script writer in a Hollywood studio. These two characters are in love in a casual but real way. They understand each other, make love and are funny together. They represent the feeling of hope and young love that O'Hara said he wanted to celebrate, against the despair that was so prevalent in his work as well as his life. Evidently, the source of the philosophy behind O'Hara's work was Alexander Pope, the eighteenth-century Roman Catholic poet. In *An Essay on Man,* Pope tries to relate man to the whole structure of the universe in order to understand his predicament. Man's future is always in doubt, he says, because no one knows what happens after death. But since nothing can be accomplished through despair, the only sensible thing is to accept reality and understand that it is part of unchanging nature. This leads Pope to conclude that "Whatever is, is right," which in turn makes it possible to hope:

> Hope humbly then, with trembling pinions soar;
> Wait the great teacher, Death; and God adore.
> What future bliss, he gives not thee to know,
> But gives that Hope to be thy blessing now.
> Hope springs eternal in the human breast;
> Man never Is, but always To be blest.

The hope for a future together that Malloy and Peggy might share is destroyed by the unexpected appearance of two characters from the underworld: a petty crook from Gibbsville who is living off forged travelers checks, and Peggy's father, Henderson, who, rather too coincidentally, is a private detective in search of the forger. These two men are like the fates that come on stage in a Greek tragedy. They soil everything they touch and bring death and destruction with them. They even destroy the relationship between Peggy and Malloy. "I love you," she says, "but as you have guessed and despite Francis Brett Young, love is not enough. It isn't even enough to know that not only do I love you, but that you also love me." The trouble is that Malloy has been corrupted by the cynicism that motivates the two men. Like them, he has learned to look at the world and say, "The hell with it." This 1930s tough-guy cynicism, representing "the current moral attitude," as O'Hara put it, of "youth in an America temporarily stunted," is not capable of nourishing anything that needs to grow. The love between Peggy and Malloy therefore withers.

Certainly O'Hara did not intend his novella to be a theological treatise, but it reflects Roman Catholic doctrine, at least as expressed by Alexander Pope. O'Hara was afraid that in revising the book he had lost its allegorical element, but it seems to be a modern version of the Book of Genesis, with Hollywood as the Garden of Eden, and Malloy and Peggy as the two innocents who allow themselves to be corrupted by the knowledge of good and evil. But O'Hara was too inventive a writer to be tied to a scheme; what he wanted was to create a living world of human beings. In *Hope of Heaven,* more than its two predecessors, he relied on dialogue for almost the whole story. Reading dialogue is like listening to a conversation, and O'Hara used it not only to reveal character but to establish relationship and atmosphere, as well as to further the story. As in the theater, where the spoken lines do all the work, dialogue in *Hope of Heaven* creates the whole world.

Even when O'Hara wants to introduce information about the sudden appearance of Peggy Henderson's father, he has Peggy tell Malloy about it:

> "I'll talk," she said, with a nice smile. She lit a cigarette, scorning my assistance, because she liked to fool with those pull-out matches. She seldom smoked. "I got the coat from my father."
>
> "Oh. Another check? Where from? Where's he spending Christmas?"
>
> "Right where he is now. Right here. Seventy-two-sixty-eight Orchard Terrace."
>
> "No!" I said. "Your father's here?"
>
> "He's here, all right. In the flesh. Not a moving picture. Not a pretty picture, either."

This brief exchange establishes the daughter's relationship to her father and underlines her confidence in Malloy, although her nervousness is evident from her smoking and the repetition of her address, which is also background information. In addition, there is atmospheric talk about Hollywood. It is the sort of scene that most writers would skip or handle in a brief exposition in order to get onto a more weighty conversation, but O'Hara can make a trivial piece of dialogue carry a great deal.

O'Hara had worked harder on *Hope of Heaven* than he had on any other piece of writing. Sometimes, in order to escape drinking companions, he had holed up by himself in a hotel where he would not be tempted. Once he spent some days at an inn up the Hudson River across from West Point where he had a room with a view and a fireplace in a cottage on the property. He finally finished the book at the Ben Franklin Hotel in Philadelphia. In rewriting, he did not go over the typescript as an editor might, making small corrections. Since most of his writing was done in his head, he would throw spoiled work away and start afresh. He typed rapidly on yellow copy paper without carbons, and the speed of his writing may help explain its pace and immediacy. When he was writing dialogue, he would speak words out loud to hear whether they sounded natural. He would also act out conversations, imitating the intonations of his characters, their grimaces and sneers.

The publication of *Hope of Heaven* in March of 1938 brought disappointing reviews. Most critics saw little development beyond the earlier work, and one reviewer thought it a "woefully empty book." While recognizing that his characters were intended to be shallow, some critics thought they had not been "studied deeply enough in their very limitation." Heywood Broun, who had not liked *Butterfield 8,* felt that O'Hara needed "to write about people who are a little more important." O'Hara was to follow this advice; in the meantime, he was pleased by Broun's recognition of his intention as a writer, for what Broun called his "talent for compression" was one of O'Hara's principal aims in the book. *"Hope of Heaven* could have been twice as long," he told an interviewer, "but because of the impressionistic style in which it is written I made it short. It is impressionistic without being in that school because it is realistic. Its realism is of the kind I applaud in other writers." *Hope of Heaven* does suffer from the faults the critics pointed out, but it is also a step forward in O'Hara's art. Often literary development occurs in books that are not successful as a whole, and this is true of *Hope of Heaven,* for especially in the uses of dialogue it goes considerably beyond the first two novels.

The book did well, and within two months of publication, 13,000 copies were sold and plans were under way for a book of short stories to follow. O'Hara was pleased: he had survived the despair of 1936 and was happy with his marriage to Belle. They were living in the big house at Quogue and the routine suited him. He and Belle were both surprised by the change in his habits. "This is John O'Hara speaking to you," he wrote Adele Lovett, "and I have been up not later than eight-twenty every morning, closing the window, turning on the heaters, and pouring coffee from the thermos bottle (my idea, you may be sure). Then I go downstairs and have a proper breakfast, read all the morning papers, and by that time Belle, the ex-early riser until she met me, is ready to come down for her oatmeal, etc." He worked in Dr. Wylie's study, with its memorabilia, fishing tackle, shotguns, copies of Galsworthy and Yale year books. O'Hara was writing short stories for *The New Yorker* and also trying to place work with the *Saturday Evening Post.* But pleasant as the life was, it wasn't settled. They had no house of their own, so when they went to New York, they either had to stay at the Algonquin or at Mrs. Wylie's apartment at 1115 Fifth Avenue at Ninety-third Street.

In April, they suddenly decided to go abroad. A Laurence Olivier movie had given them the idea, and afterwards at "21," as O'Hara later reported, it "was easy to convince ourselves that it would be a good economy, that I would be able to work, etc. and since we've been married Belle has saved a lot of money." They planned to buy a car and tour the Continent, although the threat of war made Germany, Italy and most of eastern Europe impossible. Belle's mother and sister were abroad, and they expected to meet them, as well as see old friends like Janet Flanner, Ernest Hemingway, Louise Macy and James Thurber and his wife, who were spending the year in London. They sailed in tourist class on board the *Paris* of the French Line and were rather abashed to learn that Helen Petit O'Hara was also a passenger on board. They visited her in first class and got on surprisingly well, though O'Hara drank a good deal. He noted what he called "a curious psychological reaction: the Mmes. O'Hara, in discussions about poetry, etc. present a solid front against me on almost every occasion. We get reasonably tight together, and it has worked out very well indeed, and I don't think Belle is faking." O'Hara later described the crossing as being "without incident. Rats in the hold caused an outbreak of bubonic plague, which was quickly stamped out. A time bomb exploded in the foc's'le head, but the loss of life was slight. Indeed, many passengers were not aware of the incident, for which two German spies were drumhead court-martialled and shot. A lady on B Deck was seasick all the way, and the commandant was buried at sea, with traditional honors."

They stayed at the Hotel Scribe on the Right Bank, saw Janet Flanner and Louise Macy, and drove to Senlis in the outskirts of Paris in a hired Hispano-Suiza to have lunch with Louis Bromfield. The car impressed his host; O'Hara thought the guests included "some of the prize pricks of three continents." Then abruptly, they decided to leave Paris and go to London. The plans to settle down and study French for the summer were thrown aside: "Paris was a bit too much for me," wrote O'Hara. "It wasn't so much that most French people speak French; it was that so few of them converse in English." In London, they stayed at Almond's Hotel, a small establishment in Clifford Street and around the corner from Bond Street. O'Hara called on Faber and Faber, the publishers of *Appointment in Samarra,* and it was agreed that they would bring out *Hope of Heaven* together with a number of short stories in one volume. At Faber's, O'Hara dealt with Morley Kennerly, an American and a graduate of Yale. He helped O'Hara and Belle find a place to live in a block of flats called Chesil Court in Chelsea Manor

Street, just off Cheyne Walk and the Thames Embankment. Their brand-new building with its "modern" glass entrance hall seemed out of place in their Chelsea neighborhood with its red stone town houses, where fifty years earlier such worthies as Carlyle, Rossetti and Oscar Wilde had lived. The O'Haras' apartment had "a tiny living-room, a tiny bedroom, and a tinier bedroom, tiny kitchen, tiny can, tiny hall. It rents for the not so tiny sum of 25 guineas the month, furnished, but I like it," wrote O'Hara.

He was soon feeling at home—"I am picking up a Breetish axunt"—and sometimes in the late morning he would visit one of the clubs to which he had been given a letter of introduction, and perhaps have lunch there. In the evenings, he and Belle normally dined out. There were also parties with American friends. The Thurbers had a service flat in Clarges Street, off Piccadilly, and the O'Haras often went there. One night after returning for a nightcap, O'Hara became upset when the proprietor of the service flat tried to linger after bringing the ice that Thurber had ordered. O'Hara had discovered the benefits of English privacy and class distinction.

Although O'Hara did not receive the public attention in London that Thurber did, he managed to meet some English authors. Peter Quennell, who was an admirer of the sociological thoroughness of *Appointment in Samarra,* often came by for drinks and a chat. Alec Waugh was also in London and gave a party for the O'Haras. "But everybody was there," wrote O'Hara to Adele Lovett, "from dear old Mrs. Belloc-Lowndes, who fell in love with me, to L. A. G. Strong; not to mention a Lord who seems to have committed a murder, a fairy with a beautiful wife, an Asquith with teeth that she copied from Mrs. Roosevelt, and so on." This led to other engagements, such as a dinner given for him by Strong where the guests included V. S. Pritchett. The only man O'Hara met whom he remained friends with in later years was John Hayward, a well-known bibliographer, literary editor and biographer, who for years shared a flat with T. S. Eliot. Hayward was O'Hara's exact contemporary, born three days later, and both had doctors for fathers. The two men got on, for Hayward was an enormously humorous and erudite man, and O'Hara enjoyed revealing to him the complexities of Broadway double-talk.

Alec Waugh also invited the O'Haras and the Thurbers to attend a meeting of a curious London dining club called Ye Sette of Odde Volumes. This was a bookish society which met once a month for dinner and the reading of a literary paper. It was very formal, and the uniform was white tie and tails. There were badges and insignia of membership and, according to Waugh, each of the members had a special name such as "Brother Idler, Brother Spectator, or Corinthian. The president is called 'His Oddship.'" It is hard to imagine either Thurber or O'Hara responding warmly to this facetiousness. The occasion was a strain, which O'Hara relieved as much as possible with drink. As the speeches wore on, O'Hara lit a cigarette—the only one to do so. This created a stir, and a waiter came up behind him and asked him to put it out since the toast to the King had not yet been given. What might have been an explosive moment passed, good manners triumphing over boredom and drink.

Generally, he was not so polite. In later years, O'Hara recalled his blunt criticism of English ways, and admitted that his remarks "were treated with disdain, as though they were the intemperate utterances of a youngish man who had a great deal to learn about England and as much to learn about his capacity for whiskey." Moreover, O'Hara did little to make himself accessible to the English literary world. At a time when people dressed for dinner, certainly black tie, O'Hara would come in ordinary street dress, sometimes without any tie at all. He frequently neglected to shave. In 1930s London, this sort of bohemianism did not go down well. His drinking also led people to drop him. On an ordinary evening he would sometimes go out alone to one of the neighborhood pubs in Chelsea such as the Kings Head and Eight Bells, by the river. Afterwards, he would go off, by himself or with someone he picked up, to a nightclub, in imitation of his New York habits. He liked Quaglino's and the Apéritif along Jermyn Street. Sometimes when he didn't come home, Belle would phone Morley Kennerly, and the two of them would make the rounds of the West End nightclubs in an effort to find him.

The unhappiness that led to this behavior was fed by many things. In 1938, London was full of political turmoil, and O'Hara was repelled by the fascism he encountered. Once with Joel Sayre he visited a restaurant and found it full of young people singing the Horst Wessel song. O'Hara gradually became anti-English and made a point of emphasizing his American nationality. Driving through Hyde Park in an open carriage, he shouted out, "Has anyone seen Mrs. Simpson?" in a teasing reference to the American source of Edward VIII's difficulties. Then, on the Fourth of July, irritated at not having been invited to the party at the American Embassy, O'Hara decided to throw a party for the occasion. "The cigarettes and booze were American," he later recalled, "the flowers were red, white and blue. The guests were Americans-in-London, but there were the inevitable crashers and one of them, an Englishwoman, said: 'What *is* the Fourth of July?' That was all James Thurber needed. He gave the best July 4 oration I've ever heard, and I can't remember a thing he said. He can't either."

During the three months of their stay in England, the O'Haras hardly left London, except for brief visits in the southern counties. Once while staying with a friend in Kent, and seeing a pair of oars hanging on the wall in someone's house, O'Hara embarked on a convoluted leg-pull with a detailed history of his own rowing career. In general, he showed no interest in the literary or cultural history of England, and the sightseeing that was originally planned never took place. Although an anglophile in dress and externals, O'Hara had been put off by the formality and stiffness of English society. Finally, in July, they decided to leave. "Suddenly John couldn't face another Englishman without wanting to kill him," wrote Belle to Adele Lovett, "and we felt the need for sunburn, so back to America we go." Originally booked on the *Normandie,* they switched to an earlier sailing, on the *Champlain.* "I guess we just got fed up," said O'Hara.

7. PAL JOEY

Arriving in New York O'Hara and Belle went straight to Quogue to join the Wylies. Then, only a day or so before the famous hurricane of 1938 hit the east coast, they flew to Hollywood. O'Hara joked about missing the fun of the storm: "Bodies of *total strangers* were being washed up constantly at our beach club." The move to Hollywood was designed to replenish the bank accounts that had been exhausted by travel and living abroad. At first they stayed with Belle's sister, Lucilla, then rented a furnished apartment on Carmelina Drive, north of Sunset Boulevard, in the hills above Brentwood. The palm trees, eucalyptus and fruit trees were a welcome change from London.

O'Hara first took a job at RKO, a studio that lacked the prestige of Warner Brothers or MGM, but that occasionally produced an interesting film. He was to work on a movie called *In Name Only*, a social comedy that takes place mainly on board ship and in hotels, starring Carole Lombard, Cary Grant, Kay Francis and Charles Coburn. He was soon fired by the film's director, only to be rehired two days later by the producer, Pandro Berman. O'Hara received no credit on the film, having only been hired to fix the dialogue.

His next job was at Twentieth Century-Fox, where he worked on the screenplays of several films that were about to enter production. An improvement over RKO, Fox was under the control of one man, Darryl Zanuck, who had begun as a writer but switched professions for financial reasons. As executive producer, he was the company's most powerful representative in Hollywood. To his surprise, O'Hara found that he got "along fine with Zanuck, which is strange because I'd always hated everything I'd ever heard about him, and still do, but I do not yes him and he respects me." O'Hara's arrival in Hollywood coincided with the studios' decision that the best way to make good films was to hire novelists and short-story writers instead of professional scriptwriters. That is why in the 1930s and 1940s such writers as Fitzgerald, Chandler, Faulkner, Steinbeck and Huxley found themselves in Hollywood. O'Hara was paid $750 a week, which put him in the top 20 percent bracket for screenwriters. Nearly half earned less than $250. Yet even though the studios paid high salaries to well-known novelists, they did not make good use of them. The writers were just employees and what they wrote belonged legally to the studio. The studio could use their work in any way it liked: a script could be rewritten by somebody else or it could be filed and forgotten. Serious writers could not be expected to commit themselves to work over which they had so little control; even handsome salaries could not buy the emotional investment a good writer puts into his own work.

Many writers ended up doing what amounted to editorial work. At Fox, O'Hara did what he called "polish jobs. Buffing jobs somehow seems better." The first of these was a comedy called *He Married His Wife* in which a young divorced couple decide to remarry. It starred Joel McCrea, Nancy Kelly, Roland Young and Cesar Romero. After that, he worked on a film called *Johnny Apollo.* This film, according to O'Hara, "was a whitewash of Richard Whitney and which I therefore refused to do unless I could make changes." These were agreed to and O'Hara finished the script, but "then they got a new director and he didn't think I had been strong enough on the subject of Whitney, so they threw out what I had done." Next came *I Was an Adventuress,* which was a romantic comedy about jewel robbers in the south of France and had Vera Zorina as its star. It was notable mainly for a long dance sequence choreographed by George Balanchine. O'Hara contributed material establishing the main character as a ballet dancer and also an introductory passage that led up to the dance, as well as some dialogue changes. Don Ettinger, who with Karl Tunberg had written the original script, was surprised to find O'Hara sharing screen credit with him and phoned him to ask him to withdraw his name. O'Hara angrily refused.

While work was progressing on these films, O'Hara discussed further work with Zanuck, who urged him to become a producer. "Me a producer!" he exclaimed afterwards. "In some ways I would like it, but not the work part. A producer under Zanuck is a 24 hour job." He turned the idea down but signed a new contract at $1000 a week. "I am, for me, rich —that is, I have $2000 in the bank." The first film under this new arrangement was *Down Argentine Way,* a splashy musical that made use of O'Hara's knowledge of jazz. It starred Don Ameche, Betty Grable and Carmen Miranda. Again, O'Hara was employed to polish the dialogue.

For O'Hara, working at Fox was just a job, and he seems to have had no real interest in the medium. He was more serious about films than he had been about working for newspapers, however. He asked his brother to send him some framed photographs showing him with Winchell, McClain, Hemingway and Reynolds at the Stork Club so that he could make his office look "as though somebody lived in it." O'Hara did his studio work at top speed. "I never work more than 3 hrs a day," he wrote to William Maxwell, "but I am so much faster than they are accustomed to that my boss laughs at me. 'You'll catch on,' he said to me the other day. 'I hope you don't,' I said to myself." The remaining hours at the studio O'Hara devoted to his own work.

Meanwhile, the O'Haras moved to another furnished apartment, this time at 471½ Landfair Street in Westwood. They were on a slight rise of land above the campus of the University of California at Los Angeles, in a blue and white stucco apartment building, one of many occupied for the most part by graduate students and faculty members. Later, they moved around the corner to a more substantial building at 542 Midvale, which was built in the style of a French chateau with a flower garden in the front courtyard. In the 1930s, Westwood was still almost rural, and O'Hara enjoyed the open fields in the neighborhood as well as the university atmosphere.

Soon after arriving in Los Angeles, O'Hara was stricken by an attack of ulcers, the result of heavy drinking in England. He was depressed at having to go on the wagon and said he was "as melancholy as a pregnant woman around mealtime, hating the discipline, and suddenly losing all appetite when I remember that I have to think before I eat instead of just pouring on the hot mustard and Escoffier and going to it." At first he was also made unhappy by what appeared to be a snub by old friends, especially John McClain. Belle wrote Adele Lovett that McClain was returning to New York "which in fact is no loss to us as we never see him"; in another she noted that "we see very little of anybody which I think is a bad thing."

O'Hara had company at the studio, where there was a writers table at the commissary, but generally he preferred to leave the Fox lot and drive to the Brown Derby restaurant in Beverly Hills. He was one of a group of men who met there regularly for lunch. They had a special table in the bar, in the manner of "21" in New York. Most of them were connected with Hollywood: Lewis Milestone was a director; Sir Cedric Hardwicke, Peter Lorre, Charles Butterworth and Gilbert Roland were actors; Mike Romanoff was to be famous for his own restaurant. Lorre called the group "The Creeps." It was not at all limited and others who happened to come in, such as Scott Fitzgerald, Herman Mankiewicz and Artie Shaw, were welcome to join. There was a good deal of drinking, and O'Hara would prepare himself by having a bland lunch of corned beef hash with an egg on top and a glass of milk.

Sometimes O'Hara would join Gilbert Roland afterwards for tennis at the West Side club. They had in common a liking for St. James's Scotch, and O'Hara's lack of self-promotion appealed to Roland's sense of rectitude. If there was no tennis, O'Hara might spend the whole afternoon at the Brown Derby. Then Belle would join him and they would go out to dinner, almost always at an expensive restaurant like Chasen's or Perino's where the food was excellent, although O'Hara always chose something plain. They were no longer lonely as they were when they first arrived in Hollywood and usually went out with friends. These included George Brent, the actor, and his wife; Sidney Skolsky, who wrote a column; Collier Young, the agent. Or they would be with friends from Pasadena, like the Rowans and Earls, who enjoyed dining out in Beverly Hills. Sometimes the Potters or Dorothy Parker and Alan Campbell would join them. After dinner, they would go to a nightclub. O'Hara would have been drinking slowly but steadily all this time and without noticeable results. Whiskey did not affect him immediately except to make him cheerful. Then, suddenly, it would strike, and he would be drunk in an instant. If something then happened to go wrong, he would become irritable. Sometimes he would start to clench his fists and mutter about some son of a bitch who had just entered the establishment—or who had not yet even come in but whose presence he somehow sensed. He did this once while sitting with James Thurber who, hoping to neutralize O'Hara's pugnacity, placed a glass in his fist and thus made it impossible for him to rise and strike the unsuspecting enemy. At other times, O'Hara would turn his head away and pointedly cut the person in question, especially if he came up to the table. Sometimes there were actual fights, and once Budd Schulberg rescued him from a group of angry people who had surrounded him. Usually, when these difficulties arose, Belle drove him home, gave him some milk and a bowl of cereal and put him to bed. California nightclubs closed at two in the morning, so at least there were no all-night benders.

The drinking, which was now habitual, reveals O'Hara's underlying discontent and disappointment in himself. Although he was happily married, he was not the successful figure he thought he should be, and it rankled. He was still a loner in Hollywood. Although he would attend some of the large parties, he didn't enjoy them and tended to stand apart with Belle at his side to protect him from unexpected encounters. He was fascinated by the structure of Hollywood society, but did not belong to the upper level of established actors and heads of studios. In his isolation, he sometimes seemed to enjoy being thought of as a roughneck and played the role of the American original. He wanted others to think that, like Jack London, Mark Twain and Sherwood Anderson, he saw through the sham of society and remained true to himself. Yet he would as quickly turn the other way and play the gentleman, eager to demonstrate through externals that he was one. What is endearing is that he was so transparent in revealing his inner disquiet. S. J. Perelman used him as the basis for one of his humorous stories called "The Rape of the Drape." Here O'Hara appears as Waldo Hogan, whom the narrator meets in Hollywood one day after lunch: "He stood there frozen in the middle of Vine Street, his pale Malemute eyes pinned on my jacket and his nostrils dilated. Like myself, he was a transplant—a journalist I'd known around Jack & Charlie's in New York, and a man possessed of a burning desire to walk with the mighty. Hogan's knowledge of the *Social Register* was Koranic—he could tell at a glance whether Joe Blow had prepped at Choate or St. Paul's, he was able to recite Laddie Sanford's every polo score and the name of every skipper in the Bermuda race since its inception, and he knew all the arcana of bobsledding, cotillions, and similar *goyim nachis*. Not only an expert on modes and manners was he but an oracle on men's fashions, and my jacket was a challenge to his authority. He wasted no time on salutations. 'Where'd you get that Norfolk?' he asked fiercely, and, when I told him, snorted in disbelief. 'Impossible. Brooks hasn't carried that model in years.' "

Clothes, clubs, cars—they were all part of an attempt to reassure himself, but underneath there was great solitude and unhappiness. Philip Dunne, who knew him in the 1930s, thought he was singularly friendless: he had acquaintances to have lunch with, to play tennis and drink with, but no real intimates. William Saroyan said of him: "I think O'Hara was one of the loneliest souls I have ever seen, although we gather that he affected the opposite."

More important than the casual relationships at the Brown Derby and the West Side Tennis Club was O'Hara's friendship with F. Scott Fitzgerald, who in the late 1930s was living with Sheilah Graham at the Garden of Allah and also in Encino, where he had rented a house from the actor, Edward Everett Hale. O'Hara's friendship with Fitzgerald had always been interrupted by time and distance, but he considered his reading of the galley proofs of *Tender Is the Night* to be "a major honor in my life." When the book was published, he was "shocked and probably frightened by what the critics and the public had done to it and to him."

In Hollywood, the two novelists saw a good deal of each other. They had an easy relationship, without constraint, for they had much in common—provincial origins, Roman Catholicism and admiration for the upper classes in the east. Fitzgerald noted that they shared the same "football-glamor-confession complex," but whereas he tended to romanticize the rich, O'Hara looked at them with a relatively cold eye. O'Hara was also cruder and more impulsive than the smooth Fitzgerald who said that he thought O'Hara was "in a perpetual state of having discovered it's a lousy world." Yet this concern made him more understanding than Fitzgerald. Once he was with Fitzgerald and his wife Zelda in Maryland, taking her back to the institution where she was committed for schizophrenia and, as O'Hara recalled, Fitzgerald "kept making passes at her that could not possibly be consummated. We stopped at a drug store to get him some gin. The druggist would not give it to him. I had to persuade the druggist to relent, and he got the gin. But I wanted to kill him for what he was doing to that crazy woman, who kept telling me she had to be locked up before the moon came up." O'Hara understood that Fitzgerald was caught up in a drama of his own making that would always keep him remote: "The loneliness of his private hells was so enormous that he really would have got no real relief by sharing a little of it, in other words by letting you know him better, and so he figured to keep it all for himself."

One day Fitzgerald invited Belle and O'Hara to have lunch with him in Encino. "The food was good and there was a lot to drink, but I was on the wagon and Scott was not. He was terribly nervous, disappearing for five and ten minutes at a time, once to get a plaid tie to give to my wife because she was wearing a Glen plaid suit. Once to get a volume of Thackeray because I'd never read Thackeray, another time to get some tome about Julius Caesar which he assured me was scholarly but readable —but which he knew I would never read. Then we went out and took some pictures, and when we finished that he suddenly said, 'Would you like to read what I've written, but first promise you won't tell anyone about it. Don't tell them anything. Don't tell them what it's about or anything about the people. I'd like it better if you didn't even tell anyone I'm writing another novel.' So we went back to the house and I read what he had written. He saw that I was comfortable, with pillows, cigarettes, ashtrays, a coke. And sat there tortured, trying to be casual, but unhappy because he did not know that my dead pan was partly due to my being an extremely slow reader of good writing, and partly because this *was* such good writing that I was reading. When I read it I said, 'Don't take any more movie jobs till you've finished this. You work so slowly and this is so good, you've got to finish it.' "

Fitzgerald never did finish *The Last Tycoon.* His last encounter with O'Hara occurred when he phoned to ask O'Hara to be his second in a duel. Sheilah Graham had been attacked by a writer in the *Hollywood Reporter,* and Fitzgerald wanted to defend her honor. O'Hara knew that a brawl of this sort would only create notoriety and he tried to explain that to Fitzgerald. "In other words you're saying no," Fitzgerald answered. O'Hara said he would go along but that he thought it a mistake. "That's all I want to know," answered Fitzgerald. "I thought you were my one real friend in this town. I'll get Eddie Mayer. He's diabetic and he doesn't get into fights, but he's a gentleman." Fitzgerald and O'Hara never met again, and within the year Fitzgerald died of a heart attack.

Twentieth Century-Fox eventually rewarded O'Hara for his many small polishing jobs by asking him to write the screenplay for a movie called *Moontide,* based on a novel by Willard Robertson. It was to be produced by Mark Hellinger, an old friend of O'Hara's, and the French actor Jean Gabin was to play the main role, his first in English. Others in the cast included Ida Lupino, Thomas Mitchell and Claude Rains. O'Hara, Belle noted in a letter, was "working quite hard—very hard compared to any movie work he has done before—and seems quite enthusiastic." It was the only film, O'Hara later noted, in which he had any "pride of authorship."

Set on the waterfront of a small California fishing port, *Moontide* is the story of a wandering seaman who rescues a pathetic young girl from suicide. He is falsely accused of being a murderer, is exonerated, and in the end decides to settle down and marry the girl. This happy ending differs from the conclusion of the novel, but otherwise O'Hara stuck to the original story. What may have attracted O'Hara to this work is the similarity between the roughneck sailor and himself. The sailor suffers from opposed impulses. On the one hand, he enjoys his freedom. "All my life, people have attached themselves to me—like Tiny, and my dog here. But I have attached myself to nobody. I am free. All my life, I am free— and I am not going to change now." Yet he acknowledges the argument put forth by another character who says, "Vagabondage is a juvenile manifestation. It's a remnant of adolescence, a childish flight from responsibility. But sooner or later, and sometimes suddenly, this Rover Boy spirit dies, sometimes from weariness, sometimes from boredom, sometimes from a realization of the futility of such flight, and then, at last, the man becomes an adult, the ultimate adult that God intended him to be."

Here O'Hara was reflecting his own concerns. Writing movie scripts had made him a lot of money, which he enjoyed, but he was afraid it might be a trap. "Perhaps it won't last," he wrote, "but I could easily make it last, simply by deciding now that I want it to last, and act accordingly with the studio. I never would have made this dough if I hadn't married Belle, for obvious reasons. But I am a little worried that I won't get back to my rowdy life, rowdy but apparently the kind of life that goes with my writing what I want to write, while I am married to Belle, or at least working at it the way I am now." In *Moontide,* the wandering sailor eventually decides to marry the girl he rescued, and the reasons he gives seem close to O'Hara's own: "Anna and me—no matter what else—we share some words and thoughts—maybe half a dozen. That's a lot—maybe all you can hope for. When you find somebody like that, you grab on—and hang on. You may not find another." O'Hara had made that discovery with Belle, yet he was still restless and dissatisfied, drifting back "to my loneliness—lonely for I don't know what—that's me."

When *Moontide* was produced, it received decent reviews, and Howard

Barnes in the *Herald Tribune* praised O'Hara's "sparse and elegant dialogue" which contributed "a tough, earthy quality to a none too substantial story." The film never became a financial success, but it continued to be shown from time to time in the revival houses.

Hollywood did not isolate O'Hara from New York, for friends were constantly passing through. Joseph Bryan came and so did James Thurber, whose play *The Male Animal* was opening in Los Angeles. Harold Ross was also in California, and O'Hara hoped to have a quiet conversation with him about his own work, but they went to the Trocadero nightclub instead. O'Hara later remarked: "I told Ross that hereafter I never would mention the Troc in pieces, because he would think he knew all about it." The O'Haras also gave a party for Samuel Sloan, one of his editors at Harcourt, Brace.

Most of these visits were connected with the literary activity O'Hara was constantly engaged in while working for Twentieth Century-Fox. During the time he was in Hollywood, he published nearly a dozen stories every year in *The New Yorker,* and was in touch with William Maxwell and others at the magazine about various projects and proposals. O'Hara's correspondence with *The New Yorker* was lively and often vitriolic. "Boss Ross," as he called the editor, would occasionally reject a piece that O'Hara sent, and once he replied, "I have decided to reject your rejection of this piece and to give you a chance to read it over again." O'Hara had no fear of making himself clear. "You must occasionally remind yourself," he told Ross, "that, having written probably more than 200 pieces that have appeared in your magazine, I have some idea of your requirements. I don't send you junk." Ross believed in clarity, but sometimes he let a piece of O'Hara's allusive writing he didn't fully comprehend get into the magazine. Thurber recalls his once saying in anger, "I'll never print another O'Hara story I don't understand. I want to know what his people are doing." For his part, O'Hara was bothered by the editorial queries for which *The New Yorker* was famous. "I wish to hell there would be an end to this quibbling about my use of the vernacular," he wrote. "Even if people don't get it at first, they will. I was the first person ever to do a piece about double talk, and God knows a lot of people still don't know what it is, but that was several years ago that I did the piece (in The New Yorker), and several things in that piece have become established slang. It is a point of artistry with me." He would also be annoyed when a story of his was rejected. "I write it so that The New Yorker will buy it. It won't go anywhere else," he explained. The waste irritated him, but Ross had no easy solution: he could not fill the whole magazine with O'Hara's work.

In September of 1939, O'Hara's second collection of short stories was published with the title of *Files on Parade.* It contained thirty-five stories, of which two had also appeared in *The Doctor's Son,* and of which all but two had appeared first in *The New Yorker.* About a third of the stories are better than anything he had written before. They produce a secondary effect that goes beyond the apparent point of the story. In "Olive," which takes place in a small residential hotel in New York, Colonel Browder, who is a widower, befriends Miss Bishop, a lonely girl in her thirties, and the two have tea together every afternoon just to have some company. The telephone operator, Olive, is unable to understand that the friendship is innocent and she makes insinuations that so upset the girl that she moves out. The result is that the colonel now takes tea alone. On the surface, the story seems merely a sad anecdote, but it is really about the destructiveness of people with limited imaginations; that is why it is called "Olive" and not "The Colonel and Miss Bishop." O'Hara's experience as a screenwriter may have helped him with stories such as "Olive." Just as, in Gilbert Seldes' words, "The essential thing in the moving picture is not the picture itself but the movement," so in O'Hara's stories the picture, which in literary terms would be setting or explanation, is almost entirely eliminated. In O'Hara's stories people are always talking and doing things. In "Olive," for example, there is not a single descriptive passage about the hotel or the neighborhood; we learn about the hotel and its little lobby and newsstand only through conversation that is primarily about something else. There is not a wasted line or dead sentence in the story; everything relates to the theme. Olive is not wantonly destructive: her own loneliness is legitimate and derives from the inhumanity of her job as a telephone operator. She listens in on the lives of others because she has none of her own.

Almost all of the stories are about relationships. "Trouble in 1949" shows how the institution of marriage destroys the possibility of new love and the memory of old. In "The Gentleman in the Tan Suit," the elder sister of a young wife meets her brother-in-law for the first time. In the course of their brief conversation, he insists that his marriage with her sister is fine. But as she listens, she realizes that she has abandoned her younger sister to a cruel marriage. Suddenly she bursts into tears, for she also understands that despite the husband's protests to the contrary, they are desperate. These facts are not made explicit: they are revealed allusively through what the husband says and how he says it.

Files on Parade also contains a number of stories in O'Hara's earlier style of writing in the form of monologues, telephone conversations and letters. The stories cover a wide range of experience from New York and the suburbs to Pottsville. There are also theater stories, stories about criminals and, among the best, stories about Hollywood actresses and producers on the make. O'Hara's picture of America is not a pretty one. Most of his characters are aggressive and selfish or defeated and lost. To O'Hara America is a jungle in which people use one another and cruelty is casual. This view of a self-centered society came from his own experiences. His disappointments and failures, the hypocrisy of Pottsville and the Catholic schools, the deprivations caused by his father's death, the frustrations of his love affairs all made him feel cynical. "I've never been faithful to anyone," he told Adele Lovett, and his attitude was the defensive one of somebody who had been hurt and would not risk being hurt again. Adele and Robert Lovett tried to make him believe that there were decent and altruistic people in the world, and to some extent he moderated his views, but never completely.

Ironically, O'Hara achieved one of his greatest public successes through writing stories about a man who seemed to personify his cynical view of humanity. These stories take the form of letters written by an amoral nightclub singer in the Middle West called Pal Joey, who is always in search of a pretty "mouse" to sleep with and who will use anyone, including his girls, to further his career. The first of these stories was written in 1938 just after the O'Haras returned from Europe and were in need of money. Having completed *Hope of Heaven* at the Ben Franklin Hotel in Philadelphia, O'Hara told Belle that he would go there again to work on a few stories for *The New Yorker*. Leaving her at her mother's apartment at Ninety-third and Fifth Avenue, he took a taxi south to Penn Station. He was suffering from a hangover, so on the way downtown he decided to get out and buy himself a restorative at the bar of the Pierre Hotel. After a couple of drinks, he decided it would be just as easy to stay at the Pierre as go to Philadelphia, so he checked into a room. That was the beginning of a two-day bender. On the morning of the third day, as he later recounted, he woke up and found that instead of completed stories, all he had "was the typewriter, some blank paper and a lot of empty bottles." Then the remorse set in: He asked himself, "What kind of god damn heel am I? I must be worse'n anybody in the world." Then he thought a minute: "No, there must be somebody worse than me—but who? Al Capone, maybe. Then I got it—maybe some nightclub masters of ceremony I know."

Earlier, when he was living as a reception clerk in a cheap hotel in the West Forties, he had written some sketches about a Broadway girl he had referred to as a "mouse." He had also written a piece called "Master of Ceremonies" which was published in *The Doctor's Son*, a monologue adapted from the "gangster-gambler chatter" of a nightclub introducer he had heard on Fourth Street in the Village. Thinking about these pieces, he decided to write "a piece about a nightclub heel in the form of a letter." *The New Yorker* bought the story and wanted more, so he quickly wrote "Ex-Pal" and "How I Am Now in Chi," which were also published in *Files on Parade*.

O'Hara soon grew bored with the Pal Joey stories. They weren't even original. The Broadway patter owed something to Damon Runyon and the idea of the semiliterate letter writer had already been exploited successfully by Ring Lardner in *You Know Me Al*, his stories about a Chicago baseball player. Nevertheless, the character grew on him: "The more I wrote about the slob the more I got to like him," he said. It also amused him to play with the language. At the Stork Club, he and a group of friends including Quentin Reynolds and Jimmy Cannon spoke a special lingo, half Broadway slang, half invention, and O'Hara used it in his Joey stories. His main device was to wrench the sentences around so they would sound the way a nightclub operator might talk, not write. This language, in turn, created character. "Anyway this is a rich playboy type of a chap and kind of an Ed. Arnold type," writes Joey. "He does all the talking so I do not have to tell him any lies and when he saw me and this mouse he said to join him as they are going slumming. Slumming was what he said and slumming is what he meant. From one of the top rooms in Chi we go bang to a joint that is a joint. The mouse with me is strictly no cigar and the daughter of a small town banker and have a summer home up in Mich. and I am thinking of next summer when I take her out. So she is not the one I would of pick to go with me to a joint like the one we went."

In the end, O'Hara wrote about a dozen Pal Joey stories which were published in book form in 1940 by Duell, Sloan and Pearce, a new firm founded by his editors at Harcourt, Brace. There was a good deal of O'Hara in Pal Joey, and the popularity of the stories was undoubtedly due to his understanding of the aggressive young nightclub entertainer who wants to get out of the provincial world and into the big time. O'Hara was also using a universal theme that was as old as fiction: the rogue who uses his wits to make his way in society.

Had *Pal Joey* remained a book, O'Hara would undoubtedly have continued as before, but one night at a dinner party in Hollywood, George Oppenheimer, the screenwriter, made a suggestion that changed his life. "You have a play in that Joey character of yours," said Oppenheimer. O'Hara dismissed the idea for the moment, but it kept coming back. In early 1940 he began to think that "if anybody would write a play about Joey," it would probably become as popular as *Life with Father.* Finally, he decided to write directly to Richard Rodgers in New York. Rodgers was then collaborating with Lorenz Hart, Jr., in writing musical comedies. O'Hara told Rodgers that he thought the *New Yorker* pieces about Joey "or at least the character and the life in general could be made into a book show, and I wonder if you and Larry would be interested in working on it with me." The letter arrived at a favorable moment. Since 1935, Rodgers and Hart had produced nine musical comedies together, but they were bothered by the formulas that governed their work. Musical comedies were traditionally boy-girl dramas that ended with wedding bells. Rodgers believed "that the story and the music must be closely interrelated," but he wanted to improve the quality of his work, not impair it. Rodgers and Hart had already enriched the literary side of their work by making a musical out of Mark Twain's *A Connecticut Yankee in King Arthur's Court,* and they had engaged George Balanchine in order to bring dancing of a high quality into their shows.

Rodgers and Hart were both enthusiastic about O'Hara's suggestion. The possibility of doing an unconventional and realistic musical play excited them. "Not only would the show be totally different from anything we had ever done before," wrote Rodgers afterwards, "it would be different from anything anyone else had ever tried. This alone was reason enough for us to want to do it." Rodgers quickly wired O'Hara and their correspondence began. He found that O'Hara thought of basing his play on material drawn from several of the Pal Joey stories rather than from a single episode. This required a considerable amount of new work, and the story eventually dealt with Joey's romance with a rich older woman who helps him and whom he later tries to blackmail. By May of 1940, O'Hara was in New York working on the script in consultation with Rodgers and Hart. Even from Quogue, where he spent the summer, he could easily confer with them. Because it was a collaborative effort, O'Hara found he had to rewrite a good deal, and here his Hollywood experience helped him. "Getting a musical together is one long process of backing and filling," he later wrote, "hedging and trimming." One of the first decisions he made was to eliminate all topical references in order not to have to change them later on. He was satisfied, however, that "the argot and time spirit" were preserved.

In July, casting for the principal actors began. Rodgers was already predisposed towards Gene Kelly, a young actor he'd seen in a minor role in William Saroyan's *Time of Your Life,* so he was the first to be auditioned. Kelly started off with a Rodgers and Hart song. He had momentarily forgotten who the authors were, so unintentionally appeared to be currying favor with them. But O'Hara and Rodgers, who were the only ones present, liked him and he was signed on to play Joey. O'Hara had Marlene Dietrich in mind for the role of the rich girl who falls for Joey, but Rodgers suggested Vivienne Segal, who had already played a similar part in another play, and she was chosen instead. Meantime, George Abbott, who had already directed some earlier Rodgers and Hart musicals, agreed to direct *Pal Joey.*

Half a dozen other auditions were held in July and August, and the rest of the cast was chosen. O'Hara liked June Havoc so much that he expanded the role of Gladys for her. The participants conferred frequently, especially Rodgers and Hart. They had worked out a system for their own collaboration: for love songs, Rodgers wrote the music first and then Hart would do the words; for what are called "situation numbers" that open or close scenes, Hart would give Rodgers his verses and he then wrote music for them. But before anything could be finally settled, the book had to be written and agreed to by everyone. By the end of the summer, O'Hara handed in what he considered was the final text.

In the meantime, Rodgers had been selecting others for the jobs that must be done before a musical comedy can reach the stage. Jo Mielziner, who had already worked with him on other productions, began to draw the settings. In October, Robert Alton, the choreographer, started auditions to choose seventeen chorus girls and eight men dancers. Chorus calls would bring as many as five hundred applicants, but not many were able to fulfill Alton's requirements, which included knowledge of ballet and tap-dancing. The first rehearsals with the piano began on November 11, six weeks before opening night. At that point John Koenig, the costume designer, began to supervise fittings from the warehouses of the costume company.

O'Hara, who later admitted he was in a decline at the time, imagined that his job was over. With rehearsals beginning, he decided to stay away from the theater in order not to "be that perennial Broadway nuisance, The Author." But this was not what Rodgers had in mind. "There were periods during which I didn't hear from him for several weeks, and I couldn't get him on the telephone. Finally, in desperation, I sent him a wire: SPEAK TO ME, JOHN, SPEAK TO ME." George Abbott would attempt to fix a scene that needed rewriting, but it was difficult. "I know what's wrong, but I can't do it," he would say. Finally, Hart called on O'Hara in his apartment, early one morning. A maid let him in and he went to the door of O'Hara's bedroom. "Get up, Baby. Come on, come on. You're hurting George's feelings." This statement was sufficiently bizarre to get O'Hara out of bed. After that, he attended the rehearsals.

Late on the evening of December 8, the *Pal Joey* company took the train down to Philadelphia for the final rehearsals and tryout. In addition to the actors and dancers, the stagehands and the musicians, there were three freight cars full of scenery. With O'Hara, Rodgers, Hart, Adler, Mielziner and their assistants all on hand, the hectic process of putting all the pieces together began. Neither the actors nor the stagehands had seen the settings before; the musicians had never seen the music, nor had the actors and chorus ever sung and danced with the orchestra. The lighting had yet to be arranged. Rehearsals began at eleven in the morning, when the company would arrive at the Forrest Theatre, and they would go on as late as three or four the following morning. Sometimes, while the scenery was being installed, they rehearsed at the Hotel Erlanger. There were numerous last-minute changes and the ending was altered half a dozen times before it was finally agreed to. Changes in the dialogue had to be made on the spot. Two days after they arrived, they put on the dress rehearsal. It was a disaster. But opening night was a success, and after that everyone relaxed, polishing up the details of the production.

O'Hara and Belle had decided to drive down to the rehearsals, but their car broke down in New Brunswick and they had to complete the trip to Philadelphia by train. Budd Schulberg stayed at the same hotel with them, for he had come east to hold O'Hara's hand during the tryouts. O'Hara was much in evidence in the theater, and he was interviewed by his brother Tom who was then working for the *Philadelphia Ledger.* The interview took place in a bar, and O'Hara spent much time drinking. He took the occasion to reminisce about his father bringing him to Philadelphia to go to football games and see theatrical revues starring Al Jolson. Every night after the show, he and Schulberg, Gene Kelly and Hart would go out to a bar together. "Let me buy you a stimulant," Hart would say, and they would be off. The two Irishmen and the two Jews were kindred spirits who enjoyed one another's company, although their late-night habits sometimes annoyed the more staid Rodgers and Abbott. Kelly was afraid his appearing as an unpleasant stage character would hurt him professionally, but O'Hara encouraged him by saying, "Don't worry, kid. They'll like you." Hart also had his worries, for despite his marvelous lyrics, he was a lonely man who, in O'Hara's words, "knew better than anyone else that he was a disappointment to the lady admirers who had counted on swooning." For his failure with women, Hart took solace in drink. Often Schulberg, O'Hara and Kelly had to carry him out of a bar and take him back to the hotel in a taxi.

After opening night in Philadelphia, O'Hara and his collaborators went to the nightclub at the Adelphi Hotel to wait for the reviews. O'Hara had a pile of telegrams in front of him, which he was opening nervously. Someone said, "I bet he sent them to himself." O'Hara and the others had thought of *Pal Joey* as a burlesque of the sort of second-rate nightclub they knew in New York, but the show at the Adelphi was so bad that they suddenly realized that "instead of a violent caricature we had on our hands only a somewhat underexposed photograph."

Following good notices in Philadelphia *Pal Joey* opened on Christmas night at the Ethel Barrymore Theatre in New York. O'Hara went with his family and friends. Afterwards, O'Hara and Belle went to the cast party that Larry Hart gave at his apartment on Central Park West, and there they waited for the newspapers to come out. According to Gene Kelly, O'Hara and Hart were particularly eager for the critics to recognize that the show was introducing a new seriousness to the musical theater. Someone phoned in Brooks Atkinson's review from *The New York Times* which, although it praised the work of Rodgers and Hart and the performers, seriously objected to the "odious story" and the "scabrous lyrics" of the one song that was destined to become the hit of the show, "Bewitched, Bothered and Bewildered." Atkinson ended his diatribe with this sentence: "Although *Pal Joey* is expertly done, can you draw sweet water from a foul well?" Hart was so upset by this review that he burst into tears and went into his bedroom and wouldn't come out. O'Hara was more angry than disappointed but was encouraged by the good notices that also came in.

In *The New Yorker,* Wolcott Gibbs praised the musical and said that after *Pal Joey,* "the idea of equipping a song-and-dance production with a few living, three-dimensional figures, talking and behaving like human beings, may no longer strike the boys in the business as merely fantastic." Yet many other critics were outraged by the idea of having so unpleasant a figure as Joey as the main character. Richard Watts tried to sum up the controversy by observing that it was "a novel fault in a musical show when a too strikingly drawn character is to be held against it." Citing earlier works like *The Beggar's Opera,* he made the point that "even though he is a pretty miserable specimen, Joey is by no means unbearable as a musical comedy hero. There is something so naive about his cheap caddishness, he is so essentially an innocent boob, the simple prey of any smart operator, that he emerges as an object of Olympian amusement rather than hatred." Looking back at it ten years later, O'Hara pointed out that the play created enough controversy to make people go back to see it repeatedly. In *The New Yorker,* Gibbs commented on it again after a third visit, and O'Hara claimed that others, including Robert Benchley, had seen it even more often. Admittedly, there were others who left after the first-act curtain and never came back. But *Pal Joey* brought O'Hara's vision of humanity to a wider audience than he had ever known before.

8. WAR YEARS

Pal Joey's success made O'Hara a celebrity, and he was able to live better than he had for years. Moreover, his theatrical name was now established, so he could always count on getting a high-paying Hollywood job if he needed money. For the time being, thanks to the earnings from *Pal Joey,* that was unnecessary, and he became more a man-about-town than ever. It was easy to do, for he and Belle had taken a duplex apartment at 8 East Fifty-second Street, a few hundred feet from their favorite restaurant, "21." They were in the very center of Manhattan with Saks, Bergdorf's, Cartier's, and other shops along Fifth and Madison avenues, and only a few blocks away, the great hotels that clustered at the southeast corner of Central Park—the Plaza, the Sherry-Netherland and the Pierre. Nearby were St. Patrick's Cathedral and Rockefeller Center, while the best book-shops in the city were five minutes away. They were also right in the middle of the midtown restaurant district and in the heart of New York club land, from the Racquet and University clubs uptown to the Harvard Club and the Century, ten blocks south.

According to Lucius Beebe, the O'Haras' apartment, on an upper floor of their building, was filled with "portable typewriters, sheets of copy paper, radios, a white furry dog, somewhat modernist furniture, a complete portable bar and an assortment of books." These included *Bartlett's Quota-*

tions, The New York Social Register, Dostoyevsky's *The Possessed, Who's Who in America* and *The World Almanac.* There were also copies of *The New Yorker, Newsweek, Stage, Town and Country* "and other coated-paper periodicals easily available in the middle of the carpet."

As a normal routine, O'Hara would get up in the late morning, have breakfast of lemon juice, tea and cornbread or, if the previous night required it, cereal with milk and cream. Then he read the papers and opened the mail. He would go out to have lunch, perhaps at the Colony, or at the Ritz-Carlton, which was still in business on Madison Avenue. Sometimes he would go to the Players Club, where he was a member, and spend the rest of the afternoon there playing cards or backgammon. It would then be time to change and go out to a Broadway opening or a dinner party. The evening would usually end with drinks at "21," followed by a nightclub —El Morocco, with its zebra-striped banquettes, or Larue, which was then popular with the college and boarding school set. If they felt energetic, O'Hara and Belle might go to the St. Regis and dance to the music of Emil Coleman, or go downtown to Nick's in the Village, which was famous for jazz. Usually, they were with friends: Belle's sister, Winnie, and her husband, Henry Gardiner; Charles Addams and his wife; or the Thurbers, or William Lord and his wife. It was a full social life that also had its uses. As O'Hara remarked to Lucius Beebe, "After all, you can't be an old Pre Cat boy and live a life which for two decades has been practically all New Year's celebrations without picking up a lot of dope about strange people around Broadway and Fifty-second Street." O'Hara's memory made everything useful to him. He could remember complete conversations "through the smoke and noise and babble of the bars and nightclubs" where he spent so much time. These conversations would reappear with startling freshness in his stories. Usually they were trivial, for O'Hara believed that trivialities were more revealing than conscious pronouncements. He once remarked half-jokingly, to Adele Lovett, "I have a dread of having insufficient time to waste on unimportant things in life."

O'Hara most enjoyed going to "21" because, more than any other restaurant in New York, it was like an eighteenth-century London coffee house, a place where he could regularly see people from the worlds that interested him. Walking into its carpeted front hall, with its paneled walls and leather chairs, was like entering a private clubhouse. O'Hara would be warmly greeted by Jack Kriendler and Charlie Berns or members of their two families who were responsible for the high quality and amiable atmosphere which dated from prohibition days when the place was a speakeasy. Broadway actors, Hollywood producers and directors, theater critics and newspaper columnists patronized "21." Certain writers, such as Robert Benchley, Sinclair Lewis, Ben Hecht and Robert Sherwood also went there, as did H. G. Wells and Somerset Maugham when they were in town. It was popular with New York society in general, while the cost of going to "21" discouraged hucksters and tourists. O'Hara occasionally made direct use of the material he found there. Once he saw a group of undergraduates at a neighboring table in the downstairs bar. When he found out they were from Yale, he invited them to join him and then questioned them closely about New Haven. He was eager to have up-to-the-minute information about social customs and college slang. Visitors from abroad sometimes made "21" their first stop after disembarking from the *Ile de France* or *Queen Mary*. O'Hara was once there when Hemingway appeared with André Malraux—Hemingway in bulky tweeds and wearing gold-rimmed spectacles; Malraux, sallow with a lank piece of hair over his forehead, a cigarette dangling from his lips.

For many writers and artists who could not afford to go to "21" regularly, if at all, Costello's, a former speakeasy on Third Avenue at Forty-fourth Street, became a favorite. It was an Irish saloon and restaurant combined, and not at all fashionable or elegant. *The New Yorker* was usually represented by John McNulty, Joseph Mitchell and James Thurber, who drew a series of cartoons that for years decorated its walls.

O'Hara and Belle went there frequently, usually with friends such as Charles Addams and his wife. Once, Barbara Addams told the waiter, "I'd like cantaloupe, please." O'Hara immediately corrected her and instructed her how to address waiters: "You don't say 'cantaloupe' and you don't say 'please.'" One St. Patrick's night, some years later, O'Hara went in to Costello's alone to have a drink at the bar. After a while a group of writers came out of the back room. They included Ernest Hemingway, John Hersey and John Steinbeck, with their wives. They stopped to say hello and Hemingway noticed that O'Hara's walking stick, of which he was very proud, was a real blackthorn. "He bet me fifty dollars he could break it over his head," O'Hara recalled later. "I didn't want him to try it because I understand Ernest has a silver plate in his skull, but he went ahead and broke it." O'Hara sent Hemingway a check but Hemingway returned it and told O'Hara he would replace the cane. He never did, so Steinbeck bought him one instead. The broken stick was hung up on the wall behind the bar at Costello's, a symbol of Hemingway's victory over his younger admirer and competitor.

O'Hara's constant patronage of public bars and restaurants put him on display far more than most writers. He was constantly recognized, and because he was so sensitive, was put on his mettle much of the time. He was aware of the status that was indicated in café society by friendly relations with a headwaiter or a good table at a restaurant or nightclub. He was therefore determined to hold on to his customary privileges. If, at Voisin's, he was given the wrong table, he would fuss and complain to the point of spoiling the evening for everyone else. Once at the Stork Club he refused to pay the bill because he and his guests were placed at the wrong table. In the competitive world he lived in, O'Hara believed that if you wanted something, you had to be tough to get it. Even when he first came to New York, he would make a point about having the bacon well done in a sandwich and would send food back to the kitchen if he didn't like it. He wanted the world to view him as seriously as he viewed himself, and he was upset if it did not.

Drinking always made him touchy, but even without it, his sense of himself could put him in an unshakably bad mood. Once at "21," while having dinner with friends from England whom he had not seen for a long time, he suddenly rose from the table and went to sit by himself in a corner. On another evening with William Lord and his wife, he appeared to be spoiling for a fight. Lord successfully deflected all of O'Hara's provocative remarks, but then in the taxi going home, he innocently observed that a knowledge of Latin and Greek was useful for a prose writer. O'Hara whirled round in the jump seat and started to berate Lord, and when the taxi stopped, he started to take off his coat in order to settle the matter with his fists. This kind of long brooding was very Irish, and it betrayed his insecurity and self-absorption. Generally O'Hara made no effort to hide his feelings. If he was at a party he did not like, he would make it plain he was not having a good time. He would stand next to Belle for support and be grouchy or disagreeable with people who came up to talk to him. Sometimes, however, there were hidden reasons for his surly behavior. Once at the Stork Club he cut a person who had come over to the table and when asked why he had done so, he said, "That man had no right to ignore Belle the way he did."

Sometimes O'Hara's bad behavior was cured by tactful but firm intervention by someone else. One night, William Saroyan and his wife, with Michael Arlen and his, had dinner with the O'Haras at "21" and O'Hara became increasingly scornful and aggressive. Saroyan reports: "It may have been this dangerous potential that finally compelled rather tiny and fragile Michael Arlen to demand that O'Hara cut it out, after all there were ladies at the table, a piece of behavior I found both out of order and admirable, we had all had a few drinks (too many) and the girls, so to put it, were having fun, and why spoil it for O'Hara—that's the way I felt, but suddenly it was quite clear that Arlen had done right, for O'Hara immediately settled down to his best manners, as if a child were especially grateful to a father for being corrected before it was too late."

At a much earlier time, before *Appointment in Samarra* was published, O'Hara was at a party given by Howard Dietz. He went up to say hello to M. R. Werner, who had just brought out a successful book. Then, imagining he was being snubbed, he said, "I know you snubbed me because I'm nobody and you're famous and a big shot." Werner, startled, had not intended a snub, but he came back with a quick reply: "Yes, I snubbed you because you're nobody and I'm a famous big shot," and so saying, he turned his back. O'Hara enjoyed and admired the quickness of the retort and the two men remained friends.

O'Hara's quick reversal of behavior suggests that sometimes he acted badly just to get a reaction. Certainly O'Hara was aware of his reputation. Sometimes his behavior produced comic side effects. Once at "21" he was found sitting in a corner lost in thought like Rodin's "Thinker." When asked what was worrying him, he replied, "I can't remember why I won't speak to that son of a bitch over there." He soon became well known as "the master of the fancied slight." But he could also be honestly unaware of the impression he made. Once he went up to Richard Watts at "21" and started to complain about a reference to himself that had appeared in a gossip column. Growing tired of his grievances, Watts said, "My God, John, why do you have to be so damn sensitive?" Whereupon O'Hara said, "Who me? Sensitive?" and he laughed.

But there were also humiliations. Once O'Hara found himself at a bar sitting beside a midget. Somehow they fell into a quarrel and O'Hara got ready to fight. Just then another midget materialized so there was one to his right and one to his left. Finding himself being grabbed from both sides, O'Hara pulled his shoulders back, hoping to throw off the midgets like a pair of gnats. But they pushed him and he fell on his back on the sawdust floor. The two midgets then jumped on him and began to pummel him. The bartender broke up the fight and threw O'Hara out of the bar. O'Hara was astonished and outraged. Apart from the shame of the defeat, he knew that John Steinbeck was present and had seen the whole episode. By common unspoken consent, neither of them ever mentioned it afterwards.

O'Hara's perverse behavior was a trial to his friends, and he made many enemies along the way. James Thurber wrote of his actions as sympathetically as anyone: "If he sometimes seems to exhibit the stormy emotions of a little boy, so do all great artists, for unless they can remember what it is to be a little boy, they are only half complete as artist and as man. Who wants to go through life with only easy friends? Nothing would be duller."

O'Hara had always wanted to go to Yale. Now, spending time with graduates of Yale or other prominent universities, he imagined that he had missed something important. Wolcott Gibbs had the same feeling, and James Thurber reported that Harold Ross had "a special, though inarticulate respect for Yale." O'Hara supposed that the orderly progress from boarding school to Yale gave those who had experienced it opportunities he had never enjoyed. "You may think the world begins outside of college," says one undergraduate to another in Owen Johnson's *Stover at Yale*. "It doesn't, it begins right here. You want to make the friends that will help you along, here and outside. Don't lose sight of your opportunities, and be careful how you choose." O'Hara believed that if he had gone to Yale, he would have been elected to Skull and Bones and his problems would be over. What he did not realize is that he would probably have rebelled against the system and sneered at those who did everything "for God, for country and for Yale." Indeed, in an early piece for *The New Yorker,* he commented on "that clean and stupid countenance that the regular life of college gives to those who live it."

By the time O'Hara was in his thirties, he was pleased to be taken for a Yale man. If the band played "Boola Boola" when he entered Rudy Vallee's nightclub, he was delighted. He openly called himself an "assistant Yale man" and told the famous story against himself about how Vincent Price, James Lardner and Ernest Hemingway, finding some money left over from a trip to Spain decided to use it to "start a bloody fund to send John O'Hara to Yale." O'Hara was quite aware of the slight: "It's a mean little story," he commented, "but (and?) it shows what my friends think of me." Still, Yale remained for him "my ever alma mater."

Not having been exposed to the social benefits that are supposed to come with a university education, O'Hara picked them up on the outside. He learned everything he could about colleges and their clubs and fraternities. He studied the Social Register and *Who's Who,* and he learned how to dress properly. Having been in his early days a sloppily dressed newspaper reporter, he went to the opposite extreme. Invited to a party given by Neysa McMein at fashionable Sands Point on Long Island, he arrived wearing new shoes and a spiffy cream-colored suit that looked as though it had come from a Broadway costume designer's. But he caught on quickly, and by observation and imitation, he learned how to dress. As an outsider, he put too much emphasis on the paraphernalia of upper-class life such as club ties and fraternity insignia. What he did not understand is that adults generally put away the insignia they had used as insecure undergraduates to show that they belonged. Not having enjoyed these privileges himself, O'Hara wanted every badge he could lay his hands on.

At the same time, O'Hara knew that he did not belong to the upper classes. The security and privileges of upper-class life were personally agreeable, but his own fiction made it clear that he knew they were bad for a writer. In a celebrated passage from *Butterfield 8* that seems entirely autobiographical, James Malloy speaks of his Irish background: "I want to tell you something about myself," he says, "that will help explain a lot of things about me. You might as well hear it now. First of all, I am a Mick. I wear Brooks clothes and I don't eat salad with a spoon and I probably could play five-goal polo in two years, but I am a Mick." He then goes on to explain why other Americans denigrate the American Irish: "I'm pretty God damn American, and therefore my brothers and sisters are, and yet we're not American. We're Micks, we're non-assimilable, we Micks. We've been here, at least some of my family, since before the Revolution —and we produce the perfect gangster type! At least it's you American

Americans' idea of a perfect gangster type, and I suppose you're right. Yes, I guess you are. The first real gangsters in this country were Irish. The Mollie Maguires."

Like the Italian-American and the Jewish-American, O'Hara felt that he was not quite trusted by the Protestant Anglo-Saxon majority. He was tarred by the bad reputation made for all Irish-Americans by the most violent and ill-educated members of the minority. Still, he had enough humor to joke about his origins and appearance. Invited to be an usher at a society wedding in Boston, he reported that one of the guests had explained his and his partner's presence by saying, "I believe they're the detectives, here to keep an eye on the wedding presents." Also, he could sometimes overcome his own feelings of inadequacy to realize that a true gentleman is one who is "sure enough of himself to find it unnecessary to be a snob."

O'Hara made no effort to hide his background and had a good-natured, chaffing, relationship with his mother and his sister Mary in New York. By 1940, he began to realize that it was foolish for his mother to remain in Pottsville, living alone with her younger daughter Kathleen in a house suited for a family of eight. He and Mary therefore found a modest but pleasant apartment at 107 University Place, just south of Fourteenth Street in Greenwich Village, and there he installed his mother and his Aunt Verna, together with Mary and Kathleen. O'Hara was very fond of his mother; they were friends. As she had a lively sense of humor and brought out her son's, there was always joking and laughter when they were together. When O'Hara and Belle were in California during the first year of their marriage, O'Hara told his mother he would like her to meet Belle's. He sent her some money and suggested that she and Mary invite Mrs. Wylie and her daughter Winnie to dinner and the theater. The younger generation was to be there "to cover up the conversational lapses while you two mothers in law glare at each other and think, 'You bitch, you took my prize.' " O'Hara told his mother that Mrs. Wylie was "good fun and my answer to all motherinlaw jokes. So go to it, but I don't want any trouble. Mrs. Wylie's bigger than you."

Although his own family and his in-laws had little in common, O'Hara visited his mother from time to time and brought friends like Philip Barry around to meet her. He was generally protective about the O'Hara women. When he overheard some people at Costello's making what he imagined were derogatory remarks about Kathleen, he turned on them and told them to watch what they were saying. But his attentions were sporadic, and he kept his uptown professional life separate from family involvements. As a group, his family inevitably reminded him of a world he had escaped from.

Early in 1940 O'Hara was asked to become a columnist on *Newsweek* at a fee of $1000 a week. The job provided the money he needed for living as he did in New York and the column, called "Entertainment Week," gave O'Hara the opportunity to write about anything from ballet to sports and from movies to music. Mainly he concentrated on the theater, and on plays that out-of-town readers of *Newsweek* might want to see when they came to New York. He also devoted columns to well-known Broadway individuals such as his friends George Gershwin and Robert Benchley. Of Gershwin he wrote the memorable sentence: "George died on July 11, 1937, but I don't have to believe that if I don't want to." O'Hara's column was personal and he freely mentioned his own work. He didn't even hesitate to condemn *Pal Joey* when the cast was changed and the original actors were replaced. "Under the present circumstances," he wrote, "I caution you against going to see 'Pal Joey.' " When he was interested in a subject, he was lively and entertaining, but too often he seemed bored and the writing was tired and flat. His column also suffered from an excess of name-dropping and of flattering reference to himself.

One of his most memorable articles was a highly favorable review of Orson Welles's *Citizen Kane* which he saw while efforts were being made to have it suppressed as a satirical portrait of William Randolph Hearst. O'Hara attacked the attempted censorship and said it was the best film he had ever seen. Undoubtedly his column helped create the public interest that forced the film's release, but O'Hara believed that it also caused his ultimate firing from *Newsweek* about six months later. "A man who worked for Hearst told a cowardly publisher that I was a Communist," said O'Hara, "and the publisher found a way to get rid of me."

Overshadowing O'Hara's activities from the late 1930s until 1945 was the world conflict that had begun to take shape with the Spanish Civil War. In 1938, he had tried to organize a Hollywood ambulance unit for Spain, but nothing came of it. Then, with the outbreak of war in Europe in September of 1939, he became deeply involved with events. In a letter he described how he had heard Chamberlain's declaration of war from 10 Downing Street. He ended by exclaiming: "God save Roosevelt!"

O'Hara's patriotic fervor was further strengthened when America entered the war in December of 1941, after the Japanese attack on Pearl Harbor. He was thirty-six years old, and he immediately tried to obtain a commission in the armed forces. As a close friend of Robert Lovett, who was the assistant secretary of war for air and of James Forrestal, who was undersecretary of the navy, he had useful connections, and he appealed to both men for help in getting him accepted. But they were unable to repair O'Hara's physical condition, which was unacceptable for military service. The many years of heavy drinking and neglect had produced ulcers that required active treatment, and he had startlingly bad teeth for a man so fastidious. He had begun to lose teeth in his late twenties. Those that remained were so weak that one fell out once at a dinner party when one of the guests, while joking about boxing, tapped him lightly on the jaw.

As a doctor's son, O'Hara was predictably afraid of medical involvements, but by 1943 he could no longer procrastinate, and in April he entered the Presbyterian Hospital in New York with a badly swollen jaw to have most of his teeth extracted.

O'Hara was bitterly disappointed when he failed to get into the navy. He developed a "strong sense of guilt and futility" and, as he remarked in a letter to Forrestal, "I'm reading a hell of a war." He tried to use connections to get into the army air corps, but once again he was defeated by the ulcer. He began to feel that Lovett and Forrestal "just plain didn't want me, and that's something to resent, isn't it?" Worst of all was the feeling of being left out when everyone else was doing his part. His friends Joseph Bryan and John McClain had navy commissions, as did many of the younger generation such as Al Wright, Finis Farr, Henry Fonda and John Hersey. Having missed the first World War because he was too young, he now seemed on the verge of missing the second because of physical weakness, all the more maddening because he looked like a strong man. "I feel like a jerk being out of uniform when I go to 21 and places like that, and at the Field Club here the kids I used to play tennis and golf with are all gone—or come home on leave. Right here on the property"—he was writing from Quogue—"I have two brothers-in-law, one a captain in the Medical Corps, the other a lieutenant in the artillery. The fact that I am as close to 40 as I am to 35 doesn't quite square me with myself, so I have my eye out for something or other all the time. I am starting flying lessons tomorrow, and that may be the answer. They have a Civil Air Patrol here which makes sense, and especially in recent weeks."

Even Quogue was showing signs of war. "You're not allowed to go on the beach at night; only the parking lights of your car are permitted in the village and along Dune Road. Windows on the ocean side of the houses are blacked out, and if you forget about it you're reminded by the soldiers." Gasoline and sugar shortages were becoming noticeable, much to the annoyance of O'Hara's rich Long Island neighbors—"the same greedy ones as ever," he noted, "the unthinking, unseeing dopes who for nine years have been unable to get it through their thick skulls that the President was trying to retain and not snatch away the way of life to which they had become accustomed. There was plenty of the same greed and stupidity in Wilson's time, as in Lincoln's, but never, I'm sure, so much of it in so many phases as now. There again is a reason for wishing I were in uniform; I'm so sick and tired of the civilian point of view, especially as one hears it on Long Island." His worries extended to his work. "It's a hell of a time to be a writer," he said, "or at any rate a writer who is 37 years old and very likely 4-F."

Meanwhile, through his Hollywood friend, Philip Dunne, he was given a job in the film section of the Office of the Coordinator of Inter-American Affairs, an organization headed by Nelson Rockefeller, whose purpose was to create propaganda for South America. O'Hara was named chief story editor, but was given little to do. The purpose of his group was to show that the Nazis were anti-Catholic, but the organization was so amateurish that not much was accomplished. Aside from Dunne, O'Hara also knew John Hay Whitney, the immediate coordinator, who soon left to take up a commission in the air corps. O'Hara stayed with the Rockefeller committee, as it was known informally, for only a short time. He was forced to withdraw by a series of illnesses relating to his run-down physical condition.

Nonetheless, O'Hara kept up his efforts to be taken into the services and approached Colonel William Donovan, head of the Office of Strategic Services. To his surprise, he was accepted for training in the OSS and was sent to a camp in Virginia for the first steps. There he grew a beard and, in order to preserve the anonymity required of all candidates, he used his Pottsville nickname of "Doc." Again, he was stricken with illness and had to withdraw in less than a month's time. He then tried to find something in the merchant marine or the Red Cross, but these possibilities also fell through.

One of his best remaining chances was to get a job as a war correspondent as his friends John Steinbeck, Joel Sayre and Quentin Reynolds had done. But even here he was frustrated. By the time he got around to approaching likely magazines and newspapers, most of them had already hired somebody else. "I'll be right here on my duff for keeps," he wrote to his friend Joseph Bryan. "I am so fucking sick of myself that it's a good thing I don't use a straight razor. Or live in a tall building. I am also sick of civilians, of all sexes. I just got turned down by Colliers on my feeler to go with the Navy. How do you think I'd be as a Nurse's Aide?" Then at last he secured a job with *Liberty,* a magazine he would normally have scorned. He quickly bought himself the mock uniform, without insignia, that war correspondents used and was delighted to be out of civilian dress.

In August of 1944, he flew to Honolulu and went to the Moana Hotel where war correspondents were staying. Since he had to double up, he found an acquaintance, Emmet Crozier of the *Herald Tribune,* and moved in with him. He was assigned to the Commander in Chief of the Pacific, known as CINCPAC, and was warmly greeted by Admiral Towers, who turned out to be an admirer of his work. The first days in Hawaii were taken up with inspection trips, interviews with admirals, and dining out at clubs and hotels along Waikiki Beach with dancing girls and Hawaiian orchestras in attendance. Coinciding with O'Hara's appearance in Honolulu was the arrival of the *Intrepid,* a new aircraft carrier of 41,000 tons that was later to take part in the Battle of Leyte Gulf and the invasions of Iwo Jima and Okinawa. The skipper of the *Intrepid* was Captain William Bolger, an acquaintance of Crozier's, who invited both O'Hara and Crozier to sail with him to the Far East. O'Hara gladly accepted, but when he had a look at the captain's bookshelves and found none of his books there, he remarked darkly, "I should never have come on this ship."

O'Hara and Crozier were assigned a small but neat cabin in the pilots' section. There wasn't much to do while they sailed across the Pacific. The ship was in a convoy with another large carrier, the *Franklin,* and with several destroyers and other ships as well. They were heading for Eniwetok, an atoll with a large lagoon that served as a natural harbor. O'Hara and Crozier wandered around the ship talking informally with officers and men. Occasionally O'Hara was asked if he was the writer, but he would say no. One officer, John Valentine, got him to admit it, however, and they became friends and remained so after the war. In the mornings, Crozier and O'Hara would watch the pilots practice taking off and landing on the flight deck of the carrier. In the evenings, there was a jazz band that performed below decks. The drummer had been in Duke Ellington's orchestra.

When they arrived, the correspondents were invited to visit Admiral Mitscher, the commander in chief of a forthcoming operation that was to proceed along the Philippine shore to prepare the way for MacArthur's return. O'Hara took notes on what was happening and went ashore twice, visiting the officers' club, but there was little else to do. He was older than the officers and men aboard ship, and he felt the difference. Gradually he grew restless, and after inventing an excuse to go home, he was transferred to the fuel ship *Kaskaskia,* an oil tanker that was returning to San Francisco.

Just before he left, O'Hara saw the only military action of his trip. The general alarm sounded, and he and Crozier rushed up on deck to find that an enemy plane was approaching. It was tracked with tracer bullets and then fired at by antiaircraft guns. Whether it was shot down or escaped no one was certain. A day or so later, O'Hara was swung over the side of the *Intrepid* in a boatswain's chair and trans-shipped to the *Kaskaskia.* In case of attack, an empty tanker is more dangerous than a full one because of the fumes that collect in the vacant tanks, but the return trip was uneventful. There is nothing glamorous about a tanker, and to judge from O'Hara's story "The Skipper," which derives from his experience on board, the crew members felt they were the forgotten men of the war. Perhaps O'Hara thought he had something in common with them, for the one piece he wrote for *Liberty* about his trip to the Pacific was "Nothing from Joe," which explains why soldiers and sailors don't write home. Sometimes they are worried about their wives' fidelity, or they are ashamed of having their letters read by the censors. Some don't write for fear that the letter might be their last.

O'Hara was met in San Francisco by Belle. He had missed her and the separation had proved how much he depended on her. He freely admitted that at sea he "was scared most of the time—what time I was not admiring the kids who fly our planes." The two months at sea, with regular meals and no alcohol, had made him physically fit, and to distract himself he had kept a journal that was in effect a long love letter to Belle. Not long after his return, Belle told him she was pregnant.

Since their marriage seven years earlier, they had thought without much enthusiasm about having children. Although she wanted a child, Belle knew that her weak heart made it dangerous for her to become pregnant. O'Hara claimed not to care one way or other. "I find myself becoming a kind of married bachelor," he once wrote and said that although he sometimes treated the dog as a father might a son, he was not enthusiastic about small children. Nevertheless, they had cared enough about the possibility of having children to consult gynecologists, and O'Hara reported that "Belle is upside down inside, which is more or less typical of modern girls I believe; but of course the main point is that I'm sterile and I know it." This self-deprecating conviction may have been adopted to refute any claim that drinking was damaging to his fertility.

O'Hara and Belle returned to New York and a new apartment at 27 East Seventy-ninth Street near Madison Avenue. Before that they had lived briefly at 17 West Fifty-fourth Street, but the move uptown signified a subtle change in their status as a married couple. Abandoning the midtown restaurant and nightclub world, they were entering a more domestic and residential neighborhood. The streets were well swept and the grocers, fruiterers, drugstores and flower shops all had a local feeling. A quiet part of town with double-parked limousines and nannies with prams, the upper east side was Belle's world and she was at home there. The O'Haras' new apartment was on the ground floor and therefore dark, and that suited O'Hara's sleeping habits. But Belle soon cheered it up with posters, bright cushions and modern furniture.

Belle's love and subtle mastery of their domestic life saved O'Hara, for the war years were particularly bad for him. He was frequently despondent and fractious. He had sold only one war piece to a magazine, but he wanted to use material from his Pacific trip in his writing. One idea, for which he asked Forrestal's help, was a novel about the logistics of capturing a Pacific island, including strategy and the provision of supplies. He planned to have a marine private as the central character through whose eyes everything would be seen. It is probably as well that he abandoned the idea, for he intended to call the marine Pat Fidelis, which suggests that patriotic fervor had got the better of literary judgment. O'Hara's writing was in effect a war casualty. "It was impossible to write during the war," he later observed. "Short stories that I could turn out in a couple of hours were all I could manage." In the four years of the war he published fewer than twenty short stories. "If you are the sort of egocentric, sensitive individual who chooses writing for his lifework, wartime is an emotional experience like no other. No one escapes the dreariness and the drama."

His unhappiness often led him to drink and he found himself unable to stop. Whereas formerly his drinking was followed by periods of productive and satisfying work, now all he could do was make an attempt to go on the wagon. He began drinking orange blossoms, apparently in the theory that the orange juice nullified the effect of the gin.

At the beginning of the last year of the war, O'Hara turned forty, and inevitably he compared his own career to that of others. All around him were frightening examples of the toll that illness, disappointment and drink had taken on those who tried to be writers in America. One of the most important to O'Hara was F. Scott Fitzgerald who had fallen into obscurity and died at the age of forty-four. To help re-establish Fitzgerald in his rightful position, O'Hara wrote an introduction to the *Portable F. Scott Fitzgerald* that was edited by Dorothy Parker and published in 1945. He had already written shorter pieces on Fitzgerald, but the introduction also allowed him to say something about American writing in general. Comparing Fitzgerald to Sinclair Lewis, whom he calls "Johnny One-Note" and a satirist, O'Hara states that Fitzgerald refused to follow the typecasting of so much American fiction of the 1920s and 1930s, in which the American male is regarded "as something between Will Rogers and roles played best by Walter Huston. Come down heavy on your r's, don't dress Eastern, be a tall-size hypocrite, and your creator automatically wins half the heavyweight prize. Remember, too, if you are the author, that the female sex is to be handled in pasture, once over lightly. Any other treatment just shows how you stand on the question of virility." O'Hara admired Fitzgerald for refusing to write in these clichés and for having the kind of honesty he tried to achieve in his own work. "Fitzgerald didn't feel that way, act that way, or write that way. Fitzgerald could believe that an American man and woman were capable of married love, and that if a husband heard the call of the wild it wasn't inevitably toward the direction of a plump, inexperienced organist or a plump, bored woman in a hotel with a funny quasi-Indian name. For a man who has always been around and who periodically takes an austerely moral stand, Sinclair Lewis has some strange ideas about the sack-time of American men. On the subject of extralegal love you will come across two sentences by Fitzgerald the like of which are not available in any Lewis that I recall. They read: 'For a long time afterward Anson believed that a protective God sometimes interfered in human affairs. But Dolly Karger, lying awake and staring at the ceiling, never again believed in anything at all.' "

O'Hara also reviewed another Viking Portable, this time the *Portable Dorothy Parker*. It was an opportunity to salute an old friend whose work he had long admired, and once again, his piece revealed his own artistic beliefs. Writing of two of her stories, he observed, "You go on reading both stories in spite of your awkward, embarrassed sensation of being in a room with two young people, married and in love, who at the moment of all moments ought to be left alone. I guess more than that cannot be said about the goodness of a story."

Fitzgerald was dead at an early age and Dorothy Parker had stopped writing because of drink. How would O'Hara end up? He had good work to show for the years following the publication of *Appointment in Samarra,* but except for the short stories, his reputation had not developed. *Hope of Heaven,* which he considered a big step forward, had been dismissed, and he was known mainly not for his own writing but for a musical comedy based on it. Also, he was drinking as much as Fitzgerald and Dorothy Parker. Then in 1945, his old friend Robert Benchley suddenly died at the age of fifty-six. Along with everyone else, O'Hara was shocked, and although the effects wouldn't be registered immediately, he realized, as he put it later, that "when Robert Benchley died, the party was over."

Meanwhile *Pipe Night,* O'Hara's fourth book of short stories and his first publication in five years, was brought out, indicating that his talent was very much alive. The title derives from a custom at O'Hara's club, the Players, of having dinner meetings at which some of the members, usually from the theater, provide entertainment for the others. The stories in the collection deal with so many different subjects that in his introduction Wolcott Gibbs noted that his range was a critical disadvantage. It was "too great for an editorial mind accustomed to writers, generally speaking, as rigidly typed as seals in the circus." The stories move from the upper-class world of New York and Long Island to the spurious chic of Beverly Hills, from the underworld of New Jersey to the deprived sectors of Harlem and the Bronx. Their principal theme is the conflict between social and human values. People are formed and judged by their experiences: an ex-convict can never shake his prison record; a member of the Porcellian Club at Harvard cannot resist recalling this symbol of his social superiority, even though it brings his downfall. Age traps people: the old cannot escape their mistakes; the young, lacking experience and years, are impotent. O'Hara's characters walk the streets with their emotions bottled up inside them. Usually they are only released in accidental encounters, usually with strangers, in a bar, on a train or on a street corner. Then the emotion breaks through and the hurt begins. "What the hell kind of a life is this, anyway?" says one of the characters, and he speaks for many in the book.

Social structure almost always throttles human feeling and warmth. It takes many forms, ranging from class distinction to the code of the criminal mob. Often sex makes the conflict more poignant. In "Too Young" a schoolboy falls in love with a college girl at the tennis club. He waits in the parking lot to ask her to play tennis and then overhears her conversation with the local motorcycle cop. He learns that they have been meeting frequently and he hears the cop force her into meeting him later in the day. In a flash his innocent vision of the girl is destroyed and he can do nothing. "Let me alone!" he exclaims to no one in particular. He walks off "to think thoughts that he hated and that would forever ruin his life."

In O'Hara's world people rarely succeed in breaking out of their lonely lives, and O'Hara treats their predicament with sympathy. Sometimes, a character manages to escape, if only for a moment, and then O'Hara writes with a pure rush of feeling. In "Bread Alone" a black car washer wins a baseball pool and decides to take his son Booker to watch the New York Yankees play a game. One of the batters hits a foul ball, and everyone in the stands tries to catch it. The ball falls but nobody catches it and it can't be found. At the end of the game, Booker takes the ball out of his shirt, where he has hidden it, and gives it to his father. The father throws back his head and laughs:

> "I'll be god-damn holy son of a bitch. You got it? The ball?"
> "Sure. It's for you," said Booker.
> Mr. Hart threw back his head again and slapped his knees. "I'll be damn—boy, some Booker!" He put his arm around his son's shoulder and hugged him. "Boy, some Booker, huh? You givin' it to me? Some Booker!"

The lovely inarticulateness of Mr. Hart's speech reveals the whole world of Harlem with its deprivations and hidden hopes. The best stories in *Pipe Night* all allude to a world offstage. In a front page review in *The New York Times Book Review,* Lionel Trilling noted O'Hara's use of the "precise social fact" which is there for more than accuracy or atmosphere. It signifies a set of attitudes and a complete culture. In "Graven Image," when the undersecretary pulls rank on the doorman of a Washington hotel so he can leave his car at the entrance, we know that he really is "the little man" he is described as being, despite his title. At the beginning of a story about a divorce agreement called "Civilized" the woman is offered a chair in a lawyer's office. "It was a heavy leather chair, costing a hundred dollars, surely, offering comfort but no warmth." In a story called "Can You Carry Me?" a Beverly Hills actress, noting that her caller wants a smoke says, "Cigarettes there, in the white pigskin box," and by what Trilling calls her "excess of specification," shows how she is trying to throw her weight around.

About ten of the stories in *Pipe Night* are first-rate, and the rest are at least well done. The book created a stir; O'Hara was especially moved by Lionel Trilling's review since it was the first time anyone in the academic world had written so prominently in support of his work. "I am breaking a precedent," O'Hara wrote him in thanks, "but the occasion demands it. I never write to reviewers, either to thank them or excoriate them, but I was so pleased with your piece about my book that I must express my thanks. The results began to come in on Sunday afternoon by telephone. Next day I went down to The Players and every man there, including some members I scarcely know, congratulated me, and it has been that way ever since."

The success of *Pipe Night* was followed in June of 1945 by the birth of O'Hara's daughter, Wylie Delaney O'Hara, whose mellifluous name was chosen to honor both sides of her family. O'Hara had been a nervous father, awaiting his child's birth at the Presbyterian Hospital in New York, and he celebrated her safe arrival with a good deal of drinking. Frank Sullivan found him at the Players Club and persuaded O'Hara to allow himself to be taken home. On his way, in the taxi, O'Hara suddenly turned on Sullivan and called him a "Jew Fascist." This combination of epithets astonished Sullivan, who "laughed so hard that O'Hara got laughing too" and he was delivered at his apartment building without further trouble. Soon after Wylie's birth, O'Hara left New York for Hollywood to fulfill a movie contract while Belle stayed behind to look after the baby.

O'Hara's job was to write a screenplay for Metro Goldwyn Mayer based on Sinclair Lewis' novel, *Cass Timberlaine.* The producer, Arthur Hornblow, Jr., was an old friend, as was his assistant, Collier Young. Ever since Lewis had gone out of his way to attack *Appointment in Samarra,* O'Hara had wanted to get even with him, and the job of doing the screenplay seemed to present that opportunity. He thought that *Cass Timberlaine* was a "very bad novel" so he decided to write "profiles of my characters before actually getting into the script." This procedure annoyed some of his superiors at MGM who realized that O'Hara's main intention was to show Lewis how his novel should have been written. When he finally got around to writing the script, it didn't read well. The dialogue sounded artificial and O'Hara had trouble getting his characters on and off stage. These are common failings for novelists when they turn to dramatic work, and even writers as gifted and experienced as O'Hara can fail to make the transition. Dialogue in novels and stories is usually not realistic; it only seems so in comparison to the narrative and descriptive passages that surround it. Moreover, a spoken text generally differs markedly from one that is only read.

A further problem arose when Hornblow and Young realized that O'Hara was turning in very little work for his large salary. He would occasionally appear at the MGM writers' building and even have lunch at the studio, but he did most of his work at home, and home was the Bel Air, a new resort hotel in the hills above Sunset Boulevard, with a swimming pool and pretty girls sunning themselves on the lawn and drinking in the bar. O'Hara was also enjoying the social life of Hollywood. He was a celebrity of sorts and had a number of friends of long standing. He enjoyed going to the restaurant Mike Romanoff had opened in 1941 and made it his social headquarters. The two men had much in common and Romanoff had a calming effect on O'Hara when he became upset. O'Hara often spent weekends at Palm Springs with Collier Young and his wife. O'Hara and Young would pretend they were midwestern insurance brokers or wholesale hardware salesmen and they would converse for hours about their wares and prospects during their stay at the Racquet Club. They thought they were very funny.

In the end, mixing business with friendship proved to be a mistake. Arthur Hornblow asked Young to tell O'Hara that he was going to be taken off the film. O'Hara was enraged; ever afterwards he refused to have anything to do with "Room Temperature Hornblow," as he called him. But the fault seems mainly to have been O'Hara's. John McClain scolded him, for example, telling him that his laziness as a film writer made it difficult for other writers from New York, who were resented anyhow by the studio regulars in Hollywood.

O'Hara did not take his failure with *Cass Timberlaine* seriously, nor did it matter to others in Hollywood. Not long afterwards, he went back there once again to work on a film that was being put together by Henry Fonda and James Stewart. After the war, these two actors had returned to Hollywood and set up a bachelor apartment together. Late at night, coming back from parties, they would sit up drinking and listening to jazz records. They had an idea of doing a movie together about jazz musicians, but nothing came of it until one day Burgess Meredith came by with a plan for an episodic film. It was based on the device of the inquiring reporter who goes about asking people the same question and receives a variety of answers. Meredith and Fonda decided to have a number of scenes in which separate groups of actors would act out the answers given to the reporter's question, which was "What great influence has a little child had on your life?" One of the scenes was to be devoted to a group of itinerant musicians playing along the beach at Santa Monica. Meredith and Fonda agreed spontaneously that O'Hara should be asked to write this section of the movie.

At their invitation, O'Hara came out from New York, and they met at the Bel Air to discuss the arrangements. Then O'Hara holed up at the less tempting Chateau Marmont, across the street from the Garden of Allah. He wrote an amusing skit full of slapstick in which the musicians stage a jazz contest with the hope that it will be won by the child of the local mayor so that they can obtain a license to remain in town. Instead, a glamorous girl, over six feet tall, comes along and turns out to be a wonderful trombone player. She enters the contest—and so it goes on to the end.

Meredith got United Artists to finance the film, while Fred MacMurray and King Vidor directed it. Because it was a lark and didn't take much time, a number of other actors such as Paulette Goddard, Dorothy Lamour and Victor Moore agreed to act in it while Meredith, Stewart and Fonda played in the musicians' skit. George Stevens and John Huston also directed certain sequences but preferred to remain anonymous. It was fun for the participants, but *On Our Merry Way*, as it was called, was not a success, although most reviewers enjoyed O'Hara's segment.

Hollywood was useful financially, but it was not an important part of

O'Hara's life. His real world was in New York, where he and Belle had an increasingly settled routine. They continued their patronage of the Stork Club and "21," where they would meet Hollywood friends such as Humphrey Bogart and Lauren Bacall, and where by himself O'Hara had a busy round of lunches with Wolcott Gibbs, Richard Watts, Harold Ross and others. In the afternoons he would sometimes drop in to see his mother or Mrs. Wylie. But with a growing child at home, it was no longer possible, at least for Belle, to stay up all night and sleep all morning. They began to spend more time uptown, going to local restaurants in the Sixties and Seventies. One of these was Passy on East Sixty-third Street, which was a favorite because the tourists did not go there but the rich did. O'Hara enjoyed being seen in the same room with Gloria Vanderbilt and Joan Payson; he also observed them. In their neighborhood or within easy reach were a number of friends such as the Harold Guinzburgs, the Lovetts and the Lords whom they saw regularly. John Steinbeck and his wife Elaine lived off Seventy-second Street, and the O'Haras occasionally went out to dinner with them. The two men had much in common, including their position in American letters. In a letter to Steinbeck that appears to have been written late at night after a good deal of whiskey, O'Hara let his hair down about himself and other American writers: "Writing. You and Ernest and Faulkner only. Me, of course. But room for all of us. You and I are the only ones that come out and get our whops. You know that the one is Faulkner, the genius. You are closer to him than Ern or I. Fitzgerald was a better just plain writer than all of us put together. Just words writing. But he dade. The working men are you and I. Faulkner, there is nobody like little Willie. Ern has become the modern syn-something for writing, and knows it. Has taken a Christ-awful beating because of a funny name. But what a good decent writer. When I think of all of you I want to crawl except when I think of what an honest writer I am." Steinbeck and O'Hara also talked a lot about women. They both thought they had been ill used, but were fascinated by the dependency men have on women. In the same letter, O'Hara wrote, "I always think of you as a married man, a man with a wife. Indeed I don't think of any man without a wife. Every man has a wife. The legal aspects horseshit to them." Sometimes the two men would quarrel because O'Hara stood on his dignity, but Steinbeck always phoned or sent a note and they remained good friends.

Geraldine Fitzgerald was another neighbor who would often go out with the O'Haras to a local restaurant and afterwards return with them for a nightcap. O'Hara admired her outspokenness and enjoyed being teased by her. Sometimes they would stay up very late, drinking, and O'Hara would announce that he was going riding in Central Park. He would get dressed and sit on the bed to pull on his boots. Then he would lie back, and in a minute he would be asleep. Belle would have to pull his boots off and get him properly into bed, the next day ruefully acknowledging the devotion required of her.

Dressing up seems to have been one of O'Hara's secret delights. Brendan Gill, another neighbor, recounts that late one night just as he was about to leave the O'Hara apartment, O'Hara urged him to wait as he had a treat in store. "He disappeared into the bedroom, where he remained for some twenty minutes. When he emerged, he was utterly transformed. He had taken off his ordinary clothes and decked himself out in a cowboy suit of incomparable Reno richness. He was all leather and steel holsters, and guns with nickelled butts. Above the chaps came a checked shirt and a scarf knotted about the neck, and above the big boozy face floated a surpassingly broad, high-crowned creamy sombrero." Unfortunately Gill and his wife were more amused than impressed, and they made the mistake of laughing. "O'Hara was incredulous," recounts Gill. "He saw nothing in his person to laugh about. His cheeks flushed. He was too angry to speak. As the gentle Belle, a born pacifier, fluttered about in apprehension of the storm about to break, we said our farewells and hurried off to our house in nearby Seventy-eighth Street."

After about a year, the O'Haras moved again, this time farther uptown to 55 East Eighty-sixth Street between Madison and Park. There was no change in their social life, which continued to be populated more by O'Hara's friends than Belle's. Among them were James and Helen Thurber. Mrs. Thurber said that O'Hara "was a gentle and adoring husband, but he was also a cruel and neglectful son of a bitch. He was the most contradictory person I ever met." O'Hara's friends were aware of the stresses within him and knew what Belle had to endure. They called her "Saint Belle," but in doing so they assumed that her devotion was charitable whereas it really was motivated by love and admiration.

Sometimes the O'Haras took trips out of town. In the winter they would go south to Sarasota to see the John Ringling Norths or to Hobe Sound to stay with the Lovetts. There they would see Philip and Ellen Barry, the Forrestals and the Harrimans. In the summer they occasionally visited John Valentine and his wife on Martha's Vineyard. After meeting Valentine on the *Intrepid,* O'Hara went to see his wife when he returned to America and even brought along a model of the ship so Valentine's daughters could see where their father slept. The two families became friends and the O'Haras stayed with the Valentines at their simple cottage at Chilmark, which was so isolated they had no electricity. Away from the pressures of New York and in the company of people he liked and trusted, O'Hara found the simple life relaxing. He kept other aspects of his life secret as well. O'Hara and Belle had season tickets to the New York Philharmonic concerts, but he told nobody about it because his friends preferred "to go on thinking of me as a drunken kid in a coonskin coat, and in a curious way they would have spoiled the Philharmonic for me if they'd known about it."

At the same time, when pleased with something, he could be open and demonstrative. Invited by the novelist and *Newsweek* critic Frank Norris and his wife to go to the Kentucky Derby, the O'Haras made the trip in a pair of private railroad cars made available by Norris' father who was president of the Southern Railway. At Louisville, O'Hara was pleased to score off John McClain who had gone down with the Whitneys, but in only one car. O'Hara bought some gold charms that were being sold as race souvenirs and gave one to each member of the Norrises' party as a memento of the occasion. Also at Louisville, while walking up the driveway of the country club where a party was being held, O'Hara heard the orchestra playing "I Could Write a Book" from *Pal Joey* almost as though they knew he was coming. He was delighted.

After spending the winter in town, the O'Haras went for the summer months to Quogue, where they had bought a beach house of their own right after the war. It was a simple wooden house on Dune Road overlooking the sea, low-lying because of the winds and without any shade trees. It had a large living room with a fireplace and bookshelves, and behind it a bedroom where O'Hara did much of his work, that also had a fireplace. The O'Haras hung a few charts and sailing prints on the plain wooden walls along with a few framed photographs and clippings of reviews of O'Hara's first books. A wooden staircase led to the beach, and down the way was the beach club where Belle would take Wylie to swim. For O'Hara, who did not know how to swim, the ocean was just something to look at.

Life in Quogue was quiet, and O'Hara enjoyed the self-sufficiency of the place. "I like the fact that at ten-thirty on the night of the Fourth of July I could drive around the streets of this village and see that more than half the people had turned in. I was born and brought up in a small town, and in that town there were only three houses besides my own which I would even think of entering without ringing the doorbell; in Quogue there are not even three, and I like that." But it wasn't only the small-town atmosphere that he liked. "Quogue is unique in that it is the only really family-place-cum Social Register on the Eastern Seaboard. No throwing around of money."

O'Hara didn't enjoy going to the cocktail parties given by the summer people, although he liked to play tennis and golf at the Field Club. He so rarely repaid invitations that he imagined he and Belle were becoming known as "the Sponging O'Haras." His shyness made him standoffish at large gatherings, and he much preferred small parties with a few friends. The O'Haras saw a good deal of Belle's sister Winnie and her husband, Henry Gardiner, as well as her brother, Dr. Robert Wylie, and his wife and children. O'Hara also had friends who lived in the neighborhood of

Quogue: Wolcott and Elinor Gibbs, Louis Nizer and his wife and the members of the Kriendler family who owned "21." Most of the social entertainment was homemade with cocktail and dinner parties at private houses.

One of O'Hara's closest friends on Long Island was Charles Addams, the artist and *New Yorker* cartoonist, who lived a short distance down Dune Road in Westhampton Beach. They saw each other frequently and shared a common passion for fixing up old cars. Addams had a 1926 Bugatti and a 1927 Amilcar and at one point owned a Dusenberg which John McClain sold to O'Hara and which was later owned by Philip Barry. For O'Hara, the habit of keeping old cars in order went back to his childhood in Pottsville, when he had to look after the horses and carriages. O'Hara occasionally sent Addams postcards in which he would pose as a car salesman. "Sir," begins one of them, "My Klein Mrs. Wigwam wishes to sell U Packard twins 6 with special Estherwilliams body. If so please contact Uppercu-Gliddon Co. who owns Holmes Air Cooled franchise for S.E. Block Island." Another starts: "Dear Mr. Addims: I happint to notice that you was inrested the garage last Tues. and old cars. I owing an old E.M.F. car which with cut-out and Dietz lamp. Also Welsbach burner both sides of front Head Lamp Special. Can Put radio in if nesry. If U want a Mitchell I got it. $5000. No Dozenborg they are heart to get. Reply."

Although his published writings are rarely comic, O'Hara wrote many funny letters to his friends. One he sent to Addams' wife, Barbara: "I read your letter to Belle," he begins, "in which you explained that Charlie is in Canton, Ohio, attending the funeral of his step-grandmother. 'You just couldn't make that up,' you say.

"Well, if Charlie wants you to think he is at the funeral of his step-grandmother, that's his business, I suppose. But where he made his big mistake was in picking Canton, Ohio as the town. As a true friend I think I ought to tell you that Canton, Ohio was dismantled about ten years ago and moved to northern Wisconsin, lock, stock, and barrel, where it became the plant of the Northern Wisconsin Lock, Stock and Barrel Factory. Canton, Ohio, was ploughed up and converted into a cemetery, but I don't believe Charlie's step-grandmother was being buried there as it is a dog cemetery."

O'Hara used Quogue in many of the short stories he wrote during the late 1940s, most of them appearing in *The New Yorker* and later published as a book under the title of *Hellbox*. The largest single group of stories in this collection is set in a small village like Quogue. It deals with the relationships between summer people and natives, the loneliness of a widow who wants to live vicariously through a younger person, the slow deterioration of a man who drinks his life away. A sex scandal comes to nothing because the villagers know one another too well to believe it. A wartime doctor is abandoned by his patients as soon as their original doctor returns from the service. The stories show how well O'Hara understood the solitude, endurance and decency of the villagers. The stories in *Hellbox* cover his usual wide range of material from small-town Pennsylvania to Beverly Hills, from Harvard Law School students to navy flyers. But whereas in *Pipe Night,* encounters between people suggest a potential for friendship, most of the newer stories reflect nothing but emptiness and sadness. They show that loneliness and failure are an inevitable part of living. The Hollywood stories throw these themes in high relief—the fading movie star in "Drawing Room B" who no longer gets the celebrity treatment she used to receive and takes her anger out on a would-be actor she meets on a train; the alcoholic sitting in a nightclub who wants to pick up the singer but drinks so much he loses the capacity to do so. The stories are full of love and yearning, but everything is out of synch.

O'Hara concentrates on motives. There will be a plausible reason for doing something, but the real reason is usually sexual. No one is to blame; it is simply the human condition. O'Hara used to say that you could always trust the American gentleman about money and keeping his word, but you could not trust him with women. "The Three Musketeers" illustrates this view, for the fiancée of one of three close childhood friends is sexually accosted by the other two the very first time they meet. There is less anger and more pity and understanding in these stories than in the previous collection. The book is well named *Hellbox,* since that is the box into which printers throw individual pieces of type before they are melted down again.

Hellbox was the first of O'Hara's books to be published by Random House. The change from Duell, Sloan and Pearce came partly because Samuel Sloan died only a few days after *Pipe Night* was published, and O'Hara was hesitant about continuing there without him. He had been thinking about going to another publisher when Phyllis Cerf, an old friend, ran into him and Belle at "21" and invited them to a party she was giving that night. The O'Haras accepted and not long afterwards O'Hara and Bennett Cerf began to talk about working together. O'Hara was looking for someone with whom he could have a trusting relationship, as he had with Sloan, and he wanted to work directly with the head of a house and not deal with subordinate editors. Random House, which was the creation of two men, Bennett Cerf and Donald Klopfer, seemed to offer exactly what he wanted.

The book went into several printings and did well, even though it was not so prominently reviewed as *Pipe Night* had been. Some critics attacked the book for its bleak view of mankind. Wolcott Gibbs commented on this in a letter to Charles Addams. "I know there is a good deal of complaint about John's stuff these days," he wrote, "(The reviews were certainly discouraging enough), but people are mistaken about that. A writer who never cheats, who never changes what would actually have been said to make things easy for Jim Wasserman or Squirrel Notkins, is sure to be in trouble with the critics and may even be too difficult to be quite successful in a magazine, where his stuff usually gets read by somebody who wants to get on to the newsbreaks, but he gets the facts down and I should think fuck the critics, though, of course, John can never quite see things that way, as who the hell can."

Other editors at *The New Yorker* were less enthusiastic about O'Hara than Gibbs was, so during the 1940s, his relationship with the magazine gradually deteriorated. Ross never really trusted O'Hara, and he treated Ross rather casually, referring to the magazine as "Ross's Folly" and to the building as "Ross's Quarry." O'Hara was never an in-house writer, although he was given an office in the building briefly in 1943 and again in 1946; mostly he communicated with the magazine by letter and telephone. He was "handled" by a series of fiction editors, starting with Gibbs and Katharine Angell, who by now had married E. B. White, and going on to William Maxwell, Gustave Lobrano and John Lardner, before reverting again to Mrs. White. O'Hara treated these editors in a friendly way for he understood, or pretended to understand, that the queries about his work came mainly from Ross. When sending in one story, he commented, "Here is one which Ross may think is about adultery, and by God, Ross will be right." He objected to criticism of the facts in his fiction and to attempts to improve his writing because, as he said, "I have my own ignorant style." But, he added in a letter to Mrs. White, "when my point is insufficiently clear to the Editors, you must certainly have a beef, the right to insist upon my making the point clear, a right which is implicit in the right to accept or reject."

Generally, O'Hara was reasonable about editing his work and he took a humorous line when dealing with the magazine. He told Mrs. White that he was hoping to see Ross in Hollywood so he could "tell him how a magazine should be run. For this advice, usually attended by a frozen grin, I charge nothing." Once he used a French title, explaining, "I think a little French now and then gives a writer class, and Boss Ross is impressed by class." But sometimes, he thought *The New Yorker* didn't have enough of it: "I have here a little article about high society, written as only Henry James can write them, which I am offering for sale at a good price. I am doing this to raise the general tone of the magazine, which lately has seemed rather middle-class. Let us have more little articles about nice people and in so doing draw a better type advertiser. Who likes to read about people they would not have in their own home?"

But O'Hara was also serious about his position as a writer. Because he considered *The New Yorker* the only outlet for his shorter work, a rejection meant a waste of "anywhere from a week to three weeks gone out of my life." For this reason, he was jealous of the position his pieces occupied in the magazine and chided Mrs. White on this subject. Once he became so angry that he sent her a one-line letter that ran: "My pieces don't run second." Friction also arose over the amount paid for his contributions. As *The New Yorker* became increasingly successful, Ross introduced a number of schemes that gave a bonus to writers who contributed substantially to the magazine. He still paid writers by the word, however, a system that confused many authors who were not by nature accountants. O'Hara was among these, but he was up against a magazine that for all its good will was run in an exaggeratedly businesslike way. Ross made no special concessions to length of service. In 1944, just before going to the Pacific, O'Hara asked him for an advance against future work so he could pay his income taxes. Ross refused, making O'Hara so angry that he slammed out of the office. Ross's rectitude created more discord than it was worth, but with O'Hara the issue was not so much money as human nature. O'Hara believed in loyalty and trust, confident that with them, results would naturally follow. Ross didn't care about personal loyalty; all he wanted were results. The two attitudes were implacably opposed, and a collision was inevitable.

9. A RAGE TO LIVE

The capital of Pennsylvania is Harrisburg, an industrial city in the interior of the state, located below the junction of the Juniata and Susquehanna rivers. Originally it had been a provincial market town, but when the factories were built its population was increased by immigrants from England, France, Ireland and Germany. The old part of the city has retained much of its early flavor. It was built along the river's edge with rows of town houses on treelined streets and substantial public buildings and churches. The most impressive structure was the state capitol, which was built in granite in the classical style with a dome copied from St. Peter's in Rome and an inner staircase in the rotunda modeled on the one in the Paris Opéra. Despite its imitativeness, it is a sumptuous and impressive building.

O'Hara chose this provincial American city as the setting for his new novel. The decision to write this book had gradually taken shape during the years immediately following the war. The continuing quarrels with *The New Yorker* had made him question the short story form, and he began to write what he called "novels in brief." He said that he thought he had reached the end of a period "when time was cheap and everlasting and one could say it all in 2,000 words." In 1946, when Duell, Sloan and Pearce brought out an omnibus collection of his older work called *Here's O'Hara,* readers were reminded that he had not written any extended fiction since 1939. In making the decision to write a new novel, O'Hara was influenced and encouraged by Lionel Trilling's statement, in his review of *Pipe Night,* that "for O'Hara's talents the novel is the proper form." Trilling ended his review by saying that "the novel was invented, one might say, to deal with just the matter that O'Hara loves. Snobbery, vulgarity, the shades of social status and pretension, the addiction to objects of luxury, the innumerable social uncertainties, the comic juxtaposition of social assumptions—the novel thrives on them, and best knows how to deal with them." Trilling's hopes coincided with O'Hara's own ambitions, for he wanted, as he said, to write a novel about a city that is "just short of being New York, Los Angeles, Philadelphia or Boston."

In order to begin this ambitious task, O'Hara looked for models in the work of others. He was a slow reader of fiction for he read "professionally, studiously. When I come upon a passage I admire, I go back and see how the man (almost always a man) did it." One direct influence on the novel that was to be called *A Rage to Live* was Booth Tarkington's *The Magnificent Ambersons.* "I also decided," he said in an interview, "that I would write this novel as Tarkington might have written it if this kind of treatment could have been got away with in the time Ambersons was written, and if Tarkington had been somewhat less so totally unlike me in almost every respect." Tarkington's ability to handle a large number of characters, his superlative dialogue and his ability to dramatize social distinctions made him an appealing figure for O'Hara. But an even greater influence, so he thought, was Jules Romains, the author of an immense novel in twenty-seven volumes called *Men of Good Will,* which is a panoramic view of French life from 1908 to 1933. In his portrayal of France, Romains takes up individuals and groups, tells their stories and then moves on to others, so there is no central character or necessary link between one and another. "I face the fact that this life of ours is very difficult to group around any central character," Romains explained; "that, indeed, it obstinately refused to be so grouped." He also believed that "families are not of very much importance. They are in certain cases; but they are not in the common run of life." Romains was concerned with what he called "collective life" and he warned his readers that "certain things do not lead anywhere. There are destinies which end nobody knows where, like watercourses in the desert." For this reason, many of Romains' characters simply disappear.

In 1949 O'Hara said he regarded Romains as "the greatest novelist living today," and what he most admired was the way he dealt with so many different aspects of life in the city. Romains had the range of a journalist on the city desk, and was also orderly and concise. "The newspaper influence," O'Hara claimed, "is a good one for the writer. It teaches economy of words. It makes you write faster. When you're on rewrite as I was, you can't fool around at half-past nine trying to write beautifully lacy prose." Because *A Rage to Live* is set in Harrisburg, O'Hara did not follow Romains in abandoning the family as the center of his interest. Harrisburg was much smaller than Paris, and in such a place, he thought, "there is always a family, not necessarily the richest one but the snappiest one that sets the tone in manners, sure, but also in cars and horses." O'Hara's motive in writing *A Rage to Live* was simply to record reality. He had no political or social theories to preach; he believed his attitudes would be implicit in what he wrote. He wanted people to say, "That's how it was." That, for O'Hara, *was* the message. In making the statement, he allied himself with such fiction writers of the past as D. H. Lawrence, Flaubert, Chekhov, and Turgenev, who, whatever their individual views, show what life is like in coal mining towns, provincial villages and the Russian countryside.

Having chosen Harrisburg as his site, O'Hara decided to have a woman as his central character. His earlier novels contained strong female characters—Caroline English, Gloria Wandrous and Peggy Henderson— but the books as a whole were dominated by the male point of view. O'Hara understood women well and believed they had the same longings and passions as men. He also realized that because men dominated society, women were forced to live secret lives: they could not publicly express their feelings and get away with it. O'Hara admired Thackeray's *Vanity Fair* and said he wanted to create a Becky Sharp without relying on a war for background. He claimed he had never read Tolstoy's *Anna Karenina,* but that the movie made from it influenced his portrait of Grace Caldwell Tate, the central character of his novel.

The switch to Harrisburg and to having a woman at the center of his book signified a fundamental change in O'Hara as a writer. He was no longer writing out of his personal feelings of resentment and anger. He was moving beyond that point, and when Steinbeck wrote him about *A Rage to Live,* he sensed exactly this change: "I am extremely anxious to read your new book. There are lots of reasons for this. I believe that your hatreds are distilling off and that your work is all ahead of you. For hatred is a completely self-conscious and personalized emotion and a deterrent to a clear view but it may be as necessary to developing ability as the adjectives we later learn to eliminate. But we must first learn to use the adjectives before we can know how to leave them out."

To gather material for his novel, O'Hara decided to drive to Pennsylvania in his new MG, a convertible two-seater car of which he was fond. He invited Joseph Bryan to accompany him and proposed driving through the countryside in the eastern part of the state, stopping at country hotels and visiting farms along the way. He planned to concentrate on the region west of his native Schuylkill County and to go as far north as Sunbury, up the Susquehanna River. He wanted to visit Lawrenceville in New Jersey because his character Sidney Tate was to be a graduate of the school, and he also intended to see Lafayette College in Easton, where Tate's father was to have gone. He hoped to consult old class books and yearbooks to see what the college was like in the nineteenth century.

O'Hara had known Harrisburg as a child, visiting it from his grandparents' house in nearby Lykens. When it came time to do research there, he called on his cousin, John Delaney, whose wife's family owned a large department store in the town. The Delaneys did not belong to the circle O'Hara wanted to write about, but his Aunt Bess, John Delaney's mother, knew about the inner workings of society in the town and also the relationship between money and politics in Pennsylvania. Delaney arranged to have the files of the *Harrisburg Telegraph* made available to O'Hara and introduced him to the Harrisburg Club where he could meet some of the local people. O'Hara visited the library in the capitol building and the newspaper room where he gossiped with the legislative reporters. In the evenings he would join some reporters for drinks and dinner at the Esquire Restaurant and Bar. There he learned even more about Harrisburg.

O'Hara set himself a quota of a thousand words a day and worked steadily. This discipline was necessary for a book that when published had nearly six hundred pages, more than twice as many as anything he had written before. While it contains a great deal of information about Fort Penn, as Harrisburg is called in the novel, *A Rage to Live* is really the story of Grace Caldwell, a rich and stylish woman of the town, who marries Sidney Tate, a New Yorker. They settle down on a farm outside of Fort Penn and lead an exemplary life. In love with each other, they are the envy of their neighbors. Then, unable to help herself, Grace has an affair with a young Irish building contractor, Bannon, and Sidney finds out about it. Angered and hurt, he reacts by eliminating Grace from his emotional life. It is the time of the first World War, and Sidney tries to join the navy, but is rejected. He then unexpectedly catches the new disease, polio, and dies. Shortly afterwards, the Tates' beloved child Billy also dies. O'Hara provides no explanation for these deaths: they are simply his recognition of the importance of accident or chance in life.

The second part of the novel is devoted to Grace's widowhood and her relationships with other men. She has a meaningless affair in Philadelphia and then meets the young editor of the local paper. This relationship is short-lived, but the newspaperman's wife, inflamed with jealousy, creates a scandal by trying to shoot Grace and her husband as well. Grace and her remaining children decide the time has come to leave Fort Penn.

The form of *A Rage to Live* is spoiled because the novel falls so abruptly into two parts. The relationship between Grace and Sidney is a novel in itself, and what follows is anticlimactic. Sidney Tate is too important a character to kill off halfway through. Grace, by contrast, is not strong enough to carry the rest of the book by herself. O'Hara was proud of the way he presented her in the novel. "I have given you a complete picture of Grace," he wrote to Frank Norris, "the superficial things such as a spottily good vocabulary, with a naturalistic use of grammar; her clothes, her drinks, etc. But I also have let you know how she thinks and feels *and yet at no time do I, the novelist, enter her mind.* At no time am I the omniscient, ubiquitous novelist. The God. You read that book and you *think* you have been inside her thinking moments, but the fact is that nothing is told about Grace that could not have been actually seen or actually overheard by another human being. That, my friend, is a triumph of writing. I am very proud of it, because in my own estimation it makes me really a pro."

O'Hara's technical accomplishment is impressive, but it also keeps Grace at arm's length from the reader. She remains only a mannequin: she is not involved in much of anything, and she is not an interesting woman. She is only a woman in society whose position is more important than she is. As a result, the novel tends to unravel as it goes on. What one remembers best from the book are individual scenes. At a whorehouse where Sidney goes one night, the exchange he has with the girl is touching and human. O'Hara also describes with great skill the reaction of Billy to his father's death. These scenes stand out from the rest of the book like separate short stories.

O'Hara's greatest challenge was to write about sex from a woman's point of view. Obsessed by the relations between the sexes and his own often unhappy experiences with women, he wanted to go as far as he could in examining the motives of women and to treat them with the thoroughness and frankness that was generally reserved for male characters. Inevitably, his desire to treat them honestly destroyed their romantic image. In *Butterfield 8,* Gloria Wandrous was a passive object of other people's sexual drives; in *A Rage to Live* he wanted to create a more active and positive character. He was also interested in showing that unpredictable sexual relations between men and women act as a counterweight to American society's obsession with status and social structure.

Except for Hawthorne and Dreiser, O'Hara had no one in American literature to draw on as a model for writing about sex from the woman's point of view. His success in treating this subject is therefore astounding. The novel's title is taken from a passage in Pope's second "Epistle to a Lady," which is about exceptional women who want to experience life fully before they die and who are too ambitious to accept it passively. "You purchase Pain with all that Joy can give, / And die of nothing but a Rage to live." This passionate commitment to life involves sexual frankness and O'Hara did not dodge the issue. Before the book was published, Bennett Cerf told him that he thought certain passages were too strong to print. O'Hara was intransigent and only Louis Nizer's delicate intervention induced him to make cuts.

When *A Rage to Live* was published, it was reviewed mainly for its sexual content. Orville Prescott was offended by O'Hara's characters and objected to "the nasty details of their lubricious sexual lives," and even friendly reviewers regretted what they considered was an excessive emphasis on sex. O'Hara's descriptions of sex are muted and chaste, but his characters sleep with a greater number of partners than is usual in serious books. Since he was dealing with what Freud had already made public, O'Hara felt he was only reporting the obvious. His reply to the critics was to demand that the book be considered as a whole and not be condemned for isolated passages. "Let's look at the record," he said. "Grace is a virgin when she gets married, and how many of the biddies who claimed they were shocked by the book can claim the same? She resisted every effort by the man who was her husband's best friend to get her into bed with him. In fifteen years of marriage, she had just one extramarital sexual experience, and I think that's better than the average for American women."

By today's standards, the objections of 1949 seem ludicrous and O'Hara's position is vindicated. Yet for other reasons the book is not wholly successful: it suffers from patches of dull sociological writing and is only intermittently moving. Orville Prescott also objected that O'Hara did not attain "the dignity and stature of true satire," but O'Hara was not interested in writing satire. His ambition was more comprehensive: he wanted to present human beings without prior judgment and to deal with them as sympathetically as possible. But in his first long novel, he was suffering from the growing pains of a writer who was trying something completely new.

The production and public reception of *A Rage to Live* affected O'Hara's professional life in a number of ways. He was pleased to be a Random House author, but he and Bennett Cerf soon fell to wrangling when O'Hara asked for an additional advance of $10,000 and was offered $2500 instead. This irritated O'Hara and he said so. Cerf wrote back, accusing O'Hara of taking "some kind of perverse delight in making us uncomfortable. Why?" He then chided O'Hara for slighting the firm's editors and concluded by asserting that while Random House was proud to be publishing him, "We don't intend, however, to be whipping boys and I don't see what on earth you accomplish by putting us in this position." O'Hara wrote back a point-by-point rebuttal and said that "if you have been uncomfortable after some of my comments on some of your actions, my comments were only a stimulant to your conscience." He then accused Cerf of making covert threats: "If you are saying, under your breath, get another publisher, please say it intelligibly and I'll set about to do exactly that."

Further difficulties arose with the editor, Saxe Commins, who had been assigned to O'Hara by Cerf. Commins liked to take an active part in the preparation of the final manuscript and had done so successfully with other Random House authors, but O'Hara found the process distasteful. His touchiness made him sensitive and he developed a personal dislike for Commins. "You'd better get that surgical glint out of your eye," he warned Commins before making an appointment with him. When they met, Commins showed he was upset by the language in the book and even warned him that the Society for the Suppression of Vice might get after him. O'Hara picked up a paperweight and hurled it at Commins before storming out of the office. Shortly afterwards, Cerf transferred O'Hara to another editor, Albert Erskine. "It seems impossible to please you," Cerf wrote him towards the end of 1948. But the conflict cleared the air between the two men. O'Hara learned he couldn't bully Cerf and get away with it, and Cerf learned that it would always be up to him to smooth things over and make peace again. The two men were never close, but they were generally amiable. Mainly their relationship was cemented by the great deal of money that O'Hara's books made for Random House over the years.

A far greater upheaval occurred when a hostile review of *A Rage to Live* was published in *The New Yorker.* It was written by Brendan Gill, who compared the novel to the Kinsey Report, criticized it for being "discursive and prolix" and concluded that after O'Hara's early accomplishments, the publication of *A Rage to Live* was "a catastrophe." O'Hara was never known for moderation in his opinion of hostile critics. Once, when Wolcott Gibbs remonstrated with him for making personal attacks on another reviewer. O'Hara conceded he was being excessive, but added, as an explanation, "the damn fool didn't like my book." O'Hara was only mildly irritated by Gill's review which he dismissed as "a bad one-joke wisecrack." What really enraged him was that Ross had allowed it to appear in *The New Yorker,* the one magazine with which he was closely associated.

Moreover, O'Hara soon began to think that the review was the product of a deliberate campaign being waged against him by senior people in the magazine. "If you have a moment," he wrote to Lionel Trilling, "I would like to tell you what annoys me more than the actual review: it is the influence of both Gibbs and Ross. Ross and I have had serious trouble in the past seven months, and I have written my last piece for the magazine. Gibbs read the book, wrote me a long letter saying he didn't like it and didn't want to review it (although I wish he had). When I replied briefly to his letter I used the word discursive, a word which neither Gibbs nor I have used in correspondence or personal encounter in the 21 years I have known Gibbs. But by God the word pops up in the NYer review. As to Ross's influence, you know that not a word gets in the magazine without Ross's reading and acceptance." Brendan Gill claims that James Thurber was responsible for making O'Hara believe that Ross and Gibbs were out to get him. Certainly he believed they were, but most *New Yorker* writers and editors agree that Ross was incapable of using a review to get back at a writer with whom he had quarreled or whom he didn't like personally. In the same fashion, he would never censor a piece because it had to do with a contributor.

But O'Hara's rage grew, especially following Clifton Fadiman's earlier attacks on him in the same magazine. "Ross had called me the master," he stated in an interview. "Then this clown comes along and flays me as a bumbling incompetent. You can't be both. There are various degrees of treachery, and I consider *The New Yorker*'s printing such a scurrilous review to be treachery of the lowest kind." He then made two decisions. The first was to make Gill know where he stood. They met at "21" for the first time after the review was published, and Gill went up to O'Hara, who was with Charles Addams, and suggested they have a drink together. O'Hara's eyes flashed, and he said, "I wouldn't sit down with a son of a bitch like you for anything in the world."

The second decision had to do with money. It is true that O'Hara may rightfully be thought of as the father of the modern *New Yorker* short story. For a long time he had tried to impress upon Ross and other editors at the magazine that his stories were written specifically for *The New Yorker.* This meant, he argued, that they were not suitable for publication elsewhere but were analogous to commissioned articles. O'Hara therefore tried out with Ross the idea of being paid a refusal fee, as is customary when articles are commissioned but not published. He suggested he be paid $500 for every story submitted but not printed. He added the further argument that the number of stories he published in *The New Yorker* made him like a salaried writer at a film studio who was paid whether his work was used or not. To Ross, the proposal was wholly preposterous. *"The New Yorker* is not Hollywood," he exclaimed. No resolution to O'Hara's position with the magazine had been reached by the time Gill's review was published, but for O'Hara it was enough. He refused to submit further pieces to *The New Yorker,* and for ten years the magazine went on without one of its most distinguished contributors.

Earnings from *A Rage to Live* more than made up the financial loss. This novel soon became a best seller, the first of O'Hara's to do so, and hardcover sales alone produced about $50,000 in royalties. Random House presented the author an inscribed silver cigarette box commemorating the sale of the first 100,000 copies of the book. The idea for the present came from O'Hara, who was not shy about seeking rewards, but his pleasure was unalloyed when he received the box. "I could not have done better by myself if I had done the selecting as well as the dreaming," he wrote. Over the years, he received a number of additional boxes.

Another change in O'Hara's life came from his decision to move away from New York. He and Belle were worried about Wylie's asthmatic tendencies, which were made worse by the dust in the city air. They thought of living in Saratoga Springs and in Swarthmore, Pennsylvania,

In Lykens, 1907

At the farm around 1909

Riding a pony on Mahantongo Street, with Mary Jane and Gertrude Burgen, around 1912

With sister Mary in Atlantic City, 1916

The O'Hara children, Mary, John, Martin and Joseph, around 1913

Riding Julia in Lykens around 1919

The O'Hara house, 606 Mahantongo Street, Pottsville, Pennsylvania

John and Pet O'Hara in Bermuda, 1931.

John and Belle at the West Side Tennis Club in the 1930s

In the 1930s

With Budd Schulberg at the
West Side Tennis Club, 1936

With Belle

With mandolin, wearing pyjamas and Western hat

At Quogue

In the 1940s
(P. J. Pujol, courtesy of Pennsylvania State University)

With Belle in the 1940s

With F. Scott Fitzgerald in Hollywood, 1940

With Amanda Dunne in Los Angeles

In training for the O.S.S., 1943 (Underwood & Underwood)

With Belle and Wylie at Quogue, 1949

On the bridge of the Intrepid:
Emmet Crozier, Captain Bolger, John O'Hara
(courtesy of Emmet Crozier)

O'Hara, in war correspondent's uniform,
with Belle at Quogue, 1944

Around 1948 (Katherine Young)

Observing Nicholas Ludington and his daughter Merloyd at her wedding to Seymour Lawrence, June 21, 1952 (courtesy of Seymour Lawrence)

O'Hara, Elinor and Wolcott Gibbs, Charles Addams

At National Book Award ceremonies, W. H. Auden, John F. Kennedy, Herbert Kubly,
O'Hara, 1956

With brother Thomas (left) *at the* New York Herald Tribune, *March 25, 1960*
(courtesy of Pennsylvania State University)

At Linebrook (Martin D'Arcy)

With John Steinbeck at Quogue

With Sister at "21," December 18, 1965

With Wylie at "21"

*Sister and John O'Hara with Gilbert Roland
and his wife and daughter,
Palm Springs Racquet Club, 1967
(courtesy of Gilbert Roland)*

With model in publicity shot, 1948 (Esquire)

"The Home Fleet," O'Hara's cars

With the Rolls-Royce and Pat the dog in Princeton, 1966

With Sister at Quogue

In his study at Linebrook

but in the end they settled on Princeton. Asked by friends why he hadn't chosen New Haven, O'Hara replied, "So all you guys wouldn't make fun of me." There were other reasons for getting out of New York. The break with *The New Yorker* and the negative reviews of *A Rage to Live* typified the rift that had grown between him and the world of publishers, critics and litterateurs in New York. To be continuously involved in the city's literary life was bad for his work and he realized it: "it is time," he said, "that I made '21' a restaurant instead of a career." He wanted to start a new sort of life and he wanted to work. At about the same time in his own life, Ernest Hemingway had the same idea: "To work was the only thing," he said, "it was the only thing that made you feel good, and in the meantime it was my own damned life and I would lead it where and how I pleased."

The O'Haras rented a house at 18 College Road, a pleasant tree-shaded street about half a mile from the center of town. This house, like its next-door twin into which they moved a year later, was a gray, single-story prefabricated house. It had a terrace and garden overlooking the fairways of the Springdale Golf Club. The setting was rural with graceful willow trees in the green foreground. On a hill a few hundred yards away was a Gothic tower that looked as though it belonged in Gloucestershire, although it was actually the Princeton Graduate College. The streets of Princeton were lined with substantial houses, some of them dating back two hundred years or more, while the buildings of Princeton University looked like an attempt to reproduce Oxford or Cambridge in an American setting. Nassau Hall was authentically native, but behind it were a pair of Greek temples and not far distant an English Gothic chapel so well scrubbed it looked like part of a Hollywood set. But all of this suited O'Hara. He said he wanted to live in a college town because of the library and "because I like the sports program."

The problems of settling in and making adjustments were mainly in Belle's hands. Fortunately two old friends and contemporaries at St. Timothy's School, Ann Martindell and Kate Bramwell, lived in Princeton, and they introduced the O'Haras to people they knew in the town. O'Hara had high hopes for Princeton: it was not then the suburban town it has become. There were big estates and fox hunting and the style that comes with old money. But reality kept breaking in. At cocktail parties, people would come up to him and say, "I found my daughter reading *Appointment in Samarra,* and I took it away from her." Soon O'Hara was forced to develop defenses against these upper-class Babbitts. When a woman came up to him and said, "I don't know anyone who thinks that way about sex," he looked at her with his cold blue eyes and said, "You do." At large parties the strain was greater and sometimes O'Hara behaved badly. Once at a dinner party he was seated opposite a bore he didn't like. He just sat there shaking his head and snorting like a horse. His nervousness made him drink too much and then he would have to be taken home. Treated aggressively—as celebrities often are by unknown people who want to establish their own importance—O'Hara would sometimes respond by being outrageous. He found himself forced into playing a role and enjoyed it so much it became something of a habit. Once at a dinner party in Princeton he met a marshal of the Royal Air Force, one of the most distinguished military leaders of the second World War. He and O'Hara fell to talking about London clubs. O'Hara made it appear that the air marshal did not belong to the clubs expected of him. "What! Not Whites?" The Englishman sat up for hours after O'Hara left, oppressed with the sense of his own failure.

Belle was forced to adopt a protective stance with O'Hara. At large parties she would stay by his side, and they developed a system of secret signals so they could leave in a hurry if necessary. She also defended him openly and would order people at a party not to tease him. To act in this way went against her shy nature, yet her warm smile and laugh allowed her to get away with it. More and more she built a cocoon around him to keep him from being upset by outside forces such as unwanted visitors. In time, the O'Haras solved their social problems by going only to small dinner parties where the guests were sympathetic. Before accepting, Belle would find out who else was being invited. In congenial company, O'Hara was his best self, amiable and warm, relaxed and gay. He never preened himself as an author nor did he try to dominate the conversation. He preferred to sit a little to one side and listen to what others were saying. Even on more ceremonial occasions such as the small birthday parties Belle gave him, he was always self-effacing. Halfway through the meal he would stand up. When there was silence he would say, "God bless all present," and then sit down. That was the extent of his speechmaking.

The people the O'Haras knew who were connected with Princeton University were those who already had friends among the townspeople or were a part of the society of the town. There were a few professors— Hamilton Cottier, who was also a dean; Rensselaer Lee, an art historian who was a friend of Margaretta Archbald—but mainly the O'Haras' acquaintances were "town" rather than "gown." These included J. Robert Oppenheimer, the atomic physicist and director of the Institute for Advanced Studies, who became a good friend. But most of the people O'Hara saw were not professional intellectuals. He played golf with Charles Caldwell, the football coach, and he also knew Joe Brown, a sculptor who was also the university's boxing coach. "The five men I see the most of," he once reported, "are a stockbroker, a man who runs a small industrial plant, a banker, an opinion researcher and another writer. Four Harvard men and a Yale man." Mainly it was a quiet life with a calm routine. Sometimes in the afternoons O'Hara and Belle would take the little MG and drive around Princeton exploring the low-lying farmlands and following country lanes and cowpaths. At times, O'Hara imagined he was obeying "the advice of certain protectors of American literature, who for twenty years have been saying, 'O'Hara, get lost.' " O'Hara also enjoyed walking the little black poodle, Straus, who with his litter mate Abraham had been named by Charles Addams's wife, Barbara, after the Brooklyn department store. He would sometimes have lunch at the Nassau Club, which was mainly for townspeople, but usually just played backgammon there for an hour in the afternoon. He had wanted to join a tennis club for Wylie, but someone who hated *A Rage to Live* threatened to resign if O'Hara was elected, so he never became a member. In general, the O'Haras kept to themselves and did little large-scale entertaining. Once a year, after the Harvard-Princeton or the Yale-Princeton football game, they would give a cocktail party and invite their Princeton friends as well as people from New York or Boston who were in town for the game.

When he first went to Princeton, O'Hara hoped to be invited to take some part in the life of the university, but he was ignored by the English department. The professors dismissed his books as trashy, never assigning any of them to the students of American literature. O'Hara was not the first author to discover the academic literary man's hostility to living writers. During his first year at Princeton, he attended a gathering of English professors from all over the east that was being held at the university. "They got talking about Moll Flanders and James T. Farrell, et al., and after two hours of it I thought they sounded like a bunch of prep school boys talking about fucking. They knew all about it, and they knew absolutely nothing about it from experience. They were *dirty,* with their little chuckles and knowing allusions. I was supposed to go back for two or three more sessions, but I'd had it." Years afterwards, he summed up his opinion of university professors by saying, "If I were God I would keep them out of heaven."

In the twenty years he lived in Princeton, O'Hara was never once asked to read his work or talk to any of the students. Nevertheless, he did what he could. When John Cheever gave a reading at Princeton, O'Hara made a point of going and afterwards sat with him on a couch at a reception to which students and faculty were invited. Cheever was touched by O'Hara's presence, and the two men talked in a public way about books so that the others could listen in. Once he was asked to answer questions at a luncheon meeting of the Nassau Club, but his nervousness forced him to impose conditions that made the occasion impossibly stiff. Two professors read written questions and O'Hara read written replies. One of the few pleasant occasions connected with the university arose when John McPhee, who was then undergraduate editor of the *Princeton Tiger,* asked O'Hara to contribute a piece to the magazine since he was hoping to raise its literary level. There was no money in it, but O'Hara looked through his unpublished stories and offered McPhee one called "The Favor." The undergraduates were so pleased that they ordered a silver Revere bowl and had it inscribed to O'Hara "With thanks for The Favor." O'Hara, delighted, invited McPhee to his house for drinks. "I like that sort of thing," he said.

O'Hara kept in touch with New York friends mainly by phone. He had long conversations with Bennett Cerf, Charles Addams and others whom he would also invite to Princeton for Saturday or Sunday lunch. Most of his phoning took place before the era of direct dialing, and O'Hara was often impatient with operators and receptionists. Once he placed a call to Francis Brown at *The New York Times Book Review* at lunchtime. Nona Balakian, who still happened to be in the office, answered the phone and told O'Hara that Brown was out to lunch. "Then why the hell did you pick up the phone?" demanded O'Hara.

Princeton was just over an hour from New York, so O'Hara occasionally went to town for errands and to see friends. These meetings were less casual than those formerly arranged from Eighty-sixth Street, so he and Belle would combine several engagements in a single trip—lunch with Philip Barry, for example, then dinner with Bennett and Phyllis Cerf and Dorothy and Richard Rodgers. The O'Haras began to realize that Princeton was really not a part of New York when it came time to drive home after an evening in town, or worse, when they stayed the night and lost a second day. Gradually they went in less often.

It was hard not having kindred spirits at hand, but fortunately O'Hara had one writer friend living in Princeton. He was Wilder Hobson, a younger man who was a Yale graduate and journalist. O'Hara was frequently on the phone with him, talking about a word, a publisher or a review. He could relax with Hobson and his wife, and after a drink or two, he would reach his most amiable stage and with a beatific smile would begin to sing, "I'll build a stairway to Paradise." The Hobsons and the O'Haras tried to re-create the atmosphere of New York in Princeton, but the Nassau Club, where they went for buffet suppers, was not "21." Once the silence seemed as oppressive as that of an English club during the Boer War, so O'Hara rose from the table and announced: "Ladies and Gentlemen, Mafeking has been relieved!"

Shortly before moving to Princeton, O'Hara had seriously considered joining the Central Intelligence Agency, and he gathered the necessary letters of recommendation from such friends as Robert Lovett, James Forrestal and Averell Harriman. In 1949, the CIA had not yet earned the bad reputation it had by the 1970s, and many Americans joined it as a patriotic act during the Cold War period. Writers in particular were consulted for ideas on propaganda. O'Hara probably thought of it as an opportunity for public service after having missed being in the war. Yet even before completing the application, he began to lose interest. He was shaken and discouraged by the suicide of his friend James Forrestal, who was serving as secretary of defense. O'Hara had known Forrestal for years and whenever he went to Washington he stayed at Forrestal's house. "I knew him very well," he wrote Philip Barry, "much better than people who saw him oftener than I did—but a lot of people knew him better than I did whom he did not seek out as he did me. Alone, we could always talk. And laugh." Somewhat halfheartedly O'Hara completed the CIA application forms and went down to Washington where Joseph Bryan arranged a dinner party so that he could meet some of the higher officials of the organization. In his nervousness, O'Hara drank so much he disqualified himself as a suitable CIA agent. The next morning, Katharine Bryan congratulated him on his instinctive behavior and told him that getting drunk the night before was the most sensible thing he could have done.

The year before O'Hara had given a lecture at Yale. His only earlier experience as a public speaker was at Phillips Exeter Academy when in 1945 he appeared as a guest at the Lantern Club, whose president was Forrestal's son Michael. O'Hara had been alarmed at the prospect, but relaxed when he found he could just chat with the boys and masters in the headmaster's study. When invited to speak to the members of a literary organization at Yale called the Elizabethan Club, O'Hara was delighted and told his host that as "to fee and expenses, if you know anything about me you know how I feel about Yale, and I certainly could not take any money from my friend Gilbert Troxell's club." Troxell was curator of rare books at Yale, and O'Hara had already given the library the typescript of *Butterfield 8.*

The talk was called "Writing—What's in It for Me." In a breezy anecdotal fashion O'Hara tried to dispel myths about the writer's independent life and freedom of movement, pointing out that self-discipline is the hardest kind of all. "Nobody can make you write, nobody but yourself," he said, "and if your heart's not in it, the words are no damn good." As to what you get out of it, since writing is a solitary occupation, "the true rewards, the most satisfactory ones, should be the approval that no one else can give you. Your artistic conscience will withhold the kudos sometimes after Harvard has said Well Done." O'Hara's only other university link was with Columbia, which he attended briefly when still living in New York. He enrolled in a course of American history at the School of General Studies. Work on *A Rage to Live* prevented him from continuing, but he bought a Columbia plaque and hung it up in his study. "There's my alma mater, my only college education," he would say.

When William Faulkner was in New York en route to Stockholm to receive the Nobel Prize in 1950, Bennett Cerf gave a dinner party for him and invited O'Hara and Belle to come as guests. O'Hara always had the highest admiration for Faulkner and said he was "the one author among us all who comes closest to putting it down on paper, from thought to printed word, with the least processing in between." Unlike many writers, O'Hara was always ready to praise his contemporaries when he admired their work. O'Hara was delighted to be at the party, and Phyllis Cerf placed him at her left with Faulkner, the guest of honor, at her right. O'Hara was at his best, amusing and charming, in contrast to Faulkner who was not good at dinner party small talk.

At one point Faulkner took a cigarette out of his pocket and looked around for a match. O'Hara then pulled out his gold lighter and lit it for him. Faulkner commented on the handsomeness of the lighter, and O'Hara spontaneously gave it to him, saying, "Phil Barry gave it to me, and I'd like you to have it." Faulkner took the lighter with minimal thanks, put it in his pocket and said no more about it. O'Hara was furious though he remained polite. He was not worried about the value of the lighter, but he had thought of it as a symbol. It was a memento of his friendship with Barry, who had recently died. When Faulkner returned from Sweden, Bennett Cerf met him at the Algonquin and told him that O'Hara had meant the lighter to be a symbol, a link in a chain of friendship among writers, and asked Faulkner to write him a note of thanks. But Faulkner wouldn't do it. "I didn't want his lighter. I didn't ask him for his lighter. Why should I write him a letter?"

Faulkner and O'Hara met from time to time in later years, usually through Bennett Cerf. O'Hara continued to speak well of Faulkner, but Faulkner called O'Hara "a Rutgers Scott Fitzgerald." One night, in a taxi with Robert Penn Warren and Albert Erskine, Faulkner passed a Manhattan nightclub. Erskine remarked that O'Hara was probably inside. "Yes," said Faulkner, "nursing his paranoia."

O'Hara's encounters with his near-contemporaries or immediate elders were always dramatic because of his emotional investments in the relationships. As a young man he worshipped Ernest Hemingway, and while on Cape Cod writing *Butterfield 8,* he wrote Hemingway a fan letter that was at once bristly and enthusiastic about *Green Hills of Africa,* then running serially in *Scribner's Magazine.* "I just want to say that your first instalment in Scribner's is magnificent. Swell. The nuts. Magnificent. It is what they mean by good writing. It is what I mean by the best writing." After that, they met occasionally, although Hemingway was rarely in New York. Once O'Hara sent Hemingway a drunken letter introducing an acquaintance and ending it, "You are a non-answering prick." But they never really quarreled. O'Hara recalled the best of Hemingway after he died. "I loved Ernest Hemingway," he wrote. "At home I have a photograph of us at a night club, taken about thirty years ago, and both of us are looking straight ahead at the camera; but the expression on my face shows the pleasure I took in his company—and I was no unsophisticated kid at the time."

As with Faulkner, O'Hara expressed his admiration emphatically. When Francis Brown of *The New York Times Book Review* asked him to write a piece on Hemingway's *Across the River and Into the Trees,* which had been attacked by the minnow book reviewers, O'Hara went all out. His front-page review began, "The most important author living today, the out-standing author since the death of Shakespeare, has brought out a new novel. The title of the novel is *Across the River and Into the Trees.* The author, of course, is Ernest Hemingway, the most important, the most outstanding author out of the millions of writers who have lived since 1616." O'Hara was not enthusiastic about the novel under review, but he wanted to pay homage to a writer who was being cheaply assaulted. He was immediately in trouble. Letters poured into the *Book Review* and Francis Brown was forced to print a whole page of excerpts which in O'Hara's words, said " 'Lynch O'Hara.' Not 'Lynch EH.' "

Ten years after the review, O'Hara tried to explain what he meant by saying that Hemingway was the most important writer since Shakespeare. "The various circumstances that made him the most important are not all of a purely literary nature. Some are anything but. We start with a first-rate, original, conscientious artist, who caught on because of his excellence. The literary and then the general public very quickly realized that a great artist was functioning in our midst." The publicity grew and Hemingway lent himself to it because he was "a big, strong, highly personable man. He associated himself, through his work, with big things: Africa, Italy, Spain, war, hunting, fishing, bull fighting, The Novel, Style, death, vio-lence, castration, and a teasing remoteness from his homeland and the lit'ry life. All these things make you think of Hemingway; his name is a syno-nym for writer with millions of people who have never read any work of fiction. Etc. etc. He is the father image of writing as FDR was of politics."

The first book O'Hara published after *A Rage to Live* was a short novel called *The Farmers Hotel.* It was originally written as a play, and O'Hara hoped that it might be taken by Richard Rodgers and Oscar Hammerstein III as a musical comedy. Joshua Logan, who was associated with them at the time, did not like it, however, and the idea was rejected. When the novel was finished, O'Hara went to Rodgers' office in New York and said he would like to name it *A Small Hotel* after Rodgers' song. Rodgers was pleased but said, "John, you know the correct title is 'There's a Small Hotel.' " O'Hara said nothing and left the office, but as with the Faulkner episode, he was angry that Rodgers had missed the spirit of his friendly gesture. "I don't need that son of a bitch to tell me how to name my books," he said.

The Farmers Hotel was drawn from O'Hara's Pottsville years. The hotel that serves as the setting for the novel still sits at the crossroads near the hamlet of Beckville, where O'Hara used to stop to water the horses on his way to the country farm. A three-story building, now rather run-down, it is set back on a lawn sheltered by tall shade trees and has a covered verandah where wicker chairs were once provided for the guests. The novel takes place during a fierce winter blizzard which coincides with the opening night of the old hotel under its new management. A group of very different people—a pair of Main Line society lovers in riding breeches, a nightclub pimp and his two striptease girls, a country doctor and a truck driver—take refuge there from the turmoil outside. They are ordinary people whose isolation in the inn leads them to reveal themselves and their capacity for kindness. But the harmony doesn't last: the truck driver gets drunk and starts to pick on one of the girls, and the others force him to leave. Then the Main Line couple decide they should risk going home as the storm appears to have abated. The novel ends with the news that they have been killed by the truck driver who deliberately ran into them.

This violent ending was criticized by some reviewers who thought it was meaningless and unrevealing. But O'Hara had allegorical purposes. The hotel represents the postwar world, specifically the United Nations, where people have gathered to escape the storm of war and to prepare for a harmonious present. Rich and poor, each has something to give, but the truck driver, whom O'Hara thought of as representing the Soviet Union, could not control his bullying impulses. It is a Cold War book, but there is no mention of politics or overt suggestion of a wider meaning. O'Hara was working in a difficult area, for what happens is neither fated nor accidental. The book succeeds because O'Hara's characters are convincing and real and would remain so even with a different ending. It is daring in its attempt to bring so much to bear in so short a space. It echoes what O'Hara was trying to do in *Hope of Heaven,* but uses a more limited setting as Thomas Mann did in *Mario and the Magician.* Knowing O'Hara's sensitivity to hostile reviews, John Steinbeck told him that he had written to the *Times Book Review* in answer to a criticism of the book's structure. "Don't let these neat, dry, cautious, stupid untalented leeches of the arts get you down," he wrote. "It's a hell of a good book. They just won't forgive originality and you'll have to get used to that. Have you found too that the same people who kicked the hell out of Appointment when it came out —now want you to write it over and over again?"

In its original form, *The Farmers Hotel* was one of a number of attempts O'Hara made to write for the stage. He knew the theater well as a reviewer and had many friends among actors, directors and playwrights. He thought that after the loneliness of writing fiction it would be fun to work with others as he had done when *Pal Joey* was staged. But as was already evident from his Hollywood work, dialogue that was successful in his fiction was not necessarily so in work that had to be spoken. On stage, dialogue must never be discursive; it should be vernacular and abrupt, for the actor and the set provide visually what the novelist has to give in words. In the dramatic version of *The Farmers Hotel,* for example, O'Hara has one of the characters seat the others at a table where they are all going to have a meal together. "Well, let's see," she says. "The table has room for twelve, and without Charles we're nine. Nine means two men will have to sit side by

side, somewhere." She then laboriously spells out the whole seating arrangement, character by character. This device may be acceptable in a
novel where nothing can be seen, but on stage it would better be taken care
of by gestures and a few brief directions such as "You here" and "Over
there, please."

O'Hara succeeded in getting *The Farmers Hotel* staged in summer stock
at Fishkill, a village up the Hudson River, but it never reached Broadway.
Another play, *The Searching Sun,* was put on at the Murray Theatre in
Princeton by the combined efforts of two amateur theater groups, the
Princeton Community Players and the Theatre Intime, in May of 1952.
O'Hara decided to direct it himself, but after a while a professional director, John Capsis, was engaged in his place. The opening night audience
seemed to like it, but the reviews were not favorable. The university paper,
the *Daily Princetonian,* ran a headline "Searching Sun Terribly Written" and
the critic described O'Hara's work as "an unbelievably poor piece of incompetent writing" which led O'Hara and a few others to wonder whether
he might have been kinder about a good piece of incompetent writing. *The
Searching Sun,* like another of O'Hara's plays, *The Champagne Pool,* is about
the theater itself. Both contain a good deal of knowledgeable information
about actors and playwrights as well as witty passages, but they suffer
from the self-consciousness that often creeps into works of art that are
about art itself. *The Champagne Pool* was given a reading at the Mermaid
Theatre in New York and went on for over three hours. Paul Shyre, who
was interested in producing it, said that cuts were required. O'Hara refused
to make any so the play was never produced.

Two other plays, *The Way It Was* and *Veronique* are autobiographical
and deal with Greenwich Village in the late 1920s. *The Way It Was* is about
star-crossed lovers who come to New York to make their way. O'Hara
thought it could be made into a musical by Irving Berlin. The two men met
in Berlin's "dingy office on Broadway, where he had his famous key-
changing piano. He sent out to Lindy's for sandwiches and coffee and we
had a very pleasant couple of hours," O'Hara recalled. In the end, nothing
came of it. "Irving and I have had a friendly parting of the ways. He does
not feel musically equal to some of the demands my libretto would make
upon him (although I think he could do it), and I cannot make changes that
might make for commercial success but that I would not want to put my
name to." *Veronique* is about the struggles of a young writer in New York
and deals with the contradictory demands of love and art. Like the other
plays, it lacks dramatic structure and was never staged.

Failing to get his plays on Broadway, O'Hara got them published in
book form under the title of *Five Plays.* He claimed that publication was
needed to secure copyright, but mainly it gave him an opportunity to
express his feelings about writing for the theater. "I have no hope of ever
getting a play done on Broadway," he said in the foreword, "because I will

not allow a director to rewrite it. Most directors are frustrated writers or ex-actors." This familiar and comforting notion covered up his own lack of skill as a playwright, but he was perceptive in his remarks on the deterioration of the American theater, especially on Broadway. "I am tired of hearing about creative directors, creative editors, creative producers, creative hucksters and creative artists' representatives," he wrote. "Create something, boys, and I'll direct it for you. But don't create something that Ibsen has already written." O'Hara was too realistic to believe that his plays were anything but a diversion. "It's doing something different, between turning out novels," he said. "I write a new play nearly every spring, usually after finishing a novel."

In 1952, *Pal Joey* was revived in New York, and this compensated for O'Hara's many theatrical disappointments. He had taken a lively interest in provincial productions of the musical, always hoping it would return to Broadway. The new production, organized by Jule Styne, had its trial run in New Haven and opened at the Broadhurst Theatre on Broadway in January of 1952. Harold Lang played the part of Joey, and of the original cast, only Vivienne Segal returned as Vera, the Chicago matron Joey tries to swindle. *Pal Joey* proved to be the exception to the rule that revivals are rarely successful. Even Brooks Atkinson, who had attacked the first production, acknowledged he had been wrong, and Wolcott Gibbs explained its success: "Standards apparently have changed, probably for the worse, because up to now I have met nobody who found anything embarrassing in the goings on at the Broadhurst. A few, indeed, said they considered the whole thing a little quaint, but the chances are they were just showing off."

Pal Joey won many awards this time around, including the New York Drama Critics Circle award and the Donaldson award. These were the first prizes O'Hara had ever received for his work and he was delighted. All this success did not eliminate O'Hara's native suspiciousness, however. One night at "21" Nathaniel Benchley's wife ran into O'Hara and told him that she had liked *Pal Joey* the second time even better than the first. O'Hara gave her a steely look and replied, "What was the matter with it the first time?" Although he was less involved in the production than he had been in 1941, O'Hara was interviewed and wrote an article about it for the *Herald Tribune.* Random House brought out the libretto in book form, and when rehearsals began in the summer of 1951, O'Hara came up from Quogue to be present.

During the summers, O'Hara and Belle continued to go to Quogue. O'Hara felt he belonged to the village with its little Episcopalian church and unobtrusive landscape, but he stayed apart from the other summer visitors. He did so partly because he did not have a lot of money. He might make a great deal all of a sudden, but that would be followed by months with no income. O'Hara characterized his life as "riding the plush one year, staying home and listening to the radio the next." On the whole, they lived simply. Belle cooked meals of hamburger and fresh vegetables and fruit, followed by Italian coffee. Generally they did not have wine with their meals, preferring the usual summer drink of gin and tonic.

O'Hara tended to see the same people year after year and often played golf with Charles Addams at the Field Club. He didn't like to lose and told Steinbeck that "the only times I make a good score are when I play against par and not against my competitor." Occasionally the O'Haras would go to Southampton or visit friends within easy reach, but generally they entertained only when they had a house guest. Going out could sometimes be trying. Once at an Italian restaurant where he and Charles Addams were dining, the proprietor, thinking he was being funny, came up to their table and said to O'Hara, "Have you written any dirty books lately?" O'Hara asked for the check and they left. Because of the success of the new *Pal Joey,* he was asked by a committee of the Field Club if he would write a skit that could be put on at a fund-raising benefit. O'Hara refused because he thought he was being used.

During the summer of 1953, O'Hara was involved with the television play of *Appointment in Samarra,* put on by Robert Montgomery and Herbert Bayard Swope, Jr.; he had conferences with Clifford Odets and Joshua Logan about a possible production of *The Farmers Hotel;* he flew with Belle to Martha's Vineyard and Fishers Island, and the small plane used on the Vineyard frightened him badly. All this activity was accompanied by the usual amount of drinking. During the day O'Hara usually nursed five or six weak Scotches and water.

In August he went to Wilmington to see his friend William Marvel and, for an article he was preparing, to talk to a man who had known F. Scott Fitzgerald. He stayed at the Dupont Hotel and that evening drank a good deal while talking to the two men. The next day he returned to New York. He was supposed to give a talk in a small town in Pennsylvania, but suddenly he felt ill and took a taxi to his mother-in-law's apartment on East Sixty-third Street, where the doorman let him in. He vomited and then lay down on the tile floor of the bathroom where it was cool and soothing. Fortunately, Belle's sister Winnie Gardiner was in town, and she came to the apartment and found him. She phoned Dr. Bailey to make tests to see whether O'Hara had been poisoned. The doctor reported that O'Hara was bleeding internally and ordered an ambulance and a room for him at the Presbyterian Hospital. On the way uptown, O'Hara hemorrhaged repeatedly, losing so much blood that he had to be given transfusions. A bleeding stomach ulcer was diagnosed, and with the loss of blood, O'Hara thought he was going to die. But with pipes pumping out his stomach and others giving him transfusions, he cracked, "I am a busy body, aren't I."

During all this time, Belle was at Quogue, unable to come to New York because Lili Pell, the young companion the O'Haras had employed to look after Wylie, was away for the day with the car. When Lili returned she found a note asking her to stop at Belle's room before she went to bed. She did so and found Belle on her knees by the bed, crying in distress for fear that she would lose her husband. Belle wanted to leave for New York immediately but was persuaded to wait until the next morning.

It was a close call. Dr. Bailey told O'Hara that he would have to give up drinking. He took it cheerfully, joking that being on the wagon was at least better than the "glass-sided wagon with the six white horses, and where the hell can you find six white horses nowadays?" The doctor did not outlaw drink forever, but prescribed short-term periods of abstinence. He arranged these to follow one another without interruption so that the nondrinking became habitual. Bailey told him that drink might kill him, and O'Hara joked that it was "a hell of a way for booze to treat me after I've been so kind to it."

After two weeks of recuperation at Quogue, O'Hara returned to Princeton. Apart from not drinking, he had to follow a strict routine. Only bland food was allowed: his main meal was mashed potatoes with the juice from a steak poured over it. There was no entertaining and few visitors. At about this time, he heard that his first wife Pet had died in her mid-forties. She had never remarried and had become an alcoholic. Her fate reminded him of his own mortality.

Belle, too, was frail. After taking Wylie to school in the morning, she would lie down until it was time to fetch her. She had always suffered from a malfunction of her heart, but she never talked to O'Hara about her problem because she didn't want to worry him. By the autumn of 1953, she knew she was in trouble but she kept putting off going to the doctor. Then on New Year's day, Belle and O'Hara went to a large party given by Mrs. Zilph Palmer where Belle's coat was taken upstairs. When the party was over, she had to climb the stairs to get it and nearly fainted from the effort.

O'Hara was upset and insisted she visit the doctor the following day. Belle was immediately admitted to the hospital. Her brother, Dr. Robert Wylie, was a heart specialist from New York; he came to visit her as did her sister Winnie. Belle was sure she was going to die but said nothing about it to O'Hara. Then she seemed to get better, and taking note of her improvement, the local doctor told O'Hara that she could be released from the hospital in three days. O'Hara was so pleased he even accepted a dinner party invitation for later in the week. Shortly afterwards, while the family were sitting together after dinner the phone rang. It was the doctor, who told O'Hara that Belle had died.

O'Hara immediately called Wylie and let out a terrible noise. He and Wylie clutched each other and wept, and then Wylie, who was only nine, lay down on the couch stiff as a board. For some days afterwards, she wore a little cap as a sign of her grief. The doctor then arrived, bringing with him a bag containing Belle's belongings. When he saw O'Hara he said, "What you need is a good stiff drink!" O'Hara replied, "That's the last thing I'm going to do." Keeping his temper, he suggested that before leaving the doctor have a look at the dog Straus, who had a cold.

Kate Bramwell returned immediately from Bermuda where she was on holiday, and arranged the funeral, which took place at Trinity Church, not far from the O'Haras' house. There was a great crowd of friends there, but O'Hara was too distraught to take it in. Also, he was worried about Wylie. Afterwards, he said that the only person he remembered seeing was Katharine Barnes Bryan, who had recently become separated from her husband and who was sitting by the side door when Wylie and O'Hara entered the church.

The next day, they had to go to Quogue where Belle was buried. O'Hara went through the funeral process, distracted and numbed by details. He seemed to be coping but his friends were worried. In the car on the way to Quogue, Kate Bramwell told him that he and Wylie would be all right, that Belle had refused to die until she was convinced they could make it on their own. This comforted O'Hara, but there were many bad moments. The Wylies and Gardiners stayed with him for a while, and other friends invited him for meals. Averell Harriman stopped by for a visit and Finis Farr came for a couple of weekends to keep him company. One of his best friends, Joseph Outerbridge, known as Pat, later recalled that O'Hara "was in a state of complete shock. He would call me up at eleven o'clock at night and say, 'Come on over,' and we'd sit up and talk until three A.M." He also spoke every day on the telephone to his mother in New York. Everyone remarked on his self-control, the inner strength he seemed to have tapped. But he was often despairing. He hardly knew his daughter as a person and he doubted his competence as a father. For a time he thought of having her move in with the Gardiners to be brought up with their children.

Belle's death made the world seem meaningless. It confirmed the nihilism he had experienced at his father's early death. Yet the same chance that had killed Belle had brought Wylie to life, and instinctively O'Hara responded to the living responsibilities that lay before him. What helped him most was not drinking. Early in his bereavement he poured a full bottle of Scotch down the drain as a symbol of his rejection of that solution. "If I'd been drinking then," O'Hara later recalled, "I probably would have committed suicide. But I had a nine-year-old daughter, and I said to myself: 'Here I am. My wife has just died. I've had a near fatal illness. What shall I do about this child?' Well, I had seen several bad examples of a father turning his child over to in-laws, so I decided I'd have a go at raising her alone."

10. TEN NORTH FREDERICK

It was dispiriting to have to cope without Belle, but O'Hara was kept busy with domestic arrangements. He asked Lili Pell, who had been Wylie's companion at Quogue, to help, and she agreed to leave Smith College where she was a student and come to Princeton. O'Hara obtained lodgings for her with a widow on nearby Mercer Street. Every day Lili would arrive at the house at seven, have breakfast with Wylie and drive her to school. Afterwards, she ordered the food and acted as housekeeper. Thelma Pemberton, who had been engaged by Belle, was in charge of all the cooking and housecleaning. O'Hara would get up late and while still in his pyjamas have breakfast and read the mail. He would then dress and go out, but generally was home by the time Wylie came back from school. Lili would help Wylie with her homework, have dinner with her and put her to bed before returning to her own lodgings. It was a difficult time, for everyone had to get used to the new routine.

O'Hara was a fond father, and his face would light up when Wylie came into the room. He was amused by the harmless jokes Wylie and Lili had played on him by singing under his window at Quogue and he enjoyed listening to their duets of "Falling in Love Again" and "Someday My Prince Will Come." But he really didn't know his daughter and he wasn't efficient with Band-Aids and scraped knees. They played Scrabble and other games together and gradually got to know each other. O'Hara was indulgent about bedtime and television hours, which made it hard for Lili to encourage self-discipline. He was rarely critical; instead, he held up certain ideals and would look disappointed if Wylie fell short of them. He always tried to be honest with his daughter. He encouraged her to do well and praised her when she won prizes, but he never spoke down to her or covered up things that were unpleasant. In time, O'Hara found he enjoyed being a father. His responsibility to Wylie gave him a sense of his own decency as a human being, and this was important for one so tormented by self-hatred.

Still, there were many bad moments. Sometimes O'Hara would stand by a window, staring at the rain falling on the golf course, and his face would be overcome by an immense sadness. At such moments he had to be left alone until his despair passed. At home, when he was hit by a sense of loss, he would generally go into his study to be alone. Elsewhere it was more difficult. "It is when it hits me on a train, or walking on Nassau Street or Fifth Avenue, suddenly and for no apparent reason, that I have trouble," he confided to Adele Lovett. "Then I try to go on another street, or look out the train window, anything that will change my physical position from what it was when the grief hits me without warning. I of course have had my share of grief, but never anything like this. It is like a blow in the solar plexus, paralyzing except to the brain. I was not prepared for this: I always believed that I would die first, and we had so arranged our affairs."

O'Hara's friends and neighbors continued to help, but more and more he turned to Pat Outerbridge, who made a habit of going to O'Hara's house after dinner at night. The two men would talk or watch television; sometimes they would just sit in silence together. O'Hara did most of the talking, telling stories of Pottsville and the literary life, Outerbridge provided the noncritical audience he needed. Regular journalistic work also helped him. Just before Belle died, James Kerney of the nearby *Trenton Times-Advertiser* had asked O'Hara to write a weekly book column for his paper. The fee was only $100 a column, but O'Hara liked the idea and accepted. Afterwards he was grateful because the weekly deadline helped save his sanity. In his first column he said that his policy would be "to give my friends all the best of it and blast the incompetents that I don't like." Most of the pieces were garrulous and outspoken, with a good deal of autobiographical material. After a year they were published as a book under the title of *Sweet and Sour*. At about the same time, O'Hara was asked to write a fortnightly column for *Colliers* to be called "Appointment with O'Hara." He said that he intended to "write about the theatre, movies, radio, television, music and anything else that comes under the heading of Entertainment that can safely pass through the mails. I am going to do this without using the words valid and rewarding unless I am talking about valid passports and sheriffs paying rewards." The *Colliers* series ran from early 1954 for nearly three years until O'Hara had a disagreement with the editor, Paul Smith. Neither of his two columns added much of importance to O'Hara's work, but they were useful to him when he was not in a mood to write fiction.

As he began to recover from the shock of Belle's death, O'Hara spent more and more time in New York. At first he stayed at the Roosevelt Hotel, but after a while he took a pied-à-terre where he could leave his things. He was lonely and in need of the sort of company Princeton could never provide. He knew a number of women, among them Joan Crawford, whom he would meet and take out to dinner, but as time went on he found himself increasingly attracted to Katharine Barnes Bryan, whom he had seen at Belle's funeral. The sister of two acquaintances of his, Tracy and Courtlandt Barnes, she had always been known as Sister rather than Katharine. For some years, she had been married to O'Hara's old friend Joseph Bryan, but was now living alone in New York. She was a witty, stylish and outgoing person who got on with literary people such as Dorothy Parker as well as with the social world in which she was brought up. She and O'Hara had known each other for a long time.

O'Hara had assumed he would never marry again, that he would just devote his life to Wylie and his work in Princeton. But to his amazement he fell in love with Sister: "One day when she asked me why I had done something I said 'Because I love you,' and the spontaneous declaration (which I wasn't even sure she had heard—we were in a car) told *me* what was really going on inside me." But Sister was not interested. "It *wasn't* going on inside her," O'Hara later recounted. "She didn't want it, she avoided it and carefully rejected it, and just as carefully I refrained from further declarations. I was afraid to frighten her off, and I did have to see her, more and more. Then one night in New York it had us, and we sat in Reuben's restaurant and wondered at it, and I could tell her, over and over, when I didn't have to tell her, because she knew."

After the slow beginning, O'Hara's courtship quickly moved forward. Sister was joyful and bright, and once they sat together talking for thirteen hours. Once she responded to his love, he sent her letters that openly expressed his feelings. "I need you. I started needing you, I went on to loving you, I proceed to needing you more than ever. Does it frighten you? Because if it does, let me say, let me reassure you, that you are absolved of all responsibility in the matter.

> Ever since in June I kissed her
> Valentine has been my Sister.

A month later, he was even more committed: "You now, and with great finality, are in all my thoughts, even or especially when they seem to have no connection with us. I am in love with you, and I am in life with you."

The prospect of marriage to Sister made him think of all parts of his life. "Our life should be wonderful. I am determined not to waste time with people who mean nothing to me. I want it to be spent always with you and Wylie and people who may not be important people or do important things, but who will be satisfactory to us."

O'Hara spent even more time in New York and also met Sister for weekends at the houses of mutual friends such as the Howard Dietzes. Sometimes Sister would run down to Princeton for the day and have lunch with O'Hara at his house. His humor was infectious and beguiling, and she found him physically attractive. She also welcomed his warm attentiveness. As they saw more and more of each other, O'Hara missed her more strongly when they parted. "Do you know what?" he asked in one letter. "Not to make you self-conscious, but I think I can see how you look when you read this. Smile for John, Sister; these words are a kiss." He also knew that others might criticize their romance and noted, "When people don't understand why you let me love you, remember this: I *don't* love *them.*"

By late summer Sister had decided to seek a divorce from Joseph Bryan and went to Reno for the purpose. Being apart was difficult for both of them, and O'Hara expressed himself fully on what he thought their marriage would mean. "In a sense I have staked the living of my life on you. It is too dramatic to say I am staking my life on you, although in a sense that is true. It is a fact that I am almost desperately lonely, and it is a loneliness that only two people in the world can lift, and one of the two is a nine-year-old girl who is not equipped to take any active part in helping me. The other person is, of course, you, and you are really the *only* person who in the real meaning of the word can share my life and whose life I can share. What I drew from you in strength you would get back in all the things that I believe a man should offer his wife. His real and spiritual presence. His steadfast and automatic devotion. His fierce and unquestioning loyalty. His quick sympathy and his idealization. The things that don't exist without love but that love can exist without. There's more to love than love, when it's right."

Towards the end of 1954, O'Hara went out to Reno to be with Sister when she got her divorce. Afterwards, for their own marriage, they decided on a civil ceremony at Sister's apartment on East Seventy-fourth Street. The wedding was set for January 31, 1955, which was also O'Hara's fiftieth birthday, and the only guests were the mothers and children of the two principals. Joseph Bryan contributed to the festivities by sending a telegram of congratulations signed "Frying Pan." After the marriage Sister closed her apartment and made plans to move to Princeton. By early March she was installed with her English furniture, silver knickknacks and potpourri in crystal jars. Sister was so chic and sophisticated she made the dowdy Princetonians sit up. She also shocked them by wearing slacks and by using the rough language O'Hara employed when he was in a Broadway mood. Eyebrows were raised along Nassau Street, but Sister soon charmed the provincial doubters and became involved in the life of the town.

Sister's arrival in the O'Hara household naturally created problems with Wylie who had been spoiled by her father and Lili. Sister realized the need for discipline and applied it as tactfully as she could, but Wylie was resentful and angry that Sister was taking her mother's place. The first weeks were difficult, for Wylie would run to her father to complain. Caught in the middle, O'Hara would sometimes side with Wylie. Once Sister phoned her friend Lucinda Dietz and joked, "I've got some free time to gossip. John has just sent me to my room!" Adjustments were necessary all around. Sister and O'Hara fell into the habit of playing Scrabble almost every day: he was slow but sure, she was impetuous and instinctive. The game helped them to get to know each other and resolve problems. At times, however, there were bizarre incidents. One day O'Hara went into the living room and found Sister sitting there with a strange man. Without saying anything, he stomped off. Afterwards, Sister asked him what was bothering him, and he replied, "It's quite obvious you are inviting your lover right into our house." Sister explained that the man was an upholsterer.

They both laughed, but the quarrels continued, for Sister was a spirited person who refused to sacrifice everything to domestic tranquillity. Sometimes after a quarrel, O'Hara would retire to his study and write a long summary of his own position. One began, without other salutation: *"Well,* now you read *this!"* and went on for six pages to explain why he had been late for dinner. He concluded with the observation that Sister's menstrual cycle must be the source of her unpleasantness and that he supposed he must resign himself to violent quarrels every four weeks. Not long afterwards, following another fight, O'Hara again retired to his study, but he soon emerged and going into Sister's room, exclaimed, "You know, I've made a discovery. *I've* got the curse!"

The intensity of this relationship made O'Hara resentful of any intrusion on it. Consequently he was somewhat jealous of Sister's commitments to her own children. O'Hara was amiable with his stepson, C. D. B. Bryan, known as Courtie, who had plans to be a novelist in his own right, and he offered fatherly advice and encouragement. He had less in common with his stepdaughter, Joan, but when her husband, Peter Gates, began to practice law in New York, O'Hara placed all of his legal and estate affairs in his hands. His other stepson, St. George, was to prove a source of distress. He had rebelled against his parents and had been arrested for possessing drugs in New York. Afterwards he cured himself of his addiction and went to live in Hawaii where he was accidentally drowned while sailing.

With Sister now in charge of the household, Lili Pell planned to leave as soon as Wylie's school term was over. Meanwhile O'Hara had received a call to Hollywood and he decided to take his new family with him. They took the Broadway Limited to Chicago, and there O'Hara showed Wylie and Sister the walk-up hotel he had stayed in when he was penniless in 1927. Afterwards they had lunch at the Pump Room and went to a movie before boarding the Super Chief for the rest of the journey to Los Angeles. Crossing America by train was part of O'Hara's unending research into the life of the country. He admitted that he enjoyed such sides of American life as watching a porter make up a Pullman berth. On arrival, they went to the Beverly Hills Hotel and that evening O'Hara took Wylie and Sister to Mike Romanoff's restaurant. Wylie was thrilled: "She met Gary Cooper and Darryl Zanuck and Georgie Jessell and Herbert Marshall, and saw Rocky Marciano and was entertained by Mike himself, who started things right by giving me a beautiful pair of cuff links," O'Hara reported.

The trip was part honeymoon and part work. O'Hara was to write a treatment for Twentieth Century-Fox of a movie that was to be called *The Best Things in Life Are Free.* A musical biography of three jazz musicians of the 1920s, Buddy DeSylva, Lew Brown and Ray Henderson, it was a backstage story of Tin Pan Alley and Hollywood during the prohibition era. It had the benefit of such well-known songs as "You're the Cream in My Coffee," "Button Up Your Overcoat" and "Life Is Just a Bowl of Cherries" and was more like a revue than a biography. Apart from the music, O'Hara liked the subject because it gave him an opportunity to use his knowledge of social behavior. He has Buddy DeSylva dress up as a yachtsman, but his Park Avenue girl friend tells him he looks too perfect. "You can do without the creases in the sleeves," she says. "I had it pressed," he protests. "I can see that," she says. "Next time, no creases in the sleeves." After completing the treatment, O'Hara was asked to write the screenplay. Even though he knew he would lose $75,000, he turned it down because he was working on a new novel.

While O'Hara was busy at the studio, Sister found them a place to live at 14300 Sunset Boulevard, near the Will Rogers Park in Pacific Palisades. It was a white, single-story house in a garden shaded by two old oak trees. Another garden and lawn in the back gave the house a rural feeling and made it a quiet place in which to work. Wylie was sent to a day camp where she learned to ride, and O'Hara joined the beach club at Santa Monica so that Wylie and Sister and Joan Gates, Sister's daughter who was visiting them, would have a place to swim. He also asked old friends like Burgess Meredith, Gene Kelly and Clark Gable to arrange for visits to the sets where they were working.

Soon O'Hara was back in the social world of Hollywood he had known from previous visits. After the quiet of Princeton, it was a welcome change, especially as he was always fascinated by the lives of Hollywood actors and actresses. Rather breathlessly he reported in *Colliers,* "At dinner the other night I sat next to Ginger Rogers. At that dinner my wife sat next to Clark Gable." One evening Charles Addams was in town and O'Hara gave a party for him along with Gary Cooper, Humphrey Bogart and Lauren Bacall. But O'Hara did not pick up his old routine of lunching out every day. He was too busy and Pacific Palisades was too far out for daily visits to LaRue or Romanoff's. Also, he had begun to notice that there were many people at Romanoff's he did not know. When he asked who they were, he found out they were businessmen working for the aviation and automobile industries who had made money in the war from real estate or munitions. O'Hara thought their presence reduced the glamour he had always associated with Hollywood. He was getting older and the new Los Angeles lacked charm. "I really don't like California," he wrote. "I like seasons and seasoned people."

Even so, O'Hara agreed to a new contract with Twentieth Century-Fox that called for three pictures to be done over a three-year period. He was to be given a free hand and was to work with Buddy Adler, David Brown and Herbert Bayard Swope, Jr., all old friends. The first project was a screenplay to be based on a novel by Frank O'Rourke called *The Bravados.* This book was a routine Western involving a long chase and a romantic triangle. O'Hara was interested in it because it offered him a chance to deal with an American subject that had been reduced to a cliché. "I have lived in tough towns," he said, comparing the Middle West to the Far West, "where there would be a fatal stabbing or shooting every payday, and I think that kind of controlled violence was closer to the real west than the more obviously exciting stuff we have seen and read, in which somebody is always saying, 'Reach!' "

O'Hara objected to Hollywood's habit of rewriting screenplays. He believed that if the script was allowed to stand, the story would "have its ups and downs, not all in the right places, but you will have felt at the end that you were in the presence of a story-teller telling a story, and not just examining an assembly-line product." Once again, he made the familiar argument of the writer against the director who always wants to change the text. "There is not a director in the business who is not a frustrated writer, who does not think he is better than a writer, and who knows damn well he can't write. But The Director is King, and the result is that it is the directors who are permitted to stamp their personalities on motion pictures, when it should have been the writers." To prove his point, he said that he heard people at Fox saying "that they were trying to 'put O'Hara back' in The Best Things in Life. Why did they take him out in the first place? I want to do a Western that the average guy will look at and say to himself, 'I don't know why, but I liked this one a little better than most Westerns.' "

O'Hara wrote the screenplay quickly, and the results were not satisfactory. Changes from the O'Rourke novel were required, but O'Hara's did not improve the story. The new script was static and there was not enough action. Swope and Brown treated O'Hara respectfully, and he rewrote a number of scenes. He also went along with Adler's suggestion to bring back some of the material omitted from the O'Rourke novel. Work dragged on for nearly two years. In 1957, O'Hara was asked to make further changes. By this time he realized that he could no longer work profitably on the script. He therefore withdrew and the screenplay was rewritten by Philip Yordan. Under his contract with Fox, O'Hara wrote one further treatment, but no script was ever written from it. The money he later earned from his novels made it unnecessary for him ever to work again on a screenplay.

The Hollywood work entailed travel back and forth from Princeton to the coast, and O'Hara made a number of other short trips including one to Montreal, Quebec, Ottawa and Toronto in March of 1956. Twice he returned to Pottsville, once for a dinner in honor of the *Pottsville Journal* and the other to attend the funeral of his friend Ransloe Boone. The dinner for the employees of the *Journal* was held at the Elks Hall and O'Hara gave a talk to the assembled guests. There he saw many old friends including Walter Farquhar, Wodrow Archbald and Fred Hoefel. The death of his friend and the closing of the paper may have put O'Hara in an elegiac mood, for he wrote a novella called *A Family Party* in the form of a testimonial speech given at a party in honor of a Pennsylvania country doctor. The novella is a sentimental portrait of a doctor who devoted himself to the well-being of a town which is modeled on Lykens, where O'Hara's grandparents lived. The monologue was O'Hara's earliest literary device, and *A Family Party* is remarkable mainly for the way he used it to tell a complex story. O'Hara called his novella "a simple, honest story," and it was a sign of the mood that had come over him after the death of Belle and his new responsibilities to Wylie and Sister. He was forced to confront values directly and not leave them in the background.

In the early 1950s O'Hara was mainly occupied by the writing of *Ten North Frederick,* a Gibbsville novel about Joseph Chapin, a prominent lawyer who has a secret ambition to become president of the United States. Accident and pride prevent him from getting what he wants, so he gradually drinks himself to death. His unsympathetic wife and spoiled children offer little solace, and he has only superficial friendships with the many other characters in the book. Chapin is oppressed by a sense of failure. His emotional starvation is relieved only once by a brief love affair with his daughter's roommate in New York.

Ten North Frederick is the story of a decent man of affairs who has no real interior life, who is hardworking, honest, responsible and propertied. He belongs to the upper class of Gibbsville and is limited by its values and those of the Hill School and Yale. These call for a gentlemanly aggressiveness in public life and a gentlemanly withdrawal in private. Unlike Julian

English, who was shallow and purposeless, Chapin is a man of substance and achievement, and his secret ambition uses up his energies in public life. When it all comes to nothing, he is left adrift in his own household, preferring the escape of alcohol, which helps him nurse his pride, to confronting the realities of his private life.

In *Ten North Frederick* and his other long novels, O'Hara worked from the outside, for he believed that external appearance and behavior revealed the inner person. Along with Hemingway, he was an impressionist, and belonged to the school of fiction that was founded by Gustave Flaubert and Henry James and developed in English by Joseph Conrad and Ford Madox Ford. These writers believed in giving readers the facts and letting them draw their own conclusions without full explanations. Conrad's statement from the preface to *The Nigger of the 'Narcissus'* meant so much to O'Hara that he had a portion of it copied and framed to be hung in the living room at Quogue. It reads: "My task which I am trying to achieve is, by the power of the written word to make you hear, to make you feel—it is, before all, to make you see. That—and no more, and it is everything." O'Hara differed from other impressionists in his willingness to comment directly on his characters but otherwise he was more detached than they were. Impressionism is effective only when the facts are right, and O'Hara was determined that there be no mistakes in his work. "To me," he wrote, "one of the most irritating elements in novels and plays is the sore-thumb anachronism, the Norfolk suit in 1928, the soldier-boy of 1918 saying 'You can say *that* again.' How many readers know those things are wrong? Not many; but they make me distrust everything else about the play or the novel." To avoid errors of his own in *Ten North Frederick,* he made lists of questions he needed answers to, such as "What are primaries? What is done at primaries? How is a man nominated?" He wrote Pat Outerbridge for information about private schools—"Customs for indoctrinating new boys, pleasant and unpleasant. Special treats. Special clothing regulations. Special quarters." He asked William Marvel to find out for him what subjects were required for admission to the law school at the University of Pennsylvania. He did not intend to use all this information, but it was needed to make sure that what Thornton Wilder called the "tacit assumptions" about a society were properly recognized, from knowing how to ring for a servant to knowing what kinds of curtains to hang in a living room.

O'Hara also wrote profiles of each of his characters and made charts for each one, recording dates of birth, dates of marriage, dates on which children were born and dates of anniversaries, showing how old they were on each of these occasions. He made other charts that showed how old each character was in relation to the others as of a particular date, so as to make sure they grew old at the same rate. In the pocket biographies of his characters, he included the names and dates of schools, colleges and postgraduate universities attended. For his more important characters he also listed such bits of information as the names of restaurants and clubs they would be likely to visit, sports events they might have seen, theaters, with address, names of plays and actors seen, news events, funerals, famous crimes, books published, including names of especially popular books of the time, names and addresses of schools in New York, descriptions of clothes, shops where they were bought, prices, musical events, society events and storms, droughts or floods. He also kept a journal called "So Far" in which he would record what had happened to each character in order to avoid repetition.

Most of the sort of information O'Hara recorded was similar to the kind found in *Who's Who,* and that book, along with other biographical dictionaries, was one of his most important research tools. Natural for one who was writing more and more about public life, *Who's Who* was also psychologically useful for anyone who followed a person from one year to another. Not only did it record the new achievements and new clubs joined by an important person, but information dropped from the annual entry often revealed what the subject was now ashamed of. O'Hara derived a great deal of pleasure and amusement as well as information from his reading of *Who's Who.* He knew more about people than they realized. This could be startling when, after being introduced, O'Hara might begin to question an individual closely on certain events in his past. O'Hara had a favorite character, William Fortune, whose biography was second in length only to Nicholas Murray Butler's. "I know him like a book, this Bill Fortune," said O'Hara. "He was the originator in 1892, of the Indiana Good Roads Movement. He married May Knubbe. He was a member of the committee of three that had charge of relief of over 5000 unemployed in Indianapolis during the winter of 1894. President O'Leary of the United States Chamber of Commerce wrote him a letter commending him as a citizen in 1926. Cal Coolidge also wrote him a letter. All these facts and many others of a similar nature are faithfully reported, by himself, in Who's Who. He is a wonderful man."

This is the sort of information about America that O'Hara wanted his fiction to contain. In the tradition of such writers as Dickens, Trollope, Tolstoy and Balzac, O'Hara wished to give a picture of upper-class social life as well as the commercial world on which it was based. Henry James is said never to have gone "downtown" to the source of the moneyed society he wrote about. O'Hara wanted to write about both, to combine Henry James, or Edith Wharton, with Frank Norris. Also he wanted to introduce a region of the country that though provincial was not Babbitt-like and though eastern was not polished. Above all, he wanted to talk about the private lives of Americans and to say things about the relations between men and women that no one had ever said before. But always he wrote as a novelist. Asking for political information from his brother, he noted that "since I am writing a novel rather than a Lincoln Steffens kind of work, I can always fall back on the fact that it *is* fiction, and the political machinations while important are still the second most important item in my novel. The most important is the credibility of the characters." Because he was accurate, O'Hara was often called a social historian, but he was clear about his priorities. "From Harriet Beecher Stowe to John Steinbeck," he wrote, "the author who offers social history is most effective, perhaps even *only* effective, when his concern is for his characters rather than for his conditions. The difference between a novel about sharecroppers and a novel about Ezra Bumpkin, sharecropper, is the difference between a social-history report on the one hand and, on the other, Art. The novelist ought to be, must be, on the side of Art. If he writes as a social historian first, I even doubt that his social history will be much good, since his understanding of, let us say, the sharecroppers' conditions is limited by his observations of the general and his remoteness from the particular."

O'Hara became famous for his sociological accuracy, but so strong was his concern for psychological truth, he made a fantasy out of Gibbsville, turning it into something quite different from Pottsville. Accustomed to the relative grandeur of Long Island and New York, he may have imagined that the upper classes of Pottsville lived on the same scale. It is natural when looking into the past to magnify it and see it in a more glamorous light than the facts warrant. Certainly Fort Penn and Gibbsville are more grand and sumptuous than the cities on which they are based. The Chapin house in *Ten North Frederick* was modeled on Walter Farquhar's house on North George Street across the tracks from Mahantongo Street. The actual house is a plain clapboard box perched on the top end of a small lot in a run-down section of the city, but in the novel O'Hara gives the impression that it is a substantial mansion, the equivalent of a big house in Brookline or Greenwich. Artistically, this discrepancy is of no consequence, for O'Hara was writing fiction, but it suggests that in the world of his imagination, he could go back and make Pottsville into something he could love instead of the ugly and narrow place he had to run away from in 1928.

Yet O'Hara never prettified or improved in a sentimental way. His newspaper training alone would have prevented that, for he was taught to be accurate and specific. He developed what he called "pre-paper discipline," which meant organizing everything in his head so that it would illuminate the point he wanted to make. Such training made it virtually impossible for him to be fanciful. By temperament, O'Hara was also suspicious of elaborate language. He mistrusted the poet's principal device, the metaphor, because he doubted its accuracy. " 'All the perfumes of Arabia' makes you think of all the perfumes of Arabia and nothing more," he wrote. "It is the trouble with all metaphors where human behavior is concerned. People are not ships, chess men, flowers, race horses, oil paintings, bottles of champagne, excrement, musical instruments or anything else but people. Metaphors are all right to give you an idea."

He also rejected the primacy of poetry in literature. "I have been amused rather than complimented on the occasions when a reviewer commented on the poetry in my prose. The poetry, I assure you, is entirely accidental; the good prose is not. I therefore deny that when a novelist is called a poet, or his work poetry, he is being promoted." Aiming for clarity and simplicity, O'Hara wanted to prevent the reader from being distracted by mannerisms; he wanted to absorb the reader's attention so much that he might think he was living the story instead of reading it. He called his own style "presentation" and the penalty for his stylistic modesty is an occasional lack of tension in the language. John Updike said that O'Hara's prose was "tuned to less than highest pitch" and that it "just ran on," but he explained it by saying that O'Hara thought life was so interesting there was "no need to *make* it interesting."

O'Hara thought of style mainly as a way of solving problems. Since one of the fundamentals in fiction is having convincing characters, he believed that dialogue, representing their actual voices, was of the first importance. "Nothing," he wrote, "could so quickly cast doubt on, and even destroy, the author's character as bad dialog. If the people did not talk right, they were not real people." O'Hara had developed his gift for dialogue mainly in his short stories. A more difficult problem, in the longer novels, was to structure the book so that the narrative remained alive while the necessary information was presented. As a newspaperman, O'Hara was aware of the tricks compositors used to present information in an easily digestible way. Given the more limited scope of the printed book, O'Hara became interested in paragraphing. In reading Hemingway's *A Farewell to Arms* and Gertrude Stein's *The Autobiography of Alice B. Toklas,* he was struck by the use of long unbroken paragraphs. He became conscious of "massive blocks of type that by their massiveness prepare the reader for a great collection of facts even before the reader has had a chance to read the words or sentences. This is a splendid device. For several hundred years the spoken word in novels has had all the typographical breaks, by reason of the fact that said-he and said-she are kept separate and thus subtly the reader is directed to break his attention from he to she, which is what the novelist wants him to do. But in descriptive passages, whether they are descriptive of the contents of a room, or of a fistfight, or of stream of consciousness, most novelists have been timid about risking the long, unbroken block of type. Consequently they have paragraphed descriptions that should have been kept intact."

Ten North Frederick is generally a better novel than *A Rage to Live.* The central character survives till the end of the book and provides a continuing focus of interest. Even though he is conventional, Joseph Chapin is more interesting than either Sidney or Grace Tate, and O'Hara invests him with some of the concerns that had been troubling him in his own life. The novel is obsessed with death as O'Hara was in the bad years of 1953 and

1954, and it offers a scenario of what might have happened to O'Hara had he behaved differently in his own crisis. The book also reflects O'Hara's deepening concern with values. Driven by literary ambition as a young man, he had been forced to consider what public success meant and did not mean. His move to Princeton, the death of Belle and his marriage to Sister all deepened his awareness of what was important. These autobiographical elements give the book substance, but they also limit it. Chapin seems unnecessarily paralyzed by his privacy and the failure of his secret ambition. His end is psychologically true, but he is not engaging enough for us to care, despite O'Hara's efforts to make him sympathetic. *Ten North Frederick* nevertheless shows considerable development in O'Hara's skills as a novelist.

The book was published on Thanksgiving Day of 1955. O'Hara had chosen the date with care, and most of his later books were published on the same day. The reason was that on Thursdays, Charles Poore reviewed for the daily edition of *The New York Times,* and O'Hara was eager to avoid being reviewed on another day by Orville Prescott who he thought was "so unfavorably disposed that nothing I write can expect fair consideration." When *Ten North Frederick* was published, the book reviewers at *Time* said, "O'Hara has a tape-recorder ear, a headwaiter's instinct for credit rating and a preoccupation with different means of making love." John Steinbeck publicly replied to this personal attack by calling the review in *Time* "stupid," but O'Hara, though grateful, knew that rebuttals never get the attention the original review does. He therefore wanted what he called "respectful consideration"—reviews that made an effort to consider the author's intention. He could only count on two to do so, Charles Poore and John Hutchens of the *Herald Tribune.*

O'Hara was easily upset by bad reviews, though he never made the mistake of answering one. Instead, he made sarcastic remarks about reviewers in general, dismissing them as "little old ladies of both sexes." His own petulance sometimes surprised him. "Who are these people?" he asked himself. "Why do I let them bother me?" He gave as his answer his view that "they have influence and lend it to the lunatics" who were always ready to attack him on another level. Conversely, he was enormously gratified by understanding reviews and would write to thank those who publicly admired his work. He said that what St. Clair McKelway wrote of *Ten North Frederick* in *The New Yorker* had "been decisively important to me," and explained what he meant in a letter to Robert Kirsch who had also written about him in the *Los Angeles Times:* "It is important to me to be able to read those words because finally one man, and a man I've never met, has shown that he has known what I have been doing." Yet he was never really taken in by a book reviewer's praise. "They, the reviewers, are not us," he wrote to James Gould Cozzens. "We tend to overlook that fact when we get intelligent, understanding reviews; but they are still not us.

They are as different as touch football and the genuine article. But they sure as hell talk big."

The public responded so well to *Ten North Frederick* that it soon sold over 100,000 copies. The genteel hostility of the critics did not discourage sales. The public seemed to welcome the reality of O'Hara's world and appreciated the courage with which he dealt openly with sex and drink and success or failure. Random House gave him another silver cigarette box and the novel was also nominated for the National Book Award in fiction. The other leading contenders were Robert Penn Warren's *Band of Angels* and MacKinlay Kantor's *Andersonville.* One of the judges, Mark Schorer, was strongly in favor of *Ten North Frederick;* he convinced the other two, John Brooks and Carlos Baker, to go along with him and the award was made unanimously. Except for the prize received for the Broadway revival of *Pal Joey* in 1952, it was the first recognition O'Hara had received since he was a schoolboy and he was beside himself with pleasure. He and Sister went to New York for the ceremonies which began with a press conference for the winners at the Commodore Hotel. O'Hara was inevitably asked about the prominence of sex in his novels, but he kept his temper and replied, "It's life as I see it." Among the other winners was W. H. Auden, and the speaker was Senator John F. Kennedy who urged writers to turn to public themes in their work.

When he was given the award, O'Hara began by saying that he had been waiting for twenty-two years for some recognition: "I am taking the liberty of accepting the National Book Award," he said, "not only for my current novel, *Ten North Frederick,* published by Random House, price three-ninety-five, but at least to some extent a recognition of the fact, and I immodestly call it a fact, that since 1934 I have been publishing novels and books of short stories in which I told as honestly as I could what I have seen, heard, thought, and felt about a great many of the men and women who populate this country. At the time of writing I first have to satisfy myself that I am telling the truth, then that I am telling it in the most readable, by my standards, fashion I know." At the end of his speech, he said that he would be pleased to be asked again, but he was so moved that he choked up and was not clearly heard. O'Hara enjoyed the occasion except for a woman who came up to him afterwards and stuck her tongue out at him saying, "You shouldn't have got it. *Andersonville* should have got it." Later, when asked what it was like to have won, he gave the Irish response, "It's better than a poke in the eye with a sharp stick," and then frankly admitted, "I am pleased that I got it because if I hadn't got it I'd have been sore as hell." But he refused to take it too seriously. "Any author who gets a swelled head because he has been given a prize or a plaque is a foolish man," he noted.

Even before winning the National Book Award, O'Hara was beginning to receive public attention and invitations to give lectures. He was not a good public speaker, was ill at ease on a platform and always read from a prepared text. His voice was pleasing and clear: he thought he had a Pennsylvania twang, but actually he sounded like an educated New Yorker. At the Library of Congress, where he delivered the Whittall Lecture, O'Hara spoke about the public's reaction to fiction, and especially to the familiar complaint about "those awful people" in contemporary novels. He pointed out forcefully that "it is not now, it never has been the serious author's job to make his characters nice. The author who does make his characters nice is a hack and a liar." Most of O'Hara's lecture was given over to book chat and he was described in a Washington paper as being "cheerfully bellicose." His remarks made the audience laugh and applaud a good deal "between sharply indrawn breaths."

In a talk at Rutgers, O'Hara discussed writers' backgrounds, questioning whether one was more helpful than another. He chose seven writers he admired, pointing out that they were all middle class, neither rich nor poor, and graduates of high schools. One of his more revealing talks came through an invitation from his Wilmington friends, Chancellor William Marvel and Judge Paul Leahy, to speak at a ceremony honoring a group of new citizens. O'Hara told them about his own mixed ancestry from England and Ireland, Holland and France. His forebears included "soldiers and surgeons, a poet or two, an unconvicted lawbreaker, a tribe of gipsy horse-traders, a couple of bank presidents, a bishop, a mother superior, and a nest of simple folk. There was some money made, but not great millions. We often did nothing to maintain domestic tranquillity; we sometimes did a little for the common defense; a few of us helped to promote the general welfare." He also told one anecdote that revealed his simple patriotism: "In 1918 I watched a parade. In my town we took pride in our parades, and this one I have in mind was organized in less than an hour, but it was one of the best parades I ever saw anywhere. The Third Brigade Band, the Spanish-American War Veterans Fife & Drum Corps, and the Boys Band provided the marching music. The president of the Coal & Iron Company, carrying a small flag, was at the head of the Patriotic League. The men from the car shops marched in their work clothes. The Boy Scouts, with all flags of the Allies, were up front, and the troopers of the State Constabulary on sorrels and their captain on a gray rode at the very head of the procession. The sidewalks were lined by the populace, and the parade was in honor of one man: the first Negro to be drafted for the United States Army in our Country."

Sometimes his speeches produced amusing side effects. At Yale in 1952, he gave a talk to an informal gathering at Pierson College, whose master was Gordon Haight. "I talked to the members of the college," O'Hara later recalled, "and got a little drunk. Instead of an honorarium, I suggested they give me a Pierson College tie, and by God some kid went down to J. Press and got me one. Some time later, in Princeton, Thornton

Wilder referred to me as an honorary Fellow of Pierson. I said I didn't know that, and he said, 'Oh, yes. You are.' But on a subsequent visit to the Haights I learned that I most definitely was *not.*"

One of the honors O'Hara most cherished was his election to the National Institute of Arts and Letters in 1957. The Institute, modeled on the Institut de France, was founded in 1898 and housed in a large stone building overlooking the Hudson River at One Hundred Fifty-fifth Street. Of the 250 members who represent the plastic arts, music and literature, fifty also belong to a smaller group known as the American Academy, which also has French origins. The Institute promotes the arts in the United States by awarding prizes to worthy writers and artists. For years O'Hara wanted to belong, but as election days came and went, he began to think of them as his "annual snub." He even devoted one of his columns in the *Trenton Times-Advertiser* to his failure to be elected. He was originally nomi-nated for membership in the early 1950s by Malcolm Cowley, with Marc Connelly and Robert Penn Warren seconding him. His other supporters included Louis Untermeyer, Deems Taylor and Philip Barry, but he was not elected. Then in 1956 John Hersey began a campaign on his behalf. Hersey knew that O'Hara had enemies so in his nomination statement he reminded the members of what Cowley had said earlier about the Institute, "that a body like the Institute dies if it does not make room for people about whom its members can argue with vigor, conviction and pleasure. It can also die of tardiness." With this reasoning and the backing of Thornton Wilder, William Faulkner, John Dos Passos and John Steinbeck, all of whom seconded the nomination, O'Hara was elected and taken into the Institute at a dinner in April of 1957.

O'Hara had no illusions about the place. Ernest Hemingway had refused membership when elected, and O'Hara in his private correspon-dence sometimes wondered about the qualifications of some of the mem-bers. But he thought it might regain the prestige it once had if worthy people joined it. He urged James Gould Cozzens to remain a member, in the belief that his presence would discourage the second-raters. "There will always be some smilers, some deadwood," he wrote, "but you can't keep them all out. What you *can* do is keep them to a minimum by making it awkward or embarrassing for the politickers to bring in their toadies and seat them at table with men of real standing." O'Hara was delighted with his own election, and on the day he received notification, he reported to Deems Taylor that he planned "to spend the afternoon with a razor blade, slitting the stitching in my lapel buttonholes to make way for the rosette. (Ready-made clothes, you know.)"

Ironically, O'Hara's election to the Institute coincided with attacks against *Ten North Frederick* as a book unfit to be sold on the newsstands in paperback form. In January of 1957, the police in Detroit and Cleveland banned the book as an obscene work. Notified of their action, O'Hara

replied characteristically: "From what I have heard of conditions in Detroit, I am surprised that the Detroit Police Department can spare a single
patrolman for literary duty." The newspapers in both cities attacked the
police, and the publishers, Random House and Bantam Books, successfully
defended themselves in the courts and ultimately won their case. But
O'Hara was sensitive to the issue. He had already experienced censorship
in England where Chatto and Windus declined to publish *Butterfield 8* for
fear of interference by the obscene publications division of the Home
Office. He was upset when the sexual side of his work was emphasized in
advertisements, and had already objected to what he called the "boudoir"
advertisements Random House used for *Ten North Frederick.* Like all writers,
he was alone and vulnerable, but he thought of his membership in the
Institute as "an ace in the hole against further attacks. The Institute of Arts
and Letters is not a hangout for writers of obscene books."

Yet within the year he was accused in Albany, New York, along with
Bantam Books and a number of smut magazines, of being a purveyor of
obscene literature. In New York for a dinner at the Institute, he was
warned by his lawyer to leave the state lest he be arrested and imprisoned.
Before returning to New Jersey, he wrote Malcolm Cowley at the Institute,
informing him of the obscenity charge and asking for "the moral support
of the members of the Academy and the Institute. This is a dangerous
action affecting not me alone." Cowley read the letter to the members at
the dinner, but nothing was done. He later told O'Hara that the constitu-
tion of the Institute was too cumbersome to allow it to take quick action
on matters like the Albany indictment, and O'Hara replied that the machinery should be improved so it could. The indictment was quashed by
the judge, but O'Hara still disapproved of the Institute's inaction. His
sense of loyalty was also offended. "Instead of staying out of these things,"
he wrote, "the Institute should be the first to come to the defense of a
member. The Institute need not commit itself to automatic defense of every
author and artist in the country, but having elected a man, it should
support him vigorously, if only to say to the world that membership carries
distinction."

The financial success of *Ten North Frederick,* together with his awards
and honors, began to change O'Hara's style of living. The framed certifi-
cates and the bank accounts were evidence that despite his doubts, he had
not only arrived, but that other people recognized that he had. As a sign
of his new status, O'Hara and Sister decided to move from their small
house on College Road. Like most writers, O'Hara was content to live
wherever he could write well, but Sister was eager for something better.
She found land available outside Princeton on Pretty Brook Road near
Province Line Road. This part of the township was formerly open farming
country and woods, but rich businessmen from New York and Philadelphia had gradually bought up the land to build country houses on it. After

buying a few acres, Sister engaged a Princeton architect to design a French provincial farmhouse that would be at once spacious and simple.

Built at the end of a driveway in a grove of trees, the house was made of brick painted white with a flagstone terrace by the front door and a garage to the right. Inside was a large living room with a fireplace and windows overlooking the garden in back. The room was somewhat cluttered; there was a television set, a card table and a piano, and the tables were covered with knickknacks, including the Random House cigarette boxes. The main bedrooms were on the ground floor. O'Hara's study was beyond them in a corner room with a fireplace and a small bathroom of his own which he had modeled on an A-deck bathroom from the *Queen Mary*. The study, paneled in wood with two leather armchairs facing a window, was the real center of O'Hara's life in the new house. There he collected all his memorabilia—signed *New Yorker* cartoons by Charles Addams and Thurber, photographs of Scott Fitzgerald and of Benchley, hunting horns, a model of a 1932 Dusenberg car, framed citations of his membership in the Institute and his winning of the National Book Award, a John Held drawing, photographs of the *Pal Joey* cast. The study was also a real workroom. In the corner, beneath bookcases, were two desks on one of which rested a Remington noiseless typewriter. The bookshelves were mainly filled with reference books. In addition to *Who's Who,* Burke's *Peerage,* the *Social Register, Bartlett's Quotations,* the *Statesmen's Who's Who,* there were specialized books about New York, Pennsylvania, Hollywood, Wall Street and the United States Congress, as well as references to music, medicine, sports, trains, ships and the navy. In addition, there were travel guides and atlases, gazetteers, dictionaries of French, Italian, German, Latin and Greek as well as English, biographies of public figures, the *Encyclopaedia Britannica* and the *Dictionary of American Biography,* Baird's *Manual of American College Fraternities* and the Yale Year Book for 1924, the class O'Hara might have belonged to. The other bookshelves were filled with books of fiction and nonfiction, including translations of his own work and novels he had owned since childhood, notably works by Sir James Barrie and Louisa May Alcott.

The O'Haras called their house Linebrook, combining the names of the two nearest roads. It was a suitable place for Sister to entertain, for it was large and airy and private. By now she was well known in Princeton, involved in a number of civic and charitable organizations: she ran a boutique for the Princeton Hospital and was on the board of the Neuro-Psychiatric Institute. She was a practical woman, an efficient housekeeper and enjoyed seeing people. On Friday evenings she occasionally gave dinner parties for six or eight people. She felt ill at ease with some of the more intellectual friends O'Hara had known while married to Belle, and gradually began to invite more social people. Sister also established closer relations between O'Hara and his own family. She had the kind of sense

of humor that Mary and Mrs. O'Hara appreciated. They would warn her
not to let herself be bossed around, and she would laugh and tell them she
had the situation under control. On one of her early calls to Mrs. O'Hara,
she announced herself by saying, "This is Sister O'Hara" and immediately
got the response, "And this is Mother Superior."

Although there was a strong bond between them, Sister and O'Hara
had different routines. Sister was an early riser and would be up by the
time Thelma Pemberton arrived at seven. After breakfast, she would
phone her friend Corella Bonner and they would plan the morning's activities or run up to New York for the day. Sometimes Sister would lunch out,
but she always tried to return to the house by two, since O'Hara would
then be up, although still in his pyjamas. He would have eaten his cream
of wheat cereal and coffee on a tray in his study and be ready for their daily
game of Scrabble which they played in the living room, with the television
on but the sound turned down. The game sometimes languished, but since
their two lives were otherwise much apart, this time for being together was
important. Afterwards, O'Hara would read his mail and make phone calls.
Sometimes he would dress and go out, but often he stayed in his pyjamas
all day long. He would have a series of snacks, half a sandwich and a cup
of coffee now and again. Towards the end of the afternoon, he would take
a short nap before getting up again in time for dinner with Sister. His food
was always bland, usually creamed or minced chicken, some meatloaf or
a piece of bluefish. After dinner, O'Hara and Sister would watch television
together; it was O'Hara's main connection with the world outside of Linebrook, and as an old Broadway hand, he enjoyed watching popular enter-
tainers and listening to talk shows. He knew many of the participants and
enjoyed telling Wylie and Sister what they were like. At about eleven or
twelve, when it was time for Sister to go to bed, O'Hara would go to his
study and begin his workday. The house was quiet, and alone he would
enter the world of his imagination, sitting at his desk sometimes till dawn,
adding new pages of yellow typescript to the growing pile of his novel
until it was time to go to bed.

It was an isolated life, but the routine was not rigid. Sometimes
O'Hara and Sister would go to New York for the day. They had a subscription to Friday afternoon concerts by the Philadelphia Orchestra. They
would often invite friends to join them for lunch at the Bellevue Stratford
and then go to the Academy of Music. Apart from the music, which he
loved, O'Hara found these occasions socially instructive and diverting. "I
understand there was a duPont in our box this year," O'Hara wrote to his
Wilmington friend William Marvel. "Now so far as my actual experience
went, she was inoffensive and kept her place. Nevertheless, at no time did
she let on that she knew there were two O'Haras in 'her' box. It is quite
possible to be inoffensive and yet at the same time be impertinent. If this
duPont was the person I recall, I cannot remember that any time did she

rise when we entered the box. She may have done so, but not noticeably, and what's the good of doing it if it is not observed. You know perfectly well that I am not stuffy about things, but if we can't have those little niceties at the Academy of Music, Philadelphia, Pennsylvania, then we all might as well give up. Communism is *here.*"

Meantime, O'Hara never stopped working, and that gave him satisfaction. "Good writing is pleasurable work," he noted, "but it is work and it is not easy." It had been one of the steadying influences in his life and had helped him survive the experiences of the last few years. Never again did he fall into the paralyzing bitterness he had known as a young man when he felt spurned and neglected. His work had paid off, and with the steady income he received from the sale of subsidiary rights to paperback publishers, from translations and from television options and sales, he had the satisfaction of knowing he had attained stability largely through his own efforts and determination.

This work became most intense in 1956 and 1957 when he was writing his longest and most ambitious book, *From the Terrace.* He had been planning this book for years and considered *A Rage to Live* and *Ten North Frederick* to be important mainly as preparation for this enormous novel of 897 pages. The book is a fictional biography of Alfred Eaton, the younger son of the owner of a steel mill in Port Jefferson, a small Pennsylvania city near Gibbsville. The novel traces Alfred's background, especially his father's preference for his elder brother who dies young, and the early death of two girls who loved Alfred as a young man. It then follows Alfred through an obscure preparatory school in Pennsylvania to his undergraduate years at Princeton, his experiences in World War I and his employment in a prestigious private bank in New York where he soon rises to become a partner. Eaton marries a beautiful but shallow girl from Wilmington, has three children by her and then, as the second war comes, accepts a job in Washington as assistant secretary of the navy. Meanwhile his wife becomes notoriously promiscuous, so he has an extended affair with another woman whom he eventually marries. His high-minded patriotism earns him the animosity of some of his Wall Street associates who want to profit from the war, so he is forced to resign from his banking partnership. At about the same time, he suffers from a hemorrhage and has to resign from the navy as well. Moving to California with his new wife, he finds himself at loose ends. At the age of forty-eight, with enough money to live on, he becomes a superfluous man, a person with no future.

O'Hara's intention with Eaton is to trace the life of a public man who has no introspective impulses, no interest in the arts, no religious or philosophical beliefs, whose personal life is made up of social engagements and whose psychic balance depends on a good marriage. Alfred Eaton is a public figure on a grand scale, far beyond Joseph Chapin. Through his friends Averell Harriman, Robert Lovett and James Forrestal, O'Hara was well acquainted with the lives of public men, but none of them was a model for Eaton. In 1956, just before he began to write this novel, the Suez and Hungarian crises occurred, and O'Hara began to take an interest in Anthony Eden. As Churchill's right-hand man during World War II, Eden became prominent early in his career, but after the fiasco of Suez and his own brief tenure as prime minister, he went into a decline accompanied by illness. He had never been personally popular and had violated the unwritten code of the politician by divorcing his first wife and marrying again. There are many parallels between Alfred Eaton and Anthony Eden, but also a different emphasis that arises from the American setting. Eden's story was useful mainly because it gave O'Hara an opportunity to investigate the personal side of an upper-class millionaire's life better than any domestic models known to him.

O'Hara was fascinated by rich and powerful men whose careers are devoted to the manipulation of public forces. He thought they represented a basic element in American life and in giving a portrait of one of them, he hoped to touch on a fundamental characteristic of American society during the first half of the century. The accumulation of wealth is a ruthless occupation, involving cruelty and injustice to others, even when no laws are broken. Alfred Eaton's steel mill was the product of his father's business energies, and the money that Alfred inherited came with a price attached to it. To benefit from his inheritance, Alfred had to be tough and unfeeling. His class and schooling gave him gentlemanly trappings, but ruthlessness was under the surface and inevitably affected his relationships with his family and wife. As O'Hara saw it, the objective of the American capitalist class is the same as that of the European landed aristocracy: the accumulation and preservation of wealth for the benefit of future generations. But in America there is little of the sense of social responsibility that grew out of the feudal system in Europe. Americans are restless and have little feeling for place, so the general rule has been to sell out and move on. O'Hara had Alfred Eaton, who hated his father, close the steel mill and move to New York where he entered the world of finance. In abandoning Port Jefferson, he also abandoned his mother whom he might have saved from her drunkenness just as she might have helped him save his own marriage. But Eaton gave up provincial Pennsylvania because "he was not a second-rater. He could have been the leading citizen of Port Jefferson without much competition, but it would have been avoiding life and rather cowardly. Port Jefferson was not good enough for him. He had to live in the big world, compete with the big people."

Financial men control the fates of others, but they don't do anything in a physical sense. They don't dirty their hands on the farm, they don't deal with employees at the mill, nor do they make anything. But they determine the direction society will take. Theirs is a world of polite warfare in which the main objective is gain and power. O'Hara thought human life was mainly defined by social events and believed that individualism was a luxury except for those rich enough to afford it. A man might make one slip, and find that in terms of the values he'd subscribed to, his life had suddenly come to an end. That is what happened to Anthony Eden and what happens to Alfred Eaton. It is a very American story. It is specifically the story of the moneyed upper classes in the United States. O'Hara believed that the "American aristocracy has petered out very quickly," and he blamed commercial values. "I wonder," he wrote William Marvel, "if the American aristocracy was not made flabby by the democratic materialism of the 19th Century. In the North the Woe Between the States was not generally participated in by the aristocrats, and in the South the aristocracy fought because they had to; the Yankees were just down the road a piece. And what Yankees! Men like my grandfather, who, if the USA had been England, would not have been a commissioned officer; the Irish of New York and New England and Pennsylvania; the Germans of the East and Middle West. The Northern army was a middle class army at best, and an aristocracy simply must be tested by war if it is to continue at the top."

O'Hara places Alfred Eaton's story against the social and industrial background of a half-century of American life. Without ever moving his focus away from Eaton, he brings in two world wars, shows how old money made way for new, how small towns like Port Jefferson and Gibbsville fell under the control of Wall Street, how education destroyed class distinctions, how politics, trade unionism and transportation completely transformed American society. To avoid a sociological tone, O'Hara presents everything through stories of individual human beings. He emphasizes in particular the importance of marriage in the lives of his characters. He tells stories of the many different solutions people adopt for failed marriages, but also provides instances of truly fulfilled love between men and women. For O'Hara real love was magical and physical. There is no logic to it—it just happens, usually unexpectedly, sometimes inconveniently, but there is never any doubt about its authenticity.

O'Hara was full of enthusiasm about *From the Terrace,* almost from the moment he began to write it in 1957. He had been thinking about it for a year and estimated it would take him three more to complete it, although he only required two. He hoped to write without pressure. "I am going to knock off in the summers," he said, "at least I will as much as I can. I'll use the summers for research and reading. It will be a wonderful experience." He worked on it every day, summers included, five hours a day, and he was pleased with the results, confident the book would secure his place in American literature. "I like to write," he said, "but I have never known such pleasure as I have had with this novel; brutally hard work, sure, but work with a pleasure and a purpose, the pleasure or mastery of my characters and of technique." He had charts to control what he called the "literary logistics" of handling over a hundred characters in different times and

places and he was proud of the way he managed chronology and flashbacks, including flashbacks within flashbacks. His own purpose as a novelist kept him going: "Beginning with *A Rage to Live,* I knew I had a grand
scheme, of which the individual works were each a part. My best is *From
the Terrace."*

The book was published on Thanksgiving Day of 1958 with a first
printing of 100,000 copies. O'Hara's enthusiasm for the novel was not
generally shared by the critics, although Charles Poore and John Hutchens
praised it in the New York press and Robert Kirsch of the *Los Angeles Times*
thought so well of the book he said O'Hara deserved the Nobel Prize. The
title of the review in the *New York Times Book Review*—"Something Went
Seriously Wrong"—typified the reaction of a number of critics who de-
plored the length of the book, claiming it was full of lifeless detail and
bloated with pretentious documentation. "We are deluged, suffocated,
drowned in facts, facts, facts," said Alfred Kazin. Others claimed the book
lacked point of view. "Everything is there save what matters," said Saul
Maloff, citing the absence of "controlling intelligence" and "the moral
imagination, the great novelist's unerring feeling for the dramatic center
and the crucial revelation of that which the social historian does not see
or sense; the sense of the depths beneath the teeming, glittering surface."

These serious objections became the basis on which readers were later
divided, many dismissing *From the Terrace* and the other long novels, insist-
ing that O'Hara's short stories and *Appointment in Samarra* were the only
works worth reading. Some critics even stated that he had sold out and was
pandering to the lowest levels of popular taste. O'Hara's own claims for
this novel make it necessary to judge it in terms of some of the more highly
praised books of his own time and of preceding decades that attempted to
combine public and private life in a single work. But as soon as comparison
is made—with such works of his contemporaries as Cozzens' *By Love Possessed,* Katharine Anne Porter's *Ship of Fools,* Vladimir Nabokov's *Lolita,*
Robert Penn Warren's *All the King's Men,* or with older books like Steinbeck's *Grapes of Wrath,* Hemingway's *For Whom the Bell Tolls,* or even Ford's
Parade's End and Conrad's *Nostromo*—it becomes evident that each author's
intention is so different from the others' that any attempt at ranking
becomes preposterous.

The comparison is nevertheless useful in revealing a great disadvantage in *From the Terrace,* which is the shallowness of the central character,
Alfred Eaton. In the opening pages of the novel, O'Hara makes it plain that
"Alfred Eaton is and was a simple man," and says that it would be false
to make this "attractive, handsome man more complicated than he is." By
characterizing him in this way, O'Hara prevents him from having the
depths of motivation and feeling that make for a great character in fiction.
The sacrifice was made to be honest, but it puts a strain on the book. What
is astonishing, given this handicap, is that the book is continuously inter-

esting. It contains a great deal of information, much of it becoming more absorbing with the passage of time. Yet this information never becomes unpalatable: it is always made subsidiary to the narrative and related to one of the characters. This takes skillful writing. "Because I write plain, but without the jerkiness of Hemingway-plain," said O'Hara, "most of what I do of a technical nature is not noticeable." O'Hara achieves most of his effects by good organization. Information is imparted in small doses so it never becomes obtrusive, and the narrative pace is interrupted by leaps forward and backwards which introduce surprise and also a greater understanding of what is going on. O'Hara believed that attending concerts by the Philadelphia Orchestra helped him solve some of his structural problems. "I love music. But it is not as a sensual experience that symphonies have influenced me in this novel; it is hour after hour of sitting there and listening to Brahms while my intellect contemplates the simplicities and intricacies of symphonic construction."

As lesser themes in music have to be as well written as major ones, so the success of *From the Terrace* depends largely on O'Hara's handling of secondary characters. Whether they are Eaton's fellow students or fellow businessmen, labor leaders or Wall Street brokers, they are alive and real in their own terms. O'Hara's success in characterization probably came from years of writing short stories where he learned how to be deft in presenting all sorts of people. It is a valuable attribute for a writer who wants to give a sense of the complexity of society without favoring one kind of person or set of ideas. O'Hara's characters are all *in* society: they have jobs, families, debts, whole histories that limit them and tie them down. His fictional world may lack the tension that arises from clearly opposed forces, but he is dealing with a grown-up world where people are compromised; their responsibilities bind them as well as form them.

O'Hara is at his best when dealing with the relationship between men and women. He makes no distinction between the way he forms his male and female characters and acknowledges that both have sexual urges and ambitions. O'Hara's Roman Catholicism and Jansenist training has been cited to explain why some of O'Hara's women are vicious bitches, impure vessels who seduce men and destroy them. Some women do that, and for that reason they appear in O'Hara's books, but there are others who are warm and loving.

Some readers and critics thought that O'Hara had a peculiar view of human behavior. A cartoonist depicted a New York matron rejecting a proffered O'Hara novel in a bookshop with the words, "No thank you. I don't go into O'Hara's world and he doesn't come into mine." Whether his view is just or not, it is not merely the product of journalistic reporting; it comes from a vision of humanity that is implicit in all his later work. His early disappointments gave him a low opinion of people and made him nihilistic; at the same time he had a tremendous energy and abundance.

He was sentimental, but never romantic in the manner of Scott Fitzgerald
or Raymond Chandler, and despite efforts to the contrary, he was not an
idealist. Not having read the great Russian, French and English novelists,
he was deprived of the solace and understanding they might have given
him. On the other hand, he read five newspapers a day and was drunk with
the varieties of human experience. His vision of human life was to deepen
in his last important book, *The Lockwood Concern,* but at the time of *From the
Terrace* he seems to have settled for what might be called conditional
stoicism or cautious existentialism. Like Trollope he was too busy with
particulars to make generalizations, but in his writings he expressed what
he had learned from his own life. There was no order in life; so, conversely,
there was no planned disorder. Towards the end of *From the Terrace,* Alfred
Eaton, at loose ends in his retirement from the navy, says, "I wish I had
something to do." O'Hara never had that problem.

11. PRINCETON SQUIRE

With the publication of *From the Terrace,* O'Hara joined that small number of American writers who have managed to be both serious and rich. Earlier he had had moments of affluence, but now he was earning so much he didn't know what to do with it all. The hard-cover earnings of *From the Terrace* brought in $50,000 and, since success begets success, he was able to sell the paperback rights for the book for $100,000. He earned an additional $50,000 for *Ten North Frederick* and smaller amounts for earlier books that were being republished at the same time. O'Hara had no agent except in Hollywood and England. He handled his American literary negotiations directly with Random House, and they acted as agent on his behalf with translations and subsidiary sales. He might have earned more with the help of a literary agent, but he was a tough negotiator and believed he could do as well on his own and also save the agent's fee. The new money he earned did not change his way of living, although it later changed his attitudes. He was too old to go on a splurge as he might have done had he earned the money at the age of twenty-five. He was already living comfortably; since the new money was more than he needed, he arranged to have Random House send him quarterly royalty payments of $20,000 or $25,000 and allowed the rest to accumulate in his account in order to avoid paying excess taxes.

O'Hara was also beginning to earn money from the sale of his novels to Hollywood. These sales in turn led to new paperback editions of his other books. Before 1957, only two of his novels had been filmed. These were television adaptations made by Robert Montgomery in 1952 and 1953 of *Appointment in Samarra* and *The Farmers Hotel.* O'Hara was deeply moved by the work Montgomery and Herbert Bayard Swope, Jr., did in adapting *Appointment in Samarra,* and tentatively offered it to them for a full-scale Hollywood production, but then withdrew permission, preferring to bide his time. O'Hara had also planned to work with Belle's sister's husband, H. C. Potter, on a film version of *The Farmers Hotel,* but they disagreed, so the idea was dropped.

The first feature movie to be made from his work was Columbia Pictures' version of *Pal Joey,* which was released in 1957. For O'Hara, who was experienced in Hollywood, it was strange to have nothing to do with the screenplay. He was not consulted on the toning down of the book or the switching of the locale from Chicago to San Francisco. He said he approved of Frank Sinatra as the lead since Joey was a singer and not a dancer like Gene Kelly, but he let slip a comment during the making of the film that he "understood Gene Kelly's voice was going to be dubbed in for Frankie's." The remark did not endear him to the film company so he was never asked to see the film. Later, when asked what he thought of Sinatra's performance, he replied, "I didn't have to see Sinatra. I invented him."

He was much more involved in the next film, *Ten North Frederick,* which was bought by his friends at Twentieth Century-Fox, Buddy Adler and David Brown. The rights were sold for $300,000. He was pleased when Spencer Tracy was selected to play Joseph Chapin and he urged Brown to make sure to get a director who was over forty years old. "It is not necessary to be old to write well about the old, any more than it is necessary to be a woman to write well about women. But in this case there will be moments in every sequence that could only be helped by a middle-aged man's understanding. And I don't only mean sympathetic understanding." He was glad that Philip Dunne was asked both to direct and write the script, because Dunne's Eastern background was helpful for an understanding of the novel. He was also an experienced screenwriter, and as the son of Finley Peter Dunne, author of the Mr. Dooley books, he had literary intelligence. Spencer Tracy decided to withdraw from the film, but his place was taken by Gary Cooper, while yet another friend, Geraldine Fitzgerald, was offered the role of Edith Chapin. O'Hara was upset because he thought she was too beautiful to play so ugly and unattractive a woman. He believed there was a correlation between inner and outer ugliness and said that children were right when they shrank away from ugly people.

The film received respectful reviews and won first prize at a film festival in Locarno. Acknowledging that he was not known "as a gusher,"

O'Hara surprised everybody by saying, "I have seen *Ten North Frederick* and I am more than pleased with it." His only objection was that the setting was changed from Pennsylvania to an anonymous piece of America. He also disliked the characterization of the Italian-American Bongiorno; he was not authentic in dress or speech and therefore much was lost in the portrayal of his relationship with Chapin's daughter.

With the success of his books, O'Hara was becoming, in David Brown's words, "the hottest moving picture writer today," so for his next venture he turned to a New York lawyer, Ben O'Sullivan, to handle the financial negotiations. O'Sullivan set up separate corporations for each of the films he was handling and assured O'Hara an advance and a share of the profits of each film. The first was *Butterfield 8,* which was bought by MGM and earned O'Hara $150,000. Pandro Berman produced the film and the leads were played by Elizabeth Taylor, Laurence Harvey and Eddie Fisher. The period was updated and the ending, in *Variety's* word, was "spectacularized." Elizabeth Taylor created a flurry by saying that the character she was being asked to play was "almost a prostitute and the script is the most pornographic I've ever read." Although not involved in the film, O'Hara could not bear to keep silent; he observed in print that he understood Elizabeth Taylor was eager to play the role of Cleopatra and noted that although she was still in her twenties, she had already had three husbands.

From the Terrace was bought by Twentieth Century-Fox for $100,000 and a profit-sharing arrangement. The original plan was to use the material from the novel in a series, but in the end only one film was made. Ernest Lehman was selected to write the screenplay and he visited O'Hara in Princeton to discuss it. They talked for about three hours about everything except *From the Terrace.* It was evident to Lehman that O'Hara was not really interested in the movie version. Mark Robson was chosen as producer and director and he soon made O'Hara furious by the comments he made about the film. "This guy placed a lot of bedroom wisecracks with Lyons and others such," complained O'Hara, "and now he claims to have put 'values' in the movie that the novel did not have. God help anything that is loaded with his values." Not surprisingly, O'Hara disliked what little he saw of the film, a half-hour sequence only. While he approved of Joanne Woodward who played the role of Alfred Eaton's wife, he thought that Paul Newman was miscast as Eaton. He also objected to updating the film. "It is a shame to see so much money wasted when the same money could have been used to do a picture with sense and taste," he said. "But money is no substitute for sense or taste or talent. That's a truism. But to develop the thought a little more: a man like Robson thinks he can substitute money for those other items, and that's where the danger lies. He ducks the basic problems, takes the easy way, and right away the cheapness shows through. It becomes obvious that he is out to make a money-maker, when the property has already been proved a moneymaker in the other, the novel, form. *They will not learn."* O'Hara's opinion was shared by the critics who thought the film was turgid and soggy, comparing it to *Peyton Place,* a vulgar piece of work that had some of the same ingredients. All this made little difference to O'Hara, who liked the money. He was delighted one night, after having dinner at "21," when his Hollywood agent H. N. Swanson took him on a stroll over to Broadway and showed him a theater marquee that read JOHN O'HARA'S FROM THE TERRACE in big letters.

The film that might have been the greatest success of all has never been made, although it has often been under option. When *Appointment in Samarra* was first published, it was offered to Hollywood, but it was considered too outspoken for the 1930s. The suicide ending would have been opposed by the Legion of Decency and by the Hays and Johnston offices that administered the studio's own production code. Henry Fonda wanted to play Julian English and cooperated with two efforts to produce the film, but the scripts offered contained changes of the original text that he found unacceptable. O'Hara knew the potential of the film, but because the book had a special following, he wanted to protect it. He refused to consider offering it to Twentieth Century-Fox so long as that studio was under the same management that made *From the Terrace.* "I can say in all modesty," he observed, "that if it weren't done right as a film, I wouldn't like it and a lot of people wouldn't like me." One of the things he insisted on was that the ending remain intact. "There is no other ending for this story," he wrote. "There is not even another form of suicide, such as poison or shooting. This man has to die by motor car, by Cadillac motor car. It is equally true that this whole thing must take place in 1930. I would sooner update *Wuthering Heights* than *Appointment in Samarra.* Both are firmly fixed in their periods." He therefore put a price of a million dollars on this film which, as he said, "keeps out the grocery clerks."

Not all of O'Hara's new money went into the bank. With no need to deny himself, he began buying the things that represented the good life. He bought the country gentleman clothes he considered appropriate to his new address—English caps, hacking jackets in bold patterns, shoes from Peal's of London. He owned a Jaguar which along with his MG and station wagon gave him a fleet of three cars. Like Steinbeck, he had no puritan inhibitions about treating himself to what he wanted. His pleasure in things was a sign of his appetite for life. He was also rewarding himself in an unabashedly American fashion. He had never been hypocritical about his motives for writing and he expected to be as well paid for his work as his professional friends were for theirs. While courting Sister, he had openly asserted that he had a hunch that with her he was "going to be rich and famous." Moreover, he intended with her "to keep richness and fame in their proper perspective, which means that we use them to make a good life together." Having always wanted to live well, he found he could now do so without worrying, and with gusto.

His zest for acquisitions extended to clubs. In his young days in Pottsville where he tried to form a private fraternity among his friends, O'Hara put great emphasis on clubs. They represented friendship and loyalty, but also signified achievement and success. While only twenty-four, he began having fantasies about "the suave, versatile, slightly pedantic, interestingly snobbish Prominent Clubman." Among people he admired, clubs were an accepted thing; they also represented levels of attainment. Never having achieved the status that came automatically through membership in a good college club or fraternity, he wanted to make up for it by joining adult clubs in New York and elsewhere. It was his way of overcoming the social disadvantage of having come from an undistinguished small town in Pennsylvania. Now that he could afford the initiation fees and membership dues, he eagerly added to the list of clubs he had joined by the mid-1950s.

In New York, his main club had been the Players, but in 1951 he joined the Metropolitan instead. He also belonged to the Leash, a club for dog owners, the National Press Club in Washington, the Nassau Club in Princeton and the Field Club in Quogue. He wanted to join the Coffee House Club in New York, but was blackballed the first time he was put up for it. Finding out the name of the villain, O'Hara phoned him up. The man was out, but O'Hara identified himself to the servant answering the phone and told him to deliver this message: "I know what you did." Later on, he was elected. These were all adequate clubs, but for O'Hara they did not quite represent the top drawer. He started asking friends to put him up for other clubs as well. His first choice was the Racquet & Tennis Club. In 1942 he coyly asked James Forrestal to write on behalf of his membership in "that lively mausoleum on the west side of Park Avenue somewhere in the Fifties." But he was never elected. Apart from any animosity other members may have felt towards him, some were alarmed by O'Hara's tendency to write about club life in his books; this was not what a gentleman did. Indeed, some clubs have specific rules forbidding members to mention their clubs in print. Although he failed to become a member of the Racquet Club, O'Hara developed the habit of ordering playing cards bearing the club's insignia through a friend who was a member. For many years he used them without shame or explanation while playing bridge at home.

Clubs were important to O'Hara for his writing, and he learned a great deal about them. He would know all about a club's history and tradition and would sometimes compare its social standing to that of other clubs. Most members found it unpleasant and disconcerting to be reminded of these things. Because O'Hara made them uncomfortable, they presumed he was not a gentleman. O'Hara was aware of this. When he wrote about the Philadelphia Club in his column for *Colliers* he said he had as much chance of being elected to that club as becoming a member of the College of Cardinals, noting, "And can't I hear some of the members, on reading this, saying: 'Who in blazes brought that feller in?' "

Next to the Racquet Club, O'Hara was most keen to join the Century Association in New York, a club whose members are supposed to be involved in the arts. He was proposed for membership by Philip Barry in the 1940s, but was not elected; in 1957 he became a member, thanks to the efforts of some of his Princeton friends. Even Brendan Gill, who happened to be a member of the admissions committee at the time, urged his election, saying "that a good club was one in which enemies as well as friends could find themselves at home." At his first dinner after being taken into the Century, O'Hara told Rensselaer Lee that he considered he had joined a very distinguished group of men. He was disappointed, however, to learn that the Century had no club tie, an outward sign he enjoyed. "You can always go into a club of which you are a member and wear the tie of some other club. That's real snob."

Almost every year O'Hara added a new club to his list. Edgar Scott arranged for his membership in the Philadelphia Racquet Club. His brother-in-law Tracy Barnes put him up for the Metropolitan Club in Washington, but O'Hara grew impatient with the delay and withdrew his name. O'Hara was so obsessed with the idea of clubs that he would invent one with the slightest excuse. Once when Charles Addams' wife gave Wylie a puppy, O'Hara in thanking her said he wanted to found a Quogue Leash Club and asked her whether she would care to join. Learning that his friend Outerbridge had a club of his own called the Kew-Teddington Observatory Society, O'Hara invented a club which he called the Hessian Relief Society. When he was in London, he went to Gieves to order special ties for his new club and brought them back to America. A harmless indulgence, this club was also slightly pathetic. O'Hara could not think of enough people who would want to join it, so gave out more than one tie to the few who did.

Despite his almost fanatic interest in clubs, O'Hara rarely used the ones he belonged to. He attended occasional dinners at the Century, traveling up with fellow members from Princeton, and would have lunch there once or twice a month. He felt at home and was convivial with other members, including those much younger than he was. Mainly O'Hara enjoyed the feeling of reassurance that membership in clubs gave him; it was evidence that he was approved of and acknowledged by others. At the same time, he was content to be an outsider to some organizations. "To me," he wrote to Edgar Scott, "going to the Philadelphia Club is something like going to one of Robert Oppenheimer's dinner parties (which I am doing next week); I am completely relaxed. They know, and I know, that my status is forever that of visitor. I can never be a member of the Institute for Advanced Learning or of the Philadelphia Club, but so long as *they* know that there is no one at the Institute or the P.C. who could write *From the Terrace,* I am not compelled to assert myself, and that, I suspect, is what makes for messiness."

O'Hara's new affluence also led him to travel. In September of 1959 he and Sister decided to go abroad. The trip was a conscious effort to get over his new habit of "not participating in life." Sister was always eager to get away from Princeton even though O'Hara was content to stay home and write, and she flew ahead to Germany to see her daughter Joan and her son-in-law, Peter Gates, who was stationed there in the army. Shortly afterwards, O'Hara sailed on the *Queen Mary* from New York to Southampton. He hadn't looked forward to the trip but he knew he was stale and needed a new perspective. "It is a dangerous thing for a writer to do," he wrote to Wylie, "to bury himself in his work and never stir away from it. I know that is true because I will confess to you that I am *afraid* to be alone in England, etc. I would not make this trip if I were not going to meet Sister. Now that is the danger of sitting here and burying myself in my work."

No one saw him off when he sailed from New York, but O'Hara was well supplied with books sent by friends. When he went to book a deck chair the steward recognized him and offered him a place "on the terrace." He spent his time reading and pottering about and he wrote a short story. There were a couple of "sexpots in their twenties" on board, but he found the social life a strain because it was "the first time I've been on a ship and on the wagon at the same time." One of the sexpots flirted with him, however, and that cheered him up. "I admit quite frankly that I am pleased when it happens to me," he wrote. "At 54 you better be pleased!" He was also proud of winning fifty dollars in the ship's pool and enjoyed the attentive service for which the Cunard Line was then famous.

From the boat train he went straight to the Savoy in London. He had some business appointments and then Sister arrived from Germany. They spent their time shopping, seeing plays and visiting old friends such as John Hayward. They were in London during a national election and O'Hara was pleased by Macmillan's victory because he thought the Conservatives were more pro-American than the Labour party. After a few days they took the *Queen of Scots,* the best daytime train to Scotland, from King's Cross to Edinburgh. O'Hara enjoyed the plush armchairs, the wooden table between them on which lunch was served and the old-fashioned paneling of the railway car. From Scotland they went to Dublin, where they stayed at the Shelbourne in St. Stephen's Green. It was O'Hara's first trip to Ireland, and the way was prepared for him by Geraldine Fitzgerald, who gave the O'Haras a dinner party and also introduced them to several Irish and Anglo-Irish friends of hers. O'Hara was impressed by their estates and titles, but was touched by their impermanence:

"They were a perfect picture of the fading aristocracy, with the good and the bad, the sad and the pleasant in proper mixture. Their kind is dying out, but what is to take its place?"

The O'Haras stayed a week, time enough to get an idea of the Irish character. Comparing it to Scotland, he thought Ireland was "more a country of individuals. The grooms at the Aly Khan's farm; the men driving the big wagons of the Guinness brewery; the very poor in the Dublin slums —they all, and people in their class, give the impression that they are not really working steady, but are only helping out temporarily. They wear tweed caps at a jaunty angle, cigarettes dangle from their lips, and they gaze about as if they were more concerned with other things than with this silly task, whatever it is. The Scots are not that way, and neither are the English—which may explain why so many Irish families stay poor for generation after generation."

The O'Haras returned to London for another week before sailing for home on the *Queen Elizabeth*. They had lunch with Mrs. John Hay Whitney at the ambassadorial residence in Regents Park and had a good time, but O'Hara was convinced that he "would not really be happy anywhere but in the U.S.A. There are small and large differences between life abroad and at home that would keep me from being happy elsewhere. There are many things about life in Britain and Ireland (and Bermuda and Canada) that I like, but I can borrow some of them, and I can really do without the rest. I always have."

The next year, the O'Haras repeated their trip on the *Queen Mary*. O'Hara was happy to be recognized by the headwaiter. This time they stayed at Claridge's and O'Hara was down with a cold. Nevertheless, he was able to get some business done with his agent, Graham Watson, and with Denis Cohen, chairman of the Cresset Press, which had become O'Hara's publisher after Faber and Faber refused to publish *A Rage to Live*. At one party he was approached by an eccentric old lady who had been Gorky's secretary and H. G. Wells's mistress, and who turned out to be an O'Hara fan. "She tawld me," O'Hara reported, "dat I had enreeched her life with my nowels and dat I was one of de truly great." For their last night in London they were invited to a party attended by a number of literary critics, where O'Hara revealed his dislike of critics so forcefully that some of the guests thought he had a persecution complex.

From London they flew to Paris for a week, staying at the Prince de Galles off the Champs Élysées and near the Place de l'Étoile. O'Hara's cold struck him again and he was forced to stay in his room for a few days. Twenty-two years had passed since his previous visit to Paris, and O'Hara was nostalgic. But things had changed, as he wrote to his daughter: "There is a fabulous man who is the head guy at the Ritz Bar. We used to be good friends and I even mentioned him in a book. He knew everybody, did all sorts of favors; lent money, kept secrets, etc. He was one of the very first people I wanted to see." O'Hara went to the Ritz to renew his acquaintance, "but I did not recognize George, and George did not recognize me. Only 22 years. How could *he* have changed that much? What has happened to his memory? Poor George."

The trip was not a success. O'Hara was restless and ill at ease. He hesitated to go out to restaurants because he did not drink. He didn't want to be thought of as a stupid American tourist who didn't know how to order wine, so he and Sister had most of their meals at the hotel. In his letters, he showed he was homesick. "Right now I have no desire to go abroad again at all," he said. He could hardly wait to get home. For the next few years he made no transatlantic trips, although in the summer of 1961 Wylie and Sister went abroad together and Wylie visited Copenhagen alone in 1962. These trips made O'Hara regret not having traveled much as a young man. "I would be a better writer for it," he admitted.

Wylie was now a student at St. Timothy's School in Maryland, where her mother had gone, and O'Hara wrote her often. Once he quoted the line from *Hamlet,* "This above all: to thine own self be true," as his advice to her, but otherwise, his tone was not heavy. He tried to imagine what it was like to be a young girl and gave her the love and support she needed. "Every once in a while—not too often but occasionally—you should stop and say to yourself: 'These are my years. These are the years in which I am making my future.' These years belong to you, the years before you fall in love, get married, have children and a home of your own. Time passes all too quickly, and when love and marriage and children come into your life, you will welcome them all. But these few years are your own. Treasure them." O'Hara was never censorious; usually he was funny as well as encouraging "So now you be a good girl, understand? And you work like hell, do you hear? And you just show those teachers that Wylie Delaney O'Hara is the smartest and nicest girl at St. Timothy's, and don't make a liar out of her father." Sometimes, wanting her news, he would adopt her lingo: "So shoot us the information, chum. Like soon, huh?" In helping Wylie, he told her about his own troubles. "It embarrasses me to have to report that *I* flunked a test today," he wrote about a rejection when he learned that she had failed history at school. But O'Hara did not cover up reality: when a friend of Wylie's died at school, he did not try to dismiss her grief: "Sadness is a part of growing up, of maturing, of learning to live," he wrote. Wylie never had any doubts about his affection for her: "I was born loving you," he said at the end of one letter. He was proud of her being elected president of her class at St. Timothy's. A year or so after she graduated, Sister and O'Hara gave Wylie a party at "21" instead of the usual coming-out dance that so many of her friends were given at a club or hotel. O'Hara had often taken Wylie there during school vacations before going to an afternoon movie or matinée, so "21" was special to them both and the most appropriate place for an O'Hara family party.

Travel and social life never interrupted O'Hara's work for long. Two years after *From the Terrace* was published, Random House brought out his next novel, *Ourselves to Know.* With its title drawn from the line, "And all our Knowledge is, ourselves to know," from Pope's *An Essay on Man,* it was a change from the panoramic scale and intent of *From the Terrace.* Instead of being an exposition of the public life of an extrovert, it is a psychological study of an introspective intellectual who wants to be a painter. After spending some time in Europe where he learns he lacks a true artistic gift, Robert Millhouser returns to the small Pennsylvania town where he grew up, takes charge of the family property and is elected a director of the bank. He lives a generally passive existence until he meets and marries Hedda Steele, who is thirty years younger than he is. They are strongly attracted to each other despite the age difference, and for the first time in his life Robert feels real passion. She is headstrong and impetuous, he patient and cautious, and their marriage might have succeeded had she not been unfaithful and taken a lover. The same passionate conviction that led him to love Hedda now compels him to kill her. The rest of the novel deals with his imprisonment, release and psychological evolution.

O'Hara was an indiscriminate reader, but what he read often influenced his work. At the time he was working on *Ourselves to Know,* he read *Ethan Frome* by Edith Wharton, *The Education of Henry Adams,* and Rosamond Lehmann's *Dusty Answer* and went to a production of Ibsen's *A Doll's House.* Known mainly as a social historian, O'Hara saw a parallel between his own work and that of Edith Wharton who, he noted, "wrote with understanding and precision about people in New York society, and then with the same understanding and precision created Ethan Frome." After *From the Terrace,* O'Hara wanted to write a psychological novel dealing with the same kind of violence that erupts in Edith Wharton's novel. He may also have been thinking of *Ethan Frome* when he created the character of Millhouser's mother who, like Frome's wife, controls much of his life. Placing *Ourselves to Know* back as far as the Civil War, O'Hara may have found Henry Adams' autobiography useful in defining his own feelings about knowledge and power. The economic turmoil that led to the anthracite strike of 1902 and the money panic of 1907 are the historical events in the novel that force the question of human responsibility into the open. When Millhouser acts to help his fellow citizens in their need, he gains confidence in many ways and overcomes his personal shyness and hesitancy. O'Hara also borrowed from family history in creating Millhouser.

His grandfather in Lykens, on which the fictional Lyons of *Ourselves to Know* is based, took a chance similar to Millhouser's. In 1902, "He supported the miners who were fighting for recognition of their union. He believed in capitalism, but he also believed in the miners' right to organize, and he gave evidence of his belief by allowing credit to the miners while they were out of work. It turned out to be good business: the miners were grateful. But he took the big chance. If the miners had lost, he would have lost, and he had the most to lose." Millhouser's decisiveness had less fortunate results. It gave him the courage to marry the eighteen-year-old girl Hedda, but it also made it impossible for him to deal with her as she really was—a woman whose life was dedicated to herself and especially her own sexual fulfillment. She is the embodiment of Venus who holds men in thrall, but she is also, as O'Hara said of Nora in *A Doll's House,* "a woman who would not grow up, and who thereby got herself and others into trouble."

Because the book is a psychological novel, O'Hara concentrates on the significance of the actions, on what meaning a life like Robert's may have. This concern emerges especially when Robert is in prison for the murder he has committed. Robert has by now come to believe that he is without feelings. His domineering mother had made him passive and dry, and he has killed Hedda, the source of the only true feelings he ever had. Now he feels completely empty, neither having remorse nor fearing death. He quotes Milton's phrase, "where no hope is left, is left no fear."

The idea of hope is central in O'Hara, as it was in the work of Alexander Pope. From Julian English onwards, O'Hara's characters find themselves in despair, but with Robert Millhouser, it is no longer merely a condition, it is an issue. In prison, Robert has a meeting with an old friend, a libertine now become a Roman Catholic monk, who tells Robert that in theological terms despair is a sin because it is the same as denying the existence of God. Robert refuses his friend's help and rejects Christian belief, but as the friend leaves, Robert begins to weep. This reveals that he still has feelings and therefore hope as well. Robert never commits the vulgarity of positive thinking, but at the end when he is asked about his deepest beliefs, he quotes lines from George Meredith's "Modern Love" which he has read in Rosamond Lehmann's novel *Dusty Answer:* "Ah, what a dusty answer gets the soul/When hot for certainties in this our life."

This was as explicit as O'Hara had ever been about values in his fiction. His willingness to go this far may have come from the philosophical attitudes he was developing while watching his daughter grow up. Now fifty-five, he was seeing relationships between one life and another, one story and another. In *The Lockwood Concern,* he would inquire further, if less explicitly, into the relationship between power and love; in *Ourselves to Know* he deals with the more vivid forces of passion and energy. He may have placed the novel further in the past than usual in order to justify the expression of opinion. It is an effective novel, but would have been more so had it been as short as *Ethan Frome,* since it has the force of fable. But O'Hara's complex narrative machinery got in the way. In order to justify his sources of information in the novel, O'Hara introduces a narrator who is supposed to be writing a biography of Robert as a university thesis and who is therefore able to quote early documents. As if anticipating objections about conversations that his narrator could not have heard, O'Hara wrote, "I did not exercise my right to omniscience but only my ability to present them without merely stating them. I was acquainted with two men who served in the Mexican War; I go back that far in human contacts, even though I didn't talk to them about that war. I had a dear friend called Bill Irving, who lived in Lykens, Pa., my mother's home town, and who was a Civil War veteran. In spite of the great disparity in our ages, whenever he came to Pottsville for the annual G.A.R. Encampment, he would call me up. And I spent many hours on a bench with him—he smelled very strongly of whiskey and cigars—watching the Lykens people go by and laughing and talking. I loved that old guy, and I loved that little old town, and as I got older it was not hard for me to unpeel the crusts of the decades going back to 1863."

Ourselves to Know sold well, but because it seemed to be a retreat from the contemporary world, it did not receive much critical attention. Admitting that he thought it was "not as good as *From the Terrace*" but "transitional and evolutionary" in nature, O'Hara was nevertheless disappointed by the reviews that ignored or misunderstood his experiments. Because O'Hara insisted on being readable, he disappointed critics who equate experimentation with disordered prose. They probably didn't think he was experimenting at all, but O'Hara took solace in knowing that he was. "The most fascinating thing about writing as a career," he wrote, "is that you never stop learning." Still, he was upset that his work was not taken seriously by the critics. In addition to sympathetic reviews, he thought he deserved to be awarded honorary degrees. He rather obviously placed the idea with Harvard, Yale and Princeton when he gave their libraries typescripts of his books. Yale of course mattered most, and he hoped that through his friend Gilbert Troxell, he might be honored. O'Hara's public reputation as a writer of sexy best sellers discouraged academic acceptance of his work, however, and he was never seriously considered by English departments. O'Hara risked appearing capable of trying to buy a degree and showed dubious taste when he wrote about his misfortunes over honorary degrees in his column for the *Trenton Times-Advertiser*. "There was a time," he wrote, "when I thought I was a shoo-in for at least an honorary master's (Master of Arts, not of foxhounds) at New Haven. I had always spoken well of the place and of most of its alumni. When the library asked me for some manuscripts for its American collection, I forked over gladly." He then went on to speak of his friendship with the university president, Whitney Griswold, whose wife was Margaretta Archbald's cousin. "Well the years came and went," he continued, "and every June I would laugh at the not quite screamingly funny citations that go with honorary degrees, but I must admit there was a certain bitterness in my laughter; just a touch of frustration and envy, perhaps. I am, I think, all boy, and yet I began to understand how a town girl feels: I was all right to play around with during the school year, but at Commencement the Yale Fellows always had a date with Thurber." O'Hara with universities was the same as O'Hara with clubs: he didn't know how to be a diffident gentleman. The price of his honesty was exclusion from what he most desired.

Even as he received more recognition, he grew more bitter about what he failed to achieve. The difference is visible between two lectures he gave at Rider College, a small institution in Trenton, New Jersey, in 1959, and the final talk he gave there in 1961. He was invited to give these lectures "as a neighborly gesture" and he spoke to the members of a regular evening class in American literature. O'Hara read his first 1959 lecture forcefully and the session was so successful that the second was held in the library auditorium where more people could be seated. For these two talks, O'Hara discussed the craft of writing—the use of dialogue, the role of significant detail, the importance of character and social history as compared to art. "I must remind you," he said, "that you came here tonight to hear me, and not someone else, so the things I say are me speaking and not Hemingway or Steinbeck or Cozzens or anyone else. Above all they are not the comments of a literary critic of the Marxist persuasion or of organized religion, or of the Columbia boys or the Kenyon crowd." He concluded his second lecture with a few words in praise of his profession: "It is a pleasure to write a good novel, if you are writing it for yourself as an artist. It is hard work, but hard work is a pleasure if you are your own boss, and sometimes when you are not your own boss but are doing what you like to do. When I read or hear of an author saying that he hates to write, I want to say, 'Well, why do it?' "

The third lecture, two years later, reveals a considerable change in O'Hara. The talk is self-centered and lacking in humor or charm. Much of his time was devoted to attacks on hostile critics, even a reviewer from the local paper in Trenton. There are useful comments, but they are buried beneath aggressive observations about his own worth and his contribution to American literature. The tone of this talk suggests a growing alienation from the literary world that was rejecting him. In accepting an invitation from Rider, following his failure to win honorary degrees from Harvard, Yale or Princeton, he showed that he was willing to resort to local company where he was appreciated.

O'Hara resigned from the National Institute of Arts and Letters in 1961. "I am only too eager to tell you about my resignation from the Institute," he told James Gould Cozzens after the event. "When at long last I was elected, I decided that I would wait three years and if at the end of that time I was not promoted to the Academy, I would resign from the basement. There were 29 members of the Institute, elected prior to or at the time of my election, who in my opinion did not belong there *at all.* There were five or six in the Academy who I did not think had accomplished as much as I had. Well, I forgot to resign, but then along came that ballot for the Gold Medal, or the Howells Medal, with Faulkner, Steinbeck, K. A. Porter and I think it was Kay Boyle as the fourth. Steinbeck and Faulkner were fairly obvious nominees, but the other two were preposterous. So I quit." O'Hara explained that he did not think his act was "mere petulance or peevishness" but if he stayed in the Institute he would inevitably be party to decisions, such as the nominations, he did not believe in. There was also a personal reason: "So long as I remained a member of the Institute, I would continue to be subject to the kind of snub that has sickened me since 1934," he wrote. "If I stayed in the Institute, I had only myself to blame for the slaps that would follow. So I got out." O'Hara had told Robert Oppenheimer that although he had not received many honors, he considered "membership in the Institute the only first-rate one I've had." It was not easy for him to resign, but he resisted the appeals of Glenway Wescott, the Institute's president, and of Malcolm Cowley, who tried to make him change his mind.

O'Hara was deeply affected by the death of Hemingway that same year. He was sitting with Wylie in the living room when the news was broadcast, and after fetching a photograph showing the two of them together, he sat down and wept. Earlier, when he heard that Hemingway was ill at the Mayo Clinic, O'Hara had sent him a telegram: "Whatever it is you can lick it. Good luck." The two men hardly ever saw each other— Hemingway was rarely in New York and their lives were unlike—but O'Hara was depressed by Hemingway's suicide because, as he told Wylie, "I understand it so well." He knew that Hemingway realized that his most recent work was not up to his best. *The Old Man and the Sea* was a minor work of art, but no more, and it was a *safe* work of art. It was lavishly overpraised and unreasonably overdefended by Hemingway himself, and he knew that if that was all he had to show for so many years of being respected and applauded, he was cheating, capitalizing on his legend, and he drove himself crazy with his fear of work." O'Hara understood Hemingway's life because he had also been tempted to drift. He had noted a deterioration in Hemingway and was distressed by his "petulant arrogance" and his allowing himself to be familiar with his inferiors. "He likes to get a favorable mention in Leonard Lyons' column, which is cheapness at its cheapest, and extremely costly to a man who is willing to settle for it. He comes to New York, makes an ass of himself with Earl Wilson and Toots Shor and then hurries away to what?"

Hemingway had everything O'Hara yearned for, including the Nobel Prize, but watching his last years, O'Hara could see the terrible destructiveness which he knew so well in himself but had overcome. Hemingway had been writing for *Life* a series on the two famous Spanish bullfighters, Luís Miguel Dominguín and Antonio Ordoñez. O'Hara was horrified to see Hemingway, "our ranking artist concerned with a disgusting spectacle, adopting a son-hero and wishing him dead in conflict with a former son-hero, Dominguin, whom he also wishes dead. He wants to see them die, to be there when they die, and I got the feeling he particularly wanted Dominguin to die because Dominguin had not been as easy to adopt as Ordonez. Hemingway is *afraid* to lose Dominguin in life, and rather than lose him in life he wishes him dead. The conflict between the two bullfighters, as represented by Hemingway, actually gets us away from the bull ring and could just as well have been a fight with knives between two son-heroes. It is a terrible thing to get old that way, as Hemingway has done; to feel so strongly about two young men that you want them to kill each other, to play the one you like less against the one you like more—Ordonez against Dominguin. And all the while there is this cheap, vulgar thing I spoke of: the heartiness, the rough play, the feats of strength, the explicit hint of sex orgies, the boy-did-we-raise-hell stuff, did-we-give-it-to-that-cunt, that reminds me of John Ford and John Wayne and Ward Bond on location."

Hemingway's death reminded O'Hara of his own struggle to become a mature human being; his mother's illnesses made him realize how far he had drifted from his family. Sister had tried to bring O'Hara closer to his brothers and sisters and to some degree succeeded. Of his brothers, he was fondest of Tom, who was a political reporter for the *New York Herald Tribune,* and they frequently chatted on the phone. Tom wanted to write a novel of his own, and was irritated when O'Hara suggested he use another name to avoid comparisons. Except for Mary and his younger sister Kathleen, he kept the rest of the family at arm's length. Once hearing that a brother was in the neighborhood, he went to the Princeton stadium and sat there until he thought he could go home without meeting him. One brother sat in his car outside of O'Hara's house, refusing to come in unless invited to do so. Since O'Hara was in the bathtub waiting for his brother to go away, the invitation never came. In 1961, O'Hara decided to give each of his nineteen nieces and nephews $1000 for their education. Not knowing all their names, he had Mary write a letter explaining the terms of the gift and the fact that because of taxes it was actually costing him $80,000. His relatives were pleased to be remembered, but some were offended by the way he did it. O'Hara was always closest to Mary and his mother, and talked to them frequently. They joked a good deal, for his mother refused to take him as seriously as he wanted to be taken. Once she told him she had just read a good story in *The New Yorker* and O'Hara asked who wrote it. When his mother told him it was by Irwin Shaw, he got up and prepared to leave. "Aren't we even allowed to say good-bye?" she asked.

By the spring of 1962, his mother, then eighty years old, had to be taken to St. Vincent's Hospital in New York for observation. When O'Hara visited her, he was horrified to find her so ill. He was so afraid she was going to die, he didn't want to go into her room, and when he did so he was speechless. O'Hara was so obsessed by death that the imminent death of someone else reminded him of his own mortality and his conviction that he did not have long to live. After seeing his mother at St. Vincent's he would go home and stay in bed for a whole day. For a while his mother seemed to improve, so he sent her a copy of his latest book. When later on she told him she didn't like it, O'Hara replied that if he wanted a book review he knew where to get one, and that it was just a present. Knowing that she was soon going to die, he objected to what he thought were unnecessary operations. After she finally died of cancer, he wrote of her experience, "Life was fine, death was horrible, it all evened up in the end. The Supreme Ironist at work." The funeral took place in Pottsville in May of 1962. O'Hara and Sister went, spending the night before at the hotel. After the burial service, the relatives gathered at the house of one of O'Hara's brothers. When Sister and O'Hara arrived, one of the family called out, "Oh look! Here comes John O'Hara!"

As he grew older, O'Hara accepted the flux of success and failure more calmly than he had in his violent drinking days. His sensitivity was unimpaired, but he defended himself against disappointment by developing a sense of his own importance. He was also an accomplished grudge bearer. After his rupture with *The New Yorker,* for example, he never lost an opportunity to take a dig at Harold Ross, with whom a rapprochement was impossible. When Random House was planning to bring out his *Selected Short Stories,* O'Hara wrote a preface in which he said, "I cannot pretend that I have not been grievously hurt by the magazine." Referring to the hostile reviews he had received after having long been a contributor, he noted, "The high principles they peddle in 'Notes and Comment' don't even last till the back of the book. Well, damn their eyes." This preface was not used, but O'Hara attacked the magazine in *The New York Times Book Review* for its profile of Hemingway and in one of his columns he said, "I will always go out of my way to irritate *The New Yorker.* " After Ross's death, O'Hara began to discuss with old friends the possibility of his return. Wolcott Gibbs was one of the first to act on his behalf in a letter to Gustave Lobrano, the head fiction editor: "I went down to Princeton last weekend and had lunch with O'Hara. He would really like very much to write for us again, because there is really no other place for his short stories, but his conditions, of course, are grotesque. He wants an apology, from somebody in authority, for Gill's review of his book, and he wants what you might call a punitive payment for the pieces he might have written if we hadn't annoyed him. I asked him how much he thought this would amount to, and he said that, well, in a good year he had made as much as $10,000 from us and so, since he had lost five years, he felt that morally we owed him $50,000. He has a feeling this may be a little excessive, but that it is a figure at which negotiations might start. Nothing was said about the station wagon I think he asked for once, or a private airplane and pilot, but perhaps it just skipped his mind. In any case, I felt that he wanted this intelligence passed on to you, and I do so. You might offer to pay him ten dollars and shoot Gill. Your problem, of course."

With Gibbs's death in 1958 O'Hara lost a champion at the magazine. But by 1960 a number of others, among them Roger Angell, had begun to regret openly that his work was still missing from the magazine. Finally St. Clair McKelway took up his case with vigor, and the new editor, William Shawn, proving receptive to the idea, asked what material O'Hara might have available. At this point O'Hara had no short stories on hand but was preparing a book of novellas, so he offered them. Having no carbon copies, he suggested that someone be sent down to read the novellas at Quogue. Shawn assigned the task to William Maxwell who drove down to Long Island with his wife, to stay the night. O'Hara greeted them warmly and then tactfully withdrew to allow Maxwell time to read. Maxwell chose "Imagine Kissing Pete" and Shawn quickly confirmed the purchase. By paying the generous amount of $10,000, he also succeeded in bypassing O'Hara's earlier demands. The story was scheduled for publication shortly before Random House brought out the book *Sermons and Soda-Water,* in which it was included. Eleven years had passed since his last appearance in the magazine, and O'Hara was immensely pleased to be back. He wrote one or two friends, swearing them to silence, because he was sure his return would be the subject of much literary gossip. "One of the things I like about this whole situation is the anticipation of the bafflement of the critics and the trade press. There will be a great deal of misinformation and guesswork, and I shall contribute to it because I am going to refer all questions to Shawn as editor of *The New Yorker*." His delight was mixed with an exaggerated idea of its importance. "In all modesty," he informed Bennett Cerf, "I regard this as the publishing sensation of the season."

"Imagine Kissing Pete" is one of three linked novellas that attempt to bring the world of *Appointment in Samarra* and *Butterfield 8* up to date. "I am now fifty-five years old," he wrote in his preface, "and I have lived with as well as in the Twentieth Century from its earliest days. The United States in this Century is what I know, and it is my business to write about it to the best of my ability, with the sometimes special knowledge that I have. The Twenties, the Thirties and the Forties are already history, but I cannot be content to leave their story in the hands of the historians and the editors of picture books. I want to record the way people talked and thought and felt, and to do it with complete honesty and variety." His characters, he said in a letter to Cerf, were "men and women who were a bit too young to have been disillusioned by World War One. Everybody can understand a war. But it is not so easy to understand an economic revolution; even the experts continue to be baffled by it; and the people of my time never knew what hit them or why."

The title of the book is drawn from Byron's *Don Juan*—"Let us have wine and women, mirth and laughter, / Sermons and soda-water the day after." In following the young people of the prohibition era into later decades, O'Hara adopts an elegiac tone that comes from having survived. As the narrator, Jimmy Malloy, says, "In middle age I was proud to have lived according to my emotions at the right time, and content to live that way vicariously and at a distance. I had missed almost nothing, escaped very little, and at fifty I had begun to devote my energy and time to the last but big task of putting it all down as well as I knew how." The three novellas are how people make do, how they survive with the increasingly narrow options they are offered. The first story, "The Girl on the Baggage Truck," is about a movie actress who is attracted to a suspicious Gatsby-like character and who becomes terribly disfigured in a car accident with him on the way back to New York from a weekend on Long Island. Unlike *The Great Gatsby*, which ends with the disaster, the novella shows what happens afterwards and how the maimed actress survives in Beverly Hills. The second novella, "Imagine Kissing Pete," is about a Gibbsville couple who are married on the rebound and gradually slide downhill through drink and promiscuity. Skid Row threatens to replace the world of Princeton and the country club. But then, living in a working-class factory town outside of Gibbsville, they begin to communicate for the first time and to patch up their marriage. At forty, they realize that self-hatred made them cheat on each other, and they learn to have feelings for each other. The third story, "We're Friends Again," is about the secret arrangements people make to save their lives in unhappy marriages. The solutions are often awkward and inconvenient, but they allow life to go on and feelings to be expressed. O'Hara asks more questions than he answers, and that is his intention, for at the end of the three novellas, Malloy reveals that he has missed a good deal. "I realized that until then I had not known him at all," he says of his best friend. "It was not a discovery to cause me dismay. What did he know about me? What, really, can any of us know about any of us, and why must we make such a thing of loneliness when it is the final condition of us all? And where would love be without it?"

When he first proposed the book to Cerf, O'Hara said he would like to have the three novellas published in separate volumes and boxed. Cerf approved of the idea and then, as he rarely did, O'Hara made further suggestions about the binding: "I like the rather episcopal idea of a blue or black spine and the yellow, non-episcopal flat sides—an aproned clergyman in tennis shoes." O'Hara knew he was publishing too much and thought that an unusual format would distract readers. He believed that if he had delayed publication of *Ourselves to Know*, it would have had better notices. "Most novelists are such plodders that they take longer to write one novel than I do to write two," he said.

Sermons and Soda-Water was well received, although it was not featured in the literary papers and columns. Certain critics took its publication as an opportunity to state their preference for his shorter works, and O'Hara regarded this as a threat. "Over and over again I came across a frank warning not to write any more long books," he told the students at Rider College. He was outraged and determined to write as he chose; at the same time he knew it would help his sales if long work were paced by shorter. His solution was to publish a book of short stories in between each novel. The renewal of his relationship with *The New Yorker* provoked a flood of new material. Within a week of the magazine's acceptance of "Imagine Kissing Pete" he reported to Maxwell that he had completed ten short stories and a novella. Over the next three years O'Hara published nearly thirty stories in *The New Yorker* and six in the *Saturday Evening Post.* Starting in 1961 with *Assembly,* he also published a volume of short stories every year. In 1962 came *The Cape Cod Lighter* and in 1963 *The Hat on the Bed,* a total of seventy-three stories in all. Even with new encouragement from *The New Yorker,* there were problems. Not all of the stories he submitted were accepted, sometimes because they were too long, and O'Hara's unhappiness over rejections remained unchanged. Still, the money mattered less than it had thirty years before, and with assurance of book publication, he cared less about the magazines. On his occasional trips into New York to have lunch at the Century, he would often stop by at *The New Yorker* office, which was just down the street from the club and, if Maxwell was not there, he would leave a story or two with a note. "One of those stories that are good if you buy them, but not bad if you don't," reads one. "Have a little story," reads another. Sometimes he would bring in a whole briefcase filled with stories and leave them with Maxwell to read and choose from at his leisure.

O'Hara's range of subject matter was as wide as ever. His novels caused him to be thought of as a chronicler of upper-class life in New York and Philadelphia, but other subjects dominate his short fiction. There are stories placed in eastern Pennsylvania, generally in the neighborhood of Gibbsville, that go back to his own experiences as a young man. There are also Hollywood stories and Broadway stories. These not only take in the theater, but include nightclubs and the world of gangsters and organized crime. There is hardly an aspect of American life which O'Hara does not touch on—from prostitution to teenagers, from jazz to boxing, from middle-class suburban matrons to déclassé Hollywood actresses. O'Hara's tireless curiosity about public life ensured him a range that is hardly equaled in American literature.

To some extent, the subject matter determines the theme. The Hollywood stories, for example, derive from the competitiveness and egomania that characterize the movie industry. O'Hara shows how actors, directors and producers become an appendage of the world they live in. Their characters are their ambitions; they become the mask they present to their public. Although O'Hara allows his Hollywood characters to reveal their own shallowness and the tawdriness of their ambitions, he is not satirical as are so many writers on Hollywood. Instead, he is curious and even sympathetic. He does not put his characters in pigeonholes, for he is also interested in what may happen to them next. He described one of his pieces, "Sunday Morning," as a "story of vague discontent; from here on the marriage could go anywhere, but it has reached this stage." Except in death, O'Hara did not believe in closures: there is always a future of some kind.

At the same time, especially in his stories of middle age, O'Hara gives his characters a history. Many of the Pennsylvania stories are exercises in looking back over the past. Often placed in social occasions, like weddings or funerals, they allow former entanglements to be relived or revived. Some are stories of lesser characters from the novels: a novella called "Pat Collins" could have been a subplot in *Appointment in Samarra.* Yet although they start in memory, they are not nostalgic; they confront the present and what the future may bring. In one story O'Hara's narrator Malloy speaks of the young newspaperman he once had been who "sees so much in the first few years that he begins to think he's seen it all. That makes for a very unattractive wise-guy attitude, what I call unearned cynicism." O'Hara's early fiction had this tone, but by the 1960s, he had matured as an artist, and felt that his duty was now to deal with his characters rather than get rid of them. This change came from experiences in his own life, for many of his characters have lives like his own, with broken love affairs, broken marriages, defeats, disappointments, losses, hatreds, even success in the earning of money. Sometimes, their experiences are too much for O'Hara's characters. The Park Avenue matron may have become so accustomed to vacuity that she cannot face reality at all, or the destruction of a friendship will alter the characters of the people involved so they are never the same again. The past closes many doors in the future and the physical decay of old age is a curse without redemption, but some of O'Hara's characters are capable of learning from the disasters that have overtaken them. Here O'Hara's own values become evident. "I hate cruelty and stupidity," he often said, and some of his stories are texts that illustrate his scorn for such examples of selfishness as the father who won't allow his daughter to become a doctor, or the politician who harasses prostitutes only to further his own career. But in the best O'Hara stories there is a sense of wonder and openness that goes beyond the drawing of any moral lesson.

The real point of a short story may be the atmosphere or condition of life that makes the plot possible, rather than the plot itself. O'Hara's best stories establish this atmosphere—whether it is one of boredom or spiritual undernourishment or despair—and it is what affects the reader at the end of the story. Because O'Hara relied on external details and dialogue, he was thought of mainly as a writer who dealt with social rather than spiritual concerns. But as he matured O'Hara evolved a vision that John Steinbeck was one of the first to notice: "In his early work, O'Hara hid behind a tight jaw as sensitive and gentle people are likely to do. A kind of shyness forced toughness on him. But beginning with *A Rage to Live,* he broke through his crust and achieved freedom to say what he wants to. A universal quality began to come through." O'Hara might have expressed this vision by writing in the heightened language of Thomas Wolfe or by faking what Louis Auchincloss calls a "literary doom." Instead, he stuck to the facts of his story and in an unobtrusive language tried to let them speak for themselves. His facts were primarily social—they relate to status or class or power—but O'Hara makes it clear that these are merely the external signs of an inner disquiet. O'Hara dramatizes the human condition in stories that are set in social conflict, but their point usually is not social at all.

When he published *Assembly,* O'Hara wrote exuberantly in the foreword about his joy "in discovering that at fifty-five, and in spite of aches in spine and tendons, I had an apparently inexhaustible urge to express an unlimited supply of short story ideas. No writing has ever come more easily to me, and I say that notwithstanding the fact that I have always been a natural writer." O'Hara had the energy and discipline to turn his ideas into actual stories, but inevitably, they varied in quality. All of them achieve a decent professional level and at the very least are interesting for what they say about American life. O'Hara even succeeds in writing about those who appear to have dominated their experiences. These are the successful ones, sometimes smug, often inarticulate, who seem to have control of their lives. It is astonishing how well O'Hara brings these characters to life without making fools of them.

In all, there are ten or fifteen stories in these three collections that, along with others from earlier volumes, place O'Hara among the most skillful and memorable of American short story writers. There is no direct equation between subject and success, for art is unpredictable and in short stories the elements often come together in mysterious ways—in a story about a Hollywood hairdresser, or one about a young man's love for an older girl in Gibbsville, or another about a woman's suicide on board a transatlantic liner, or in a story about a young car salesman's despair on the very day he has made his greatest success. When the elements fuse, the stories are moving and true and enduring.

More and more O'Hara experienced life vicariously through his writing. Princeton winters followed Quogue summers, and he lived an increasingly conventional life. The relative isolation of the house on Pretty Brook Road also kept social engagements to a minimum. Sister liked giving dinner parties and luncheons for ten or twelve people, but they were formal and gracefully superficial. The guests were worldly people, old friends who would come down from New York, or some of the richer or more prominent citizens of Princeton, including two governors of New Jersey, Richard Hughes and Robert Meynor, whom O'Hara came to know. Sister and O'Hara enjoyed being with celebrities: they liked to associate with other successful people. But except for the politicians, people of this kind did not nourish O'Hara as a writer, and his friendships lacked the vitality of his Hollywood evenings with Schulberg and Odets or his nights in New York with McKelway and Gibbs.

O'Hara's isolation made him increasingly fearful of new acquaintances. Always afraid of being used, he angrily refused to sign copies of his books for someone he knew when he learned that they were being given away as presents. At larger parties, he was somewhat aloof, and he would generally try to find a corner where he could sit and drink coffee. People he knew would come up to him and pause for a chat, but others thought he was trying to hold court like a king. The reason O'Hara preferred to sit was that he was suffering from a series of back ailments that had plagued him since 1959. In that year he had a seizure that was never diagnosed except for finding that it was not a slipped disc. He was supposed to wear a steel brace, but it was so cumbersome he usually wore a pink cloth corset and carried a cane. "So far no bra," he noted in a letter.

Still, there was a lot of fire left in O'Hara during the early 1960s. Invited to a party for the screening of the movie of *Ten North Frederick,* he sat grumpily at a table, alone with Sister. Finally Howard Dietz and his wife arrived and Sister asked them to sit down, which they did. "Thank God you came," whispered Sister to Lucinda Dietz, "He wouldn't let anybody else sit down here!" O'Hara had a definite idea of the impression he made and he rather enjoyed his eccentricities. Just to get out of the house, he would sometimes drive into Princeton with the black gardener, Willard Van Lieuw, who was often covered with mud and dirt from his work. They would go into a shop together and look at ties or shirts. O'Hara, who generally bought his clothes by phone from New York, would sometimes examine a lot of merchandise, and then decide to buy nothing. One annoyed proprietor told O'Hara that the shop could do without his custom. O'Hara continued to go there, however, because he believed he had every right to examine and choose what he liked. He rarely had any money with him so when he wanted to buy something, he would ask Willard to pay. Willard was accustomed to the routine and would have already borrowed money from Thelma Pemberton who in turn was reimbursed by Sister from the stack of $100 bills that O'Hara kept ready in a drawer for emergencies.

O'Hara's visits to the shopping center of Princeton made some people think he enjoyed throwing his weight around. If crossed, he would not hesitate to say what he thought, and he was impatient with bureaucratic and bookkeeping regulations. He would never put on a false smile or pretend to agree to something. He believed that people deserved to have

his frank opinions. He rarely spoke hastily so that when people heard what
he said they knew he meant it. Those who were unused to direct speech
were sometimes hurt, but he thought he was complimenting them by being
honest. He modified his behavior only with those he liked and trusted.
They could get away with anything, and he would never speak harshly to
them.

Underneath the brusque behavior was compassion. Unable to express
his distress at someone else's discomfort, because pain frightened him and
reminded him of his own vulnerability, he would get angry at its cause
instead. His behavior was understandable, but not easily appreciated. With
someone he liked and trusted, he would go out of his way to be considerate. Asked by the Princeton sculptor Joe Brown to sit for a bronze bust,
O'Hara agreed and because he found Brown a warm and sympathetic
person, he climbed without complaint the three flights of stairs that led to
his studio. After a while Sister phoned Brown and asked whether the
sittings might be held elsewhere because it was hard for O'Hara, with his
bad back, to climb so many steps. Sister also asked Brown not to tell
O'Hara that she had telephoned because he disliked having a fuss made
over him.

His insecurity made him constantly wary, but sometimes he could be
spontaneously uninhibited. Once while standing on the platform of the
Trenton railroad station, he looked through the window of the train in
front of him and noticed that "an austere woman" was reading *Sermons and
Soda-Water.* "I knocked on the window," wrote O'Hara, "and she was
understandably confused until I pantomimed 'book' with my hands and
pointed to myself. She got it, got all excited, and spoke to her husband in
the chair adjoining hers. He was delighted, recognized me right away, and
so did a woman who was in the other neighboring chair. Then the people
in the other chairs, overhearing the excitement, all laughed and waved to
me. So I clasped my hands like a prizefighter, and took off my hat and
bowed. I'm sure I'll get a letter from my reader on the other side of the
Pullman windows. It was fun."

Meantime, O'Hara's interest in travel revived. In February of 1962, he
and Sister decided to go to Bermuda. He reported that winters in Princeton
made Sister "stir-crazy," although he claimed to be indifferent to them,
quoting James J. Hill's comment, "I got no use for a man it never snowed
on." The trip was successful enough to justify another one the next year
when they took the Cunard liner *Franconia* for a three-week Caribbean
cruise to eleven ports, some of which he had visited thirty years before on
the *Kungsholm.* The O'Haras returned to Princeton for a week and then
went south to Bermuda again, where they stayed at Cambridge Beaches,
a cottage hotel in the quiet parish of Somerset. Sister enjoyed these excur-
sions as a break from managing a household and she looked forward to
eating in the dining room. But when O'Hara discovered their cottage at

Cambridge Beaches was equipped with a kitchen and pantry, he arranged
to have their meals sent in. The weather was blustery, so O'Hara spent
much of his time writing. He saw enough of the island to make him gloomy
about its future and he told an interviewer that he feared there would be
gambling within five years. He said that Bermuda was "giving up the
things which attracted people 30 or 40 years ago," citing the tawdry goods
in the shops that had replaced English woolens and tweeds.

O'Hara's growing misanthropy led him to ask Edgar Scott to put him
up for the Brook Club in New York. "I am disheartened by the number
of creeps who have been creeping into the Century," he explained. "They
will not get in The Brook, and maybe I won't either, but I had to make the
try." In the end, he was not elected because the members didn't want to
appear to condone what he had written about clubs. O'Hara made up for
his disappointments by buying a Mercedes Benz to go along with his MG,
station wagon and Jaguar. At the annual cocktail parties held at Linebrook
after the Harvard-Princeton or Yale-Princeton football games, no domestic
cars were ever seen in the driveway. O'Hara and his friends preferred the
high quality of expensive English or German cars or the unostentatious
honesty of Fiats and Renaults.

The early 1960s also brought him a certain amount of public attention.
When *The Hat on the Bed* was published, he was named short story writer
of the year by the New Jersey Association of Teachers. He was invited by
the Pennsylvania Historical Society to take part in what was called a
"Conversation with John O'Hara" in which he answered questions put to
him by two professors from the University of Pennsylvania. His friend
Richardson Dilworth also made him an honorary citizen of Philadelphia
at a ceremony at Princeton on his fifty-sixth birthday. This was nearer to
what he liked, for the two previous recipients of the honor were the
presidents of Germany and Ireland. He was even awarded an honorary
degree—not by an important university, but by American International
College in Springfield, Massachusetts. Unfortunately, bad weather prevented him from attending the ceremony so he never actually received the
degree which had to be accepted in person. His greatest public notice came
in 1963 when he was featured on the cover of *Newsweek*. He was photo-
graphed at Princeton and Quogue and interviewed repeatedly for the story
by Richard Boeth. The effort was worth it, for the magazine published an
intelligent and balanced report, the first extensive treatment his life and
work had received in a national magazine. He was fifty-eight and had
published twenty-two books.

The attention was pleasant but the big prize still eluded him. O'Hara
thought that Hemingway's death made him the leading American candidate for the Nobel Prize. He was able to give reasons for his conviction.
"If I live and keep on doing what I am trying to do, I really think I will
get it," he told his daughter. "Why? Because after 1948 I had sense enough

to take a look at my work as a body of work, and to look at my future. It did not happen overnight, but I came to realize that if I was going to leave a real, lasting mark, I could not do it with individual, isolated books. They all had to have a kind of continuity, a theme, a purpose. And so I wrote with a consciousness of the historical-social values that are found in the work of all the important novelists. And if I win it it will be at least partly by default, because the other major American novelists either have no big sense of history or they confuse history-sociology with propaganda."

O'Hara's ambition for the Nobel Prize increasingly consumed him. "I want the Nobel prize, as Joe DiMaggio said in quite another connection, so bad I can taste it. And as long as I live and can be wheeled up to the typewriter, I'll try; by God, I'll try." He knew indirectly from T. S. Eliot that he had been nominated twice for the prize and comparing himself with other likely American candidates—Robert Frost, James Gould Cozzens, Robert Penn Warren and John Steinbeck—he thought he had a good chance. But then in 1962, the prize was awarded to Steinbeck. O'Hara took the news in characteristic fashion, sending Steinbeck a wire that read, "Congratulations. I can think of only one other author I'd rather see get it." He expressed no feelings of jealousy and within days of learning of Steinbeck's good fortune, he acknowledged that "he wrote well and truly of half a decade of his time" and that "when he writes about what he knows about, he is vital and strong." O'Hara also realized that Steinbeck's selection made it unlikely that another American writer would win the prize in the near future. He felt that his motivation for writing had been removed and was resigned to being a "sort of American Somerset Maugham," as he said, "Too old to take up fox hunting, afraid to take up whiskey again, and with no desire to look elsewhere for feminine companionship."

But within two years his ambitions had revived and the competitiveness that gave him the energy to work asserted itself again. "It's no secret that I am *working* to get the Nobel," he informed Bennett Cerf. "I am not making speeches or writing letters or giving interviews, like James T. Farrell and Graham Greene. I am constantly at work, not only quantitatively but also maintaining as high standards as are within my power, and this has been going on for some time." He was aware that his chances were not good, but by now the habit of wanting it was ingrained. Why? "Because it's there, and I am here, without it."

It was never to be. His friends and family gingerly teased him for his vanity. Apart from questions of merit, his failure to win the Nobel Prize was partly due to the lack of enthusiasm his work evoked in the intellectual community, where only Lionel Trilling defended him. His financial success, his growing conservatism, his links with the upper classes—all these made him an unlikely candidate, especially in such a decade of social turmoil as the 1960s.

One prize he did receive was the Award of Merit for the Novel, which was bestowed on him by the American Academy of Arts and Letters in 1964. He was so moved that he wept with joy when John Hersey phoned to give him the good news. "No one can imagine the depth of my pleasure at the news you brought me," he wrote afterwards to Hersey, adding that the award represented "the high point of my professional career." It also led him to rejoin the Institute later in the year. At the May ceremonial at the Academy, Hersey presented the medal on behalf of his colleagues and spoke of O'Hara's amazing energy. "What comes through in his work, above all, is this vitality—O'Hara's joy in having the fate of being a writer." The medal had previously been awarded to Theodore Dreiser, Thomas Mann, Ernest Hemingway and Aldous Huxley, and in his acceptance speech, O'Hara paid tribute to them all, adding that he hoped they were "not made uncomfortable by my presence" in the group they formed together. The prize meant much to him because it was given him by his fellow professionals. O'Hara could not resist pointing out that his early work had been violently attacked and that at least some of "the liberties that the younger writers enjoy today were paid for by me, in vilification of my work and abuse of my personal character." He also made the point that he was always experimenting in his work, although the critics might not notice it, and concluded by saying that "as long as I live, or at least as long as I am able to write, I will go to the typewriter with love of my work and at least a faint hope that once in a great while something like today will happen to me again. We all know how good we are, but it's nice to hear it from someone else."

12. THE LOCKWOOD
CONCERN

After 1964, O'Hara reduced his publishing to one new book a year. But writing was so much a habit with O'Hara he did not feel alive unless he had a novel in progress, and he was probably unaware that the quality of his work was deteriorating. Of his last five novels, only *The Lockwood Concern* is successful. *The Big Laugh, Elizabeth Appleton, The Instrument* and *Lovey Childs* are all hasty and superficial. *The Big Laugh* and *The Instrument* deal with Hollywood and Broadway, *Elizabeth Appleton* is about academic life in a small college town, and *Lovey Childs* is concerned with a corrupt household of women on Philadelphia's Main Line. While admirable as attempts to extend his range, the four books are ill conceived and only occasionally interesting. The fault seems to be due to O'Hara's habit in later years of beginning to write without knowing where he was going. *The Big Laugh* started out as a short story, but then grew into a novel. Instead of reconsidering what he was writing, O'Hara allowed himself to be lazy and vain. *"The Big Laugh* is a short story in novel length," he wrote, "not padded, but let loose, and employing a short story technique. And, incidentally, it will sell a million. By my standards it is not a novel, but has to be called a novel because of its length. I wonder how many critics will catch on to *that.* I would guess exactly 0." It was easier to outsmart a reviewer and make a lot of money than to start over again, but the result is that O'Hara never wrote the Hollywood novel that might have been expected of him. "I unhesitatingly put it among my minor novels," he told John Hutchens, and he was right.

The Big Laugh and The Instrument are extensions of the theme of Pal Joey, but halfway through O'Hara seems to have realized that his leading characters were more interesting than the one-dimensional character Joey is. He therefore planned to describe them in a different way. "The characters and events as they developed have made this change necessary," he wrote, but he never made the change. In these two books the Hollywood and Broadway settings seem true, for O'Hara knew his material, but neither the academic world of Elizabeth Appleton nor the Main Line society of Lovey Childs is convincing. All four books read as though they were written perfunctorily: the narrative passages are wordy and there is little dramatic development. In Elizabeth Appleton, the professors spout sociology, history and economics uninterruptedly to show they are intellectuals, but they are not like any professors in real life.

Still, the themes are interesting and relate to O'Hara's main concerns. The books deal with spontaneity and intuition, especially in relation to art and sex. The question is: how far can you trust your instincts? They help you to be honest with yourself, which in turn teaches you that in order to survive you have to be tough, but the human price is high. Instinct can also lead to money and success and even artistic fulfillment, but without love, without caring, it brings emptiness—the big laugh. In Elizabeth Appleton, O'Hara approached the same question through a character who is willing to put human values first, but the novel collapses into sentimentality. O'Hara himself used to weep while reading out loud the part of this novel in which the central character renounces ambition and praises teamwork. He thought the speech was profoundly noble, whereas it only showed how far O'Hara had allowed himself to go in oversimplifying reality.

The main fault of these books is O'Hara's failure to create convincing people. Louis Auchincloss once commented on the oddness of some of O'Hara's characters: "In the strange angry world that he describes, the characters behave with a uniform violence, speak with a uniform crudeness and make no appreciable effort to control lusts which they regard as ungovernable. The most casual meeting between a major and a minor character will result either in an angry flare-up or a sexual connection, or both. It is impossible for an O'Hara character to order a meal in a restaurant or to take a taxi ride without having a crude exchange with the waiter or driver. Even the characters from whom one might expect some degree of reticence—the rich dowagers, for example—will discuss sex on the frankest basis with the first person to bring the subject up. And in Gibbsville or Fort Penn the first person to bring it up is the first person they meet." These comments are an exaggeration of O'Hara's characters in his serious books but they apply readily to the people in these lesser novels. There is no doubt that the publication of these books helped create the caricature of O'Hara as a writer obsessed with social niceties and crude sex.

Although they did not receive good or prominent reviews, these novels sold well. By now, with paperback sales, foreign earnings and movie rights, O'Hara was earning hundreds of thousands of dollars a year. In 1963 alone he paid an income tax of $135,000. The money did not change him, for he didn't believe his earning powers were permanent. He was still a tough negotiator over contracts, and wanted to get what he could while it was available. He would grumble about taxes and complain that he was not earning as much as William Dean Howells did. On the other hand, he was not grasping and was even careless about money. Once when cleaning out his desk in New York he came across two checks for $20,000 representing royalties from *Pal Joey* which he had forgotten to deposit in the bank. He thought of foreign earnings and Hollywood income as play money— "pretend-money in a pretend-world."

O'Hara liked to use his money for the pleasure it would bring him and his family. He had always wanted a Rolls Royce and had promised himself that if he won the Nobel Prize he would buy one with the proceeds. But when it seemed unlikely that he would win it, he decided to buy the car anyhow. He went to New York to inspect the Rolls showroom and then, with feigned casualness, he ordered what he wanted by phone. It was a four-door Silver Cloud III, painted dark green. He asked that his initials be painted on the door and sent in his check for $17,300. Most of his rich friends had Bentleys, which is the same car as the Rolls except for the Rolls's distinctive radiator grille. But O'Hara decided he could not afford this kind of inverse snobbery. "None of your shy, thumb-sucking Bentley radiators for me," he wrote. "I got that broad in her nightgown on *my* radiator and them two R's, which don't mean rock 'n' roll. Maybe I ought to start going to the Friday concerts again. Who dat? Man, dat Johnny O'Hara, from Pottsville, writes like a son of a bitch, he do."

O'Hara was delighted with his new toy. "Mine all mine, not owned by a corporation!" he exclaimed, and when, within the year, his friend Richard Hughes, governor of New Jersey, arranged to provide him with the state license plate of "JOH-1" he was as pleased as a little boy. Not long afterwards, the Hugheses and the O'Haras were invited for dinner by Bennett Cerf in New York, and the governor offered to have a state trooper drive them into town together in the governor's car. But O'Hara persuaded him to have the trooper drive the Rolls instead. O'Hara was like a latter-day robber baron showing off what his money could buy. He also had a gold cigarette case on which the seals of his various clubs were embossed. He would leave it casually on the coffee table, always happy to explain what they signified. He knew his display was vulgar, but he was honest enough to reveal his feelings.

Within ten days of receiving his car, he drove up to New York to show it to Bennett Cerf. The occasion was a lunch with Cardinal Spellman, part of whose diocesan headquarters in the Villard House on Madison Avenue and Fifty-second Street were rented out to Random House. One advantage of the place was the large courtyard in front of the building which could be used for parking; whenever O'Hara planned a trip he would phone Cerf to ask that space be set aside for him. On his first visit with the Rolls, O'Hara arrived like royalty and his photograph was taken with the cardinal. After lunch, O'Hara presented him a check for one of his mother's favorite Catholic charities. O'Hara's subsequent appearances at Random House were sometimes memorable. Once, finding no place for his car, he stormed into the office where he so terrified the receptionist that she fell down the stairs and had to be taken to a hospital. Another time, one of the editors, irritated by O'Hara's ostentatiousness, placed a plastic dog's stool on the front seat of the car while it was parked in the courtyard. O'Hara's attempt at swank were never wholly successful. Once when he was stuck in traffic on Sixth Avenue, his brother Tom passed him in the street and called out, "Get a horse, O'Hara." Without looking at him, O'Hara raised his hand in a little wave.

In September of 1965 O'Hara took Sister and the Rolls to England. They sailed on the *Queen Mary* and stayed at Claridge's in London. O'Hara enjoyed chatting with the owners of other Rolls Royces that were parked outside of the hotel in Brook Street. He had business appointments with his agent, Graham Watson, and with Robin Denniston of Hodder and Stoughton, his new English publishers, but mainly he followed his usual routine which was to get up late and play Scrabble with Sister before going out to shop along Piccadilly or in the Burlington Arcade. He loved visiting expensive shops like Swaine and Adeney's, Fortnum and Mason's, Jackson's and the places along Bond Street. One day he took his friend Rensselaer Lee to lunch at the Garrick Club, where he had a card provided by the Century in New York, and he enjoyed using his car to drive Lee back to his hotel.

After a few days in London, O'Hara and Sister were joined by Wylie, who flew over. All three set off in the Rolls with a chauffeur engaged for the driving. They went out through the Cotswolds, stopping at Woodstock and Broadway, to North Wales. They then drove north to Cumberland, staying at Windermere for a few days, before going on to Scotland where they put up at the famous golf hotel at Gleneagles. Then they drove down the Clyde to Stranraer where they took the ferry to Ireland. They stayed for nearly a week at the Shelbourne Hotel in Dublin. After that, they drove across Ireland to Limerick and County Clare before heading south to Cork. This was the country of O'Hara's ancestors but he had no interest in looking up family trees. He simply wanted to show Wylie something of her origins.

On the whole, the trip was oddly formal. O'Hara's nervousness about the unknown made him plan everything in advance and he was upset when something went wrong. One night at a theater in London he was unprepared for the custom of serving tea during the interval between the acts and so became flustered. He was happier when things were predictable, so he rigidly insisted on dining at the hotel where they were staying. Occasionally, when he was tired, Sister and Wylie would go to a restaurant alone, like two children released from school. O'Hara did little sightseeing, preferring to stay at the hotel where he would read and write letters. He was often recognized, and this pleased him, for it rarely happened in America. The car also made an impression. O'Hara later recalled the comment of a boy in Cork who observed, " 'Tis a massive car, massive." Exactly one month after leaving New York, they boarded the small Cunard liner, the *Sylvania,* at Cobh and prepared for the return journey. As the Rolls was hoisted on board from the tender, O'Hara looked over the side and recalled the last time he had been in Cobh as a young steward on board the *George Washington,* carrying bags full of dirty laundry onto a similar tender. "A cycle was completed," he said.

O'Hara's income and living habits made him increasingly conservative. As a self-made man who handled his own business affairs, he adopted upper-class values and attitudes and rejected those of the working-class Irish who only reminded him of the deprivations of his youth, and who he thought were held back mostly by their own prejudices and ignorance. His own hardships during the depression had made him a Democrat and he was a fervent supporter of Franklin Roosevelt. But only once, during the 1930s in Hollywood, was he actively involved in the political Left, and that was at a time when all concerned people were opposed to the tyrannical abuses of the movie moguls and the extreme conservatism of southern California, not to mention the rise of fascism in Europe. O'Hara's political convictions were mainly formed by personal experience and intuition. He hated tyranny and the abuse of power. As early as 1933 in a feature article for the *Herald Tribune,* he criticized the lazy stagehands of a Broadway production whose union threatened to close a play and thereby deprive the much harder working actors and actresses of their comparatively smaller earnings. His personal approach to politics put him against all bullies, Republican or Democrat. He attacked Martin Dies and Joseph McCarthy, the anti-Communist witch-hunters, with the same scorn with which he attacked what he called the Kennedy and labor-union fascists. In 1962, he summarized his position in a letter to John Hutchens who was then employed by the strike-bound *Herald Tribune.* "This strike is a terrible thing and only more firmly entrenches me in the Conservative position I took ten years ago. Labor fascism, which was one of the causes of my change, is here to stay, I fear, a long time. You probably do not know, for example, that in Philadelphia tonight the transit workers are going to pull a city-wide wildcat strike at the very peak of the Christmas shopping rush, although they have a contract that says no strike before Jan. 14. You and I and thousands of us who were pro-labor as the decent thing to be are now left on the curbstone, in the cold, while the fascists of labor continue their strike spirals. Meanwhile, of course, we are getting closer and closer to universal unionism, so that opposition and protest are getting to be impossible. Watch next year, when there is going to be a moribund effort to require voting machines in big unions. Meanwhile, too, we are getting into the Kennedy brand of fascism under the direction of the attorney general. Almost the most shocking event of 1962, although it will not get on any roundups, was the handling of General Walker. I don't like Walker, but the permanent discrediting of a man by having him branded a kook is right out of Hitler and Mussolini. It made me think of Silone and Fontamara, and it is of a piece with other things the Kennedy people have done and are still doing."

While attacking the bullies, O'Hara was especially irritated by fake liberals, those who from invulnerable positions risked nothing in their support of left-wing causes. He had known many such people during the 1930s in Hollywood and he was indignant when educated people supported what he thought were dubious causes. O'Hara had no illusions about politicians or union leaders, and it maddened him to see upper-class people give them their support. In California he once attended a party given for Eleanor Roosevelt and came away convinced she was a bigot. He mistrusted Adlai Stevenson, mainly because "the people behind him are going to give us a government that will make the New Deal look like McKinleyism, and I subscribe to the Jeffersonian doctrine that the least governed is the best governed." Because he thought they were prisoners of their supporters, he was also scornful of John Lindsay and Jacob Javits, the liberal Republicans from New York. Moreover, he came to believe that liberals were just as conformist as fascists, and he did not trust their slogans or their methods.

O'Hara was always more interested in the personalities of the politicians than in the issues. He was a friend of quite a number of them, notably Averell Harriman, Richardson Dilworth and Richard Hughes and Robert Meynor from New Jersey. On the night Hughes was re-elected governor, O'Hara went to visit the official residence "Morven" in Princeton where the ward heelers and television and radio journalists had gathered to await the returns. He was fascinated by the human side of the process. An individualist himself, he admired those few politicians, like Truman and Goldwater, who were willing to make unpopular statements. He came to believe that "the conservative movement is the gathering-place for individuals"; that was the main reason for his adherence to the Republican party towards the end of his life.

He freely admitted that it was "more fun" to be conservative than liberal. In 1964 he was given an opportunity to express his views publicly when Harry F. Guggenheim, the proprietor of the Long Island journal *Newsday,* asked him to write a weekly column for his paper and syndicate. There were no restrictions on subject matter and the pay was $1000 per column plus half-share of the syndicate income. Since his engagement coincided with a national election, O'Hara wrote about the campaign. He was one of the few American writers to come out in favor of Barry Goldwater against Lyndon Johnson. He made himself famous, or infamous, for saying, "I think it's time the Lawrence Welk people had their say. The Lester Lanin and Dizzy Gillespie people have been on too long. When the country is in trouble, like war kind of trouble, man, it is the Lawrence Welk people who can be depended on, all the way. Those men and women who voted for Nixon have not vanished from the earth. Most of them are still around, and most of them will vote for Goldwater." This support of a sentimental bandleader and his politically regressive followers shocked O'Hara's admirers who thought he had sold out. In a letter O'Hara privately explained his position. "The thing is, we finally have a candidate who speaks for the Lawrence Welk American, the sons and grandsons of George F. Babbitt, and they *are* America. I don't like their clothes, their glasses, their cars, their manners, their clichés. But I like them. They are good people when the chips are down. If one of their number had made the Cuba decision instead of Kennedy, we would be hearing about fascism, militarism, warmongering, etc. But Kennedy was a paid-up member of the other crowd, so he is revered as a courageous statesman. Actually Kennedy was a sarcastic, smart-aleck little prick."

In his column, O'Hara became a shameless name-caller. He conformed to all conservative positions and indiscriminately supported William Buckley, the Police Benevolent League and Ronald Reagan; he was against gun controls, in favor of smoking and opposed to Martin Luther King. He used words like "jerkism" and "liberalistic" to describe his opponents and their views. His irresponsible performance canceled out such decent objections as he may have had to the Democratic party and the labor union movements. Within a year, as a result of canceled subscriptions, O'Hara's column was dropped.

Apart from irritating people, O'Hara's political conservatism damaged him personally. A number of his friends began to avoid him for fear of getting into political arguments. In Princeton, O'Hara was already isolated from writers and intellectuals, but now old friends like John Steinbeck and Budd Schulberg hesitated to see him. He had not become a political bore, nor did he lecture people as so many Goldwater fanatics did, but he tended to be a little heavy-handed and disapproving of those whose political views he disliked.

These were signs of a deeper change underneath that made him socially less attractive: he was growing old and a bit lazy. "When you pass sixty," he said, "you just naturally become conservative. It's a lot easier to be a conservative." He expanded on this statement by adding, "If I were twenty-one years old I probably would be a good deal more concerned about race problems and poverty and other problems than I am, because if I were twenty-one I would be more alive to what's going on." O'Hara realized he didn't have the time or energy to be politically engaged. "My concern right now is here, writing."

O'Hara's alienation from the prevailing values of his time tended to make him irritable and he also became a sporadic crank. One source of annoyance was Random House, who continued to be his publisher. Generally he got along well with "Cerfie" as he sometimes called Bennett Cerf, and contract negotiations were concluded to his satisfaction, but now and again he would blow up over the way he was being treated. He became so irritated by the rudeness with which American businessmen make their phone calls that he bluntly informed Cerf: "No more of this 'Get O'Hara on the phone,' and then keep O'Hara waiting while Big Shot picks up the phone." He went on: "Time and again I have answered the phone, the secretary or operator says, 'Mr. Cerf calling,' then a minute or two or three later you get on the phone and say 'Who's this? . . . Oh, O'Hara.' Well, since you don't seem to pay much attention to what I say on the phone, anyway, there is not much point in my submitting to this discourtesy." He informed Cerf that he would not accept any more calls placed by an operator. "Just make the call the way I do; and try to bear in mind that aside from considerations of courtesy, I regard my time as important as you do yours." Even relatively unimportant matters would set him off as when New American Library published a paperback edition of *Appointment in Samarra* with an afterword by Arthur Mizener, a man who had attacked his work in *The New York Times Book Review.* "I want you to go to the telephone on receipt of this letter," he informed Cerf, "and tell the New American Library that the Mizener comments must be killed immediately. I don't give a damn whether it means killing the whole edition. At this moment you are very close to losing an author," he continued. "This is one of the most outrageous performances I have ever known, and in future, if there is a future, no deal is to be made for reprint of anything of mine without my being consulted in all details." Usually O'Hara's outbursts were justified, but he could also see the humor of his rage. Once when discussing present work with Cerf, he observed, "I know I ought to stick to short stories, but if I did the critics would be left without my novels to compare unfavorably to my short stories, and their reviews would lose a lot of vitality. I am always thinking of other people. That is why, everywhere you go, you hear me called Lovable Jack. When you hear people speak of Lovable Jack, they mean me. When you hear *me* speak of Lovable Jack, I'm talking about money, that's how modest I am."

O'Hara's crustiness was so deep it affected his whole life. At home,

one of the cleaning women, Pearl, had the annoying habit of unplugging
the desk lamp when she vacuumed O'Hara's study and leaving it unat-
tached after she finished. O'Hara asked Thelma Pemberton to speak to her
about it, but the very next time she vacuumed Pearl forgot again. O'Hara
went to Thelma to complain that the cleaning woman had "fucked up"
once more. Thelma told her to plug in the lamp right away. When Pearl
didn't come back from the study, Thelma followed her there. O'Hara was
sitting in his desk chair with the plug in his hand, and every time Pearl
tried to take it from him, he would swivel around out of reach. Having
made it clear what he thought of Pearl, O'Hara gave the plug to Thelma
and the incident was closed. On another day, just after the study had been
vacuumed, a parcel arrived for O'Hara who opened it on the floor of his
study, pulling paper and sawdust out of the box onto the newly cleaned
rug. Pearl and Thelma came in to clean up the mess, and seeing them
scurrying about on their hands and knees like a pair of rabbits, O'Hara
took down one of his hunting horns and began to blow it.

Sometimes he would be unexpectedly coarse. He told dirty stories that
shocked people, and occasionally he would do what other people would
only think of doing. In the old Ritz on Madison Avenue he found a
bathroom that was being renovated, so he went in and urinated on the floor
even though, or perhaps because, the toilet was missing. He could also be
very stuffy when introducing his literary and theatrical friends into his
club world. Every summer he would arrange at least one lunch party at the
National Golf Links in Southampton and if he was taking friends like
Charles Addams or Joan Fontaine, he would lecture them in the Rolls on
the way over not to be loud or to drink too much in the genteel premises
of his club.

O'Hara's ideas about how to behave often confused outsiders. "That
John lives up to a strict code is admirable," said Bennett Cerf, "but, unfortunately, he has expected his friends to live up to it, too. This has not
always been easy, since there are some secret clauses in the code he has
never bothered to explain. There was one period of three months in my
otherwise placid relationship with him when he didn't speak to me, though
to this day I have not the slightest idea what I did or said that angered
him." When told of Cerf's comment, O'Hara replied, "He knows what he
did."

Even as late as 1964 O'Hara said, "My version of noblesse oblige is
'fuck you.' " At the same time, he was always yearning for love and
attention, wanting to be the first to know of a friend's return from a trip,
hurt if he heard about it from someone else, wanting to have birthday
parties and to receive presents. As in many imaginative artists, the spirit
of the child was alive in him at all times and kept his emotional resources
replenished. His friends knew of and respected the depths of his feelings
which were revealed in the timbre of his voice and the magnetism he

exuded when he was with those he liked. A number of them expressed their gratitude to him by asking him to be godfather to their children. The aggressiveness and self-pity he sometimes showed were the price he paid for being open. O'Hara himself knew how troublesome it was to reveal his feelings. "We will always lose out to the cold fishes," he said.

His fierce emotionalism was also painful. He knew that when he left a party at least one person could be counted on to say, "How does that son of a bitch deserve such a wonderful wife?" For this reason, especially as he grew older, he spent more and more of his time in his study. Also, he was aware that he was in the autumn of his own life. Autumn had always been an important season for him; it had meant new beginnings, new music, new plays, new work—"The new and exciting start, and so much going to happen in the quickly darking evenings." Now that he was approaching his sixties, he felt, as he wrote Sister, that the pleasure of autumn was probably not "newness at all but rather my eagerness to return once again to my favorite season, the stimulating season, the thinking season, the feeling season. For there is no doubt that for me the smell of the burning leaves and the earlier dusk and longer nights bring an atmosphere that more nearly matches my natural mood, in which a not unpleasant sadness is an important factor. Summer is to me, since my middle teens, an artificial time, when thought and feeling are suspended. Whenever you don't understand me, it may help if you remember that I like dour weather. It does not depress me; it is, I suppose, more truly representative of my view of life itself. And the beauties of autumn are more real to me than the glaring spectacle of summer. I am an autumnal man (as distinguished from a fall guy!). I have always been able to find reasons for loving the autumn, but perhaps the best reason is simply that I do."

O'Hara's study was the center of his life. There in the quiet hours after midnight he could enter the world of his imagination that was on the walls of the room as much as on paper. With its mementos, photographs of old friends, reminders of newspaper and theater years, its diplomas for work well done, it was an evocation of the past. For hours O'Hara would sit at his desk with his newspaperman's yellow copy paper and no carbon recording the past as though it were today's news. In a sense, that is what it was for him: he lived in an imaginary world of early twentieth-century New York and Pennsylvania and his fictional characters were like the actual people who had appeared in the day's feature stories or personal columns. This world engaged him far more than the world beyond the walls of his study. He had made money and was socially acceptable, but now that he had the things he yearned for, he was no longer interested in them. "When I go to parties," he wrote, "I nearly always sit and talk to my wife. I like to put on my country-squire uniforms and watch people for a little while, but very few people can hold my attention for long. The ones who interest me are those that are waiting to be put down on paper." Having begun to write out of anger and disappointment with the external world, he now preferred the fictional world he could create and control. Yet he did not abandon objectivity, even though his early bitterness was replaced in his fictional imagination by a more balanced view of life. "After I became reconciled to middle age and the quieter life I made another discovery," he has Jimmy Malloy say in "Imagine Kissing Pete," and this was "that the sweetness of my early youth was a persistent and enduring thing, so long as I kept it at the distance of years. I wanted none of it ever again, but all I had I wanted to keep."

There was nothing gloomy about O'Hara's withdrawal. His work gave him great joy: it was the absolute center of his consciousness. He liked to think of himself as belonging to a sodality of writers who like himself were devoted to their lonely careers of creating literature from the world of the imagination. "I often think of you," he wrote to James Gould Cozzens, "at work in Williamstown, and of Dos Passos, at work in Virginia, and of myself, here in Princeton. As I used to think of Faulkner in Oxford and Hemingway in Cuba, and Steinbeck in Pacific Grove. Well, I wonder how it's going for Cozzens, I would say to myself. But it was nice to think of you at work, occupied in the same way I was occupied. Steinbeck is wasting his time extravagantly, especially right now, I am told. He has *been* wasting his time. Is that any business of mine? Yes, it is. There are only a few of us whose time is worth much, and when one of us piddles it away, it somehow seems to me an act of disloyalty to the others."

O'Hara was now more isolated from other writers than he had ever been before. Wilder Hobson's death in 1964 deprived him of the friendship of the one author he knew who lived in Princeton. But he kept up with others and showed concern for those he admired, especially when he knew they were in the kind of trouble he had known earlier in his life. When Cozzens received a nasty review, O'Hara immediately wrote him. "I hope you are good and tough," he said. "I have been somewhat toughened by unfavorable reviews through the years, but my wife touts off the worst of them even now. I can get very depressed by a review that is unfair, unreasonable, and totally destructive, as the one in the Times of your book was. Steinbeck has been a friend of mine since 1936, and last year he was badly wounded—trying not to show it, and showing it every minute—by the attacks on him following the Nobel prize. He did not know what hit him. He had been (like you) accustomed to respectful reviews throughout most of his career, and when there was an occasion for jubilation They suddenly turn on him." Sometimes O'Hara also gave good advice to friends, as he did to John Hersey when his book *The White Lotus* was receiving bad notices. "The only reply to critics is, curiously, the same reply to the hostile and to the friendly. It is work. I have repeatedly told my stepson to be *engaged* in work at the moment of publication of his novel.

Do anything—a play, short stories, another novel—but be doing something. I am not so sure that amor vincit omnia, but work keeps us going. It is a reply and an answer."

When O'Hara was able to help a friend in a more active way, he would do so. During the summer of 1963 he learned that John Steinbeck had been in the Southampton Hospital for an operation on his retina. Immediately he wrote Elaine Steinbeck offering to drive over from Quogue to the Steinbecks' place at Sag Harbor every afternoon to read to his friend. It would have been easy to send condolences, but O'Hara was imaginative and kind enough to know the sort of help that was really needed. Steinbeck accepted the offer and the reading sessions helped bring the two men closer than ever. When Steinbeck was well enough no longer to need to be read to he wrote O'Hara, "If I pretended great pain—couldn't you come over again? I really can't drive yet. I wish you would. There are a number of things I can't discuss with anyone else but you."

The most enduring product of O'Hara's last years as a novelist is *The Lockwood Concern,* which alone among his final novels has the status of serious work. It is the story of four generations of a Pennsylvania family that in the nineteenth century established itself and became rich and powerful in a town outside of Gibbsville. The history of the family begins in violence, for the Lockwoods were tough and ruthless, and money was linked with bloodshed. The founder of the family fortune, Moses Lockwood, kills a robber who was breaking into his room; then he shoots a man in the street who he thinks is a vengeful debtor trying to kill him. Lockwood always acts first; he is impulsive and unimpeded by thought. The family fortune is built on blood and the family's happiness is sacrificed to alliances that will build up the line. O'Hara concentrates the novel on George Lockwood, born in 1873, and who represents the third generation. He benefits from the fortune gathered by his father and grandfather and he follows their ruthless methods in building up what he was left. "The Lockwoods took Swedish Haven by storm," Lockwood tells his daughter at the end of the novel. "The brute force known otherwise as the almighty dollar. And there was never anyone here that dared to oppose us."

The Lockwoods are never accepted, however, partly because of their small-town origins, partly because of the violence. This erupts once again in George's generation when his weak and amiable younger brother shoots his mistress and commits suicide in New York. Social ostracism increases the Lockwoods' sense of family solidarity, but it exacts a price from the individuals involved. George Lockwood is always planning. Nothing with him is spontaneous; he has no real pleasure in the present because he is always organizing the future. During his life he only loves one woman, but he never marries her; he never even knows what happiness is. With others in his circle he plays God, manipulating them for the good of the family or for what immediate pleasure they can give him. But his wives bore him, and except for sex, he abandons them as human beings. His mistresses are also objects for him, appendages to his own ego. Only his son escapes him, but in doing so he makes his father hate him. "He's wanted to be free of me, and now he is," says George Lockwood. "But anybody who wants to be free of me makes me want to be free of them."

O'Hara thought of *The Lockwood Concern* as "an old-fashioned morality novel, as are all my longer novels." On the surface, the story of George Lockwood is clear enough in these terms, for O'Hara characterized Lockwood as "completely self-centered, enormously selfish, enjoyed life, in his way." The novel opens with Lockwood building a mansion in the country that symbolizes the family "concern," which is an attempt by the Lockwoods to establish an enduring family line in the manner of a European barony. Lockwood has his property enclosed by a high wall surmounted by spikes. On the day the house is ready for occupancy a small child falls from a tree and is impaled on one of the spikes. His death is matched by Lockwood's own, at the end of the novel, when Lockwood slips and falls down a secret staircase he had built in the center of the house. He is blinded by his fall and dies alone in the dark at the bottom of the stairs. O'Hara said he believed in the "Almighty system of checks and balances and compensations," so the secret staircase was "a symbol of Lockwood's secretiveness, withdrawal, superiority complex," and it gave O'Hara what he called an "instrument of retribution."

But the morality of art is always secondary. Morality tends to freeze art and force reality into patterns that are not necessarily true. *The Lockwood Concern* would hardly hold our attention if it were only a fable of punishment. Despite his comment on morality, O'Hara had too much respect for reality ever to want to preach. In George Lockwood he created a character who was individual and complex. Although he is hard and selfish and demanding, there is something admirable about him. He has energy and the vitality that makes him survive while his weak younger brother does not. He is representative of the American man of action without whom society would collapse. Had he been introspective, and thought of the human consequences of what he was doing, he probably would have become ineffectual. O'Hara was fond of quoting Joseph Conrad's remark from the foreword to *Victory,* that "thinking is the greatest enemy of perfection" insofar as it paralyzes "the readiness of mind and the turn of hand that come without reflection and lead the man to excellence in life, in art, in crime, in virtue and for the matter of that, even in love." So it is no use to say that Lockwood and other rich Americans should give up their pursuit of wealth and power. On the contrary, if they did so, they would be emasculated. O'Hara links the rise of the rich in America to the impulsive energy and ambition that set a man apart from, and usually above, his fellow men. As an artist O'Hara had undergone this experience in his own career. Fundamentally then, he is dealing not just with the acquisition or preservation of money, but with human values and the human price that must be paid for any individual act. That is the underlying theme of *The Lockwood Concern.*

Because he resisted simple moralizing, O'Hara was able to treat the rich people of his fiction with rare compassion and understanding. Having once been poor and resentful of the privileges of the rich and then having become rich and known what it was like to have money, he had a double vision that made it impossible for him to slip into the relatively easy stance of the satirist. He chose the harder task of trying to present the rich as people. Brendan Gill said of him, "O'Hara had a passion for the rich and well-born, which is not to say that he didn't see through them as well as into them." O'Hara was also forthright in his choice of subject: "I am fascinated by the rich and how they live, and I go with them every chance I get," he said. To do so was anyhow part of his social, as distinct from his artistic, ambition, and he was proud of his connections. But apart from the snobbery, he liked the rich as people "because they wear well and they don't feel any envy or hostility." He preferred the old rich—men and women "whose fathers, at least, lived on the income of their income, the people who can buy anything but don't. You see a large band of them assembling at a wedding, for instance, and there is a wholesale display of politeness, a fair uniformity of attire among the men, and an exhibition of fashion among the women. If you, like me, are an outsider, for you they start conventional. But then you see a little more of them and then still a little more, and then you begin to see the holes in the lining. Pretty soon you realize that the moths have been really industrious—and it's time you got so yourself, if you are a novelist." He knew that although they were considerate and well-mannered, they had "their own private hells."

Occasionally he would find among the rich someone who represented to him a kind of ideal—a man of substance and achievement who was also a human being, capable of combining kindness and toughness. Barklie Henry, who was also a friend of Hemingway's, was such a person. A graduate of Harvard and Oxford and a trustee of many important institutions including the Institute for Advanced Studies in Princeton, he preserved a boyishness and innocence that made him appealing. Like Fitzgerald, who had a similar attitude towards the rich, O'Hara sometimes tried to idealize those he admired, such as Nicholas and Merloyd Ludington from Philadelphia. "She was indeed the Golden Girl that I often tried to put on paper along with Nick," O'Hara wrote of the Ludingtons in 1969, "but so far they have eluded me, and perhaps that is just as well." More than any of his contemporaries, O'Hara plunged into the complex social and economic world of the ruling classes of modern America and made it real in ways that no one had done before him. He went further than his predecessors because he was willing to reveal the underside of the life of the American rich that other writers fudged through ignorance or covered up through gentility.

"I seem to be the only American author who gets around in these circles and over the years has observed the people in them," O'Hara observed in a letter to William Marvel. "It is not easy to see them plain. Most of our authors never see them at all, and the few who do see them come ill prepared, with erroneous impressions created by other authors either on the glamorous or downgrading side. Then there are the aristocrats' distorted views of themselves. I loved Mrs. Wylie and Mrs. Barnes, but the Southern lady and the Yankee lady kidded themselves. They blinded themselves to unpleasant facts, as though that would make the unpleasant facts go away. Mrs. Wylie denied that she knew anyone like Grace Caldwell Tate; Mrs. Barnes did not so much deny their existence as to maintain that those things were not discussed. So if I had been a less determined son of a bitch, I might have been deceived by my mothers-in-law. I suppose I am the only American author since Edith Wharton who has given these people a hard but not unsympathetic look, and it is my artistic duty to write what I have seen. And what I have seen is very discomforting for the future of an American aristocracy. Hell, it has no future. But as a group, or class, the aristocrats are generally easier to associate with, so long as they mind the manners they were taught in childhood and retain some of the early principles. And it is important to get down some record of them."

It took O'Hara longer to finish *The Lockwood Concern* than most of his others novels. At sixty, he could "stay at the typewriter for four hours, but not six, and never again eight." He interrupted work on this book occasionally for other tasks and thought of making it longer, but in the end he sent the typescript to Random House as it was. When it was published, *The Lockwood Concern* was not well received. Certainly it did not get the attention it deserved, but that may be explained by the flood of other O'Hara books which had dulled the public's receptiveness to his work. Reviewers complained about its length, the social detail, its lack of vitality compared to novels set in the present and its apparent misanthropy.

The Lockwood Concern is the fourth of a series of novels that attempt not only to create a fictional region representative of America in the twentieth century, but also to study the American man of action during this period. From Sidney Tate onwards, through Joseph Chapin and Alfred Eaton to George Lockwood, O'Hara presents the psychology of the individual American who is engaged in society and commerce and who is an insider rather than an outsider. Because he did not belong in Pennsylvania, Tate was somewhat ineffectual in his role, while Chapin was his opposite, the product of a small community who had an inappropriately grand ambition. Alfred Eaton is Chapin on a large scale, but he is so external a man that when he is prematurely retired there is nothing for him to do. George

Lockwood is more interesting than all of these: he is at once more aggressive and more thoughtful, and he is more introspective than any of the others. As his "concern" begins to collapse owing to the disaffection of his children, he begins to realize what has happened to his life and what the family obsession has cost in human terms. But it is too late. Like the others, Lockwood comes to his end with a sense of futility and emptiness.

It is easy to say that America as a land of promise has failed these men only because they failed themselves, that they have been so single-minded in their pursuit of money that they have lost the power to care for others and are therefore isolated from humanity. That is of course true, but a person's creative impulses cannot be satisfied by domestic harmony nor by involvement in altruistic enterprises. O'Hara sees that aside from money, modern America has no system of rewards that can engage a mature person's interest. An attractive reward must create a new involvement and a new kind of responsibility. The award or prize is useless unless it has a future life. In England and the Continent, the award of a title frequently brought with it the responsibility of an estate, which in turn allowed the recipient of the honor to devote his energies to the continuing benefit of the society or land which he held as its trustee for future generations. Founded on egalitarian principles, the United States has no equivalent system and perhaps by definition can never have one. It is an American reality therefore that at the end of the line there is just a vacuum. Psychologically, it is evident that the drive for individual excellence does not blend with the impulse for love. The two are like oil and water; they will not mix.

If the American dream fails for those who achieve it materially, what of those who don't even get those rewards? Rich and poor alike seem to have to make do with a few moments of joy or loyalty or affection that come almost in violation of the system.

As the "private hells" of the upper classes relate to passion, O'Hara drew a great deal from his own experiences and from the difference between himself and the rich to write his books. "I've never stopped to consider happiness before," says George Lockwood at the end of the novel. But O'Hara had not only considered it, he had known it, and in losing it when he lost Margaretta Archbald, he came close to nihilism. Unlike the rich who always have something to fall back on, he fell into the worst period of his life and was plagued by alcohol and destructive impulses. Eventually the wound was healed, thanks to his marriages to Belle and Sister, but he had suffered too much to put faith in ideals. Yet he was saved from cynicism because he had learned about love and also learned the solace of work. He knew they were opposed tendencies and he ordered his life as best he could to take advantage of each. It was a pragmatic solution, but the turmoil of his life even afterwards shows how much he was pulled in opposite directions. The best he could do was avoid generalities and stick to observable facts. "One of my troubles, I suppose," O'Hara wrote, "is that I have never gone around talking about—which is to say, writing about—Man, with a capital M, or Mankind. More simply, I think about and write about the individual man."

O'Hara still had enough energy left over from his writing to keep involved in the world. In 1964, he was asked to be a guest of honor for a weekend at the Bohemian Grove in California. He was interested in joining the Bohemian Club in San Francisco and understood that a visit to the Grove was a preliminary to being asked to join. The other guest was the attorney general, Robert Kennedy. "Now *there's* a little prick for you," O'Hara observed characteristically. He returned to California again in 1968 for a couple of weeks at Palm Springs where he met his old friend Gilbert Roland at the Racquet Club and also had lunch with Mrs. Dwight Eisenhower, which led to an afternoon spent with the former president. The two men got on easily and sat together in front of a television set watching a golf tournament with the sound turned off. For two hours they chatted, as O'Hara recalled, "on sports, politics, history, current events, our ailments, Pennsylvania, in an atmosphere that was relaxed and reasonably sprinkled with helling and damning." Shortly afterwards, O'Hara was invited to a White House dinner in honor of the presidential scholars, to which a number of writers and public figures were asked, including John Glenn, the astronaut; Stan Musial, the baseball player; Jonas Salk, the polio vaccine inventor and, among the writers, Marianne Moore, S. J. Perelman, Louis Auchincloss and John Updike. O'Hara had been outraged by what he called Robert Lowell's "impudent refusal" to attend an earlier Festival of the Arts at the White House on the grounds that his presence might be interpreted as a sign of political support for Lyndon Johnson and the Vietnam war. "I was better brought up than the poet Robert Lowell, who apparently was not taught that when the President of the United States invites you to the White House, you damn well go." At the Hay-Adams Hotel, O'Hara was spotted by his fellow Pennsylvanian and fellow *New Yorker* contributor John Updike, who was to read at the dinner and therefore had a White House limousine to take him to the party. Updike offered O'Hara a ride, which he accepted, although it was somewhat embarrassing that the younger Updike had the car and not O'Hara. Conversation between the two was rather stiff, but O'Hara was suffering from backache and was tired from the trip. Still, he was honored to be invited and at the party spent most of his time with another Pennsylvanian, Marianne Moore.

O'Hara's presence at such events drew attention in the press. Often the inference was made that O'Hara was a social climber, a man born on the wrong side of the tracks. "A couple of years ago," he said of a series of articles written about him for the *New York Post,* "a local herring-wrapper devoted a whole week, a full page a day, to create an image of me as a lush, a sex maniac, a social climber, and a boy from the wrong end of the right street, like having a 2000-number on Park Avenue." He decided to put an end to this erroneous view of his upbringing by writing a piece called "Don't Say It Never Happened" for the *Herald Tribune* book section, in which he pointed out that while he had been poor, so too he had been expensively brought up and that his family belonged to the best society in Pottsville. The facts were worth putting down, but the violence of the protest naturally suggested that O'Hara's insecurity was as great as ever.

Although the O'Haras continued to go to New York from time to time, usually for errands or for parties like Truman Capote's famous dance at the Plaza in 1966, they began to change their habits. Even though he enjoyed traveling first-class, staying at the best hotels and eating at the best restaurants, O'Hara was gradually withdrawing from the hurly-burly he had known and loved in New York. Philadelphia now began to take its place. "I find that my social life is more and more restricted to the town where I live and visits to Philadelphia, which makes it possible to avoid writers and people in show biz." He had become disenchanted with New York. "My N.Y. is past history," he wrote. "N. Y. is all glass and parking lots, with no building, residential or otherwise, safe from the wrecker's big iron ball. And this vitreous construction is being done to give office space to men that I don't want to know, engaged in activities that I mistrust." Finding similar changes that upset him in Princeton, he added, "I am an anachronism, getting to be more so all the time. It is really amazing how consistently I disagree with what passes for Progress."

O'Hara enjoyed the Princeton-Philadelphia-Quogue world because it was at once gracious and easy. The houses he visited were large and old and cool, with broad lawns stretching away from flagstoned terraces and often with farmland and horses adjacent. Inside, the furniture was old but good, with bright, clean slipcovers, oriental rugs, English sideboards, glistening brass andirons and fire buckets and with silver cigarette boxes on the coffee tables. Such houses represented order and stability; for O'Hara, they were above all restful. The conversation was usually amiable, complacent and discreet. It was a world O'Hara had always yearned for, and it pleased him to be accepted, although his satisfaction also made him dull and a bit pompous. This led some of his acquaintances to quip that O'Hara became impossible when he gave up drinking. Living in the world of country gentlemen, O'Hara never talked about his own work, but he did not hesitate to say what he thought about other things. His predicament was somehow touching and absurd. "Here is a man," commented one of his friends, "with his God-given talent and the guts to use it and the very people he looks up to are not fit to shine his shoes. I think he would still like to have his talent, but to be born Jock Whitney."

O'Hara's pompous side was generally repressed, but once in his *Colliers* column, he let go: "I have lived an extremely full life," he wrote, "experiencing exquisite pleasure and all but unbearable sorrow and pain; loving some, hating a few, pitying many and scorning the contemptible; joyful of my accomplishments and stung by my failures. Throughout it all I have been pleased by the circumstance that has enabled me to earn my living at the job I love best—writing." The best answer to this was produced by Wolcott Gibbs in a letter to James Thurber: "He sounds like Lincoln's Second Inaugural. It must be wonderful to think of yourself so majestically and even more wonderful to have no misgivings about putting it all down for a national magazine. Can you imagine issuing an equivalent statement about yourself? I personally have led an extremely irritating life . . . putting up with people as best I can; doubtful of my accomplishments and on the whole resigned to my failures. Throughout it all, I have been astonished by the circumstance that has enabled me to average thirty thousand dollars a year at a job that I can't help feeling is a little comic. I am a complex, semi-educated man, and a great many things still shock me, including unbuttoning the pants in public. Now you try."

Although O'Hara gave up traveling by ship, he continued to visit England, and during the late 1960s, he flew to London four times, generally for a stay of about a week. The trips were connected with business, and O'Hara discussed his new work with his agent and publishers. He and Sister always stayed at Claridge's and they would spend time shopping at Asprey's or Swaine and Adeney's. Moving about was a strain for O'Hara because of his weak back. Generally he was tolerant of the need for the trip and the pleasure it gave Sister, but there was no gaiety or sense of adventure. Their evenings were subdued: they went to the theater, but often would leave after the first act, and while he enjoyed going to restaurants such as the Ivy, he ate so sparingly there that he got little immediate pleasure from the occasion.

O'Hara knew hardly any English writers, although he had lunch with Kenneth Allsop and John Braine and met several others at a party given by his agent, Graham Watson, when he and Steinbeck both happened to be in London at the same time. He did, however, become a member of the Savile Club, which was closer to Claridge's and easier to negotiate than the Garrick with its long outside staircase. He was not treated as a celebrity, although he was interviewed. One newspaper story was headlined "Bored by Fame." The reporter wrote, "Now 62, O'Hara is a rather disgruntled almost cantankerous figure. He finds London tiresome. He finds being celebrated a bore. He does not like having his picture taken if it can be prevented."

In 1967, O'Hara was invited to be guest of honor at a lunch at the Dorchester organized by Foyle's bookshop to celebrate the paperback publication of *The Lockwood Concern* by the New English Library. Foyle's luncheons were usually given for politicians, public figures and theater people, so it was unusual to have a writer of O'Hara's stature, especially an American. Nervous about addressing an audience of four hundred people, O'Hara wrote out his remarks in full. The guests included such notables as Prince Faisal of Saudi Arabia, John Paul Getty, Margaret Leighton and, among the writers present, William Plomer and Edna O'Brien. O'Hara gave a rambling talk about his own experiences in England. Halfway through the talk, he found he was unable to continue so he handed the text to John Moore, a novelist who was acting as chairman of the occasion, and asked him to finish, which he did. The most telling passage of the talk appeared at the end when O'Hara said, "I do not feel that I lose face by publicly acknowledging our debt to the English middle class. From you we acquired a sense of decency and fair play, respect for the rule of law and standards of conduct that add up to civilized behavior. We inherited these virtues and we do not always follow the rules or meet the standards, and neither do you." At the conclusion of the speech, the book editor of the *Sunday Express* replied on behalf of the listeners and spoke of O'Hara's own work. "By some standards his work is shocking, but his aim is not to shock or disgust. It is to show things as they are."

Although the Foyle's lunch was not a critical honor, it was the last formal recognition O'Hara was to receive. He had been nominated in 1966, along with Vladimir Nabokov and Katherine Anne Porter, for the Gold Medal for Fiction to be presented by the National Institute of Arts and Letters, but did not win the prize. He was moved by Lionel Trilling's nomination, however. "In one respect I have won already," he told Trilling. "I have the most prestigious sponsor, and I thank you."

As always, writing was foremost in O'Hara's mind. In 1964, he wrote in the foreword to *The Horse Knows the Way* what amounted to a farewell to the short story, citing the greater importance of his novels. "The real work is in writing novels, and the real satisfaction is in real work," he wrote to William Marvel. Then, rather grandly, he added: "I have been given the power to write the symphonies, and it must not be dissipated in Flights of the Bumblebee and Moonlight Sonatas. The stories could be just as bad for me as all those nights in 21 and the Stork Club, because it is almost as easy for me to write a story—and a good one—as it was to laugh it up at 21." But every other year a new collection of short stories was published: *The Horse Knows the Way* in 1964, *Waiting for Winter* in 1966, *And Other Stories* in 1968.

The three books cover familiar territory, from New York and the eastern seaboard to Gibbsville and on to Hollywood. The themes are characteristic: love and hate in married life, the violence that underlies the placid surfaces of small towns, sexual secrets masked by gentility, and the way human beings exploit one another. *The Horse Knows the Way* is in the vein of O'Hara's previous three books, but there is greater emphasis on the old and dying than before. The play of time, the burden of the past and fear of the future are often beautifully brought out. In one story, a well-known actress agrees to meet a young girl, the daughter of an old admirer, who wants to go into the theater. The actress invites her for lunch at her hotel apartment and stages everything to impress the young girl. But the girl arrives quite drunk, disclaims any real interest in the theater and half passes out in the bedroom. Instead of being irritated, the older woman sees in the girl her own youthful nervousness and treats her with warmth and kindness. O'Hara is most effective when he explores the inner lives of people who exist behind the facade of their social bearing, behind the masks they put on to help keep their emotions down. In a story called "James Francis and the Star," O'Hara writes: "They were impulsively silent, the busyness of their thoughts for once dominated by the nearness of an emotion." The sentence represents O'Hara's method in so many of his stories—a world of talk and action that flourishes mainly to keep feelings under control.

Waiting for Winter is notable for its Hollywood stories, which include some of the best he ever wrote, especially two long stories, "James Francis and the Star" and "Natalie Jackson." Hollywood is prototypical as a setting for impermanent lives and suspect relationships—friendships and affairs that exist more for career purposes than for real feelings. It is easy to be satirical about Hollywood's shallowness, but O'Hara prefers to show how tenuous and fragile everyone's life is. There is so little certainty in the film world that people exaggerate their importance to give themselves courage. O'Hara sees his Hollywood characters with a compassionate eye, and he acknowledges the courage of actresses and writers who, knowing their own vulnerability, still have the guts to go on.

O'Hara deals with an analogous theme in his stories about the half-world that exists between love and friendship in contemporary life. The search for a passionate and enduring love is so exhausting and frustrating that some of O'Hara's characters seek release in something that will temporarily satisfy their desires without creating any illusions about the future. The theme goes back to *Butterfield 8* where Gloria Wandrous and Eddie Brunner have a relationship that comforts them although they know it can't last. In a novella called "A Few Trips and Some Poetry" included in *And Other Stories,* the narrator tells the girl he makes love to from time to time and in different places that he is her "permanent, sporadic lover." O'Hara explores this relationship in several stories. Without permanent entanglements, men and women can trust one another like friends. But deeper feeling creeps in, and along with it, jealousy. " 'Loving without love' was no more satisfactory than 'love without loving,' " he notes, and so sums up modern life.

O'Hara is also concerned with the ordinary problems of living. The Gibbsville stories reveal deprivation and frustrations. People are unable to find anything interesting to do with their lives. Trapped, they nurse hidden anger or retreat into fantasy. They search for happiness and understanding in clandestine affairs but rarely find either. Some of O'Hara's characters learn to communicate with one another and in recognizing their common fears and hatreds, they find a basis for understanding and love, but O'Hara is too honest to believe that many people are capable of doing this.

His interest in lesbianism, expressed mainly in the novel *Lovey Childs,* seems also an effort to explore another possible solution to human misery. Criticized for this interest, O'Hara responded that lesbianism was a common phenomenon and therefore a legitimate subject. In his stories, however, lesbianism is presented as unnatural, a dangerous and predatory habit women fall into only when disappointed in love with men. But he is too understanding to make an absolute judgment. His last published story called "We'll Have Fun" is about two outcasts, a coachman made obsolete by the automobile, and a lesbian, who vow to live up to the story's title.

O'Hara's last collections of stories are on the whole better than the later novels, *The Lockwood Concern* excepted. But they lack the urgency and immediacy of his early work. One reason for this is that O'Hara changed his principal method of narration. By 1963, he noted that "having been one of the early practitioners of the oblique and the plotless, I have recently been getting action back into my stories." This meant that he began to "tell" his stories rather than let them rely on exchanges of dialogue. It also suited his mood, for increasingly he enjoyed going over the past with his friends. His published stories are like reminiscences, long rambling stories about a seemingly limitless supply of characters drawn from his experiences in Pennsylvania, Hollywood and Long Island. Inevitably these reveries lack the immediacy of stories using current dialogue. O'Hara may also have used this method of narration because he knew he was out of touch with the world. His ear was not in tune with the spoken language of the 1960s as it had been with that of the 1930s and 1940s.

A number of his last stories appeared in the *Saturday Evening Post.* Don Schanche, who was an admirer, asked him if he would contribute, and O'Hara invited him to Princeton to read what was available. He spent an afternoon reading through ten stories and offered to take four of them. O'Hara agreed, with the proviso that the sale was final and not subject to confirmation by a committee of editors. The price was fixed at $2500 for a ten-page story, $3500 for longer ones. The sexual prudery of the *Post* was well known, and O'Hara was hardly the sort of writer to alter his material for a *Post* audience. The livelier stories, such as those about Hollywood, were never accepted by magazines, but in some of the others it is evident that he was already writing what amounted to *Saturday Evening Post* stories. O'Hara's link with Schanche led him to publish a series of articles in *Holiday* when Schanche later became its editor. Most of them were reminiscential pieces about old cars, jazz bands and sport. Individual essays rather than personal columns, they were given the inclusive name of "The Whistle Stop" and were O'Hara's last venture into journalism.

For O'Hara, writing was a compulsive occupation. With the material he had available, he simply kept on writing, story after story, novel after novel, unable to stop. Inevitably, he suffered from a waning appreciation of his work. By publishing so much, O'Hara also robbed himself of the tranquillity that might have led to better work. His constant public exposure led one reviewer to comment: "Every year of late, sure as death, taxes and visiting mothers-in-law, comes a new O'Hara, sometimes a novel, sometimes a collection of short stories. And every year, sure as the fact that Princeton is in New Jersey and America is now in Vietnam, come the O'Hara reviews. At this point in our nation's literary epoch, it's hard to tell which is more archetypal—the work or the critiques."

As the years went by, O'Hara became increasingly dependent on Sister as she did on him. They quarreled, for they were peppery individuals, but they adored each other. O'Hara's needs were simple but definite, and Sister supplied them, giving him the support and tenderness he wanted. She prepared red leather scrapbooks in which she pasted photographs and reviews of all of his books, and she created the domestic tranquillity he required for his work. The routine was trying, but she was good-humored about it. Once her daughter phoned her from New York and asked what she was doing. "Creaming chicken," Sister replied, "creaming chicken." In return, O'Hara gave her his own love and devotion. "I have chosen to make my life work a thing that is by nature a solitary occupation," he wrote, "but I can waste away without the people I love, you and Wylie." His support meant so much that when he died Sister cried out, "What shall I do? He was my Rock of Gibraltar." O'Hara was possessive about Sister, for as he was obsessed by death, he knew he had a limited time remaining and wanted his days and weeks to be with her.

O'Hara was also fiercely attached to Wylie, for as he wrote her, "The greatest pleasure I have in life is the responsibility of being your father." After St. Timothy's, Wylie attended Bennett College and later lived in New York where she took a secretarial course. In 1966, she became engaged to a young Yale graduate, Dennis Holahan, and their marriage became the occasion of O'Hara's last big social splurge. Months were spent in preparation for the wedding, and hundreds of invitations were sent out, for it was to be a grand affair with bridesmaids and ushers in morning coats. O'Hara became involved in the arrangements, for fashionable weddings were his specialty and he wanted the best for his daughter. The ceremony was held at the church of St. Vincent Ferrer at Lexington and Sixty-sixth. Always the supportive father, O'Hara lit cigarettes for himself and Wylie as they waited nervously together in the baptistry for the wedding march to begin. The reception was held around the corner at the

Colony Club and there, attired in morning clothes, O'Hara sat like a king in his court. In addition to his many friends from Long Island, Princeton, Philadelphia and New York, members of his own family were invited. Two of O'Hara's young nephews from Pottsville made the mistake of getting drunk and O'Hara passed on his displeasure to Mary. But with a guest list that included Saltonstalls, Vanderbilts and Whitneys as well as Claude Rains, George Kennan and Truman Capote, the disruption was a small thing.

Increasingly O'Hara concentrated his attention on his immediate family and friends. He was delighted by the birth of his grandson Nicholas and for a moment thought of entering him "with the Class of 1992" at Yale, although he did not act on this impulse, thinking it "rather impertinent." When Wylie brought Nicholas and his little sister Belle to visit, O'Hara surprised everyone by playing joyfully with the two children and letting them pull his ears without complaint.

When O'Hara heard a friend was in trouble, he would quickly offer to help, and more than one of them received checks for $1000 when they were in need. Although he read little of his younger contemporaries, he kept an eye out for the work of writers whose subject was like his own, notably Cheever, Updike and Irwin Shaw; reviews of their books were pasted into the scrapbooks along with his own. If he was enthusiastic about someone or his work, he would offer to help. He always tried to be specific, as when he told a young apprentice newspaperman that he should learn how to mirror-read so that he could read type quickly. He would also praise writers whose work he admired. "There is nothing new or particularly harmful about literary back-scratching," he declared, "so long as it's done out in the open."

In the meantime, O'Hara's health was gradually deteriorating. His back still bothered him, and his neglect of his teeth caused him to have the few survivors removed. "I could live on beer and liverwurst sandwiches," he wrote, "but I am afraid to take a glass of beer. If they had told me I had cancer I was going to be less abstemious, a word which, like facetious, contains all the vowels in their proper order."

His forced immobility and bad diet made him put on weight. In his late fifties he had looked distinguished, with his dark hair parted near the center and sleeked down over his head, and wearing either the heavy tweeds of the country gentleman or the banker's blue suit and gold watch chain. But by 1965 he had become heavy-jowled and puffy and his color was bad. He moved slowly, somewhat bent over, leaning on a cane. He also became something of a hypochondriac, going from one doctor to another and having tests at the Presbyterian Hospital. All that could be discovered was his chronic hypertension and a general state of depression that may have been made worse for not having the kind of release that alcohol formerly gave him. Then in 1968, after a visit to Richardson Dilworth in

Philadelphia, he fell going to get his car in an underground garage. He was rushed to the Pennsylvania Hospital where he had stitches taken over his right eye and a splintered elbow attended to. Because his fall knocked him out, he had no memory of the incident and thought he had suffered a heart attack, but the attending physician stated that he was suffering instead from overweight and a vascular disease. He noted that the accident had made O'Hara "irritable (which is usual), antagonistic and suspicious." O'Hara resisted the doctor's suggestion that he take exercise but agreed to do so when the doctor became insistent. He gave the doctor "an impression of overwhelming pessimism."

Not long afterwards, back in Princeton, he suffered from a mild stroke which half-blinded him in his right eye. It also prevented him from realizing he was rambling as he told stories. His depression grew worse and he was convinced he would soon be dead. When Wylie returned for a visit, she was distressed to see that he had allowed himself to go to pieces. She chided him and urged him to take swimming lessons at a Princeton gymnasium. He agreed to do so and his spirits and health improved. Then, after another hospital checkup, he was diagnosed as having diabetes. This naturally discouraged him, and he admitted to his old friend Frank Sullivan that there wasn't "very much I do care about nowadays."

O'Hara's health problems slowed him down, but there were still dinner parties in Princeton and occasional visits to New York such as for dinner and an evening at the theater with the Cerfs. Knowing he was unwell, Cerf did not invite O'Hara to his own seventieth birthday party at Mount Kisco in Westchester. O'Hara was resentful, however, and told Cerf so. Cerf replied that he thought the drive would be too tiring and O'Hara accepted the explanation. He then sent Cerf seventy American Beauty roses. The Kriendlers of "21" gave a party in August of 1969 to mark the thirty-fifth anniversary of the publication of *Appointment in Samarra*, but otherwise, both at Quogue and Princeton, the O'Haras' life was quiet. A visitor to the house on Dune Road found O'Hara patiently shining his shoes, reverting to his horseman's love of leather and discoursing on the use of a bone to produce a high gloss.

He kept in touch with the outside world mainly through television, newspapers and correspondence. In 1967, he made what was to be a farewell visit to Pottsville when his childhood friend Edward Fox gave a cocktail party in his honor at the Pottsville Club. Because of his back, O'Hara had to sit quietly and greet the guests who came up to him. Some thought he was being lofty, but O'Hara didn't notice. "For the first time since 1927, when I left Pottsville," he wrote, "I had a good time there, recalling people's middle names and old sweethearts and so on. On our way back to Princeton I said to Sister that I enjoyed the feeling of rediscovering my roots, indeed of really discovering them for the first time."

It was an elegiac time, marked by the death of old friends. O'Hara attended the funerals and memorial services of as varied a group as Tim Costello, whose Third Avenue speakeasy had once been a haunt, John McClain, his former roommate in New York, and Robert Oppenheimer, his Princeton friend and director of the Institute for Advanced Studies. As he was always concerned for his future reputation, he agreed to an interview for an article by Don Schanche which was published in *Esquire.* "I respect and trust you," said O'Hara, "and at 63 it is time I got a piece written about me that the obit boys can be guided by."

In February of 1970, he was visited by Wylie, her husband and children, and felt sufficiently improved in health to fly to London as a birthday present for Sister. There he talked to his publishers and agent, and with Sister saw a few old friends and a few new plays. Back in Princeton, he resumed his swimming lessons at the remarkably early hour of ten-thirty in morning. He planned for future social events, including a trip to New York in honor of Adele and Robert Lovett's wedding anniversary. Shortly after his step-granddaughter Amanda Bryan was born, he invited her parents, Courtie Bryan and his wife, to bring her for a visit. On the last night of their stay, O'Hara went as usual to his study to work, planning to "play possom" the next morning so as to avoid the wearisome routine of farewells. While writing at his desk, he complained of pains in his chest, left arm and shoulder and decided to go to bed early. Before retiring herself, Sister looked in on him and found him sleeping soundly as she did again in the morning as the Bryans were preparing to leave. She phoned her friends to make the day's plans and went out for her errands. When she returned she went into his room and found that he was dead. On that Saturday morning, April 11, 1970, he was only sixty-five years old.

Sister's friends and relatives came quickly to support her, and Wylie came east for the funeral. The service was held at the Princeton chapel and was conducted by the university chaplain. It was a bright clear day, and as the limousines, including O'Hara's own dark green Rolls, gathered near the large Gothic structure, they brought people representing many phases of O'Hara's life. In addition to members of his own and Sister's families, John Hay Whitney and his sister Joan Payson were there, as was Governor Hughes of New Jersey and the president of the university. Bennett Cerf was in California, but his wife came, along with Donald Klopfer of Random House and Mrs. John Steinbeck. Some curious students from the university also attended the service as did many of O'Hara's old friends from Princeton. The only writer present was Joel Sayre; the only artist, Charles Addams. In itself, the funeral showed how far O'Hara had drifted away from the world of literature and the arts.

O'Hara was buried in the old Princeton Cemetery, which is operated by the Presbyterian Church off Witherspoon Street. It is an ancient burial ground containing the graves of many Princeton worthies including university presidents and such notables as Aaron Burr. O'Hara was buried in a plot nearby the grave of Grover Cleveland, former president of the United States. Sister later had a pair of simple granite stones erected under a flowering hibiscus tree, and on her husband's she had placed this inscription:

JOHN O'HARA
JANUARY 31, 1905
APRIL 11, 1970
BETTER THAN ANYONE ELSE
HE TOLD THE TRUTH
ABOUT HIS TIME HE
WAS A PROFESSIONAL HE WROTE
HONESTLY AND WELL

The newspaper obituaries emphasized O'Hara's stormy life and personality rather than his work. At a memorial service held at Random House a month later, Bennett Cerf and Charles Poore stressed the familiar themes of O'Hara's lovable but irascible nature. Wylie read a letter from her father which revealed a warmth the general public hardly knew existed.

By the time of his death, O'Hara's reputation as a writer was falling and he no longer commanded the audiences, either popular or literary, of his early days. The question that arises is whether his social ambitions and upper-class habits fundamentally damaged his work. The French painter Fernand Léger is said to have remarked, "Either a comfortable life and lousy work or a lousy life and beautiful work." This is one of those half-truths that among our own novelists is contradicted by such different writers as Nathaniel Hawthorne and Henry James. Yet there is certainly an element of truth in it. O'Hara's social attitudes became increasingly like those of the rich he wrote about. He was a snob and became an outspoken political conservative. Yet it is a common critical error to equate an author with his subject and to assume that, as with O'Hara, because he wrote about the rich, or even liked them personally, he also spoke for them. O'Hara was a profoundly divided man, and in his study late at night, free of the concerns of his daily life, he allowed his basic human instincts to dominate his work. Although he liked upper-class life, he was too honest to accept its values in his writing. It was not easy for him to strike a balance between these opposed forces, but in his best work there is a tension between the two aspects of his nature—between his social views and his artistic honesty. This tension reflects his simultaneous admiration and distaste for the rich, as well as the conflict between his ambition and his love for other human beings. Gerald Murphy, a rich painter who knew both Fitzgerald and O'Hara, once said, "It is not what we do but what we do with our minds that counts, and for me only the invented parts of our life had any meaning." O'Hara would probably have agreed.

Often compared to Anthony Trollope and George Moore, O'Hara was like them because he dealt with the ordinary realities of his society. He did not write about peripheral people as Hemingway often did, nor did he dwell in a world of grotesques with Faulkner. In the tradition of Lewis and Dreiser and Anderson, he confronted the materialistic world of middle-class America, and as the spiritual heir of Edith Wharton, he explored the world of society with an intensity few others have even attempted. Yet he was more than the social chronicler who comes to mind in a comparison with Trollope or Moore. He was a man of tremendous feeling who tried to understand how such forces as ambition, sexual passion and jealousy, as well as kindness and love, affect all human beings. There was a turbulence and violence in all his best work, just as there was in him. His vision of humanity was not hopeful, but he put value in loyalty, in communication between individuals and in imaginative kindness. He is a writer about people far more than a chronicler of society. O'Hara's world is not only a mirror of reality but a product of his own feelings and intelligence.

O'Hara's industry—his obsession with writing—was a curse as well as a blessing, for he wrote too much and the quantity of his work confused his public and caused him to be undervalued. His public statements and vanity turned people against him and he was resented and underrated, usually by his inferiors and often by his own associates. By now, however, it is clear what his best work consists of—thirty or forty short stories and novellas, for their artistic delicacy and a psychological acuteness unsurpassed in American literature; *Appointment in Samarra,* for its youthful vitality and honesty; *From the Terrace,* for its ambition, thoroughness and immense readability; and *The Lockwood Concern,* for confronting most completely the values that tormented him through his life. These works make O'Hara one of the half-dozen most important writers of his time.

O'HARA'S PUBLICATIONS

This list is restricted to original books published by John O'Hara in the United States. It does not include anthologies or other special editions, nor does it include periodical publication of stories or articles. Readers wishing a more detailed listing of O'Hara's writing should consult *John O'Hara: A Descriptive Bibliography* by Matthew J. Bruccoli. Translations and English editions are not listed here, but a complete collection is housed in the John O'Hara Collection at Pennsylvania State University.

Appointment in Samarra, New York: Harcourt, Brace, 1934. Novel.
The Doctor's Son and Other Stories, New York: Harcourt, Brace, 1935. Stories.
Butterfield 8, New York: Harcourt, Brace, 1935. Novel.
Hope of Heaven, New York: Harcourt, Brace, 1938. Novel.
Files on Parade, New York: Harcourt, Brace, 1939. Stories.
Pal Joey, New York: Duell, Sloan & Pearce, 1940. Stories.
Pipe Night, New York: Duell, Sloan & Pearce, 1945. Stories.
Hellbox, New York: Random House, 1947. Stories.
A Rage to Live, New York: Random House, 1949. Novel.
The Farmers Hotel, New York: Random House, 1951. Novel.
Sweet and Sour, New York: Random House, 1954. Articles.
Ten North Frederick, New York: Random House, 1955. Novel.
A Family Party, New York: Random House, 1956. Novella.

From the Terrace, New York: Random House, 1958. Novel.

Ourselves to Know, New York: Random House, 1960. Novel.

Sermons and Soda-Water, New York: Random House, 1960. Novellas.

Five Plays, New York: Random House, 1961. Plays.

Assembly, New York: Random House, 1961. Stories.

The Big Laugh, New York: Random House, 1962. Novel.

The Cape Cod Lighter, New York: Random House, 1962. Stories.

Elizabeth Appleton, New York: Random House, 1963. Novel.

The Hat on the Bed, New York: Random House, 1963. Stories.

The Horse Knows the Way, New York: Random House, 1964. Stories.

The Lockwood Concern, New York: Random House, 1965. Novel.

My Turn, New York: Random House, 1965. Articles.

Waiting for Winter, New York: Random House, 1966. Stories.

The Instrument, New York: Random House, 1967. Novel.

And Other Stories, New York: Random House, 1968. Stories.

Lovey Childs: A Philadelphian's Story, New York: Random House, 1969. Novel.

BOOKS PUBLISHED POSTHUMOUSLY

The Ewings, New York: Random House, 1972. Novel.

The Time Element and Other Stories, New York: Random House, 1972. Stories.

Good Samaritan and Other Stories, New York: Random House, 1974. Stories.

"An Artist Is His Own Fault": John O'Hara on Writers and Writing, ed. by Matthew J. Bruccoli, Carbondale, Illinois: Southern Illinois University Press, 1977. Literary articles, speeches, reviews and interviews.

Selected Letters of John O'Hara, ed. by Matthew J. Bruccoli, New York: Random House, 1978. Letters.

Two by O'Hara, New York: Harcourt Brace Jovanovich, 1979. Screen treatment and play.

NOTES

The information gathered for this book comes from three main sources. The first of these is correspondence, much of it already gathered in the John O'Hara Collection at Pennsylvania State University. The second is published material, such as newspaper clippings, magazine articles and reviews. Again, these are well represented at Pennsylvania State University. The third source consists of interviews that I conducted with friends and acquaintances of John O'Hara's, all over the United States and in England.

I have tried to use O'Hara's own autobiographical writings as much as possible. He never wrote a formal book of memoirs, but his reminiscences appear in the columns he wrote for such journals as *Colliers, Holiday* and *Newsweek.* He also wrote articles about his childhood for the *New York Herald Tribune.* The articles from two other columns were published in book form under the titles of *Sweet and Sour* and *My Turn.* During his lifetime, a number of biographical articles were written about O'Hara. The most useful of these are a series written for the *New York Post* by Beverly Gary and an article by Don Schanche published in *Esquire.*

Because of the books already written about John O'Hara, especially those by Matthew J. Bruccoli and Finis Farr, I have cited these works where appropriate rather than manuscript collections so that readers may have easy access to the material. This is particularly true of O'Hara's correspondence, most of which has been collected by Professor Bruccoli in his *Selected Letters of John O'Hara.* The various letters that were not known or collected by Professor Bruccoli I have cited according to their ownership. I have also cited Professor Bruccoli's collection of O'Hara's articles, reviews and interviews entitled *"An Artist Is His Own Fault."*

The notes that follow refer only to written documents and not to verbal reports, even if these are placed between quotation marks. I have indicated at the beginning of the notes for each chapter the names of individuals who have given me verbal information, and usually the source is indicated in the text itself.

For the sake of readability I have not cluttered the text with numbered notes. Instead, I have listed the sources in order against the number of the page on which the quotations appear. Occasionally I have quoted from a document without indicating excisions. Again, this has been done in order to avoid an unsightly text. In no case, however, have I changed the order of the sentences or omitted material that would seriously modify the citation in question.

CHAPTER 1.   POTTSVILLE

Information about John O'Hara's family came principally from interviews with his brothers and sisters, notably Mary O'Hara, Joseph O'Hara, Martin O'Hara, James O'Hara and Kathleen O'Hara Fuldner. I am also indebted to the widow of O'Hara's brother Thomas and to their daughter Ellen. In addition to the information I gathered during visits to Pottsville, I have read a number of local histories of Schuylkill County, Pennsylvania and Pottsville. I have also been guided by Charles Bassett's series of articles entitled "O'Hara's Roots," which were published in *The Pottsville Republican* and which have been republished under the title of "John O'Hara: Irishman and American" in *John O'Hara Journal,* I, 2, Summer 1979.

Page
  1   Arthur Pottersman, "The World, I Think, Is Better Off That I'm a Writer," *London Sun,* September 21, 1963; reproduced in Matthew J. Bruccoli, ed., *"An Artist Is His Own Fault": John O'Hara on Writers and Writing,* Carbondale, Illinois, 1977, p. 220 (hereafter cited as *Artist Own Fault*).

  1   Quoted in Beverly Gary, "John O'Hara—A Post Portrait," *New York Post,* May 22, 1959 (hereafter cited as *Post Portrait*).

  1   JOH to Kyle Crichton, August 1933, in Matthew J. Bruccoli, ed., *Selected Letters of John O'Hara,* New York, 1978, p. 77 (hereafter cited as *Letters*).

  3   JOH to Mrs. Courtlandt D. Barnes, n.d. (1953), Joan Gates Collection.

  4   JOH to Thomas O'Hara, December 30, 1963, *Letters,* p. 436.

  4   *Ibid.,* p. 437.

  4   *Ibid.*

  6   JOH to Charles Poore, n.d., Wylie O'Hara Doughty Collection.

  6   John O'Hara, *My Turn,* New York, 1965, p. 208.

  7   John O'Hara, "What's Wrong," *Newsweek,* June 9, 1941, p. 60.

  7   John O'Hara, *My Turn,* p. 208.

  7   John O'Hara, "Aged Muser Sighs for Old Days," in "The Conning Tower," *New York World,* June 21, 1929, p. 15.

  7   John O'Hara, "Dancing School," *New York Herald Tribune,* August 3, 1930, II, p. 7.

  7   *Ibid.*

  8   *Ibid.*

8   John O'Hara, "Reflections of a Non-Travel Writer," *Holiday*, January 1966, p. 28.

8   *Ibid.*

8   *Ibid.*, p. 29.

8   *Ibid.*

8   John O'Hara, *Sweet and Sour*, New York, 1954, p. 113.

8   *Ibid.*, p. 115.

9   *Ibid.*, p. 114.

9   John O'Hara, "From Winter Quarters, N.Y.," *Ringling Brothers and Barnum and Bailey Circus Magazine and Program*, 1948, p. 60.

9   Beverly Gary, *Post Portrait*, May 19, 1959.

9   John O'Hara, "Secrets Barred in 'All Quiet,' " *The Morning Telegraph*, June 19, 1930, p. 2.

10   *Ibid.*

10   John O'Hara, "Appointment with O'Hara," *Colliers*, April 29, 1955.

10   John O'Hara, "Why Manchester Roots for Small-Town Doctor," *New York Daily Mirror*, March 9, 1950, p. 2.

11   John O'Hara, *Sweet and Sour*, p. 10.

12   John O'Hara, Talk at Foyle's Literary Luncheon, London, 1967; reproduced in *Artist Own Fault*, p. 115.

13   Don Schanche, "John O'Hara Is Alive and Well in the First Half of the Twentieth Century," *Esquire*, August 1969, p. 146 (hereafter cited as Schanche, "John O'Hara," *Esquire*).

13   Thomas O'Hara, letter to his children, May 26, 1970, Mrs. Thomas O'Hara Collection.

14   *Ibid.*

14   John O'Hara, *The Doctor's Son and Other Stories*, New York, 1935, p. 282.

CHAPTER 2.   SCHOOLS

For information about the coal mining region I am indebted to such books as Anthony Bimba's *The Molly Maguires*, New York, 1934, and George G. Korson's *Songs and Ballads of the Anthracite Miners*, New York, 1927. Through the kindness of Martin O'Hara and Vincent Balitas, I saw most of the places mentioned in this chapter and I visited O'Hara's schools in New York City and Kutztown. In addition to the printed sources cited below, I gathered information through conversations with Joseph and Martin O'Hara and with various of O'Hara's childhood friends, notably Joseph Farley and Frank Sugrue, both of Fordham Prep; Wodrow Archbald, Admiral John Bergen, Edward Fox, James B. Reilly, Robert Root, Marian Sheafer, Mrs. Russell Suender and Theodore Toussaint, all of Pottsville.

Page

16   *Fordham University, Bulletin of Information, St. John's College High School*, 1921, p. 21.

16   *Ibid.*, p. 24.

16   *Ibid.*, pp. 24–25.

17   *Ibid.*, p. 41.

17   Beverly Gary, *Post Portrait*, May 20, 1959.

19   John O'Hara, "Celibacy, Sacred and Profane," *Holiday*, August 1967.

19   John O'Hara, "Appointment with O'Hara," *Colliers,* July 22, 1955.

20   John O'Hara, *The Doctor's Son,* p. 25.

20   George G. Korson, *Songs and Ballads of the Anthracite Miners,* New York, 1927.

20   Anthony Bimba, *The Molly Maguires,* New York, 1934, p. 66.

21   John O'Hara, *The Cape Cod Lighter,* New York, 1962, p. 15.

21   John O'Hara, "When Big Bands Were Big," *Holiday,* April 1967, p. 26.

21   *Ibid.*

22   *Ibid.*

23   John O'Hara, "When Dinner Coats Were Tucks and Young Men Toddled," *New York Herald Tribune,* August 30, 1931, II, p. 9.

23   John O'Hara, "Appointment with O'Hara," *Colliers,* December 23, 1955.

24   *Ibid.* Sentence order is here reversed.

24   John O'Hara, "A High Priest of Jazz Sets Down His Life Story," *New York Herald Tribune,* November 2, 1947, p. 6.

24   JOH to Robert Simonds, April 20, 1923, *Letters,* p. 7.

24   John O'Hara, *The Cape Cod Lighter,* p. xii.

24   JOH to Robert Simonds, postmarked April 28, 1923, *Letters,* p. 8.

24   JOH to Robert Simonds, postmarked May 26, 1923, *Letters,* p. 10.

25   JOH to Robert Simonds, April 28, 1923, *Letters,* p. 9.

25   JOH to Robert Simonds, postmarked May 26, 1923, *Letters,* p. 5.

25   JOH to Robert Simonds, postmarked May 26, 1923, *Letters,* p. 10.

25   JOH to Robert Simonds, n.d., *Letters,* p. 3.

25   JOH to Robert Simonds, n.d., Pennsylvania State University Library.

25   JOH to Robert Simonds, postmarked April 28, 1923, *Letters,* p. 9.

25   JOH to Robert Simonds, n.d., *Letters,* p. 12.

25   JOH to Robert Moses, December 4, 1961, *Letters,* p. 378.

25   *Ibid.*

26   Schanche, "John O'Hara," *Esquire,* p. 146.

CHAPTER 3.   APPRENTICE JOURNALIST

Many of the same individuals cited in the notes for chapter 2 provided information for this chapter as well, notably Mary, Joseph, Martin and James O'Hara and O'Hara's cousin, Polly McKee. Katherine Bowman Werner and Peter Sterner were especially helpful in telling me about O'Hara's early experiences as a newspaperman. Wodrow Archbald and his sister Margaretta Archbald Kroll also provided useful information. I have also relied on documents by O'Hara that have been reproduced in Matthew Bruccoli's biography, *The O'Hara Concern,* 1975.

Page

27   Preface to an article for *Sports Illustrated,* typescript, Time, Incorporated, Collection.

27   John O'Hara, "Famous Author Writes of His Early Days on Journal," originally published in the *Pottsville Journal;* reproduced in Matthew J. Bruccoli, *The O'Hara Concern,* New York, 1975, p. 34.

27   John O'Hara, "A Cub Tells His Story," originally published in the *Pottsville Journal;* reproduced in Bruccoli, *The O'Hara Concern,* p. 32.

28   Edward A. Roberts, Jr., "The Curtain Falls on O'Hara's Stage," *National Observer,* November 30, 1974.

28   John O'Hara, "Famous Author Writes of His Early Days"; reproduced in Bruccoli, *The O'Hara Concern,* p. 35.

28   W. L. Werner, quoted in "John O'Hara Recalls a Hero," *New York Herald Tribune,* April 5, 1960, p. 18.

29   Quoted in "Pal Joey Is Just a Boob to His Creator," *New York Post,* January 8, 1941, p. 3.

29   John O'Hara, "Famous Author Writes of His Early Days"; reproduced in Bruccoli, *The O'Hara Concern,* p. 35.

29   JOH to Robert Simonds, n.d., *Letters,* p. 4.

30   John O'Hara, *Sweet and Sour,* pp. 53–54.

30   John O'Hara, *Files on Parade,* New York, 1939, p. 277.

30   Beverly Gary, *Post Portrait,* May 19, 1959.

31   JOH to Robert Simonds, postmarked April 20, 1923, *Letters,* p. 7.

31   JOH to F. Scott Fitzgerald, January 25, 1933, *Letters,* p. 76.

31   JOH to Thomas O'Hara, postmarked February 12, 1934, *Letters,* p. 85.

31   JOH to Robert Simonds, n.d., Pennsylvania State University Library.

32   John O'Hara, "Why Manchester Roots for Its Small-Town Doctor," *New York Daily Mirror,* March 9, 1950, p. 2.

32   JOH to Bennett Cerf, December 14, 1964, *Letters,* p. 467.

32   John O'Hara, "Why Manchester Roots," *New York Daily Mirror,* March 9, 1950, p. 28.

32   JOH to Robert Simonds, postmarked March 25, 1925, *Letters,* p. 14.

33   *Ibid.,* p. 15.

33   JOH to Wylie O'Hara, September 29, 1959, *Letters,* p. 303.

33   JOH to William Maxwell, January 4, 1966, *Letters,* p. 481.

33   John O'Hara, "Don't Say It Never Happened," *New York Herald Tribune Books,* April 8, 1962; reproduced in *Artist Own Fault,* p. 213.

34   "Who's Who Gives O'Hara Chance to Startle Strangers," *New York World Telegram,* March 18, 1941, p. 3.

34   Walter S. Farquhar, "O'Hara Reverts to Speed," in "Musings" in *Pottsville Republican;* clipping in John O'Hara Collection, Pennsylvania State University Library.

34   John O'Hara, "A Cub Tells His Story," reproduced in Bruccoli, *The O'Hara Concern,* p. 33.

35   John O'Hara, "Appointment with O'Hara," *Colliers,* March 18, 1955.

35   JOH to Thomas O'Hara, May 20, 1932, *Letters,* p. 64.

35   John O'Hara, in "The Conning Tower," *New York World,* December 1, 1927.

36   John O'Hara, in "The Conning Tower," *New York World,* December 13, 1927.

36   JOH to Robert Simonds, n.d., *Letters,* p. 16.

36   JOH to Wylie O'Hara, September 30–October 4, 1959, *Letters,* p. 306.

36   John O'Hara, "Watch the O'Fearnas Go By," *Newsweek,* October 21, 1940, p. 61.

36   John O'Hara in "The Conning Tower," *New York World,* July 15, 1927, p. 13.

37   JOH to Robert Simonds, August 1, 1927, Pennsylvania State University Library.

37   *Ibid.*

37   JOH to Robert Simonds, n.d., *Letters,* p. 22.

37   JOH to Finis Farr, December 6, 1968, *Letters,* p. 511.

37   JOH to Robert Simonds, postmarked November 1, 1927, *Letters,* p. 25.

37   *Ibid.*

37   Schanche, "John O'Hara," *Esquire,* p. 147.

37   JOH to Thomas O'Hara, postmarked February 25, 1928, Mrs. Thomas O'Hara Collection.

CHAPTER 4.   NEW YORK

For information about O'Hara's journalistic work in New York, I consulted such books as *The World of Swope,* 1965, by E. J. Kahn, Jr., Stanley Walker's *City Editor,* 1934, *The Best in 'The World,'* edited by John K. Hutchens and George Oppenheimer, 1973, Robert T. Elson's *Time, Inc.,* 1966, various books on *The New Yorker,* especially Brendan Gill's *Here at The New Yorker,* 1975, and James Thurber's *The Years with Ross,* 1959, and the various newspapers to which O'Hara contributed either as an employee or as a free-lance writer. In addition to visiting many of the places named, I read a number of books about New York life during the period covered. I am particularly indebted to Cecil Beaton's *New York,* 1938, Stephen Graham's *New York Nights,* 1927, Ward Greene's *Ride the Nightmare,* 1930, *Prodigal Women* by Nancy Hale, 1942, A. J. Liebling's *Back Where I Come From,* 1938, and Stanley Walker's *The Night Club Era,* 1933. I also spoke to a great many people who gave me information about O'Hara and the era, notably, Niven Busch, Noel Busch, the late Robert Cantwell, Emily Hahn, Nancy Hale, Ann Honeycutt, John K. Hutchens, Alice Leone Moats, Adele and Robert Lovett, the late Joel Sayre, Helen Thurber, Richard Watts, Jr., and M. R. Werner.

Page
39   John O'Hara, "Bleeck's: John O'Hara Recalls a Cave of Journalistic Greats," *New York Herald Tribune,* April 24, 1963, p. 28.

39   JOH to Thomas O'Hara, April 10, 1928, *Letters,* p. 30.

40   John O'Hara, unpublished preface to *Butterfield 8,* reproduced in *Artist Own Fault,* p. 124.

40   JOH to Robert Simonds, March 8, 1928, *Letters,* p. 29.

41   John K. Hutchens and George Oppenheimer, *The Best in 'The World,'* New York, 1973, p. xxi.

41   *Ibid.*

41   Stanley Walker, *City Editor,* New York, 1934, p. 41.

41   JOH to Robert Simonds, n.d., *Letters,* p. 34.

42   A. J. Liebling, *Back Where I Come From,* New York, 1938, p. 17.

42   Joel Sayre, "John O'Hara, a Reminiscence," *Washington Post,* October 3, 1973.

43   Beverly Gary, *Post Portrait,* May 20, 1959.

43   John O'Hara, "Cesar Romero and the Three Dollar Bills," *New York Journal,* June 13, 1936.

43   JOH to Adele Lovett, n.d., Mrs. Robert A. Lovett Collection.

43   Wolcott Gibbs, "Profile: Henry Robinson Luce," *The New Yorker,* November 28, 1936, p. 25.

43   JOH to Robert A. Lovett, n.d. (1938), Robert A. Lovett Collection.

43   JOH to Robert Moses, January 10, 1974, *Letters,* p. 300.

44   Unpublished interview, September 16, 1964, author's collection.

44   Wolcott Gibbs, "Watch Out for Mr. O'Hara," *Saturday Review,* February 19, 1938.

44   JOH to Robert Simonds, n.d., *Letters,* p. 33.

44   John O'Hara, "The Man's Side," *Vanity Fair,* August 1931, p. 47.

45   JOH to Robert Simonds, n.d., *Letters,* p. 37.

45   John O'Hara, "Appointment with O'Hara," *Colliers,* April 1, 1955.

45   JOH to Wylie O'Hara, n.d., *Letters,* p. 319.

45   JOH to William Maxwell, April 7, 1966, *Letters,* p. 482.

46   Babette Rosmond, *Robert Benchley,* New York, 1970, p. 91.

46   "Pal Joey Is Just a Boob to His Creator," *New York Post,* January 8, 1941, p. 3.

46   Wolcott Gibbs, "Watch Out for Mr. O'Hara," *Saturday Review,* February 19, 1938.

47   Nancy Hale, *Prodigal Women,* New York, 1942, p. 444.

47   JOH to Katharine Angell, n.d., *Letters,* p. 40.

48   Brendan Gill, *Here at The New Yorker,* New York, 1975, p. 390.

48   *Ibid.,* p. 392.

48   *Ibid.*

48   *Ibid.*

48   Ben Hecht, *Charlie,* New York, 1957, p. 49.

48   John O'Hara, "The Alumnae Bulletin," *The New Yorker,* May 8, 1928, p. 101.

49   JOH to Mark Schorer, February 17, 1959, *Letters,* p. 289.

49   Wolcott Gibbs, preface to John O'Hara, *Pipe Night,* New York, 1945, p. ix.

49   John O'Hara, "Spring 3100," *The New Yorker,* September 8, 1928, p. 56.

49   Gibbs, preface to *Pipe Night,* p. ix.

49   JOH to Katharine Angell, n.d., Pennsylvania State University Library.

49   John O'Hara, "The Coal Fields," *The New Yorker,* October 29, 1928, pp. 85–88.

50   John O'Hara, "The Tournament," *The New Yorker,* June 8, 1929, p. 81.

50   O'Hara, unpublished preface to *Butterfield 8,* reproduced in *Artist Own Fault,* pp. 124–125.

50   JOH to Harold Ross, n.d., *Letters,* p. 35.

51   Brendan Gill, *Here at The New Yorker,* pp. 159–160.

51   James Thurber, *The Years with Ross,* Boston, 1959, p. 6.

51   JOH to Katharine Angell, n.d., *Letters,* p. 43.

51   B. A. Bergman, "O'Hara Never Forgot a Friend or an Insult," *Philadelphia Bulletin,* April 19, 1970.

51   Wolcott Gibbs, "Watch Out for Mr. O'Hara," *Saturday Review,* February 19, 1938.

52   John O'Hara, *My Turn,* pp. 159–160.

53   John O'Hara, *Sweet and Sour,* p. 4.

53   *Ibid.*

53   Dale Kramer, *Heywood Broun,* New York, 1949, p. 203.

53   O'Hara, *Sweet and Sour,* p. 19.

54   JOH to *The New Republic,* January 15, 1940, *Letters,* p. 88.

54   John O'Hara, "Radio Recollections," *Morning Telegraph,* June 21, 1930, p. 2.
54   John O'Hara, "The Unholy Three," *Morning Telegraph,* July 6, 1930.
54   JOH to Kyle Crichton, n.d., *Letters,* p. 44.
54   John O'Hara, Letter to the Editor, *New York Herald Tribune,* January 26, 1962.
54   John O'Hara, "Movie Fans Like Me Should Know All," *New York Evening Journal Magazine,* May 9, 1936.
54   Beverly Gary, *Post Portrait,* May 20, 1959.
55   Jim Bishop, *The Mark Hellinger Story,* New York, 1952, p. 199.
55   Cleveland Amory, *Celebrity Register,* New York, 1967, p. 470.
55   JOH to Robert Simonds, n.d., *Letters,* p. 33.
55   JOH to Robert Simonds, n.d., *Letters,* p. 55.
55   John O'Hara, "Anything for Joe?" *Liberty,* December 9, 1944, p. 20.
56   Thomas O'Hara to Finis Farr, quoted in Finis Farr, *O'Hara, a Biography,* Boston, 1973, p. 134.
56   Finis Farr, *O'Hara, a Biography,* p. 136.
56   JOH to Thomas O'Hara, postmarked February 12, 1934, *Letters,* p. 84.
57   JOH to Robert Simonds, postmarked July 3, 1931, *Letters,* p. 47.
57   *Ibid.*
57   JOH to Kyle Crichton, n.d., Princeton University Library.
58   JOH to Kyle Crichton, n.d., *Letters,* p. 49.
58   JOH to Kyle Crichton, August 18, 1931, *Letters,* p. 50.
58   *Ibid.*
58   Kyle Crichton to John O'Hara, September 1, 1931, Princeton University Library.
58   JOH to Robert Simonds, n.d., *Letters,* p. 55.
58   *Ibid.*
58   JOH to Robert Simonds, n.d., *Letters,* p. 71.
58   JOH to Robert Simonds, n.d., *Letters,* p. 53.
58   JOH to Robert Simonds, postmarked January 17, 1932, *Letters,* pp. 57–58.
58   JOH to Robert Simonds, n.d., *Letters,* p. 56.
59   Finis Farr, *O'Hara, a Biography,* p. 148.
59   JOH to Robert Simonds, n.d., *Letters,* p. 69.
59   JOH to F. Scott Fitzgerald, June 25, 1933, *Letters,* p. 76.

CHAPTER 5.   APPOINTMENT IN SAMARRA

Aside from the information gathered from the sources cited below, most of the material for this chapter comes from letters and interviews with Niven Busch, Lucinda Dietz, Averell Harriman, William Lord, Adele and Robert Lovett, Gertrude Macy, Eugene O'Hara, the late S. J. Perelman, Meta Rosenberg, Ruth Sato, Irving and Jean Stone, Kathrine White, Mildred Gilman Wohlforth and Frank Zachary.

Page
60   JOH to Paul Scheetz, n.d., reproduced in Bruccoli, *The O'Hara Concern,* p. 88.
61   *Pittsburgh Bulletin-Index,* July 12, 1933, p. 6.
62   JOH to Thomas O'Hara, October 23, 1933, *Letters,* p. 81.
62   *Ibid.*
62   *Ibid.*

62   Beverly Gary, *Post Portrait,* May 20, 1959.

62   JOH to Thomas O'Hara, postmarked February 12, 1934, *Letters,* p. 84.

62   Robert Van Gelder, "John O'Hara Who Talks Like His Stories," *New York Times Book Review,* May 26, 1940, reproduced in *Artist Own Fault,* p. 177.

62   JOH to Thomas O'Hara, postmarked February 12, 1934, *Letters,* p. 84.

63   Van Gelder interview, *Artist Own Fault,* p. 178.

63   JOH to F. Scott Fitzgerald, n.d. (April 1934), *Letters,* pp. 92–93.

63   JOH to David Brown, September 6, 1960, *Letters,* p. 345.

63   *Ibid.,* pp. 344–345.

64   F. Scott Fitzgerald, "Echoes of the Jazz Age," *The Crack-up,* New York, 1945, p. 20.

64   John O'Hara, *Appointment in Samarra,* New York, 1934, p. 115.

65   JOH to Thomas O'Hara, August 16, 1934, *Letters,* p. 96.

65   John O'Hara, *Appointment in Samarra,* pp. 256–257.

66   John O'Hara, Talk at Foyle's Literary Luncheon, reproduced in *Artist Own Fault,* p. 108.

66   John O'Hara, introduction to *The Portable F. Scott Fitzgerald,* New York, 1945, reproduced in *Artist Own Fault,* p. 147.

66   JOH to Gerald Murphy, July 30, 1962, *Letters,* p. 402.

67   Frank MacShane, *The Life of Raymond Chandler,* New York, 1976, p. 96.

67   Sinclair Lewis, "Nostalgia for the Nineties," *Saturday Review,* October 6, 1934.

67   JOH to Mark Schorer, February 17, 1959, *Letters,* p. 288.

67   Dorothy Parker statement is in John O'Hara Collection, Pennsylvania State University Library.

67   Fitzgerald statement is in John O'Hara Collection, Pennsylvania State University Library.

67   Quoted in Bruccoli, *The O'Hara Concern,* p. 110.

67   Joseph F. Lowry, "Dear John (O'Hara): All Is Forgiven, Love, Gibbsville," *The Pennsylvania Sampler,* ed. by Paul B. Beers, Harrisburg, 1970, p. 122.

67   JOH to Walter Farquhar, n.d. (1935), *Letters,* p. 106.

67   John McClain, "On the Sun Deck," *New York Sun,* August 21, 1935, p. 22.

68   JOH to Gerald Murphy, July 30, 1962, *Letters,* pp. 401–402.

68   John O'Hara, Rider College Lectures, reproduced in *Artist Own Fault,* p. 26.

68   *The Kungsholm Cruise News,* No. 4 , Pennsylvania State University Library.

68   *Ibid.,* No. 6.

68   John McClain, "On the Sun Deck," *New York Sun,* April 12, 1934, p. 29.

69   JOH to Thomas O'Hara, postmarked June 4, 1934, *Letters,* pp. 93–94.

69   John O'Hara, "Hello Hollywood Goodbye," *Holiday,* May 1968.

69   John O'Hara, "Appointment with O'Hara," *Colliers,* July 22, 1955.

70   JOH to Wylie O'Hara, postmarked August 12, 1959, *Letters,* p. 299.

70   JOH to Thomas O'Hara, August 16, 1934, *Letters,* p. 96.

72   John O'Hara, "Appointment with O'Hara," *Colliers,* February 19, 1954.

73   JOH to Ruth Sato, postmarked February 10, 1955, *Letters,* p. 101.

73   *Ibid.*

73   JOH to Robert Simonds, n.d. (November 1931), *Letters,* p. 53.

74   O'Hara, *The Doctor's Son,* p. 294.

74   JOH to Charles A. Pearce, n.d. (March 1935), *Letters,* p. 104.

74   JOH to Charles A. Pearce, n.d. (April 1935) *Letters,* p. 104.

74   JOH to Charles A. Pearce, August 16, 1934, *Letters,* p. 94.

74   JOH to F. Scott Fitzgerald, n.d. (October 1935), *Letters,* p. 109.

74   *Ibid.*

74   JOH to Adele Lovett, June 15, 1935, Mrs. Robert A. Lovett Collection.

74   JOH to F. Scott Fitzgerald, n.d. (October 1935), *Letters,* p. 109.

74   JOH to Charles A. Pearce, August 4, 1935, *Letters,* p. 108.

76   JOH to Adele Lovett, n.d. Mrs. Robert A. Lovett Collection.

76   *Ibid.*

76   John McClain, "On the Sun Deck," *New York Sun,* August 21, 1935, p. 22.

76   JOH to F. Scott Fitzgerald, n.d. (October 1935), p. 110.

76   *Ibid.*

76   John O'Hara, unpublished preface to *Butterfield 8,* reproduced in *Artist Own Fault,* p. 125.

77   *New York Times,* June 24, 1931.

77   John O'Hara, *Butterfield 8,* New York, 1935, p. 185.

78   *Ibid.,* p. 111.

78   *Ibid.,* p. 110–111.

78   William Saroyan, quoted in Bruccoli, *The O'Hara Concern,* p. 157.

78   John Chamberlain, *New York Times,* October 17, 1935.

78   Quoted in O'Hara, "Remarks on the Novel," 1957, reproduced in *Artist Own Fault,* p. 100.

78   *Danville Morning News,* clipping in John O'Hara Collection, Pennsylvania State University Library.

78   JOH to F. Scott Fitzgerald, n.d. (October 1935), *Letters,* p. 109.

78   Clifton Fadiman, "Disappointment in O'Hara," *The New Yorker,* October 19, 1935.

79   John O'Hara, "Hello Hollywood Goodbye," *Holiday,* May 1968, p. 55.

79   JOH to Harold Ross, December 1935, *Letters,* pp. 110–111.

CHAPTER 6.   HOLLYWOOD

Several books on Hollywood were valuable for this chapter, above all, Leo Rosten's *Hollywood,* 1941, which provided a wealth of facts about the time when O'Hara was in California. Gilbert Seldes's books such as *The Movies Come from America* and *The Great Audience* were also useful, as was Sheilah Graham's *Garden of Allah.* I spoke to a number of people who knew O'Hara in Hollywood and am indebted to Edwin Earl, Sheilah Graham, Dorothy Laughlin, Warren Leslie, Stephen Longstreet, Felicia Paramore, Allen Rivkin, Gilbert Roland, George Rowan, Robert Rowan, William Saroyan, the late Joel Sayre, Budd Schulberg, Helen Asbury Smith and Elizabeth Wilson. For information concerning O'Hara's second wife, Belle Wylie, I spoke to members of her family, including her sisters and brother, Winifred Gardiner, Lucilla Potter and Robert Wylie, as well as to Wylie O'Hara Doughty, the daughter of Belle and John O'Hara. Adele and Robert Lovett were also very helpful. For developments in the O'Hara family at this time, I learned much from Kathleen O'Hara Fuldner and Mary O'Hara. For information about the O'Haras' trip to England, I am grateful to Morley Kennerly, Pamela Milburne, V. S. Pritchett, Peter Quennell, and Helen Thurber.

Page
80   JOH to F. Scott Fitzgerald, n.d. (April 1936), *Letters,* p. 116.
81   JOH to Charles A. Pearce and Samuel Sloan, received September 19, 1936, *Letters,* p. 123.
81   John O'Hara, "Personal History," *Newsweek,* September 2, 1940, p. 48.
81   F. Scott Fitzgerald to John Peale Bishop, May 1935; reproduced in Andrew Turnbull, ed., *The Letters of F. Scott Fitzgerald,* New York, 1963, p. 367.
81   F. Scott Fitzgerald to John O'Hara, quoted in letter from O'Hara to Fitzgerald, n.d. (April 1936), *Letters,* p. 116.
81   JOH to Kyle Crichton, n.d. (August 1933), *Letters,* p. 77.
81   JOH to Charles A. Pearce, n.d. (Spring 1936), *Letters,* p. 120.
81   JOH to F. Scott Fitzgerald, n.d. (August 1936), *Letters,* p. 116.
82   *Ibid.*
82   Leo G. Rosten, *Hollywood,* New York, 1941, p. 52.
82   *Ibid.,* p. 45.
83   John O'Hara, *My Turn,* p. 179.
83   JOH to Charles A. Pearce and Samuel Sloan, n.d. (Summer 1936), *Letters,* p. 120.
83   F. Scott Fitzgerald to anonymous recipient, September 1935; reproduced in *Letters of F. Scott Fitzgerald,* p. 530.
84   John O'Hara, "Hello Hollywood Goodbye," *Holiday,* August 1968, p. 55.
84   John O'Hara, "Appointment with O'Hara," *Colliers,* January 6, 1956.
84   John McClain, "The Happy Days," *New York Journal American,* August 23, 1964.
85   Sheilah Graham, *The Garden of Allah,* New York, 1970, p. 146.
85   Nathaniel Benchley to the author, May 24, 1978.
87   JOH to Charles A. Pearce, received February 28, 1936, *Letters,* p. 113.
87   JOH to F. Scott Fitzgerald, n.d. (April 1936), *Letters,* p. 117.
88   JOH to John Steinbeck, reproduced in Elaine Steinbeck and Robert Wallstein, eds., *Steinbeck, A Life in Letters,* New York, 1975, p. 123.
88   John O'Hara, "Hello Hollywood Goodbye," *Holiday,* May 1968, pp. 55, 125.
88   John O'Hara, "The Follies of Broadway," *Holiday,* February 1967, p. 25.
90   Finis Farr, *O'Hara, a Biography,* p. 188.
91   John O'Hara, "Quogue," *Hampton Pictorial,* July 27, 1951, p. 8.
92   JOH to Adele Lovett, postmarked January 3, 1938, Mrs. Robert A. Lovett Collection.
92   JOH to Adele Lovett, n.d., Mrs. Robert A. Lovett Collection.
92   *Ibid.*
93   Alexander Pope, *An Essay on Man,* I, x, 94.
93   *Ibid.,* I, iii, 91–96.
93   John O'Hara, *Hope of Heaven,* New York, 1938, pp. 178–179.
94   *Ibid.,* p. 180.
94   Robert Van Gelder, "John O'Hara," reproduced in *Artist Own Fault,* p. 179. An indirect quotation.
94   John O'Hara, *Hope of Heaven,* pp. 66–67.
95   Alfred Kazin, "Smeared with Glitter," *New York Herald Tribune Books,* March 20, 1938.
95   Clifton Fadiman, *The New Yorker,* March 19, 1938.

95   Heywood Broun, "It Seems to Me," *New York World,* March 31, 1938.
95   Margaret Altschul, "John O'Hara at Home," *Greenwich (Connecticut) Time,* April 1, 1938.
95   JOH to Adele Lovett, n.d., Mrs. Robert A. Lovett Collection.
96   JOH to Adele Lovett, April 1938, Mrs. Robert A. Lovett Collection.
96   JOH to Adele Lovett, postmarked April 18, 1938, Mrs. Robert A. Lovett Collection.
96   JOH to Samuel Sloan, n.d. (April 1938), *Letters,* p. 129.
96   JOH to Samuel Sloan and Charles A. Pearce, May 3, 1938, *Letters,* p. 134.
97   JOH to Adele Lovett, May 9, 1938, Mrs. Robert A. Lovett Collection.
97   JOH to William Maxwell, April 30, 1938, *Letters,* p. 132.
97   JOH to Adele Lovett, May 9, 1938. Mrs. Robert A. Lovett Collection.
97   Alec Waugh, *My Brother Evelyn,* New York, 1967, p. 248.
98   John O'Hara, Talk at Foyle's Literary Luncheon, reproduced in *Artist Own Fault,* p. 106.
98   John O'Hara, "Appointment with O'Hara," *Colliers,* July 8, 1955.
99   Belle O'Hara to Adele Lovett, July 1938, Mrs. Robert A. Lovett Collection.
99   JOH to Samuel Sloan, n.d., Harcourt Brace Jovanovich files.

CHAPTER 7.   PAL JOEY

For this chapter I consulted many of the same sources as for the last. For information about the movies on which O'Hara worked during this period I consulted the library of the American Academy of Motion Picture Arts and Sciences, and for other aspects of O'Hara's life in Hollywood I am indebted to Amanda and Philip Dunne, Adele Lovett, Gilbert Roland, Gloria Romanoff, the late S. J. Perelman, Budd Schulberg and Collier Young. The principal source of information on the musical side of *Pal Joey* is Richard Rodgers's book *Musical Stages.* I also consulted numerous individuals involved in the preparation of the stage version of this story, among them George Abbott, Gene Kelly and Richard Rodgers, and I learned a good deal from Kathrine White, Richard Watts, Jr., Richard Lockridge and Kathleen O'Hara Fuldner.

Page
100   JOH to John Hayward, received November 22, 1938, *Letters,* p. 141.
101   JOH to Adele Lovett, January 2, 1940, Mrs. Robert A. Lovett Collection.
101   *Ibid.*
101   *Ibid.*
101   *Ibid.*
101   *Ibid.*
102   JOH to William Maxwell, n.d. (1939), *Letters,* p. 153.
102   JOH to Samuel Sloan, n.d. (May 1939), *Letters,* pp. 147–148.
102   Belle O'Hara to Adele Lovett, n.d. (1939), Mrs. Robert A. Lovett Collection.
102   Belle O'Hara to Adele Lovett, April 6, 1939, Mrs. Robert A. Lovett Collection.
104   S. J. Perelman, *Baby, It's Cold Outside,* New York, 1971, pp. 27–28.
104   Quoted in Bruccoli, *The O'Hara Concern,* p. 157.
104   John O'Hara, "In Memory of Scott Fitzgerald," *New Republic,* March 3, 1941, reproduced in *Artist Own Fault,* p. 136.

104   John O'Hara, "Hello Hollywood Goodbye," *Holiday,* May 1968, p. 55.

104   F. Scott Fitzgerald, "The Notebooks," *Antaeus,* 32, Winter 1979, p. 108.

104   *Ibid.,* p. 109.

105   JOH to William Maxwell, June 7, 1963, *Letters,* p. 432.

105   John O'Hara, "In Memory of Scott Fitzgerald," reproduced in *Artist Own Fault,* p. 135.

105   *Ibid.,* p. 137.

105   John O'Hara, "Introduction" to *Portable Fitzgerald,* reproduced in *Artist Own Fault,* pp. 144, 145.

106   Belle O'Hara to Adele Lovett, May 1, 1941. Mrs. Robert A. Lovett Collection.

106   John O'Hara, "Appointment with O'Hara," *Colliers,* February 5, 1954.

106   John O'Hara, screenplay for *Moontide,* American Academy of Motion Picture Arts and Sciences., p. 63.

106   *Ibid.* p. 64.

106   JOH to Adele Lovett, January 2, 1940, Mrs. Robert A. Lovett Collection.

106   *Moontide* script, p. 116.

106   JOH to Adele Lovett, January 2, 1940, Mrs. Robert A. Lovett Collection.

107   JOH to William Maxwell, n.d., Pennsylvania State University Library.

107   JOH to Harold Ross, n.d. (January 1939), *Letters,* p. 142.

107   *Ibid.*

107   James Thurber, *The Years with Ross,* Boston 1959, p. 13.

107   JOH to William Maxwell, received March 14, 1939, *Letters,* p. 144.

107   JOH to William Maxwell, received February 8, 1939, *Letters,* p. 143.

108   Gilbert Seldes, *The Movies Come from America,* New York, 1937, p. 16.

109   JOH to Adele Lovett, January 2, 1940. Mrs. Robert A. Lovett Collection.

109   "Pal Joey Is Just a Boob to His Creator," *New York Post,* January 8, 1941, p. 3

109   Earl Wilson, "It Happened Last Night," reproduced in *Artist Own Fault,* p. 181.

109   "Pal Joey Is Just a Boob to His Creator," *New York Post,* January 8, 1941, p. 3.

109   Earl Wilson, "It Happened Last Night," reproduced in *Artist Own Fault,* p. 181.

109   Jack Keating, "John O'Hara's World of Yale, Society and Sex," *Cosmopolitan,* September 1960, p. 62 (hereafter cited as Keating, "John O'Hara's World").

110   John O'Hara, "The Erloff," *Pal Joey,* New York, 1939, p. 111.

110   John O'Hara, "Joey Comes of Age," *New York Herald Tribune,* November 23, 1952, IV, p. 1.

110   JOH to William Maxwell, n.d. (January 1940), *Letters,* p. 156.

110   JOH to Richard Rodgers, n.d. (January 1940), *Letters,* p. 158.

110   Richard Rodgers, *Musical Stages,* New York, 1975, p. 100.

111   *Ibid.,* p. 199.

111   Quoted in Lucius Beebe, "Stage Asides," *New York Herald Tribune,* January 12, 1941, VI, pp. 1, 2.

111   *Ibid.*

112   John O'Hara, "On Larry (Lorenzo, Jr.) Hart," *New York Times,* February 27, 1944, II, p. 1.

112   Rodgers, *Musical Stages,* p. 199.
112   John O'Hara, "On Larry (Lorenzo, Jr.) Hart."
112   *Ibid.*
112   *Ibid.*
113   Brooks Atkinson, "The Play: Christmas Night Adds 'Pal Joey' and 'Meet the People' to the Musical Stage," *New York Times,* December 26, 1940.
114   Wolcott Gibbs, "Upturn," *The New Yorker,* January 4, 1941.
114   Richard Watts, Jr., "The Theatre: No Longer a Winter of Discontent," *New York Herald Tribune,* January 5, 1941.

CHAPTER 8. WAR YEARS

The war years were unsettled and unsettling for O'Hara, and he was often on the move from New York to California and back. It was an exceptionally social time. The range of O'Hara's acquaintance can be gathered from the names of those of his friends who saw him during this period and who have told me about him. In New York and Long Island, they included Charles Addams, Ellen Barry, Lucinda Dietz, Brendan Gill, John Hersey, Henry and Winifred Gardiner, Robert and Adele Lovett, Mrs. L. B. Norris, Robert Payne, Edgar Scott, Elaine Steinbeck, Herbert Bayard Swope, Jr., Richard Watts, Jr. and Jerome Weidman. In Hollywood his friends included David Brown, Geraldine Fitzgerald, Leonora Hornblow, Gloria Romanoff, Gloria Sheekman and Collier Young. Those who have given me specific information about O'Hara's war activities include Joseph Bryan III, Emmet Crozier, Philip Dunne, Fred Porcelli, Mrs. John Valentine and Jean Valentine.

Page
115   Lucius Beebe, "Stage Asides," *New York Herald Tribune,* January 12, 1941, VI, pp. 1, 2.
116   *Ibid.* p. 1.
116   Benjamin Welles, "John O'Hara and His Pal Joey," *New York Times,* January 26, 1951, IX, p. 2.
116   JOH to Adele Lovett, January 2, 1940. Mrs. Robert A. Lovett Collection.
117   JOH to the Editor of *Holiday,* December 1959, *Letters,* p. 316.
118   William Saroyan to the author, June 1, 1978.
119   The descriptive phrase "master of the fancied slight" has been attributed to many people, among them Joel Sayre, Bennett Cerf and Richard Watts, Jr.
119   James Thurber, quoted in Beverly Gary, *Post Portrait,* May 24, 1959.
119   Thurber, *The Years with Ross,* p. 173.
119   Owen Johnson, *Stover at Yale,* New York, 1912, p. 22.
119   John O'Hara, "Conversation with a Russian," *The New Yorker,* March 29, 1930.
119   John O'Hara, "Harvard List," *Newsweek,* February 9, 1942, p. 63.
119   *Ibid.*
119   JOH to Adele Lovett, February 3, 1948, Mrs. Robert A. Lovett Collection.
120   John O'Hara, *Butterfield 8,* pp. 67, 68.
121   JOH to Edgar Scott, December 18, 1963, Edgar Scott Collection.
121   John O'Hara, *Sweet and Sour,* p. 58.

121 JOH to Katharine Delaney O'Hara, n.d. (1939), Kathleen O'Hara Fuldner Collection.

122 John O'Hara, "An American in Memoriam," *Newsweek,* July 15, 1940.

122 John O'Hara, "Complaint Department," *Newsweek,* October 19, 1941.

122 John O'Hara, *My Turn,* p. 5.

122 JOH to William Maxwell, n.d. (late 1939), *Letters,* p. 152.

123 JOH to James Forrestal, February 7, 1942, *Letters,* p. 166.

123 JOH to Folkestone, May 31, 1942, *Letters,* p. 168.

123 JOH to Gilbert Roland, July 13, 1942, *Letters,* p. 171.

123 *Ibid.,* p. 172.

123 *Ibid.*

124 JOH to Joseph Bryan III, April 25, 1944, Pennsylvania State University Library.

125 JOH to Frank Sullivan, November 16, 1944, *Letters,* p. 187.

126 JOH to Adele Lovett, January 2, 1940, Mrs. Robert A. Lovett Collection.

126 JOH to Adele Lovett, n.d. (1938), Mrs. Robert A. Lovett Collection.

126 Keating, "John O'Hara's World," p. 62.

126 John O'Hara, Talk at Foyle's Literary Luncheon, reproduced in *Artist Own Fault,* p. 113.

127 John O'Hara, introduction to *Portable Fitzgerald,* reproduced in *Artist Own Fault,* p. 151.

127 *Ibid.*

127 John O'Hara, "Dorothy Parker, Hip Pocket Size," *New York Times Book Review,* May 28, 1944, reproduced in *Artist Own Fault,* p. 160.

128 JOH, quoted in *The New York Times,* November 16, 1958.

128 Wolcott Gibbs, preface to John O'Hara, *Pipe Night,* p. x.

128 John O'Hara, "Nothing Missing," *Pipe Night,* p. 73.

128 John O'Hara, "Too Young," *Pipe Night,* p. 48.

129 John O'Hara, "Bread Alone," *Pipe Night,* p. 85.

129 Lionel Trilling, "John O'Hara Observes Our Mores," *New York Times Book Review,* March 18, 1945, p. 1.

129 John O'Hara, "Graven Image," *Pipe Night,* p. 125.

129 John O'Hara, "Civilized," *Pipe Night,* p. 145.

129 John O'Hara, "Can You Carry Me?," *Pipe Night,* p. 31.

129 Trilling, "O'Hara Observes Our Mores," p. 1.

129 JOH to Lionel Trilling, March 21, 1945, Diana Trilling Collection.

130 Frank Sullivan to Katharine Barnes O'Hara, May 31, 1974, Saratoga Springs Historical Society.

130 JOH to David Brown, February 6, 1959, *Letters,* p. 262.

131 *Ibid.*

132 JOH to John Steinbeck, June 2 or 3, 1949, *Letters,* p. 224.

132 *Ibid.,* p. 225.

133 Brendan Gill, *Here at The New Yorker,* New York, 1975, p. 269.

133 JOH to John K. Hutchens, n.d. (1957), John K. Hutchens, Collection.

133 John O'Hara, "Quogue," *Hampton Pictorial,* July 27, 1951, p. 8.

133 JOH to John Steinbeck, June 2 or 3, 1949, *Letters,* p. 225.

133 JOH to Joseph Bryan III, dated August 1948 by recipient, Pennsylvania State University Library.

135   JOH to Charles Addams, September 26, 1947, Charles Addams Collection.
135   JOH to Charles Addams, September 28, 1947, Charles Addams Collection.
135   JOH to Barbara Addams, dated August 1948 by Charles Addams, Charles
       Addams Collection.
136   Wolcott Gibbs to Charles Addams, n.d., Charles Addams Collection.
137   Quoted in *An Artist Is His Own Fault*, pp. 159, 161.
137   JOH to Wolcott Gibbs, n.d., Pennsylvania State University Library.
137   JOH to Katharine Angell White, May 1, 1946, *Letters*, p. 198.
137   JOH to Katharine Angell White, December 26, 1945, *Letters*, p. 196.
137   JOH to Gustave Lobrano, n.d. (Summer 1946), *Letters*, p. 198.
137   JOH to Katharine Angell White, n.d. (November 1946), *Letters*, p. 199.
137   JOH to Katharine Angell White, n.d. (1947), *Letters*, p. 202.
138   JOH to Katharine Angell White, n.d. (1947), *Letters*, p. 201.

CHAPTER 9.   A RAGE TO LIVE

Information about O'Hara's connections with Random House has come primarily
from Phyllis Cerf Wagner, Donald Klopfer and Louis Nizer. For his sometimes
tempestuous relationship with *The New Yorker* I have consulted: Charles Addams,
Roger Angell, Gardner Botsford, Noel Busch, the late Robert Cantwell, Clifton
Fadiman, Brendan Gill, Milton Greenstein, Emily Hahn, Nancy Hale, E. J. Kahn,
Jr., William Maxwell, the late St. Clair McKelway, the late S. J. Perelman, Irwin
Shaw, Helen Thurber and R. E. M. Whittaker. Concerning O'Hara's move to
Princeton I have gathered information from many who knew him there, among
them Carlos Baker, Gerald and Kate Bramwell, Joe Brown, John Cheever, Hamilton
Cottier, John Davies, Richardson Dilworth, Jr., Verna Hobson, Rensselaer Lee,
Richard Ludwig, Ann Martindell, John McPhee, the late Joseph Outerbridge and
Thelma Pemberton. I have also consulted a number of people about other aspects
of O'Hara's life during this period: Nona Balakian, Ellen Barry, John Delaney,
Winifred Gardiner, Lucilla Potter, Hamilton Southworth, Paul Shyre, Herbert Bay-
ard Swope, Jr., and Robert Wylie.

Page
139   JOH to Katharine Angell White, n.d. (1947), *Letters*, p. 202.
139   John O'Hara, unpublished preface to *Selected Short Stories*, reproduced in *Artist
       Own Fault*, p. 122.
140   Lionel Trilling, "John O'Hara Observes Our Mores," *New York Times Book
       Review*, March 18, 1945, p. 29.
140   Harvey Breit, "Talk with John O'Hara," *New York Times Book Review*, Septem-
       ber 4, 1949, reproduced in *Artist Own Fault*, p. 183.
140   John O'Hara, "The Novelists Read," *New York Times Book Review*, August 21,
       1949, p. 3., reproduced in *Artist Own Fault*, p. 164. Although O'Hara deni-
       grated the work of women novelists, half the books he cited were written
       by two women, Rosamond Lehmann and Edith Wharton.
140   JOH to Frank Norris, July 22, 1949, *Letters*, p. 226.
140   Jules Romains, preface to *Men of Good Will*, I, New York, 1933, p. ix.
140   *Ibid.*, p. x.
140   *Ibid.*, p. xi.

140 JOH to Frank Norris, July 22, 1949, *Letters,* p. 227.

140 Breit, "Talk with John O'Hara," reproduced in *Artist Own Fault,* p. 183.

141 *Ibid.*

141 John O'Hara, "Appointment with O'Hara," *Colliers,* June 25, 1954.

141 John Steinbeck to John O'Hara, June 8, 1949, reproduced in Elaine Steinbeck and Robert Wallstein, eds., *Steinbeck, A Life in Letters,* p. 359.

142 JOH to Frank Norris, July 22, 1949, *Letters,* pp. 227–228.

144 Orville Prescott, "Books of The Times," *New York Times,* August 16, 1949.

144 Keating, "John O'Hara's World," *Cosmopolitan,* p. 60.

144 Prescott, "Books of The Times," *New York Times,* August 16, 1949.

144 Bennett Cerf to John O'Hara, November 29, 1948, Columbia University Library.

144 *Ibid.*

144 JOH to Bennett Cerf, November 30, 1948, *Letters,* pp. 214, 215.

145 JOH to Saxe Commins, n.d. (Summer 1948), *Letters,* p. 207.

145 Brendan Gill, "The O'Hara Report and the Wit of Miss McCarthy," *The New Yorker,* August 20, 1949.

145 Wolcott Gibbs, "Watch Out for Mr. O'Hara," *Saturday Review,* February 19, 1938.

145 JOH to Fletcher Markle, August 20, 1949, *Letters,* p. 230.

145 JOH to Lionel Trilling, August 19, 1949, Diana Trilling Collection.

146 Jack Keating, "O'Hara's World," *Cosmopolitan,* p. 60.

146 JOH to Bennett Cerf, n.d. (1949), Columbia University Library.

147 Beverly Gary, *Post Portrait,* May 22, 1959.

147 JOH to Janet Troxell, n.d. (June 1949), *Letters,* p. 229.

147 Ernest Hemingway, *Green Hills of Africa,* New York, 1935, p. 72.

147 John O'Hara, "Appointment with O'Hara," *Colliers,* February 5, 1954.

148 John O'Hara, "Appointment with O'Hara," *Colliers,* August 20, 1954.

148 John O'Hara, *Sweet and Sour,* p. 52.

149 JOH to John Hutchens, February 21, 1963, John K. Hutchens Collection.

149 JOH to Richardson Dilworth, May 31, 1966, *Letters,* p. 485.

150 JOH to Philip Barry, November 10, 1949, Ellen Barry Collection.

151 JOH to Herman Liebert, January 29, 1948, *Letters,* p. 203.

151 John O'Hara, "Writing—What's in It for Me?" reproduced in *Artist Own Fault,* pp. 59–60.

151 *Ibid.,* p. 70.

151 Kenneth D. Munn, "A Writer's Look at His Town, Career and Future," *Princeton Packet,* November 23, 1961, reproduced in *Artist Own Fault,* p. 211.

151 John O'Hara, Rider College Lectures, reproduced in *Artist Own Fault,* p. 50.

152 Joseph Blotner, *Faulkner,* New York, 1974, II, p. 1522.

152 Robert Penn Warren to the author, May 29, 1978.

152 JOH to Ernest Hemingway, n.d. (1935), *Letters,* p. 107.

152 JOH to Ernest Hemingway, January 15, 1938, John F. Kennedy Library.

152 John O'Hara, "The Wayward Reader," *Holiday,* December 1964, p. 31.

153 John O'Hara, "The Author's Name Is Hemingway," *New York Times Book Review,* September 10, 1950, p. 1, reproduced in *Artist Own Fault,* p. 165.

153 JOH to John Steinbeck, September 18, 1950, *Letters,* p. 232.

153 JOH to William Maxwell, September 23, 1960, *Letters,* p. 348.

154   John Steinbeck to JOH, November 26, 1951, reproduced in Steinbeck and
        Wallstein, eds., *Steinbeck: A Life in Letters*, p. 432.
154   John O'Hara, *Five Plays*, p. 66.
155   William M. Dwyer, "All About Books," *Trenton Times-Advertiser*, April 26,
        1970.
155   John O'Hara, *Five Plays*, p. xii.
155   JOH to Bennett Cerf, January 29, 1957, Columbia University Library.
155   *New York Times* clipping, John O'Hara Collection, Pennsylvania State Uni-
        versity Library.
156   John O'Hara, *Five Plays*, pp. xiii, xiv.
156   *New York Times* clipping, John O'Hara Collection, Pennsylvania State Uni-
        versity Library.
156   Wolcott Gibbs, "Fine Low Fun," *The New Yorker*, January 12, 1952,
        p. 38.
156   Nathaniel Benchley to the author, May 24, 1978.
157   JOH to Robert Simonds, September 13, 1948, *Letters*, p. 212.
157   JOH to John Steinbeck, September 18, 1950, *Letters* p. 233.
158   JOH to Joseph W. Outerbridge, n.d. (August 1953), *Letters*, p. 240.
158   *Ibid.*
159   Don Schanche, "John O'Hara," *Esquire*, p. 149.
159   *Ibid.*

CHAPTER 10.   TEN NORTH FREDERICK

For details of O'Hara's personal life after the death of his wife Belle and his later
marriage to Sister, I am indebted to members of the immediate families, above all
to Wylie O'Hara Doughty, Joan Gates, C. D. B. Bryan, Courtlandt D. Barnes, Mary
O'Hara and to close friends such as Mrs. Bertram Bonner, Gerald and Kate Bram-
well, the late Joseph Outerbridge, James Kerney, Jr., Thelma Pemberton and Lili
Pell Whitmer. During this period O'Hara made his last extended visit to Holly-
wood, and I am grateful to Lauren Bacall, David Brown, Mary Crosby, Henry
Fonda, Hayes Goetz, Gene Kelly and Herbert Bayard Swope, Jr., for information.
Meanwhile, he was engaged in numerous activities, literary and other, about which
I learned much from John Chamberlain, Malcolm Cowley, the late James Gould
Cozzens, Averell Harriman, John Hersey, John K. Hutchens, William Marvel and
Isabel Wilder.

Page
161   JOH to Adele Lovett, February 1, 1954. Mrs. Robert A. Lovett Collection.
161   John O'Hara, *Sweet and Sour*, p. 7.
161   John O'Hara, "Appointment with O'Hara," *Colliers*, February 4, 1954.
162   JOH to Mrs. Courtlandt D. Barnes Sr., n.d., Joan Gates Collection.
162   *Ibid.*
162   JOH to Katharine Barnes Bryan, June 19, 1954, Joan Gates Collection.
162   JOH to Katharine Barnes Bryan, June 17, 1954, Joan Gates Collection.
163   JOH to Katharine Barnes Bryan, June 17, 1954, a second letter, Joan Gates
        Collection.
163   JOH to Katharine Barnes Bryan, July 22, 1954, Joan Gates Collection.
163   JOH to Katharine Barnes Bryan, November 27, 1954, Joan Gates Collection.

165   JOH to Joseph W. Outerbridge, June 8, 1955, *Letters*, pp. 242–243.

165   John O'Hara, treatment of *The Best Things in Life Are Free*, American Academy of Motion Picture Arts and Sciences.

165   John O'Hara, "Appointment with O'Hara," *Colliers*, May 28, 1954.

166   JOH to Joseph W. Outerbridge, June 8, 1955, *Letters*, p. 243.

166   JOH to David Brown, July 30, 1956, *Letters*, pp. 250–251.

166   JOH to Herbert Bayard Swope, Jr., October 11, 1956, *Letters*, pp. 257–258.

166   *Ibid.*, p. 258.

166   *Ibid.*

168   JOH to Charles Poore, February 27, 1960, *Letters*, p. 324.

168   John O'Hara, notes accompanying typescript of *Ten North Frederick*, Princeton University Library.

168   JOH to Joseph W. Outerbridge, July 21, 1955, *Letters*, p. 246.

169   "Who's Who Gives O'Hara Chance to Startle Strangers," *New York World Telegram*, March 8, 1941, p. 3.

169   JOH to Thomas O'Hara, July 21, 1955, Mrs. Thomas O'Hara Collection.

170   John O'Hara, Rider College Lectures, reproduced in *Artist Own Fault*, p. 29.

170   John O'Hara, "The Author's Name Is Hemingway," reproduced in *Artist Own Fault*, p. 171.

170   John O'Hara, *Butterfield 8*, p. 298.

171   JOH to Louise ——— (unknown recipient), January 22, 1958, *Letters*, p. 269.

171   John K. Hutchens, "John O'Hara from Pottsville, Pa." *New York Herald Tribune Books*, December 4, 1955, reproduced in *Artist Own Fault*, p. 190.

171   John Updike, "The Doctor's Son," *The New Yorker*, November 6, 1978, p. 213.

171   John O'Hara, Rider College Lectures, reproduced in *Artist Own Fault*, p. 4.

171   *Ibid.*, pp. 19–20.

172   JOH to Donald Klopfer, February 4, 1951, *Letters*, p. 234.

172   "Member of the Funeral," *Time*, December 26, 1955.

172   John Steinbeck, Letter to the Editor, *Time*, December 26, 1955.

172   JOH to John K. Hutchens, n.d. (1957), John K. Hutchens Collection.

172   JOH to John K. Hutchens, February 28, 1957, John K. Hutchens Collection.

172   JOH to Charles Poore, October 23, 1958, *Letters*, p. 280.

172   JOH to Robert Kirsch, December 28, 1958, *Letters*, p. 282.

172   JOH to James Gould Cozzens, August 4, 1964, *Letters*, p. 459.

173   John K. Hutchens, "National Book Awards—1956," *New York Times Book Review*, February 12, 1956.

173   John O'Hara, National Book Award acceptance speech, reproduced in *Artist Own Fault*, p. 81.

173   JOH to Carlos Baker, January 10, 1966, Carlos Baker Collection.

173   John O'Hara, "Appointment with O'Hara," *Colliers*, March 30, 1956.

174   John O'Hara, Whittall Lecture, reproduced in *Artist Own Fault*, p. 91.

174   Mary McGrory, "Author O'Hara Defends Characters 'Mid Applause," unidentified Washington newspaper clipping, John O'Hara Collection, Pennsylvania State University Library.

174   John O'Hara, untitled talk, John O'Hara Collection, Pennsylvania State University Library.

174   JOH to John Hersey, May 16, 1965, John Hersey Collection.

175   JOH to Deems Taylor, January 23, 1957, *Letters*, p. 261.

175   Malcolm Cowley statement, American Academy and Institute of Arts and Letters.

175   JOH to James Gould Cozzens, June 19, 1963, Princeton University Library.

175   JOH to Deems Taylor, January 23, 1957, American Academy and Institute of Arts and Letters.

176   *Bantam Books Press Release,* Mary Jane Clement, January 1957, Pennsylvania State University Library.

176   JOH to Donald Klopfer, June 20, 1956, Columbia University Library.

176   JOH to David Brown, January 29, 1957, University of Wyoming Library.

176   JOH to Malcolm Cowley, December 17, 1957, *Letters,* p. 268.

176   JOH to Malcolm Cowley, December 1, 1957, *Letters,* pp. 284–285.

178   JOH to William Marvel, n.d., William Marvel Collection.

179   JOH to John K. Hutchens, n.d. (1957), John K. Hutchens Collection.

180   John O'Hara, *From the Terrace,* New York, 1958, p. 411.

181   JOH to William Marvel, September 5, 1961, William Marvel Collection.

181   JOH to Bennett Cerf, January 29, 1957, Columbia University Library.

181   JOH to Charles Poore, October 23, 1958, *Letters,* p. 278.

182   JOH to David Brown, December 9, 1961, *Letters,* p. 380.

182   Alfred Kazin, "The Great American Bore," *Contemporaries,* Boston, 1952, p. 168.

182   Saul Maloff, "What's Happened to O'Hara?" *New Republic,* January 5, 1959.

182   John O'Hara, *From the Terrace,* p. 5.

183   JOH to William Maxwell, August 4, 1963, *Letters,* p. 422.

183   JOH to John K. Hutchens, n.d. (1957), John K. Hutchens Collection.

183   Cartoon by Franklin Folger, *New York Times Book Review,* January 1956.

184   John O'Hara, *From the Terrace,* p. 881.

CHAPTER 11.   PRINCETON SQUIRE

During this period, O'Hara was involved with Hollywood only for the making of movies from his novels. Information about these ventures was provided by, among others, David Brown, Philip Dunne, Henry Fonda, Ernest Lehman, Ben O'Sullivan, H. N. Swanson and Herbert Bayard Swope, Jr. O'Hara's return to *The New Yorker* was made possible largely through the efforts of Roger Angell, William Maxwell and the late St. Clair McKelway, who gave me details about how it occurred. O'Hara's English travels were given direction by such friends and acquaintances as Walter Allen, Geraldine Fitzgerald and Graham Watson, with whom I have conversed. In Princeton, he began to change the quality of his acquaintances and to befriend such individuals as Governor Richard Hughes and Governor Robert Meynor of New Jersey. At the same time, he became increasingly involved with his family, and especially with his daughter, Wylie.

Page

186   *New York Herald Tribune,* May 18, 1957, IV, p. 3.

186   *Newsweek,* June 12, 1961.

186   JOH to David Brown, April 12, 1957, University of Wyoming Library.

186   "Novelist Likes the Film Translation," *New York Herald Tribune,* May 18, 1958.

187   David Brown to John O'Hara, March 28, 1961, University of Wyoming Library.

187   *Variety,* clipping in Library of American Academy of Motion Picture Arts and Sciences, *Manchester Guardian,* October 15, 1959.

187   JOH to Bennett Cerf, June 20, 1961, Columbia University Library.

188   A. H. Weiler, "Passing Picture Scene," *New York Times,* May 31, 1959, II, p. 5.

188   JOH to David Brown, September 6, 1960, *Letters,* p. 344.

188   *Ibid.,* p. 345.

188   JOH to Katharine Barnes Bryan, November 2, 1954, Joan Gates Collection.

189   John O'Hara, "William Powell Wades Through Pain and Prison at Paramount," *New York Morning Telegraph,* June 7, 1930, p. 3.

189   JOH to James Forrestal, July 18, 1942, *Letters,* p. 173.

190   John O'Hara, "Appointment with O'Hara," *Colliers,* July 9, 1954.

190   Brendan Gill, *Here at The New Yorker,* New York, 1977, p. 277.

190   John O'Hara, "Put Up Your Dukes," *Holiday,* November 1966, p. 25.

191   JOH to Wylie O'Hara, September 29, 1959, *Letters,* p. 302.

191   *Ibid.*

191   JOH to Wylie O'Hara, September 30–October 4, *Letters,* p. 304.

191   *Ibid.,* p. 305.

191   *Ibid.,* p. 306.

191   *Ibid.*

192   JOH to Wylie O'Hara, October 18, 1959, *Letters,* pp. 311–312.

192   JOH to Wylie O'Hara, October 23, 1959, *Letters,* p. 312.

192   JOH to Wylie O'Hara, October 15, 1959, Wylie O'Hara Doughty Collection.

192   JOH to Wylie O'Hara, October 17, 1959, Wylie O'Hara Doughty Collection.

193   JOH to Wylie O'Hara, n.d., Wylie O'Hara Doughty Collection.

193   JOH to Wylie O'Hara, October 17, 1960, Wylie O'Hara Doughty Collection.

193   JOH to Wylie O'Hara, n.d., Wylie O'Hara Doughty Collection.

193   JOH to Wylie O'Hara, n.d., Wylie O'Hara Doughty Collection.

193   JOH to Wylie O'Hara, n.d., Wylie O'Hara Doughty Collection.

193   JOH to Wylie O'Hara, n.d., Wylie O'Hara Doughty Collection.

193   JOH to Wylie O'Hara, n.d., *Letters,* p. 386.

193   JOH to Wylie O'Hara, n.d., *Letters,* p. 392.

193   JOH to Wylie O'Hara, September 22, 1959, *Letters,* p. 301.

194   John O'Hara, Rider College Lectures, reproduced in *Artist Own Fault,* p. 29.

194   John O'Hara, untitled speech to new citizens, Wilmington Court House, Pennsylvania State University Library.

195   JOH to Wylie O'Hara, November 17, 1959, *Letters,* p. 315.

195   John O'Hara, *Ourselves to Know,* New York, 1960, p. 385.

195   *Ibid.,* p. 406.

196   JOH to Charles Poore, February 27, 1960, *Letters,* p. 323.

196   JOH to Charles Poore, April 21, 1959, *Letters,* p. 294.

196   JOH to Wylie O'Hara, September 30–October 4, 1959, *Letters,* p. 306.

196   John O'Hara, *Sweet and Sour,* p. 70.

196   *Ibid.,* p. 71.

197   John O'Hara, Rider College Lectures, reproduced in *Artist Own Fault,* pp. 11–12.

197   *Ibid.,* p. 31.

197   JOH to James Gould Cozzens, June 19, 1963. Princeton University Library.

198   *Ibid.*

198   JOH to Robert Oppenheimer, n.d., Library of Congress.

198   JOH to Wylie O'Hara, postmarked July 11, 1961, Wylie O'Hara Doughty Collection.

198   JOH to Hoke Norris, April 3, 1960, *Letters,* p. 330.

198   JOH to William Maxwell, September 23, 1960, *Letters,* p. 349.

198   *Ibid.*

200   JOH to William Maxwell, January 4, 1966, *Letters,* p. 481.

200   John O'Hara, unpublished preface to *Selected Short Stories,* reproduced in *Artist Own Fault,* pp. 121, 122.

200   John O'Hara, *Sweet and Sour,* p. 24.

200   Wolcott Gibbs to Gustave Lobrano, n.d. (1933), Jack Cobbs Collection.

201   JOH to David Brown, August 4, 1960, University of Wyoming Library.

201   JOH to Bennett Cerf, August 2, 1960, Phyllis Cerf Wagner Collection.

201   John O'Hara, *Sermons and Soda-Water,* II, New York, 1960, p. 72.

201   JOH to Bennett Cerf, April 23, 1960, *Letters,* p. 334.

202   John O'Hara, *Sermons and Soda-Water,* II, New York, 1960, p. 72.

202   *Ibid.,* III, p. 66.

202   JOH to Bennett Cerf, April 23, 1960, *Letters,* p. 334.

202   JOH to Bennett Cerf, April 7, 1960, *Letters,* p. 332.

203   JOH to William Maxwell, n.d., William Maxwell Collection.

203   *Ibid.*

204   JOH to William Maxwell, April 4, 1961, *Letters,* p. 374.

204   John O'Hara, *Assembly,* New York, 1961, p. 229.

205   John Steinbeck, untitled statement on O'Hara, American Academy and Institute of Arts and Letters.

205   John O'Hara, foreword to *Assembly.*

206   JOH to William Marvel, July 2, 1959. William Marvel Collection.

206   JOH to Wylie O'Hara, January 1962, *Letters,* p. 384.

206   JOH to John K. Hutchens, February 21, 1963, John K. Hutchens Collection.

208   JOH to Edgar Scott, November 5, 1962, *Letters,* p. 411.

208   JOH to Wylie O'Hara, July 11, 1961, Wylie O'Hara Doughty Collection.

208   JOH to Robert Kirsch, December 28, 1958, *Letters,* p. 283.

208   JOH to William Marvel, October 28, 1962, William Marvel Collection.

208   *Ibid.*

208   JOH to Bennett Cerf, March 31, 1964, *Letters,* p. 449.

208   JOH to William Marvel, December 28, 1963, William Marvel Collection.

210   JOH to John Hersey, February 27, 1964, *Letters,* p. 443.

210   John Hersey, "Presentation of the Award of Merit Medal for the Novel to John O'Hara, American Academy of Arts and Letters, May 20, 1964," American Academy and Institute of Arts and Letters.

210   John O'Hara, "Acceptance of the Award of Merit for the Novel," reproduced in *Artist Own Fault,* pp. 103–105.

CHAPTER 12.   THE LOCKWOOD CONCERN

For information about O'Hara's last years, I have been helped mainly by his old friends and his family, for in this reclusive period he made few new acquaintances. Mostly he saw his Princeton neighbors and friends in Philadelphia. He extended himself in correspondence, but he relied mainly on such people as Charles Addams, Joan Fontaine, Bennett and Phyllis Cerf, Joseph W. Outerbridge, William Marvel and the Edgar Scotts. For information about his English trips I am grateful to Graham Watson, his agent, and Robin Denniston, his publisher.

Page
211   JOH to Katharine Barnes O'Hara, July 30, 1961, Joan Gates Collection.
212   JOH to John K. Hutchens, August 14, 1961, John K. Hutchens Collection.
212   JOH to Katharine Barnes O'Hara, July 8, 1961, Joan Gates Collection.
212   Louis Auchincloss, "Marquand and O'Hara: The Novel of Manners," *The Nation,* November 19, 1960, p. 384. O'Hara's reply to this article was an angry letter to Auchincloss: "Since you have taken it upon yourself to pass judgment on my importance as a novelist, I can best reply by pointing out that you have obviously read all of my novels, and I have not read one of yours. I don't know anything about your importance as a lawyer, but in my league you are still a bat boy, and 43 is pretty old for a bat boy." See C. D. B. Bryan, "Under the Auchincloss Shell," *New York Times Magazine,* February 11, 1979, p. 35.
213   JOH to John K. Hutchens, June 18, 1962, John K. Hutchens Collection.
213   JOH to Edgar Scott, April 20, 1965, Edgar Scott Collection.
213   *Ibid.*
215   John O'Hara, "Reflections of a Non-Travel Writer," *Holiday,* January 1966, p. 24.
215   JOH to John K. Hutchens, December 13, 1962, John K. Hutchens Collection.
216   JOH to J. Donald Adams, September 28, 1956, *Letters,* p. 254.
216   John O'Hara, *My Turn,* p. 192.
217   *Ibid.,* p. 13.
217   JOH to William Marvel, July 20, 1964, William Marvel Collection.
217   Don Schanche, "John O'Hara," *Esquire,* August 1964.
218   JOH to Bennett Cerf, November 5, 1960, *Letters,* p. 351.
218   JOH to Bennett Cerf, March 11, 1964, Columbia University Library.
219   Keating, "John O'Hara," *Cosmopolitan,* September 1960.
219   JOH to Don Schanche, December 24, 1964, *Letters,* p. 468.
220   JOH to William Marvel, December 12, 1962, William Marvel Collection.
220   John O'Hara, "Appointment with O'Hara," *Colliers,* September 29, 1956.
220   JOH to Katharine Barnes O'Hara, July 27, 1961, Joan Gates Collection.
220   John O'Hara, *Sermons and Soda-Water,* II, pp. 71, 72.
220   JOH to Finis Farr, November 19, 1966, *Letters,* p. 487.
221   JOH to James Gould Cozzens, November 27, 1962, Princeton University Library.
221   JOH to James Gould Cozzens, August 4, 1964, *Letters,* p. 459.
221   JOH to John Hersey, January 21, 1965, *Letters,* p. 471.

222   John Steinbeck to John O'Hara, reproduced in Steinbeck and Wallstein, eds., *Steinbeck: A Life in Letters,* p. 770.

222   John O'Hara, *The Lockwood Concern,* New York, 1965, p. 354.

223   *Ibid.,* p. 353.

223   JOH to William Maxwell, January 4, 1966, *Letters,* p. 480.

223   *Ibid.*

223   *Ibid.*

223   *Ibid.*

223   Joseph Conrad, "Author's Note," *Victory* (all editions).

224   Brendan Gill, Century Memorials, *The Century Association Yearbook,* 1971.

224   John O'Hara, *Sweet and Sour,* p. 54.

224   John O'Hara, "Appointment with O'Hara," *Colliers,* April 16, 1954.

224   Associated Press Biographical Service, No. 4211, October 1, 1964, John O'Hara Collection, Pennsylvania State University Library.

224   John O'Hara, *Sweet and Sour,* p. 155.

224   *Ibid.,* p. 154.

224   JOH to Gertrude Macy, October 5, 1969, Gertrude Macy Collection.

225   JOH to William Marvel, December 5, 1961, William Marvel Collection.

225   JOH to Bennett Cerf, n.d. (January 1965), *Letters,* p. 472.

226   John O'Hara, *The Lockwood Concern,* p. 351.

227   JOH to William Marvel, October 28, 1962, William Marvel Collection.

227   JOH to Richardson Dilworth, August 5, 1964, *Letters,* p. 460.

227   John O'Hara, "Hello Hollywood Goodbye," *Holiday,* May 1968.

227   John O'Hara, *My Turn,* p. 153.

227   *Ibid.,* p. 151.

227   John O'Hara, "Don't Say It Never Happened," reproduced in *Artist Own Fault,* p. 215.

228   John O'Hara, foreword to *And Other Stories,* New York, 1968, p. vii.

228   JOH to Katharine Barnes O'Hara, July 11, 1961, Joan Gates Collection.

228   Quoted in Cleveland Amory, *Celebrity Register,* New York, 1967, p. 469.

229   John O'Hara, "Appointment with O'Hara," *Colliers,* March 2, 1956.

229   Wolcott Gibbs to James Thurber, n.d. (1956), Ohio State University Library.

229   "Bored by Fame," *Evening Standard,* May 3, 1967.

230   O'Hara, Talk at Foyle's Literary Luncheon, reproduced in *Artist Own Fault,* p. 118.

230   Quotation provided by Ben Perrick, Foyle's Bookshop, London.

230   JOH to Lionel Trilling, November 16, 1966, Diana Trilling Collection.

230   JOH to William Marvel, December 28, 1963, William Marvel Collection.

231   John O'Hara, *Waiting for Winter,* New York, 1966, p. 203.

231   John O'Hara, *And Other Stories,* p. 120.

232   JOH to Don Schanche, May 18, 1963, *Letters,* p. 430.

233   Press clipping; author's collection.

233   JOH to Katharine Barnes O'Hara, July 23, 1961, Joan Gates Collection.

233   JOH to Wylie O'Hara, September 22, 1959, *Letters,* p. 301.

233   JOH to Wylie O'Hara Holahan, October 29, 1968, *Letters,* p. 513.

234   O'Hara, *Sweet and Sour,* p. 22.

234   JOH to William Marvel, July 2, 1959, William Marvel Collection.

234   JOH to William Maxwell, January 10, 1965, *Letters,* p. 469.

235   Dr. Frank Elliott to the author, May 5, 1978.

235   *Ibid.*

235   JOH to Frank Sullivan, October 20, 1969, Historical Society of Saratoga Springs.

235   JOH to Alfred Wright, March 21, 1968, *Letters,* p. 508.

237   Calvin Tomkins, *Living Well Is the Best Revenge,* New York, 1971, p. 148.

237   *Ibid.* p. 122.

INDEX